STAND OUT

Evidence-Based Learning for College and Career Readiness

BASIC

THIRD EDITION

LESSON PLANNER

ROB JENKINS

STAC

Australia • Brazil • Mexico • Singapore • United Kingdom • United States

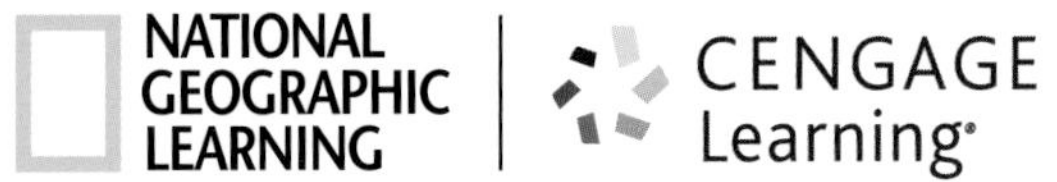

Stand Out Basic: Evidence-Based Learning for College and Career Readiness, Third Edition
Rob Jenkins and Staci Johnson
Lesson Planner

Publisher: Sherrise Roehr

Executive Editor: Sarah Kenney

Development Editor: Lewis Thompson

Assistant Editor: Patricia Giunta

Director of Global Marketing: Ian Martin

Executive Marketing Manager: Ben Rivera

Product Marketing Manager: Dalia Bravo

Director of Content and Media Production: Michael Burggren

Production Manager: Daisy Sosa

Media Researcher: Leila Hishmeh

Senior Print Buyer: Mary Beth Hennebury

Cover and Interior Designer: Brenda Carmichael

Composition: Lumina

Cover Image: Portra Images/Getty Images

Bottom Images: (Left to Right) Jay B Sauceda/Getty Images; Tripod/Getty Images; Dear Blue/Getty Images; Portra Images/Getty Images; Mark Edward Atkinson/Tracey Lee/Getty Images; Hero Images/Getty Images; Jade/Getty Images; Seth Joel/Getty Images; LWA/Larry Williams/Getty Images; Dimitri Otis/Getty Images

Lesson Planner
ISBN 13: 978-1-305-65521-8

National Geographic Learning/Cengage Learning
20 Channel Center Street
Boston, MA 02210
USA

Cengage Learning is a leading provider of customized learning solutions with office locations around the globe, including Singapore, the United Kingdom, Australia, Mexico, Brazil, and Japan. Locate your local office at: **international.cengage.com/region**

Cengage Learning products are represented in Canada by Nelson Education, Ltd.

Visit National Geographic Learning online at **NGL.Cengage.com**
Visit our corporate website at **www.cengage.com**

Printed in the United States of America
Print Number: 02 Print Year: 2016

ACKNOWLEDGMENTS

Ellen Albano
Mcfatter Technical College, Davie, FL

Esther Anaya-Garcia
Glendale Community College, Glendale, AZ

Carol Bellamy
Prince George's Community College, Largo, MD

Gail Bier
Atlantic Technical College, Coconut Creek, FL

Kathryn Black
Myrtle Beach Family Learning Center, Myrtle Beach, SC

Claudia Brantley
College of Southern Nevada, Las Vegas, NV

Dr. Joan-Yvette Campbell
Lindsey Hopkins Technical College, Miami, FL

Maria Carmen Iglesias
Miami Senior Adult Educational Center, Miami, FL

Lee Chen
Palomar College, San Marcos, CA

Casey Cahill
Atlantic Technical College, Coconut Creek, FL

Maria Dillehay
Burien Job Training and Education Center, Goodwill, Seattle, WA

Irene Fjaerestad
Olympic College, Bremerton, WA

Eleanor Forfang-Brockman
Tarrant County College, Fort Worth, Texas

Jesse Galdamez
San Bernardino Adult School, San Bernardino, CA

Anna Garoz
Lindsey Hopkins Technical Education Center, Miami, FL

Maria Gutierrez
Miami Sunset Adult, Miami, FL

Noel Hernandez
Palm Beach County Public Schools, Palm Beach County, FL

Kathleen Hiscock
Portland Adult Education, Portland, ME

Frantz Jean-Louis
The English Center, Miami, FL

Annette Johnson
Sheridan Technical College, Hollywood, FL

Ginger Karaway
Gateway Technical College, Kenosha, WI

Judy Martin-Hall
Indian River State College, Fort Pierce, FL

Toni Molinaro
Dixie Hollins Adult Education Center, St Petersburg, FL

Tracey Person
Cape Cod Community College, Hyannis, MA

Celina Paula
Miami-Dade County Public Schools, Miami, FL

Veronica Pavon-Baker
Miami Beach Adult, Miami, FL

Ileana Perez
Robert Morgan Technical College, Miami, FL

Neeta Rancourt
Atlantic Technical College, Coconut Creek, FL

Brenda Roland
Joliet Junior College, Joliet, IL

Hidelisa Sampson
Las Vegas Urban League, Las Vegas, NV

Lisa Schick
James Madison University, Harrisonburg, VA

Rob Sheppard
Quincy Asian Resources, Quincy, MA

Sydney Silver
Burien Job Training and Education Center, Goodwill, Seattle, WA

Teresa Tamarit
Miami Senior Adult Educational Center, Miami, FL

Cristina Urena
Atlantic Technical College, Fort Lauderdale, FL

Pamela Jo Wilson
Palm Beach County Public Schools, Palm Beach County, FL

ABOUT THE AUTHORS

Rob Jenkins

I love teaching. I love to see the expressions on my students' faces when the light goes on and their eyes show such sincere joy of learning. I knew the first time I stepped into an ESL classroom that this is where I needed to be and I have never questioned that resolution. I have worked in business, sales, and publishing, and I've found challenge in all, but nothing can compare to the satisfaction of reaching people in such a personal way.

Staci Johnson

Ever since I can remember, I've been fascinated with other cultures and languages. I love to travel and every place I go, the first thing I want to do is meet the people, learn their language, and understand their culture. Becoming an ESL teacher was a perfect way to turn what I love to do into my profession. There's nothing more incredible than the exchange of teaching and learning from one another that goes on in an ESL classroom. And there's nothing more rewarding than helping a student succeed.

Along with the inclusion of National Geographic content, the third edition of **Stand Out** boasts of several innovations. In response to initiatives regarding the development of more complexity with reading and encouraging students to interact more with reading texts, we are proud to introduce new rich reading sections that allow students to discuss topics relevant to a global society. We have also introduced new National Geographic videos that complement the life-skill videos **Stand Out** introduced in the second edition and which are now integrated into the student books. We don't stop there; **Stand Out** has even more activities that require critical and creative thinking that serve to maximize learning and prepare students for the future. The third edition also has online workbooks. **Stand Out** was the first mainstream ESL textbook for adults to introduce a lesson plan format, hundreds of customizable worksheets, and project-based instruction. The third edition expands on these features in its mission to provide rich learning opportunities that can be exploited in different ways. We believe that with the innovative approach that made **Stand Out** a leader from its inception, the many new features, and the new look; programs, teachers, and students will find great success!

Stand Out Mission Statement:

Our goal is to give students challenging opportunities to be successful in their language learning experience so they develop confidence and become independent lifelong learners.

TO THE TEACHER

ABOUT THE SERIES

The **Stand Out** series is designed to facilitate *active* learning within life-skill settings that lead students to career and academic pathways. Each student book and its supplemental components in the six-level series expose students to competency areas most useful and essential for newcomers with careful treatment of level appropriate but challenging materials. Students grow academically by developing essential literacy and critical thinking skills that will help them find personal success in a changing and dynamic world.

THE STAND OUT PHILOSOPHY

Integrated Skills

In each of the five lessons of every unit, skills are introduced as they might be in real language use. They are in context and not separated into different sections of the unit. We believe that for real communication to occur, the classroom should mirror real-life as much as possible.

Objective Driven Activities

Every lesson in **Stand Out** is driven by a performance objective. These objectives have been carefully selected to ensure they are measurable, accessible to students at their particular level, and relevant to students and their lives. Good objectives lead to effective learning. Effective objectives also lead to appropriate self, student, and program assessment which is increasingly required by state and federal mandates.

Lesson Plan Sequencing

Stand Out follows an established sequence of activities that provides students with the tools they need to have in order to practice and apply the skills required in the objective. A pioneer in Adult Education for introducing the Madeline Hunter WIPPEA lesson plan model into textbooks, **Stand Out** continues to provide a clear and easy-to-follow system for presenting and developing English language skills. The WIPPEA model follows six steps:

- **W**arm up and Review
- **I**ntroduction
- **P**resentation
- **P**ractice
- **E**valuation
- **A**pplication

Learning And Acquisition

In **Stand Out**, the recycling of skills is emphasized. Students must learn and practice the same skills multiple times in various contexts to actually acquire them. Practicing a skill one time is rarely sufficient for acquisition and rarely addresses diverse student needs and learning styles.

Critical Thinking

Critical thinking has been defined in various ways and sometimes so broadly that any activity could be classified to meet the criteria. To be clear and to draw attention to the strong critical thinking activities in **Stand Out,** we define these activities as ***tasks that require learners to think deeper than the superficial vocabulary and meaning.*** Activities such as ranking, making predictions, analyzing, or solving problems, demand that students think beyond the surface. Critical thinking is highlighted throughout so the instructor can be confident that effective learning is going on.

Learner-Centered, Cooperative, and Communicative Activities

Stand Out provides ample opportunities for students to develop interpersonal skills and to practice new vocabulary through graphic organizers and charts like VENN diagrams, graphs, classifying charts, and mind maps. The lesson planners provide learner-centered approaches in every lesson. Students are asked to rank items, make decisions, and negotiate amongst other things.

Dialogues are used to prepare students for these activities in the low levels and fewer dialogues are used at the higher levels where students have already acquired the vocabulary and rudimentary conversation skills.

Activities should provide opportunities for students to speak in near authentic settings so they have confidence to perform outside the classroom. This does not mean that dialogues and other mechanical activities are not used to prepare students for cooperative activities, but these mechanical activities do not foster conversation. They merely provide the first tools students need to go beyond mimicry.

Assessment

Instructors and students should have a clear understanding of what is being taught and what is expected. In **Stand Out**, objectives are clearly stated so that target skills can be effectively assessed throughout.

Formative assessments are essential. Pre and post-assessments can be given for units or sections of the book through *ExamView*—a program that makes developing tests easy and effective. These tests can be created to appear like standardized tests, which are important for funding and to help students prepare.

Finally, *learner logs* allow students to self-assess, document progress, and identify areas that might require additional attention.

SUPPLEMENTAL COMPONENTS

The **Stand Out** series is a comprehensive one-stop for all student needs. There is no need to look any further than the resources offered.

Stand Out Lesson Planners

The lesson planners go beyond merely describing activities in the student book by providing teacher support, ideas, and guidance for the entire class period.

- **Standards correlations** for **CCRS, CASAS,** and **SCANS** are identified for each lesson.
- **Pacing Guides** help with planning by giving instructors suggested durations for each activity and a selection of activities for different class lengths.
- **Teacher Tips** provide point-of-use pedagogical comments and best practices.
- **At-A-Glance Lesson Openers** provide the instructor with everything that will be taught in a particular lesson. Elements include: the agenda, the goal, grammar, pronunciation, academic strategies, critical thinking elements, correlations to standards, and resources.
- **Suggested Activities** go beyond what is shown in the text providing teachers with ideas that will stimulate them to come up with their own.
- **Listening Scripts** are integrated into the unit pages for easy access.

Stand Out Workbook

The workbook in the third edition takes the popular **Stand Out Grammar Challenge** and expands it to include vocabulary building, life-skill development, and grammar practice associated directly with each lesson in the student book.

Stand Out Online Workbook

One of the most important innovations new to the third edition of **Stand Out** is the online workbook. This workbook provides unique activities that are closely related to the student book and gives students opportunities to have access to audio and video.

The online workbook provides opportunities for students to practice and improve digital literacy skills essential for 21st century learners. These skills are essential for standardized computer and online testing. Scores in these tests will improve when students can concentrate on the content and not so much on the technology.

Activity Bank

The Activity Bank is an online feature that provides several hundred multilevel worksheets per level to enhance the already rich materials available through **Stand Out**.

DVD Program

The **Stand Out Lifeskills Video Program** continues to be available with eight episodes per level; however, now the worksheets are part of the student books with additional help in the lesson planners.

New to the third edition of **Stand Out** are two National Geographic videos per level. Each video is accompanied by four pages of instruction and activities with support in the lesson planners.

Examview

ExamView is a program that provides customizable test banks and allows instructors to make lesson, unit, and program tests quickly.

STANDARDS AND CORRELATIONS

Stand Out is the pioneer in establishing a foundation of standards within each unit and through every objective. The standards movement in the United States is as dominant today as it was when **Stand Out** was first published. Schools and programs must be aware of on-going local and federal initiatives and make attempts to meet ever-changing requirements.

In the first edition of **Stand Out**, we identified direct correlations to SCANS, EFF, and CASAS standards. *The Secretaries Commission on Achieving Necessary Skills* or SCANS and *Equipped for the Future* or EFF standards are still important and are identified in every lesson of **Stand Out**. These skills include the basic skills, interpersonal skills, and problem-solving skills necessary to be successful in the workplace, in school, and in the community. **Stand Out** was also developed with a thorough understanding of objectives established by the *Comprehensive Adult Student Assessment Systems* or CASAS. Many programs have experienced great success with their CASAS scores using **Stand Out**, and these objectives continue to be reflected in the third edition.

Today, a new emphasis on critical thinking and complexity has swept the nation. Students are expected to think for themselves more now than ever before. They must also interact with reading texts at a higher level. These new standards and expectations are highly visible in the third edition and include *College and Career Readiness Standards*.

Stand Out offers a complete set of correlations online for all standards to demonstrate how closely we align with state and federal guidelines.

IMPORTANT INNOVATIONS TO THE THIRD EDITION

New Look

Although the third edition of **Stand Out** boasts of the same lesson plan format and task-based activities that made it one of the most popular books in adult education, it now has an updated look with the addition of the National Geographic content which will capture the attention of the instructor and every student.

Critical Thinking

With the advent of new federal and state initiatives, teachers need to be confident that students will use critical thinking skills when learning. This has always been a goal in **Stand Out**, but now those opportunities are highlighted in each lesson.

College And Career Readiness Skills

These skills are also identified by critical thinking strategies and academic-related activities, which are found throughout **Stand Out**. New to the third edition is a special reading section in each unit that challenges students and encourages them to develop reading strategies within a rich National Geographic environment.

Stand Out Workbook

The print workbook is now more extensive and complete with vocabulary, life skills, and grammar activities to round out any program. Many instructors might find these pages ideal for homework, but they of course can be used for additional practice within the classroom.

Media And Online Support

Media and online support includes audio, video, online workbooks, presentation tools, and multi-level worksheets, ExamView, and standards correlations.

CONTENTS

Numeracy/ Academic Skills	CCRS	SCANS	CASAS
• Writing numerals 1-10 • Writing telephone numbers • Dictation • Focused listening • Class application • Test-taking skills	SL1, SL2, L2, RF2, RF3	**Many SCAN skills are incorporated in this unit with an emphasis on:** • Listening • Speaking • Writing • Sociability • Acquiring and evaluating information • Interpreting and communicating information	**1:** 0.1.1, 0.1.4, 0.2.1 **2:** 0.1.1, 0.1.4, 0.2.1 **3:** 0.1.5, 7.4.7 **R:** 7.4.1, 7.4.2, 7.4.3
• Writing numerals 1-31 • Writing dates • Focused listening • Teamwork skills • Reviewing • Evaluating • Developing study skills	RI1, RI7, SL1, SL2, SL4, L1, L2, L5, RF2, RF3	**Many SCAN skills are incorporated in this unit with an emphasis on:** • Basic skills • Acquiring and evaluating information • Interpreting and communicating information • Seeing things in the mind's eye • Sociability	**1:** 0.1.1, 0.2.1 **2:** 0.1.2, 0.2.1, 1.1.3, 4.8.7 **3:** 0.1.2, 0.2.1 **4:** 0.1.2, 0.2.1, 1.1.3, 4.8.7 **5:** 0.1.2, 0.2.1, 2.3.2 **R:** 0.1.1, 0.2.1, 7.4.1, 7.4.2, 7.4.3 **TP:** 0.1.1, 0.2.1, 4.8.1
• Interpreting a bar graph • Telling time • Focused listening • Scheduling • Reviewing • Evaluating • Developing study skills	RI1, RI7, SL1, SL2, SL4, L1, L2, L5, RF2, RF3	**Many SCAN skills are incorporated in this unit with an emphasis on:** • Acquiring and evaluating information • Organizing and maintaining information • Interpreting and communicating information • Basic skills • Reflect and Evaluate	**1:** 0.1.4 **2:** 0.1.5 **3:** 0.1.5 **4:** 0.2.1, 0.2.4, 2.3.1 **5:** 0.1.2, 0.2.1, 1.1.3, 2.3.3 **R:** 0.1.5, 2.3.1, 2.3.2, 2.3.3, 7.4.1, 7.4.2, 7.4.3 **TP:** 0.1.5, 2.3.1, 2.3.2, 2.3.3, 4.8.1

CONTENTS

Numeracy/ Academic Skills	CCRS	SCANS	CASAS
• Using U.S. measurements: pounds, gallons • Working in a group • Focused listening • Skimming • Categorizing and organizing information • Teamwork skills • Reviewing • Evaluating • Developing study skills	RI1, RI7, RI9, W1, W2, SL1, SL2, SL4, L1, L2, L5, RF2, RF3	**Many SCAN skills are incorporated in this unit with an emphasis on:** • Acquiring and evaluating information • Organizing and maintaining information • Interpreting and communicating information • Allocating human resources • Basic skills • Seeing things in the mind's eye	**1:** 1.3.8 **2:** 1.3.8 **3:** 1.1.1, 1.3.8 **4:** 1.3.8 **5:** 1.3.8 **R:** 1.3.8, 7.4.1, 7.4.2, 7.4.3 **TP:** 1.88, 4.8.1
• Using U.S. measurements:clothing sizes • Maintaining inventories • Counting U.S. money • Calculating totals • Writing checks • Asking for information' • Focused listening • Test-taking skills • Reviewing • Evaluating • Developing study skills	RI1, RI7, SL1, SL2, SL4, L1, L2, L5, RF2, RF3	**Many SCAN skills are incorporated in this unit with an emphasis on**: • Acquiring and evaluating information • Organizing and maintaining information • Interpreting and communicating information • Basic skills • Allocating money • Serving clients and customers	**1:** 1.3.9 **2:** 1.1.9, 1.2.1, 1.3.9 **3:** 1.1.9, 1.2.1, 1.3.9 **4:** 1.1.6, 1.3.9, 4.8.1, 6.1.1 **5:** 1.1.9, 1.2.1, 1.3.9, 4.8.3 **R:** 1.1.9, 1.2.1, 1.3.9, 7.4.1, 7.4.2, 7.4.3 **TP:** 1.3.9, 4.8.1
• Interpreting a bar graph • Creating a bar graph • Test-taking strategies • Focused listening • Dictation • Reviewing • Evaluating • Developing study skills	RI1, RI7, SL1, SL2, SL4, L1, L2, L5, RF2, RF3	**Many SCAN skills are incorporated in this unit with an emphasis on:** • Acquiring and evaluating information • Organizing and maintaining information • Interpreting and communicating information • Basic skills • Creative thinking • Participating as a member of a team	**1:** 1.3.7, 7.2.3 **2:** 1.4.1, 1.4.2, 1.9.4 **3:** 1.1.3, 2.2.3, 2.2.5, 6.7.2 **4:** 0.1.2, 0.2.4 **5:** 1.1.3, 1.9.1, 1.9.4, 2.2.1, 2.2.2, 2.5.4 **R:** 2.2.3, 7.4.1, 7.4.2, 7.4.3 **TP:** 2.2.3, 4.8.1

CONTENTS

Numeracy/ Academic Skills	CCRS	SCANS	CASAS
• Focused listening • Test-taking skills • Reviewing • Evaluating • Developing study skills	RI1, RI2, RI7, W1, SL1, SL2, SL4, L1, L2, L5, RF2, RF3	**Many SCAN skills are incorporated in this unit with an emphasis on:** • Acquiring and evaluating information • Organizing and maintaining information • Interpreting and communicating information • Basic skills • Self-management • Responsibility	**1:** 3.1.1, 3.1.3 **2:** 0.1.2, 0.2.1, 3.1.1 **3:** 2.3.1, 3.1.2, 3.3.1 **4:** 3.1.1 **5:** 3.1.3 **R:** 3.1.1, 3.1.2, 3.1.3, 3.3.1 **TP:** 1.3.9, 4.8.1
• Focused listening • Making graphs • Reviewing • Evaluating • Developing study skills	RI1, RI7, SL1, SL2, SL4, L1, L2, L5, RF2, RF3	**Many SCAN skills are incorporated in this unit with an emphasis on:** • Acquiring and evaluating information • Organizing and maintaining information • Interpreting and communicating information • Basic skills • Self-management	**1:** 0.2.1, 4.1.8 **2:** 0.1.6, 4.8.1 **3:** 4.1.3, 4.1.8, 4.4.4 **4:** 4.4.4 **5:** 4.4.4, 4.8.1, 4.8.3 **R:** 4.1.3, 4.1.8, 4.4.1, 4.8.1, 4.8.3, 7.4.1, 7.4.2, 7.4.3 **TP:** 2.2.3, 4.8.1.
• Identifying quantities and sizes • Calculating totals • Reading telephone numbers • Interpreting a bar graph • Focused listening • Test-taking skills • Organizational skills • Reviewing • Evaluating • Developing study skills	RI1, SL1, SL2, SL4, L1, L2, RF2, RF3	**Many SCAN skills are incorporated in this unit with an emphasis on:** • Acquiring and evaluating information • Organizing and maintaining information • Interpreting and communicating information • Basic skills • Self-management	**1:** 0.2.1, 0.2.2, 7.1.4 **2:** 1.1.6, 1.2.1, 1.3.1, 1.6.4, 7.1.4 **3:** 2.1.1, 2.2.1, 7.1.4 **4:** 0.2.1, 3.5.9, 6.7.2, 7.1.1, 7.1.2, 7.1.4 **5:** 4.1.1, 4.4.4, 7.1.1, 7.1.4 **R:** 7.4.2, 7.4.3 **TP:** 2.2.3, 4.8.1

For other national and state specific standards, please visit: **www.NGL.Cengage.com/SO3**

INTRODUCING STAND OUT, Third Edition!

Stand Out is a six-level, standards-based ESL series for adult education with a proven track record of successful results. The new edition of *Stand Out* continues to provide students with the foundations and tools needed to achieve success in life, college, and career.

Stand Out now integrates real-world content from National Geographic

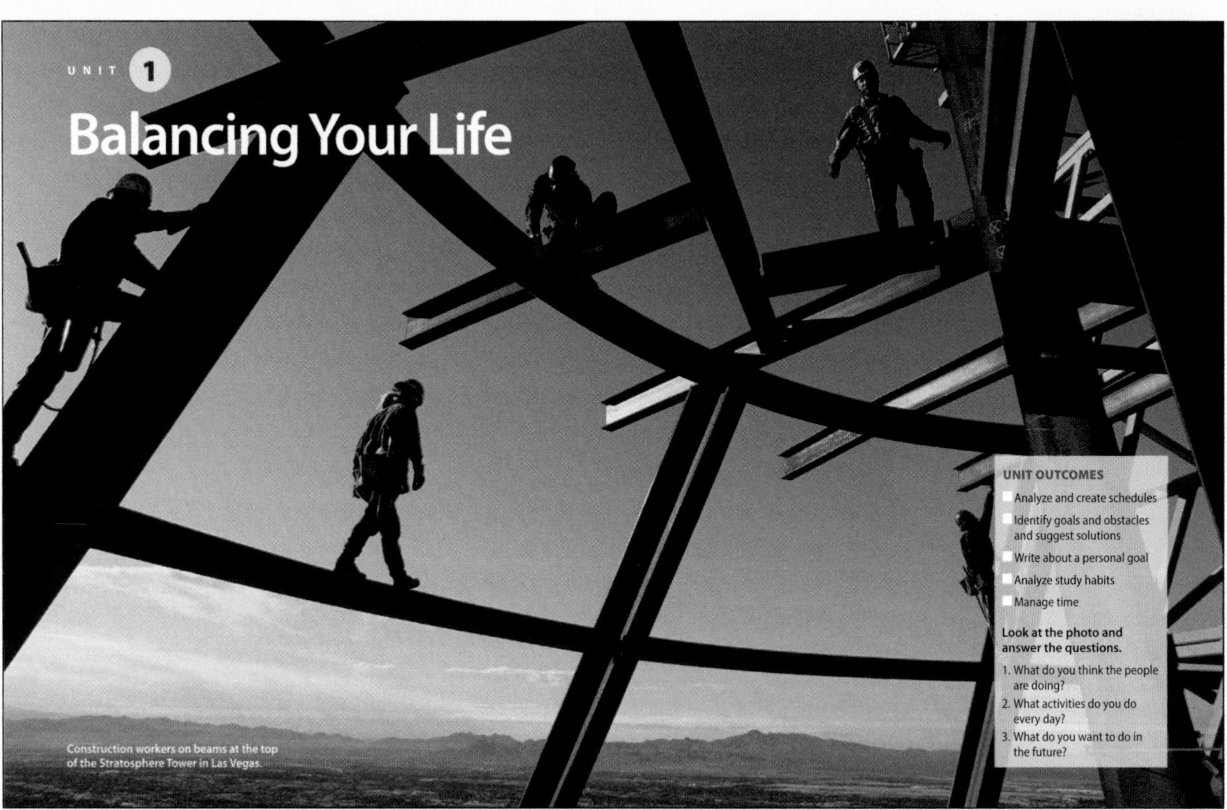

UNIT 1
Balancing Your Life
Construction workers on beams at the top of the Stratosphere Tower in Las Vegas.
UNIT OUTCOMES
Analyze and create schedules
Identify goals and obstacles and suggest solutions
Write about a personal goal
Analyze study habits
Manage time
Look at the photo and answer the questions.
1. What do you think the people are doing?
2. What activities do you do every day?
3. What do you want to do in the future?

- *Stand Out* now integrates high-interest, real-world content from National Geographic which enhances its proven approach to lesson planning and instruction. A stunning National Geographic image at the beginning of each unit introduces the theme and engages learners in meaningful conversations right from the start.

Stand Out supports college and career readiness

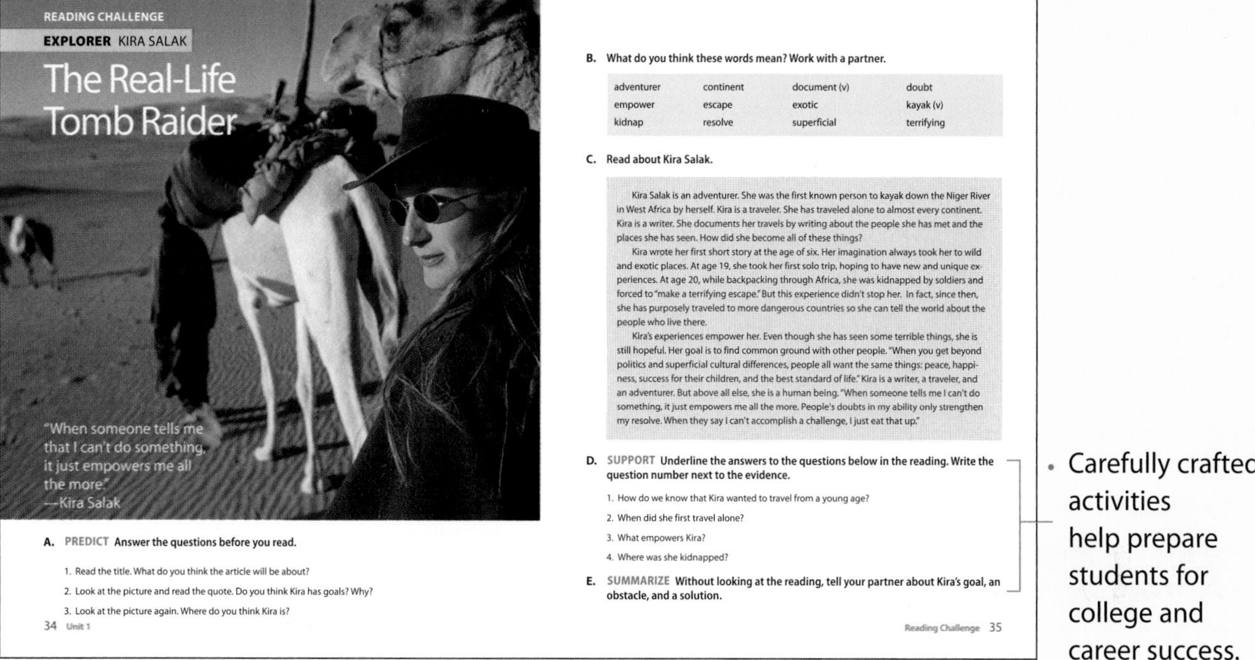

READING CHALLENGE

EXPLORER KIRA SALAK

The Real-Life Tomb Raider

"When someone tells me that I can't do something, it just empowers me all the more."
—Kira Salak

A. PREDICT **Answer the questions before you read.**

1. Read the title. What do you think the article will be about?
2. Look at the picture and read the quote. Do you think Kira has goals? Why?
3. Look at the picture again. Where do you think Kira is?

34 Unit 1

B. What do you think these words mean? Work with a partner.

adventurer	continent	document (v)	doubt
empower	escape	exotic	kayak (v)
kidnap	resolve	superficial	terrifying

C. Read about Kira Salak.

Kira Salak is an adventurer. She was the first known person to kayak down the Niger River in West Africa by herself. Kira is a traveler. She has traveled alone to almost every continent. Kira is a writer. She documents her travels by writing about the people she has met and the places she has seen. How did she become all of these things?

Kira wrote her first short story at the age of six. Her imagination always took her to wild and exotic places. At age 19, she took her first solo trip, hoping to have new and unique experiences. At age 20, while backpacking through Africa, she was kidnapped by soldiers and forced to "make a terrifying escape." But this experience didn't stop her. In fact, since then, she has purposely traveled to more dangerous countries so she can tell the world about the people who live there.

Kira's experiences empower her. Even though she has seen some terrible things, she is still hopeful. Her goal is to find common ground with other people. "When you get beyond politics and superficial cultural differences, people all want the same things: peace, happiness, success for their children, and the best standard of life." Kira is a writer, a traveler, and an adventurer. But above all else, she is a human being. "When someone tells me I can't do something, it just empowers me all the more. People's doubts in my ability only strengthen my resolve. When they say I can't accomplish a challenge, I just eat that up."

D. SUPPORT **Underline the answers to the questions below in the reading. Write the question number next to the evidence.**

1. How do we know that Kira wanted to travel from a young age?
2. When did she first travel alone?
3. What empowers Kira?
4. Where was she kidnapped?

E. SUMMARIZE **Without looking at the reading, tell your partner about Kira's goal, an obstacle, and a solution.**

Reading Challenge 35

- Carefully crafted activities help prepare students for college and career success.

- **NEW Reading Challenge** in every unit features a fascinating story about a **National Geographic explorer** to immerse learners in authentic content.

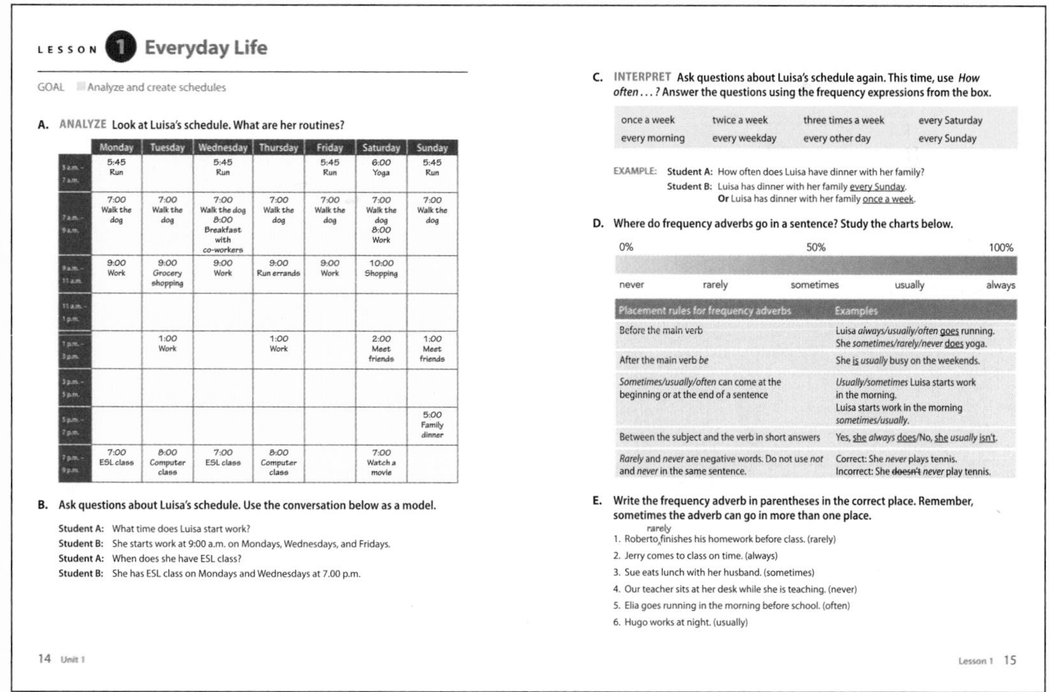

LESSON 1 **Everyday Life**

GOAL Analyze and create schedules

A. ANALYZE **Look at Luisa's schedule. What are her routines?**

	Monday	Tuesday	Wednesday	Thursday	Friday	Saturday	Sunday
5 a.m. - 7 a.m.	5:45 Run		5:45 Run		5:45 Run	6:00 Yoga	5:45 Run
7 a.m. - 9 a.m.	7:00 Walk the dog	7:00 Walk the dog	7:00 Walk the dog 8:00 Breakfast with co-workers	7:00 Walk the dog	7:00 Walk the dog	7:00 Walk the dog 8:00 Work	7:00 Walk the dog
9 a.m. - 11 a.m.	9:00 Work	9:00 Grocery shopping	9:00 Work	9:00 Run errands	9:00 Work	10:00 Shopping	
11 a.m. - 1 p.m.							
1 p.m. - 3 p.m.		1:00 Work		1:00 Work		2:00 Meet friends	1:00 Meet friends
3 p.m. - 5 p.m.							
5 p.m. - 7 p.m.							5:00 Family dinner
7 p.m. - 9 p.m.	7:00 ESL class	8:00 Computer class	7:00 ESL class	8:00 Computer class		7:00 Watch a movie	

B. Ask questions about Luisa's schedule. Use the conversation below as a model.

Student A: What time does Luisa start work?
Student B: She starts work at 9:00 a.m. on Mondays, Wednesdays, and Fridays.
Student A: When does she have ESL class?
Student B: She has ESL class on Mondays and Wednesdays at 7.00 p.m.

14 Unit 1

C. INTERPRET **Ask questions about Luisa's schedule again. This time, use *How often . . . ?* Answer the questions using the frequency expressions from the box.**

once a week	twice a week	three times a week	every Saturday
every morning	every weekday	every other day	every Sunday

EXAMPLE: **Student A:** How often does Luisa have dinner with her family?
Student B: Luisa has dinner with her family every Sunday.
Or Luisa has dinner with her family once a week.

D. Where do frequency adverbs go in a sentence? Study the charts below.

0% — 50% — 100%
never — rarely — sometimes — usually — always

Placement rules for frequency adverbs	Examples
Before the main verb	Luisa *always/usually/often* goes running. She *sometimes/rarely/never* does yoga.
After the main verb *be*	She is *usually* busy on the weekends.
Sometimes/usually/often can come at the beginning or at the end of a sentence	*Usually/sometimes* Luisa starts work in the morning. Luisa starts work in the morning *sometimes/usually*.
Between the subject and the verb in short answers	Yes, she *always* does/No, she *usually* isn't.
Rarely and *never* are negative words. Do not use *not* and *never* in the same sentence.	Correct: She *never* plays tennis. Incorrect: She ~~doesn't~~ *never* play tennis.

E. Write the frequency adverb in parentheses in the correct place. Remember, sometimes the adverb can go in more than one place.

1. Roberto (rarely) finishes his homework before class. (rarely)
2. Jerry comes to class on time. (always)
3. Sue eats lunch with her husband. (sometimes)
4. Our teacher sits at her desk while she is teaching. (never)
5. Elia goes running in the morning before school. (often)
6. Hugo works at night. (usually)

Lesson 1 15

- **EXPANDED Critical Thinking Activities** challenge learners to evaluate, analyze, and synthesize information to prepare them for the workplace and academic life.

- **NEW Video Challenge** showcases **National Geographic footage and explorers**, providing learners with the opportunity to synthesize what they have learned in prior units through the use of authentic content.

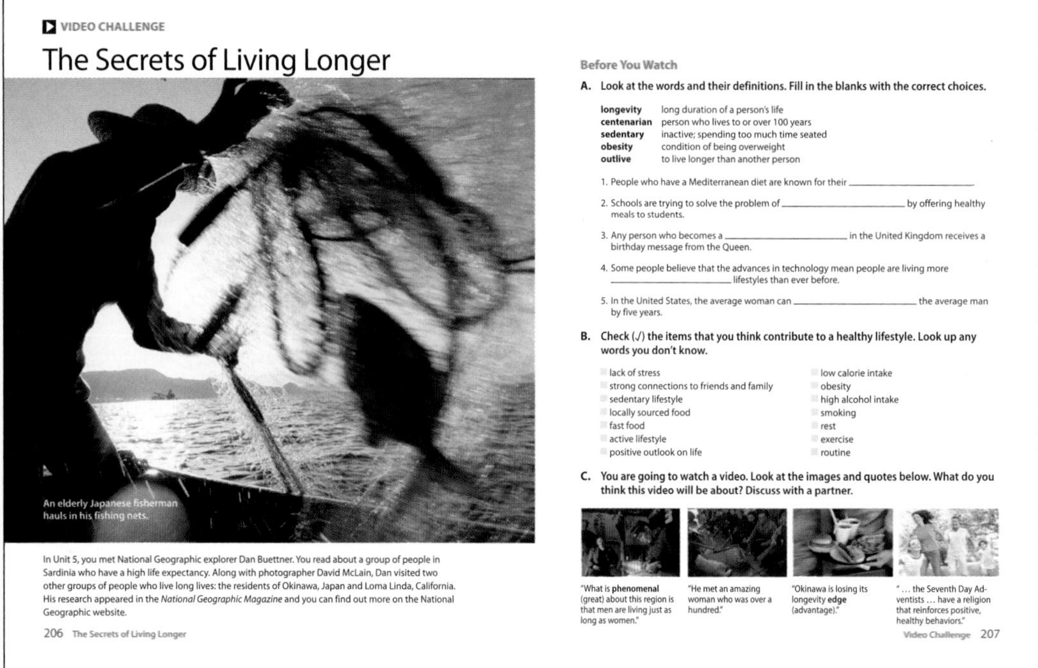

VIDEO CHALLENGE

The Secrets of Living Longer

An elderly Japanese fisherman hauls in his fishing nets.

In Unit 5, you met National Geographic explorer Dan Buettner. You read about a group of people in Sardinia who have a high life expectancy. Along with photographer David McLain, Dan visited two other groups of people who live long lives: the residents of Okinawa, Japan and Loma Linda, California. His research appeared in the *National Geographic Magazine* and you can find out more on the National Geographic website.

206 The Secrets of Living Longer

Before You Watch

A. Look at the words and their definitions. Fill in the blanks with the correct choices.

longevity long duration of a person's life
centenarian person who lives to or over 100 years
sedentary inactive; spending too much time seated
obesity condition of being overweight
outlive to live longer than another person

1. People who have a Mediterranean diet are known for their ________.
2. Schools are trying to solve the problem of ________ by offering healthy meals to students.
3. Any person who becomes a ________ in the United Kingdom receives a birthday message from the Queen.
4. Some people believe that the advances in technology mean people are living more ________ lifestyles than ever before.
5. In the United States, the average woman can ________ the average man by five years.

B. Check (✓) the items that you think contribute to a healthy lifestyle. Look up any words you don't know.

- lack of stress
- strong connections to friends and family
- sedentary lifestyle
- locally sourced food
- fast food
- active lifestyle
- positive outlook on life
- low calorie intake
- obesity
- high alcohol intake
- smoking
- rest
- exercise
- routine

C. You are going to watch a video. Look at the images and quotes below. What do you think this video will be about? Discuss with a partner.

"What is **phenomenal** (great) about this region is that men are living just as long as women."

"He met an amazing woman who was over a hundred."

"Okinawa is losing its longevity **edge** (advantage)."

"... the Seventh Day Adventists ... have a religion that reinforces positive, healthy behaviors."

Video Challenge 207

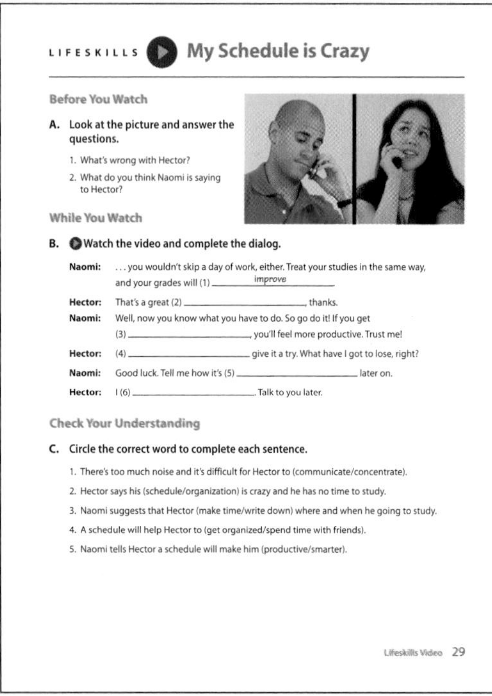

LIFESKILLS My Schedule is Crazy

Before You Watch

A. Look at the picture and answer the questions.

1. What's wrong with Hector?
2. What do you think Naomi is saying to Hector?

While You Watch

B. Watch the video and complete the dialog.

Naomi: . . . you wouldn't skip a day of work, either. Treat your studies in the same way, and your grades will (1) ___improve___.
Hector: That's a great (2) ________, thanks.
Naomi: Well, now you know what you have to do. So go do it! If you get (3) ________, you'll feel more productive. Trust me!
Hector: (4) ________ give it a try. What have I got to lose, right?
Naomi: Good luck. Tell me how it's (5) ________ later on.
Hector: I (6) ________. Talk to you later.

Check Your Understanding

C. Circle the correct word to complete each sentence.

1. There's too much noise and it's difficult for Hector to (communicate/concentrate).
2. Hector says his (schedule/organization) is crazy and he has no time to study.
3. Naomi suggests that Hector (make time/write down) where and when he going to study.
4. A schedule will help Hector to (get organized/spend time with friends).
5. Naomi tells Hector a schedule will make him (productive/smarter).

Lifeskills Video 29

- The **Lifeskills Video** is a dramatic video series integrated into each unit of the student book that helps students learn natural spoken English and apply it to their everyday activities.

Pages shown are from *Stand Out*, Third Edition Level 3

- **NEW Online Workbook** engages students and supports the classroom by providing a wide variety of auto-graded interactive activities, an audio program, video from National Geographic, and pronunciation activities.

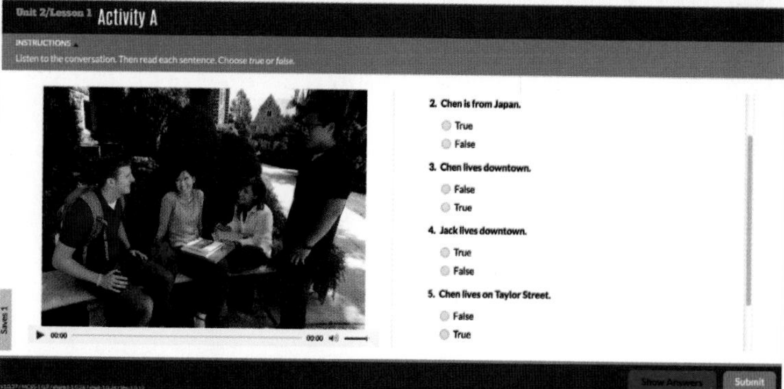

- **UPDATED Lesson Planner** includes correlations to **College and Career Readiness Standards (CCRS), CASAS, SCANS** and reference to **EL Civics** competencies to help instructors achieve the required standards.

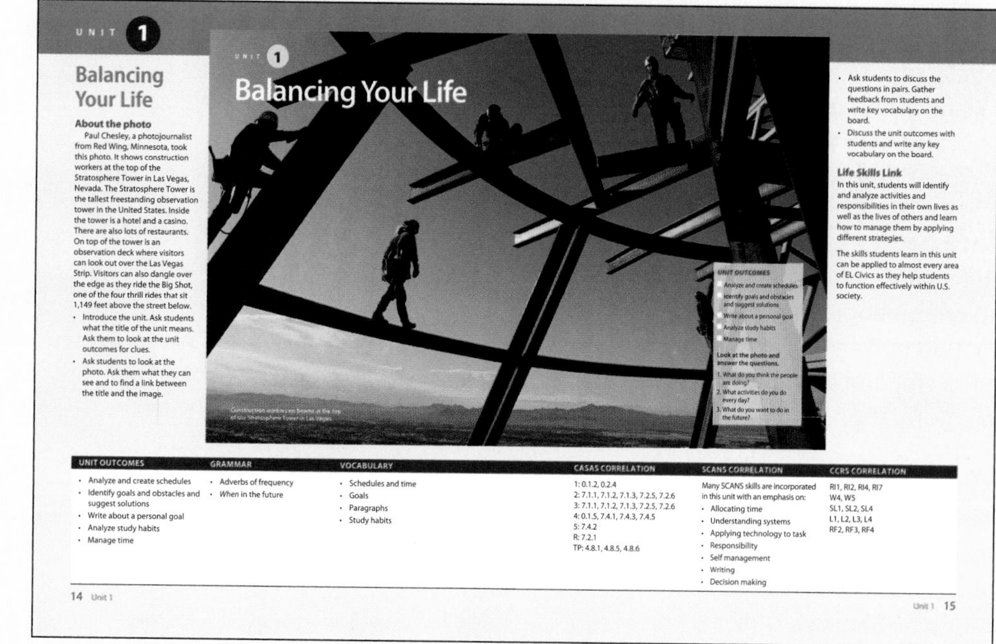

UNIT 1

Balancing Your Life

About the photo

Paul Chesley, a photojournalist from Red Wing, Minnesota, took this photo. It shows construction workers at the top of the Stratosphere Tower in Las Vegas, Nevada. The Stratosphere Tower is the tallest freestanding observation tower in the United States. Inside the tower is a hotel and a casino. There are also lots of restaurants. On top of the tower is an observation deck where visitors can look out over the Las Vegas Strip. Visitors can also dangle over the edge as they ride the Big Shot, one of the four thrill rides that sit 1,149 feet above the street below.

- Introduce the unit. Ask students what the title of the unit means. Ask them to look at the unit outcomes for clues.
- Ask students to look at the photo. Ask them what they can see and to find a link between the title and the image.

- Ask students to discuss the questions in pairs. Gather feedback from students and write key vocabulary on the board.
- Discuss the unit outcomes with students and write any key vocabulary on the board.

Life Skills Link

In this unit, students will identify and analyze activities and responsibilities in their own lives as well as the lives of others and learn how to manage them by applying different strategies.

The skills students learn in this unit can be applied to almost every area of EL Civics as they help students to function effectively within U.S. society.

UNIT OUTCOMES	GRAMMAR	VOCABULARY	CASAS CORRELATION	SCANS CORRELATION	CCRS CORRELATION
• Analyze and create schedules • Identify goals and obstacles and suggest solutions • Write about a personal goal • Analyze study habits • Manage time	• Adverbs of frequency • *When* in the future	• Schedules and time • Goals • Paragraphs • Study habits	1: 0.1.2, 0.2.4 2: 7.1.1, 7.1.2, 7.1.3, 7.2.5, 7.2.6 3: 7.1.1, 7.1.2, 7.1.3, 7.2.5, 7.2.6 4: 0.1.5, 7.4.1, 7.4.3, 7.4.5 5: 7.4.2 R: 7.2.1 TP: 4.8.1, 4.8.5, 4.8.6	Many SCANS skills are incorporated in this unit with an emphasis on: • Allocating time • Understanding systems • Applying technology to task • Responsibility • Self management • Writing • Decision making	RI1, RI2, RI4, RI7 W4, W5 SL1, SL2, SL4 L1, L2, L3, L4 RF2, RF3, RF4

14 Unit 1

Unit 1 15

- **Teacher support** *Stand Out* continues to provide a wide variety of user-friendly tools and interactive activities that help teachers prepare students for success while keeping them engaged and motivated.

Stand Out supports teachers and learners

LEARNER COMPONENTS

- Student Book
- Online workbook powered by MyELT
- Print workbook

TEACHER COMPONENTS

- Lesson Planner
- Classroom DVD
- Assessment CD-ROM
- Teacher's companion site with Multi-Level Worksheets

Welcome

Welcome

- Introduce the unit. Greet students by saying *Hello* and *Hi.*
- Ask students to look at the photos. Elicit the greetings people say to each other when they meet for the first time. Write any useful vocabulary on the board.
- Discuss the unit outcomes with students. Ask them if they know anyone's phone number or any classroom instructions. Write any useful vocabulary on the board next to the vocabulary for greetings you elicited earlier.

Life Skills Link

In this unit, students will learn how to greet people they meet for the first time. They will also learn how to ask for and give a specific piece of information.

Workplace Link

All lessons and units in *Stand Out* include basic communication skills and interpersonal skills important for the workplace. They are not individually identified. Other workplace skills are indicated. They include, collecting and organizing information, making decisions and solving problems, and combining ideas and information.

PRE-UNIT

Welcome

UNIT OUTCOMES

- Greet people
- Say and write phone numbers
- Follow instructions

UNIT OUTCOMES

- Greet people
- Say and write phone numbers
- Follow classroom instructions

GRAMMAR

- The verb *Be*
- Contractions with *Be*

VOCABULARY

- Alphabet and numbers
- *hello, hi, goodbye, bye*
- Classroom verbs: *listen, point, repeat, read, write*

EL CIVICS

The skills students learn in this unit can be applied to all EL Civics competency areas with a particular focus on the following:

- Communication

CASAS

Lesson 1: 0.1.1, 0.1.4, 0.2.1
Lesson 2: 0.1.1, 0.1.4, 0.2.1
Lesson 3: 0.1.5, 7.4.7
Review: 7.4.1, 7.4.2, 7.4.3

SCANS

Many SCANs skills are incorporated in the unit with an emphasis on:

- Listening
- Speaking
- Writing
- Sociability
- Acquiring and evaluating information
- Interpreting and communicating information

CCRS

SL1, SL2, L2, RF2, RF3

LESSON 1 Say hello!

GOAL ■ Greet people

A. Listen.

CD 1 TR 1-2

hello	hi	goodbye	bye

B. Listen again. Repeat the words. Point to the correct picture in Exercise A.

CD 1 TR 1-2

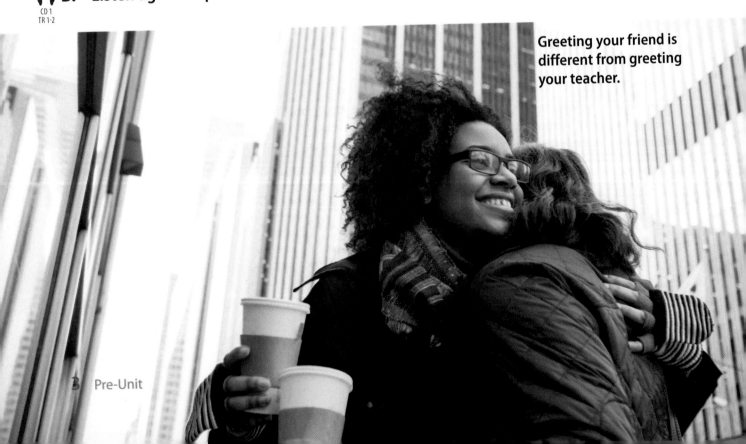

Greeting your friend is different from greeting your teacher.

AT-A-GLANCE **PREP**

Goal: Greet people
Grammar: *I'm* (contraction)
Pronunciation: /m/
Academic Strategy: Dictation
Vocabulary: Greeting words

Agenda

- Practice introductions.
- Introduce greetings.
- Review the alphabet.
- Write your name and a classmate's name.

Resources

Multilevel Worksheet: Lesson 1, Worksheet 1
Workbook: Pre-Unit, Lesson 1
Audio: CD 1, Tracks 1–6
Heinle Picture Dictionary: Wave, Greet, Smile, pages 40–41
Stand Out Basic Assessment CD-ROM with ExamView®

Pacing

- 1.5 hour classes
- 2.5 hour classes
- 3⁺ hour classes

STANDARDS CORRELATIONS

CCRS: SL2, L1, L2, RF2, RF3
CASAS: 0.1.1, 0.1.4, 0.2.1
SCANS: **Basic Skills** Listening, speaking, writing
EFF: **Communication** Speak so others can understand

Preassessment *(optional)*

Use the Stand Out Basic Assessment CD-ROM with ExamView® to create a pretest for the Pre-Unit.

Warm-up and Review

2–5 mins.

Shake hands and introduce yourself to students as they enter the classroom. Say: *Hi*, or *Hello, I'm* ______ (your name).

Introduction

2 mins.

Write the day of the week, the date, and the lesson's agenda on the board. Say the date while pointing to it and have students repeat it. State the goal: *Today, we will greet our classmates.*

Presentation 1

5 mins.

Write your name on the board. Greet a few students. Show them the American way to shake hands (curl fingers, make eye contact, etc.). Have students open their books and point to the picture of the teacher and student shaking hands.

A. Listen.

Play the conversations two times. After the first time, write *hello, hi, goodbye,* and *bye* on the board. Point to these words while students listen the second time.

LISTENING SCRIPT (CD 1 TR 1–2)

1. **Ms. Adams:** *Hello.*
   Orlando: *Hi.*
2. **Ms. Adams:** *Goodbye.*
   Orlando: *Bye.*

Practice 1

3 mins.

Play the conversations three more times. Point to the words on the board when you hear them on the recording. Have students do the same in their books.

B. Listen again. Repeat the words. Point to the correct picture in Exercise A.

Play the conversations three more times. Show students how to point to the people talking in the picture. Then, ask students to repeat the target words in Exercise A after you say them.

Evaluation 1

3 mins.

Observe students as they point to the people in the pictures and listen for correct pronunciation of the target words.

Presentation 2

10–15 mins.

Say the following: *Hi, I'm* ______ (your name). *Nice to meet you.* Shake hands with a few students and introduce yourself again. The objective of this lesson is to have students learn *hi, hello, goodbye,* and *bye,* as well as introduce them to the contraction *I'm.* The expression *nice to meet you* is used to establish the context. If students are ready, they may also say this phrase.

Play the first conversation between Orlando and Ms. Adams in Exercise C (CD 1, Track 3). Point to the pictures of the people talking.

Practice 2

7–10 mins.

C. Listen and point to the picture. Who is speaking?

Play the recording and ask students to point to the person speaking.

> **LISTENING SCRIPT**
>
> 
>
> CD 1
> TR 3–4
>
> *The listening scripts match the conversations in Exercise E.*

D. Listen and repeat.

Do a mini lesson on pronunciation. Some students may have difficulty pronouncing the final /m/ in *I'm.* Emphasize that it is important to close the lips to produce this sound.

> **PRONUNCIATION**
>
> **Final /m/**
>
> The instructor should not expect acquisition of pronunciation points after students' first exposure to them. Students may understand the concept of what is being taught; however, it is likely, especially at this level, that additional practice will be necessary for students to master the target pronunciation.
>
> In this case, /m/ is familiar to most languages although in some languages /m/ as a final consonant is not pronounced. Make sure students can produce an /m/ sound and then, apply it to *I'm.* Students may do this well in isolation, but when they try to follow the sound with their name, they may drop the /m/.

> **LISTENING SCRIPT**
>
> 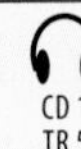
>
> CD 1
> TR 5
>
> */m/ . . . /m/ . . . /m/*
> *I'm Orlando.*
> *I'm Ms. Adams.*
> *I'm Amal.*
> *I'm Hang.*
> *I'm a student.*

E. Listen again and read.

Have students listen to the conversations again (CD 1, Tracks 3–4). This time have them read along with the text silently. At this point, they are only expected to learn the target vocabulary, not the entire conversation. Ask students to underline the target vocabulary from Exercise A in the two conversations, as well as the contraction *I'm.*

Evaluation 2

7–10 mins.

Ask four students to come to the front of the class and write the target words: *hello, hi, goodbye,* and *bye.* Then, erase the words from the board, ask students to close their books, and give them a quick dictation of the four words.

> **BEST PRACTICE**
>
> **One-word dictation**
>
> Dictation at this level does not need to involve more than a few isolated words. However, the instructor might give the word in a sentence and then, ask students to write only the target vocabulary that they hear within the sentence.
>
> As students become more competent, they will begin to write entire sentences or paragraphs. When this occurs, they should learn to listen to a phrase or sentence and repeat it mentally before attempting to write it. Students learning a second language often find it hard to write and listen at the same time, so this strategy of dictation is important. To prepare students for more extensive dictation, say each word three times. Ask students to listen only the first time, to write the second time, and to confirm their writing the third time.
>
> Dictation helps students remember the new vocabulary, more so than if they were to merely listen, recognize, and repeat it.

C. Listen and point to the pictures. Who is speaking?

CD 1 TR 3-4

Orlando

Ms. Adams

Amal

Hang

D. Listen and repeat.

CD 1 TR 5

CONTRACTIONS

I am = *I'm*

/m/

I'm Orlando.
I'm Ms. Adams.
I'm Amal.
I'm Hang.
I'm a student.

E. Listen again and read.

CD 1 TR 3-4

Ms. Adams:	Hello. I'm Ms. Adams.
Orlando:	Hi, Ms. Adams. I'm Orlando. Nice to meet you.
Ms. Adams:	Nice to meet you, too.
Orlando:	Bye.
Ms. Adams:	Goodbye.

Hang:	Hi. I'm Hang.
Amal:	Hello, Hang. I'm Amal.
Hang:	Nice to meet you.
Amal:	Nice to meet you, too.
Hang:	Bye now.
Amal:	Bye.

F. Listen and repeat. Write the alphabet and your name.

CD 1 TR 6

Aa Bb Cc Dd Ee Ff Gg Hh Ii

Jj Kk Ll Mm Nn Oo Pp Qq Rr

Ss Tt Uu Vv Ww Xx Yy Zz

I'm Amal.

G. Write.

Hi Hi

Hello Hello

Goodbye Goodbye

H. Write your name and a classmate's name. Then, talk to four more classmates.

Answers will vary.

Hi. I'm ____________________. (your name)

Hello. I'm ____________________. (classmate's name)

Presentation 3

15–20 mins.

Scribble your name on the board, intentionally making it hard to read. Next to your scribble, write your name again. This time, do it neatly and legibly. Ask students to tell you which example is easier to read. Use a thumbs-up to indicate *better*. As students identify which handwriting is better, circle the example they choose.

From this explanation, students will understand that some writing is more acceptable than others.

F. Listen and repeat. Write the alphabet and your name.

Play the recording twice. The first time students only listen. The second time they listen and repeat each letter.

LISTENING SCRIPT

CD 1 TR 6

A B C D E F G H I J K L M
N O P Q R S T U V W X Y Z

Write *I'm Amal.* on the board and spell the name a few times out loud until students begin to spell it with you. Refer students to the grammar box on page 4 and help them to see how the contraction works. Don't spend too much time on this contraction because it is only exposure at this point.

Write the alphabet on the board; quiz students by pointing to a letter and allowing them to call it out. Help with pronunciation, paying particular attention to the vowels. Invite a few students to the board. As you say a letter, have them point to it.

For shorter classes, ask students to do Exercise G for homework.

BEST PRACTICE

Volunteers

The first time you invite students to the board, you may want to ask for volunteers. Once all the students understand the activity, call on some of the quieter students to respond. Getting students up in the front of the classroom is a great way to help prepare them for the classroom presentations they will be giving at the end of each unit.

Practice 3

5 mins.

G. Write.

Evaluation 3

5 mins.

Check students' work while they complete Exercise G to make sure they stay within the lines in the book.

Refer students to *Stand Out Basic Workbook, Pre-Unit, Lesson 1* for more practice with contractions and *I'm*.

Go to the *Activity Bank* online for suggestions on promoting digital literacy and using the Internet to enhance this lesson.

Application

5–7 mins.

H. Write your name and a classmate's name. Then, talk to four more classmates.

After students write their own names and a classmate's name, ask them to read what they have written to the class. Then, ask for a few volunteers to do the short conversation in front of the class. Finally, ask students to meet and greet four other students in the class.

MULTILEVEL WORKSHEET

Lesson 1, Worksheet 1: Say *Hello* and *Goodbye*

INSTRUCTOR'S NOTES

AT-A-GLANCE **PREP**

Goal Say and write phone numbers
Grammar: *am* and *is*
Academic Strategy: Focused listening
Vocabulary: Numbers

Agenda

- Review names.
- Learn numbers and phone numbers.
- Identify spoken numbers.
- Make a phone list.

Resources

Multilevel Worksheet: Lesson 2, Worksheet 1
Workbook: Pre-Unit, Lesson 2
Audio: CD 1, Tracks 7–10
Heinle Picture Dictionary: Numbers, pages 2–3; The Telephone, pages 16–17

Pacing

■ 1.5 hour classes ■ 2.5 hour classes
■ 3+ hour classes

STANDARDS CORRELATIONS

CCRS: SL2, RF3
CASAS: 0.1.1, 0.1.4, 0.2.1
SCANS: **Basic Skills** Writing, listening, speaking, reading
Information Acquire and evaluate information, organize and maintain information, interpret and communicate information
EFF: **Communication** Read with understanding, convey ideas in writing, speak so others can understand, listen actively
Interpersonal Cooperate with others

Warm-up and Review 10–12 mins.

Write the following conversation on the board:

A: *Hello, I'm __________. What's your name?*
B: __________, _-_-_-_-_.

Show students how to insert their names and spelling in the blanks. Have students walk around the room and practice this conversation with ten classmates. Then, ask them to practice it again, this time writing down the names of five people.

Introduction 2 mins.

Write the day of the week, the date, and the lesson's agenda on the board. Say the date while pointing to it and have students repeat it. State the goal: *Today, we will say and write phone numbers.*

Presentation 1 5 mins.

Count students off, using the numbers one to ten. See how well students already know their numbers by playing the game "Stand Up and Share." Ask all students to stand. Say *two*. All the students who are the number two should repeat the number and sit. Repeat the activity until all students are sitting.

A. Listen and point. Who is speaking?

Before playing the recording, describe the pictures using a few details. Students won't understand all the words, but it is good exposure. Write *phone* and/or *telephone* on the board. Then, play the recording. Have students point at the speakers.

> **LISTENING SCRIPT** CD 1 TR 7
>
> **Lien:** *Hello?*
> **Matías:** *Hi, Lien. This is Matías.*
> **Lien:** *Hello, Matías. How are you?*
> **Matías:** *Fine, thanks.*

B. Listen and repeat. Point to each number. Then, write all the numbers.

Play the recording three times. First, have students listen and point to the numbers. The second time, ask students to repeat each number. Finally, have students write the numbers.

> **LISTENING SCRIPT** CD 1 TR 8
>
> *0 1 2 3 4 5 6 7 8 9 10*

Practice 1 3 mins.

Play the recording again (CD 1, Track 8). Ask students to write the numbers below the examples. Ask students to also write Lien's name and phone number.

Evaluation 1 3 mins.

Observe students writing in their books.

LESSON 2 Phone numbers

GOAL Say and write phone numbers

A. Listen and point. Who is speaking?

CD 1 TR 7

B. Listen and repeat. Point to each number. Then, write all the numbers.

CD 1 TR 8

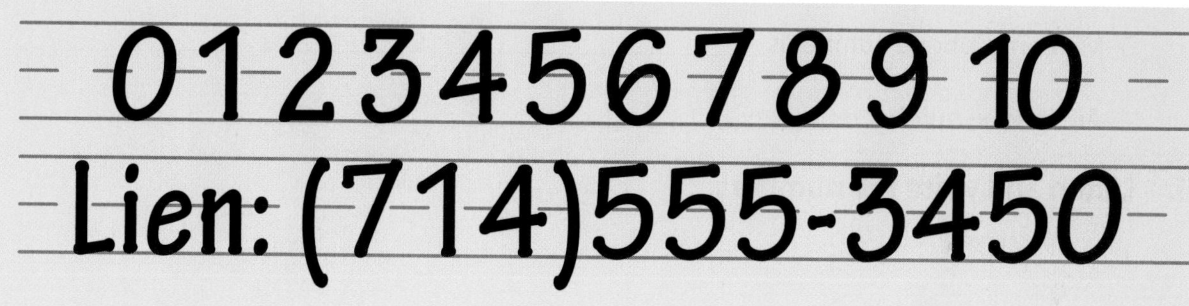

0 1 2 3 4 5 6 7 8 9 10

Lien: (714)555-3450

C. Listen and circle.

CD 1 TR 9

1. Mai	2. Paulo	3. Ms. Banks	4. Ali
(714) 555-7682	(352) 555-6767	(808) 555-4512	(915) 555-4576
(714) 555-3450	(352) 555-1415	(808) 555-6755	(915) 555-3466
(714) 555-7689	(352) 555-2655	(808) 555-3456	(915) 555-3455

D. Write.

1. Mai's phone number is (714) 555-3450.
2. Paulo's phone number is (352) 555-6767.
3. Ms. Banks' phone number is (808) 555-3456.
4. Ali's phone number is (915) 555-3455.

E. Listen and write the numbers.

CD 1 TR 10

1. (617) 555-6823
2. (617) 555-4293
3. (508) 717-8791
4. (508) 717-6342
5. (714) 424-8912
6. (714) 232-1134

Presentation 2

12–15 mins.

Dictate a few numbers (zero to ten only) and ask students to write the numbers they hear. Ask for volunteers to come to the board and write the numbers they heard.

Practice 2

5–7 mins.

C. Listen and circle.

Play the recording and ask students to circle the correct phone number.

LISTENING SCRIPT

1. *(714) 555-3450*
2. *(352) 555-6767*
3. *(808) 555-3456*
4. *(915) 555-3455*

CULTURAL NOTE

Phone numbers

Phone numbers are grouped differently in different countries. This may be a new concept to students. Also, when spoken, numbers in the United States are often said one number at a time and not in combination; for example, *five-five-five* pause *three-seven-six-five*. However, it is also correct to say *five-five-five* pause *thirty-seven*, *sixty-five*. Write different phone numbers on the board. Say the numbers in a variety of ways. Ask students to indicate when you are speaking with correct rhythm and when you are not.

Evaluation 2

5 mins.

D. Write.

Ask students to copy the numbers from Exercise C.

BEST PRACTICE

Evaluation

The evaluation stage of a lesson plan is important because this is where the instructor determines if students have mastered the concept they have just practiced. If they are still having problems with the target language, students may need additional practice activities before moving on.

E. Listen and write the numbers.

Play the recording twice. You should do this as a class, allowing students to talk among themselves and check answers as they go.

LISTENING SCRIPT

1. *(617) 555-6823*
2. *(617) 555-4293*
3. *(508) 717-8791*
4. *(508) 717-6342*
5. *(714) 424-8912*
6. *(714) 232-1134*

For shorter classes, ask students to do Activities F, G, and H for homework.

INSTRUCTOR'S NOTES

Presentation 3

15–20 mins. ■■■

F. Read the phone list.

Read the phone list with students. Check for comprehension by asking: *What is _____ 's phone number?* Ask students about each person on the list.

Go over the grammar box with students. The grammar presented here is a tool needed to understand the upcoming practice. This grammar box is intended to be only exposure at this time. Students should not be expected to completely understand the concept of conjugating the verb *Be* after this introduction.

For shorter classes, ask students to do Exercise G for homework.

Practice 3

10–15 mins. ■

G. Ask your partner for the phone numbers from Exercise F and write.

Students have not yet learned to form questions, but they can start by helping each other complete sentences.

This activity can be an information gap activity if you decide the students are ready. Ask students to work in pairs. Have Student A cover the phone list. Student A will read the name of the person in Exercise G. Student B will read the numbers and Student A will write. Then, have students change roles.

Evaluation 3

2 mins. ■

Ask students to check their answers by looking back at the chart in Exercise F.

Refer students to *Stand Out Basic Workbook, Pre-Unit, Lesson 2* for more practice with *I am* and *it is.*

Go to the *Activity Bank* online for suggestions on promoting digital literacy and using the Internet to enhance this lesson.

Application

5–7 mins. ■■■

H. Make a class phone list.

Some students may not have phones and others may not want to share their numbers publicly. If this is a problem, ask for volunteers to share their numbers with the class. As they share their numbers, classmates can write what they hear.

MULTILEVEL WORKSHEET

Lesson 2, Worksheet 1: Write Phone Numbers

INSTRUCTOR'S NOTES

Exercise G: Collect and organize information

F. Read the phone list.

PHONE LIST Ms. Adams' English Class	
Name	**Phone Number**
Hang	(714) 555-3450
Andre	(714) 555-1333
Shiro	(714) 555-9812
Sara	(714) 555-4545
Taylor	(714) 555-1237

G. Ask your partner for the phone numbers from Exercise F and write.

Student A: Hang
Student B: (714) 555-3450

The Verb *Be*

I *am* ...

The phone number *is* ...

Student A

Andre (714) 555-1333

Shiro (714) 555-9812

Student B

Sara (714) 555-4545

Taylor (714) 555-1237

H. Make a class phone list. Answers will vary.

PHONE LIST	
Name	**Phone number**
(my name)	

LESSON 3 Class work

GOAL ■ Follow instructions

A. Listen. CD 1 TR 11

B. Listen again and point. CD 1 TR 11

Classroom Instructions

Read all instructions.

Write your name.

Listen carefully.

AT-A-GLANCE **PREP**

Goal: Follow classroom instructions
Grammar: Action verbs, imperatives
Pronunciation: Final /t/
Academic Strategies: Test-taking strategies, focused listening
Vocabulary: *read, write, listen, repeat*

Agenda

- Review numbers and counting.
- Learn new vocabulary for classroom actions.
- Take a practice test.
- Show that you understand classroom instructions.

Resources

Multilevel Worksheet: Lesson 3, Worksheet 1
Workbook: Pre-Unit, Lesson 3
Audio: CD 1, Tracks 11–14
Heinle Picture Dictionary: Listen, Read, Write: pages 20–21

Pacing

- 1.5 hour classes
- 2.5 hour classes
- 3⁺ hour classes

STANDARDS CORRELATIONS

CCRS: SL2, RF2, RF3
CASAS: 0.1.5, 7.4.7
SCANS: **Basic Skills** Listening, speaking, reading, writing
EFF: **Communication** Speak so others can understand, listen actively

Warm-up and Review

5 mins.

Take out five pencils. Count them slowly. Repeat the exercise until students begin to count with you. Say: *Repeat.* Do the same thing with small numbers of books and sheets of paper and say: *Write the number.* Pantomime the action. Check what students write.

Introduction

2 mins.

Write the day of the week, the date, and the lesson's agenda on the board. Say the date while pointing to it and have students repeat it. State the goal: *Today, we will learn to follow instructions.*

Presentation 1

7–10 mins.

Establish context by asking students to look at the pictures in Exercise A on page 3. Ask how many people are in the pictures. Compare the class to yours. Ask how many students are in your class.

BEST PRACTICE

Establishing a context

The *Stand Out* approach recommends that all target language be presented in context. Context helps students connect with the vocabulary.

Here, the classroom itself establishes a good context. Help students identify items in the picture. The vocabulary may not be the objective of the lesson so no repetition is necessary, but students should begin to see a relationship between the work they do in class and their real lives.

A. Listen.

Ask students to listen to Ms. Adams. Write the word *poster* on the board. Ask: *Where is the poster?* If students can't respond, help them find the poster in the picture.

LISTENING SCRIPT

CD 1 TR 11

Hello, class. Today, we will discuss three important things you need to know to participate in class and to learn English. This is a poster. It says you should always listen carefully, read all instructions, and write your name on every sheet of paper. Please repeat these words—listen . . . read . . . write. Again—listen . . . read . . . write. Thank you.

Practice 1

5–7 mins.

B. Listen again and point.

Play the recording again (CD 1, Track 11) and ask students to point to the words as they hear them. Play the recording three times.

Evaluation 1

5–7 mins.

Observe students pointing.

Presentation 2

7–10 mins.

With the books closed, pantomime the five actions shown in Exercise C. Write the five words on the board. When you think students are comfortable with the new vocabulary, pantomime the actions again and have them identify what you are doing.

C. Write the actions.

Prepare students for Exercise C by pantomiming the actions for individual students. Do this for *listen, point, read,* and *write*.

D. Listen and repeat.

Briefly read the grammar box with students. Explain as necessary using examples.

Also, teach students the proper way to pronounce a final /t/.

PRONUNCIATION

Final /t/

Because the imperatives in this unit are often single-word sentences, and since sentences in English often end with the mouth open and relaxed, this is a good time to demonstrate the final /t/.

In many other languages, final consonants, especially at the end of sentences, end with the tongue or the lips touching. This often makes it difficult to hear the final sound completely. In English, on the other hand, the tongue or lips touch and then, release. With /t/ the release explodes with air, making it relatively easy to hear the final sound. This release of air most often occurs at the end of a sentence or phrase before a pause.

Practice the pronunciation of the final /t/ sounds of *write, point,* and *repeat* until students begin to mimic your pronunciation.

LISTENING SCRIPT

CD 1 TR 12

/t/ /t/ /t/
write . . . write . . . write . . . write
point . . . point . . . point . . . point
repeat . . . repeat . . . repeat . . . repeat

Practice 2

5–7 mins.

E. Practice the actions in Exercise C.

Ask students to work in pairs. Another way to do this activity is to have students stand up and talk to five different students.

BEST PRACTICE

Inside/outside circles

Pair work can take many forms. Changing pairs after each practice is useful because students are more likely to speak clearly with each new partner, tending to concentrate on their language production more with each partner change.

One technique of having students change partners is called "Inside/Outside Circle." In this activity, students form two circles with the same number of students in each. One circle is inside the other. Students face one another and speak to the person they are facing. When indicated by the instructor, one circle shifts one space clockwise so students are lined up with a new partner.

For classrooms with limited space, students can be in two lines across the front of the classroom. The students in one line face the students in the other and form pairs. Then, when indicated, one of the lines shifts. The last person at the end of the line moves to the front of the line.

Evaluation 2

3 mins.

Observe the activity and ask a few pairs to come to the front and do the activity for the class.

C. Write the actions.

repeat	read	listen	write	point

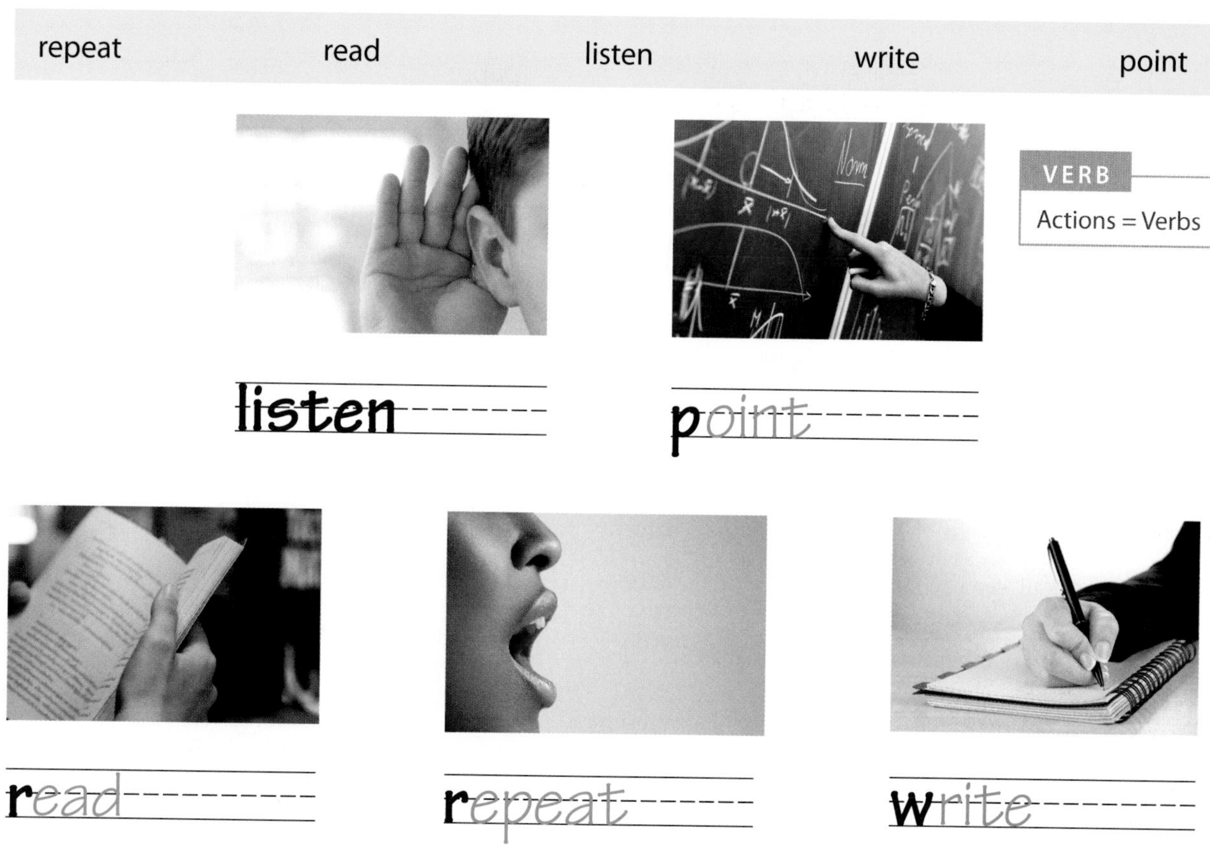

VERB

Actions = Verbs

D. Listen and repeat.

CD 1 TR 12

/t/

Write.

Point.

Repeat.

E. Practice the actions in Exercise C.

EXAMPLE

Student A: Listen.

Student B:

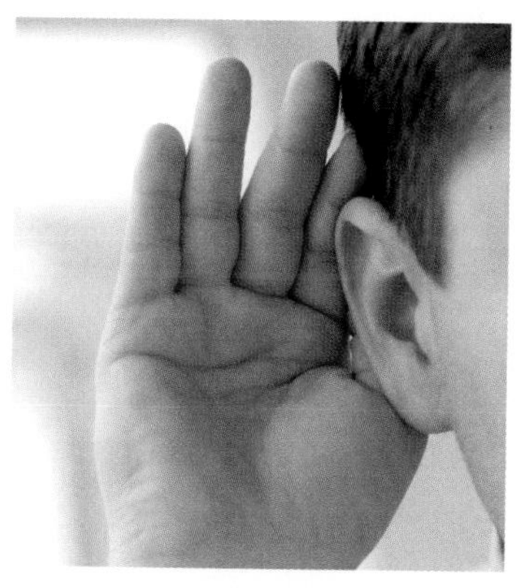

F. Read and complete.

Circle.

1. pencil
   a. pen b. (pencil) c. paper
2. paper
   (a. paper) b. pen c. pencil

Check (✓).

3. pencil
   ☐ pen ☑ pencil ☐ paper
4. pen
   ☑ pen ☐ paper ☐ pencil

G. Listen and circle the answers.

CD 1 TR 13

1. a. point b. repeat (c. listen) d. read e. write
2. (a. point) b. repeat c. listen d. read e. write
3. a. point b. repeat c. listen d. read (e. write)
4. a. point (b. repeat) c. listen d. read e. write

H. Listen and check (✓) the answers.

CD 1 TR 14

1. ☐ a. point ☐ b. repeat ☑ c. listen ☐ d. read ☐ e. write
2. ☑ a. point ☐ b. repeat ☐ c. listen ☐ d. read ☐ e. write
3. ☐ a. point ☐ b. repeat ☐ c. listen ☐ d. read ☑ e. write
4. ☐ a. point ☑ b. repeat ☐ c. listen ☐ d. read ☐ e. write

I. Follow the instructions.

1. Circle the phone number.

   02219 ((212) 555-7763) 04/08/09 7.1.2015

2. Check (✓) the answer.

   2 + 2 = ______ ☐ 3 ☐ 5 ☑ 4

3. Write the name of your teacher.

   Answers will vary.

Presentation 3

7–10 mins.

Introduce three new words to the students with their books closed: *pencil, pen,* and *paper*. Use items in the classroom to demonstrate this vocabulary. These words are not the target vocabulary, but they are associated with the act of writing. Consequently, they further expand the linguistic context. Ask students what words are associated with reading. Help them, if necessary, to say *book(s)*. Do the same for *point* (finger), *listen* (ear), and *repeat* (mouth).

Tell students that you are going to give them a test. Write the word *test* on the board. Briefly drill students by showing or pointing to the objects previously introduced and asking students to respond with the correct verb.

F. Read and complete.

Tell students that you will show them ways to take written tests and that they will take tests like this in the class from time to time. Go over circling and checking.

Practice 3

10 mins.

G. Listen and circle the answers.

Do the first item with students.

> **LISTENING SCRIPT**
>
> CD 1 TR 13
>
> 1. *listen*
> 2. *point*
> 3. *write*
> 4. *repeat*

H. Listen and check (✓) the answers.

Explain to students that they should listen for other words associated with the target vocabulary, too. Do the first item with students.

> **LISTENING SCRIPT**
>
> 
>
> CD 1 TR 14
>
> 1. *People use their ears to listen for important information.*
> 2. *The teacher is pointing with her finger at the poster in front of the class.*
> 3. *I need a paper and a pencil so I can write a letter.*
> 4. *Students, open your mouths and repeat the words clearly.*

> **BEST PRACTICE**
>
> **Listening**
>
> Students are often under the misconception that in order to do listening tasks they must understand every word. Actually, a lot of listening, even by native speakers, involves focused listening where the person listening decides on meaning from just a few key words. Exercises such as Exercise H allow students to develop this listening strategy by listening for key words and filtering out words they may not understand.

Evaluation 3

2 mins.

Ask students to compare their answers with a partner.

Refer students to *Stand Out Basic Workbook, Pre-Unit, Lesson 3* for more practice with action verbs.

Go to the *Activity Bank* online for suggestions on promoting digital literacy and using the Internet to enhance this lesson.

Application

5–7 mins. 

I. Follow the instructions.

> **MULTILEVEL WORKSHEET**
>
> Lesson 3, Worksheet 1: Classroom Instructions

INSTRUCTOR'S NOTES

Personal Information

About the Photo

Yoan Valat took this photo in Paris, France. It shows people lining up to have their photo taken in order to participate in an art performance by the French artist JR. The performance—*Inside Out: The People's Art Project*—has visited many different cities around the world since 2011, and it involves local people having their portrait taken and displayed in public. JR believes the performance allows people to make a personal statement and display it for the world to see. Around 200,000 people have already taken part in JR's performance in over 100 countries around the world.

- Introduce the unit. Ask students to look at their own forms of personal identification such as ID cards or licenses. Then ask them what type of information they see. Have them look at the unit outcomes for clues.
- Ask students to look at the photo. Ask them to find a link between the unit title and the image. Discuss as a class.

People line up to have their photo taken for an art performance.

UNIT OUTCOMES	GRAMMAR	VOCABULARY	EL CIVICS
• Identify people • Express nationalities • Express marital status • Say and write addresses • Say and write dates	• Simple present tense • The verb *Be* • Contractions with *Be* • *Wh-* questions	• Months of the year: *month, day, year* • Marital status: *single, married, divorced* • Address vocabulary: *city, state, zip code*	The skills students learn in this unit can be applied to all EL Civics competency areas with a particular focus on the following: • Communication

AVX
VOLONTAIRES
DES FORCES
FRANÇAISES LIBR
MORTS
POVR L'HONNEV
UNIT OUTCOMES
Identify people
Express nationalities
Express marital status
Say and write addresses
Say and write dates
Look at the photo and answer the questions.
1. Where are the people in the pictures from?
2. How old are they?

- Ask students to discuss the questions in pairs. Ask students if they can find answers to the questions on their own forms of personal identification.
- Discuss the unit outcomes with students. Ask them if any of the information in the outcomes is contained in their own forms of personal identification. Write any key vocabulary on the board.

Life Skills Link

In this unit, students will learn how to identify themselves and give snippets of information pertaining to their identity. They will also learn how to ask for this information from other people.

Workplace Link

All lessons and units in *Stand Out* include basic communication skills and interpersonal skills important for the workplace. They are not individually identified. Other workplace skills are indicated. They include, *collecting and organizing information, making decisions and solving problems,* and *combining ideas and information.*

CASAS	SCANS	CCRS
Lesson 1: 0.1.1, 0.2.1 Lesson 2: 0.1.2, 0.2.1, 1.1.3, 4.8.7 Lesson 3: 0.1.2, 0.2.1 Lesson 4: 0.1.2, 0.2.1, 1.1.3, 4.8.7 Lesson 5: 0.1.2, 0.2.1, 2.3.2 Review: 0.1.1, 0.2.1, 7.4.1, 7.4.2, 7.4.3 Team Project: 0.1.1, 0.2.1, 4.8.1	Many SCANs skills are incorporated in the unit with an emphasis on: • Basic skills • Acquiring and evaluating information • Interpreting and communicating information • Seeing things in the mind's eye • Sociability	RI1, RI7, SL1, SL2, SL4, L1, L2, L5, RF2, RF3

LESSON 1 What's your name?

GOAL ■ Identify people

CD 1
TR 15

A. IDENTIFY Listen and point.

What's his name?
His name is Amal.

What's her name?
Her name is Ms. Adams.

What are their names?
Their names are Hang and Elsa.

What's your name?
My name is ...

B. Practice the conversation. Use the questions in Exercise A to make new conversations.

Student A: What's his name?
Student B: His name is Amal.

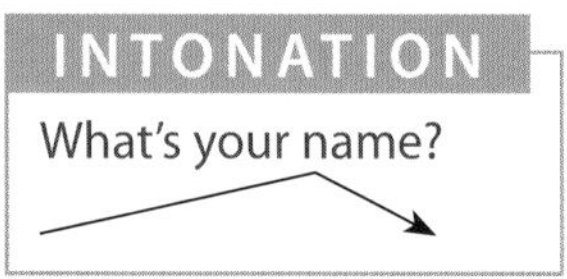

AT-A-GLANCE **PREP**

Goal: Identify people
Grammar: Subject pronouns
Pronunciation: Rising and falling intonation
Vocabulary: Subject pronouns, students

Agenda

- Review greetings.
- Ask for student names.
- Learn *I, you, he, she, we,* and *they.*
- Practice asking questions.

Resources

Multilevel Worksheets: Lesson 1, Worksheets 1 and 2
Workbook: Unit 1, Lesson 1
Audio: CD 1, Tracks 15–17
Heinle Picture Dictionary: Wave, Greet, Smile, pages 40–41
Stand Out Basic Assessment CD-ROM with ExamView®

Pacing

■ 1.5 hour classes ■ 2.5 hour classes
■ 3+ hour classes

STANDARDS CORRELATIONS

CCRS: L1, L2, SL2, SL4, RF2, RF3
CASAS: 0.1.1, 0.2.1
***SCANS:* Basic Skills** Reading, writing, listening, speaking
***EFF:* Communication** Speak so others can understand

Preassessment *(optional)*

Use the Stand Out Basic Assessment CD-ROM with ExamView® to create a pretest for Unit 1.

Warm-up and Review 2–5 mins.

Review greeting one another. Write on the board: *I'm* ________ (your name). *Nice to meet you.* Review the American style of shaking hands. Ask students to circulate around the room shaking hands with their classmates, giving their names, and saying: *Nice to meet you.*

Introduction 2 mins.

Write the day of the week, the date, and the agenda on the board. Say the date while pointing to it and have students repeat. State the goal: *Today, we will learn to identify our classmates.*

Presentation 1 10–15 mins.

Ask a few students, male and female, for their names. Then, ask the class for the names of the students who have just responded. Then, say: *His name is* ________ (name). *Her name is* ________ (name).

Write these questions on the board: *What's his name? What's her name? What's your name?* Practice them with the students. Have students practice by doing a question-and-answer chain:

Student A: *What's your name?*
Student B: *(student name).*
Student C: *What's his/her name?*
Student D: *(student name).*

Then, Student D starts with a new student.

Ask students to open their books and look at the four pictures.

A. IDENTIFY Listen and point.

After listening to the recording, students will listen to you. Read the sentences in random order. Ask students to point to the appropriate picture. Help them distinguish *he* and *she.*

LISTENING SCRIPT

CD 1 TR 15

Here are pictures of four people I know at school. His name is Amal. He is a student. Her name is Ms. Adams. She is a teacher. Their names are Hang and Elsa. They are students.

Create a dialog with the questions on the board.

Student A: *What's your name?*
Student B: *(name). I am a student.*
Student A: *What's his/her name?*
Student B: *(name). He/She is a student.*

Practice 1 7–10 mins.

B. Practice the conversation. Use the questions in Exercise A to make new conversations.

Ask students to walk around the room and talk to ten classmates. Ask them to write the students' names on a sheet of paper. Encourage students to spell out names and not write the information for their partner.

Evaluation 1 5–7 mins.

Ask for students to demonstrate the dialog.

Presentation 2

10–15 mins.

C. Listen and repeat.

Look at the illustrations and the words below them with students.

LISTENING SCRIPT

CD 1 TR 16

I
You
He
She
We
They

I am a student.
You are a student.
He is a student.
She is a student.
We are students.
They are students.

D. RELATE Look again at the pictures in Exercise A. Write.

Have students write the correct pronouns. This is still the presentation stage so do the exercise as a class.

Model this same pattern with students in the class. For example, walk up to one male student and say to the class: *His name is* ______. Use proper stress and rhythm as you do this. Encourage students to respond: *He is a student.* Do the same with a few more students. Have a volunteer ask the question about a different student this time and you give the answer. Then, ask for two students to model the exercise using another classmate.

INTONATION

Rhythm with questions

Help students hear the intonation patterns of the question: *What's your name?* This pattern will be repeated throughout the unit. When asking *Wh-* questions, the speaker's pitch should go down. Model the intonation for the class and have students repeat. Then, have students practice asking each other the question in pairs and monitor.

For shorter classes, ask students to do Exercise D for homework.

Practice 2

5–7 mins.

Have students walk around the room asking for their classmates' names. Have them continue practicing until you stop them.

Evaluation 2

3–5 mins.

Ask for volunteers to demonstrate the two sentences for each answer.

INSTRUCTOR'S NOTES

CD 1
TR 16

C. Listen and repeat.

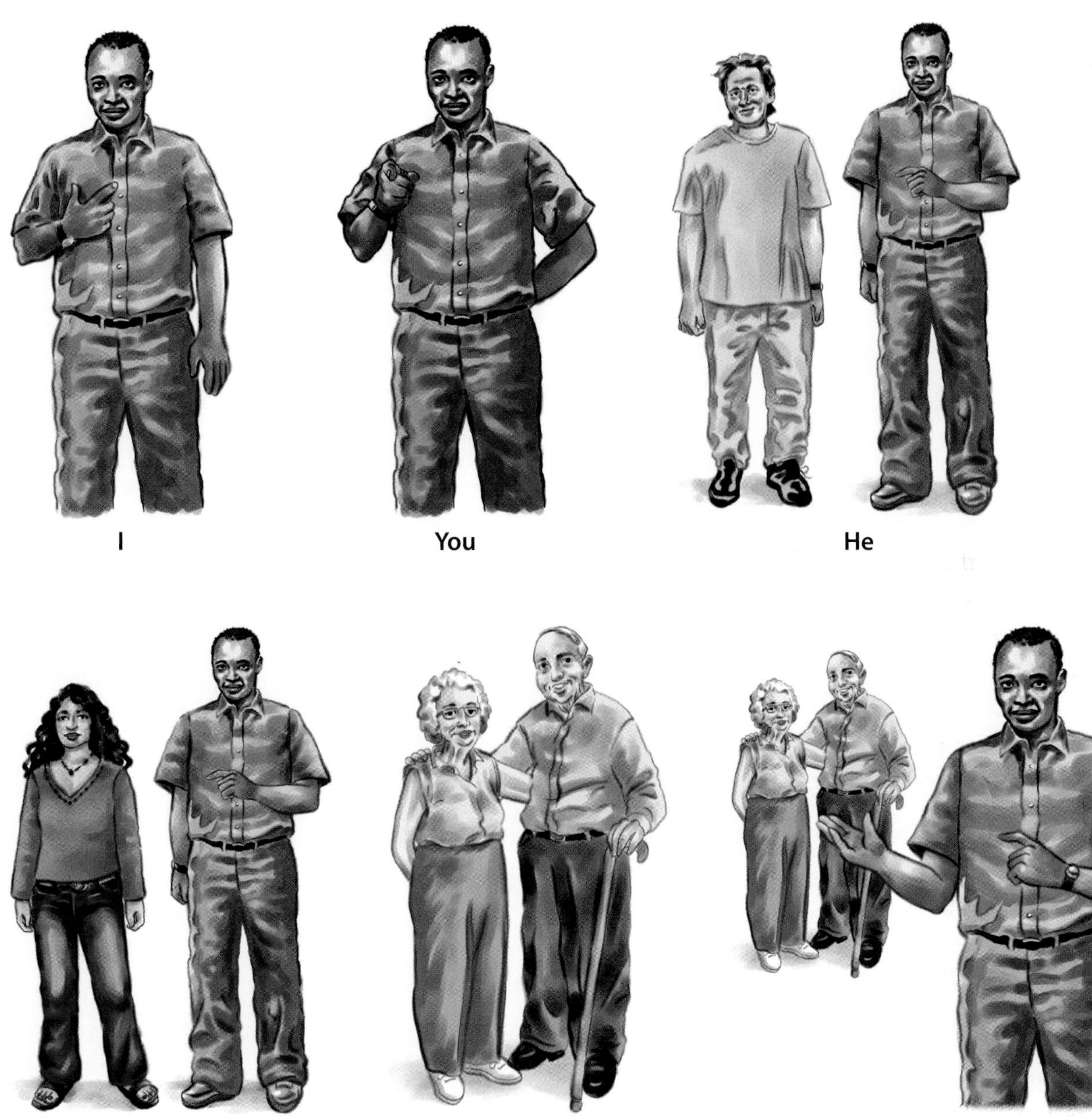

D. RELATE Look again at the pictures in Exercise A. Write.

1. His name is Amal. ____He____ is a student.
2. Her name is Ms. Adams. ____She____ is a teacher.
3. Their names are Hang and Elsa. ____They____ are students.
4. My name is ____Answers will vary.____. ____I____ am a student.

WORKPLACE CONNECTION
Exercise G: Collect and organize information

CD 1
TR 17

E. Listen and point.

Hang: Hi, Satsuki.
Satsuki: Hello, Hang.
Hang: Elsa, this is Satsuki. He is a student.
Elsa: Hello, Satsuki. I am a student, too.
Satsuki: Nice to meet you.

THIS IS ...
We use *This is ...* to introduce people.

F. Practice the conversation in Exercise E.

G. CLASSIFY Work with a partner. Write classmates' names.

Answers will vary.

Pronoun		Name
I	I am a student.	(your name)
You	You are a student.	(your partner's name)
He	He is a student.	
She	She is a student.	
We	We are students.	
They	They are students.	

Presentation 3

10–15 mins.

E. Listen and point.

Ask students who the women in the picture are. Ask them if you use *he* or *she* with women and girls. Play the recording. Go over each line with the students. Ask them to repeat after you. Practice the conversation as a class; you read Hang's lines, half the class reads Satsuki's lines, and the other half reads Elsa's line. Then, ask for three students to demonstrate the conversation in front of the class.

> **LISTENING SCRIPT**
>
> 
> CD 1 TR 17
>
> *The listening script matches the conversation in Exercise E.*

Practice 3

5–7 mins.

F. Practice the conversation in Exercise E.

Divide students into groups of three and have them practice the conversation, switching roles each time they practice.

Evaluation 3

3–5 mins.

Ask groups to present the dialog in front of the class.

Refer students to *Stand Out Basic Workbook, Unit 1, Lesson 1* for more practice with subject pronouns.

Go to the *Activity Bank* online for suggestions on promoting digital literacy and using the Internet to enhance this lesson.

Application

5–7 mins.

G. CLASSIFY Work with a partner. Write classmates' names.

Ask students to work in pairs. Show them how to do this activity by using a student as your partner. Write: *He is a student. She is a student. They are students.* Then, have students replace the pronouns *he, she,* and *they* with names and write sentences in their notebooks. For example, instead of writing *He is a student,* they write *Nicolai is a student.*

Have students, in pairs, complete Exercise G, using classmates' names. Then, have them practice saying sentences such as: *Brian and Jason are students.*

BEST PRACTICE

Presenting dialogs

The first levels of *Stand Out* use dialogs. In the *Stand Out* approach, dialogs should be used as opportunities for students to use the language and become familiar with pronunciation and vocabulary.

The following steps demonstrate how to present dialogs effectively:

1. Present the dialog in context in its entirety, allowing students to hear the model either by you or by listening to the recording.
2. Have students repeat each line as a class. Work on rhythm and other pronunciation features.
3. Have students take one role while you take the other role and then, reverse roles.
4. Ask one student to practice the dialog with you. Then, reverse roles.
5. Ask two or three students to demonstrate for the class.
6. Add substitutions where appropriate or when called for and repeat the above steps.

MULTILEVEL WORKSHEETS

Lesson 1, Worksheet 1: Say *Hello!*

Lesson 1, Worksheet 2: Use Subject Pronouns

CRITICAL THINKING

CLASSIFY

Classifying is an important skill. Classifying is a way of organizing things into groups based on similarities and differences.

When students learn how to classify, they are able to show they understand the relationships and concepts.

Classification activities can be organized in the following steps:

1. Provide students with a list of items to be classified.
2. Ask students how the items are different. Then, ask how they are similar.
3. Have students determine categories that the items can be put into.
4. Explain that in order to do the previous step, we need to think about the one thing the items have in common.
5. Ask students to complete the categories.
6. Ask students to explain their choices.

AT-A-GLANCE **PREP**

Goal: Express nationalities
Grammar: Simple present tense
Academic Strategy: Focused listening
Vocabulary: *from, native country, birthplace*

Agenda

- Review asking questions.
- Ask: *Where are you from?*
- Listen for countries of origin.
- Ask classmates: *Where do you live?*

Resources

Multilevel Worksheet: Lesson 2, Worksheet 1
Workbook: Unit 1, Lesson 2
Audio: CD 1, Tracks 18–24
Heinle Picture Dictionary: Nationalities, pages 44–45

Pacing

■ 1.5 hour classes ■ 2.5 hour classes
■ 3+ hour classes

STANDARDS CORRELATIONS

CCRS: RI7, SL2, SL4, L1
CASAS: 0.1.2, 0.2.1, 1.1.3, 4.8.7
SCANS: **Basic Skills** Reading, writing, listening, speaking
Information Acquire and evaluate information, organize and maintain information, interpret and communicate information
Interpersonal Work with cultural diversity
EFF: **Communication** Speak so others can understand, listen actively
Interpersonal Cooperate with others

Warm-up and Review

8–12 mins.

Write on the board: *What's your name*? Remind students to use correct pronunciation and intonation. Ask students to walk around the room and ask their classmates this question. They may record the information on a sheet of paper.

Introduction

2 mins.

Write the date and agenda on the board. Ask students what day it is. If you have a world map, show them what state or region they live in and where the city is. State the goal: *Today, we will express our nationalities.*

Presentation 1

7–10 mins.

List countries on the board. Make sure you include the native countries of all the students. Circle your native country and put a check mark next to it. Ask students to come up and do the same for their native countries. Ask students to find their country on a map. If most students are from the same country, have them tell their hometown.

Have students open their books and ask where Sara is from. Ask for a volunteer to find Cuba on a world map. Ask students to repeat the sentences in the speech bubbles.

A. Read and listen.

Play the recording and ask students to listen. Then, play it again and ask them to point to the speech bubble when they hear each statement.

LISTENING SCRIPT

CD 1 TR 18

Mr. Jackson: *Hello. I'm Mr. Jackson. What's your name?*
Sara: *My name is Sara. I'm new in the class.*
Mr. Jackson: *Nice to meet you. Where are you from, Sara?*
Sara: *I'm from Cuba.*
Mr. Jackson: *That's great! Welcome to the class.*

B. Write.

Ask students to write information about Sara. Walk around the room and check their work. One-word answers are expected at this level, not complete sentences.

Practice 1

5–7 mins.

C. Ask your classmates.

Ask students to walk around the room and ask several classmates what their names are and where they are from.

Evaluation 1

7–10 mins.

D. SURVEY Ask about other classmates.

Ask one student what another student's name is and where the student is from. Then, ask the student about a different student. Every time you hear a new country, point to it on the list.

LESSON 2 Where are you from?

GOAL ■ Express nationalities

A. Read and listen.

CD 1
TR 18

B. Write.

1. What's her name? ___Sara___
2. Where is she from? ___Cuba___

C. Ask your classmates. Answers will vary.

1. What's your name?
2. Where are you from?

D. SURVEY Ask about other classmates. Answers will vary.

1. What's his name? What's her name?
2. Where's he from? Where's she from?

E. **PREDICT** **Look at the picture and answer the questions.** Answers will vary.

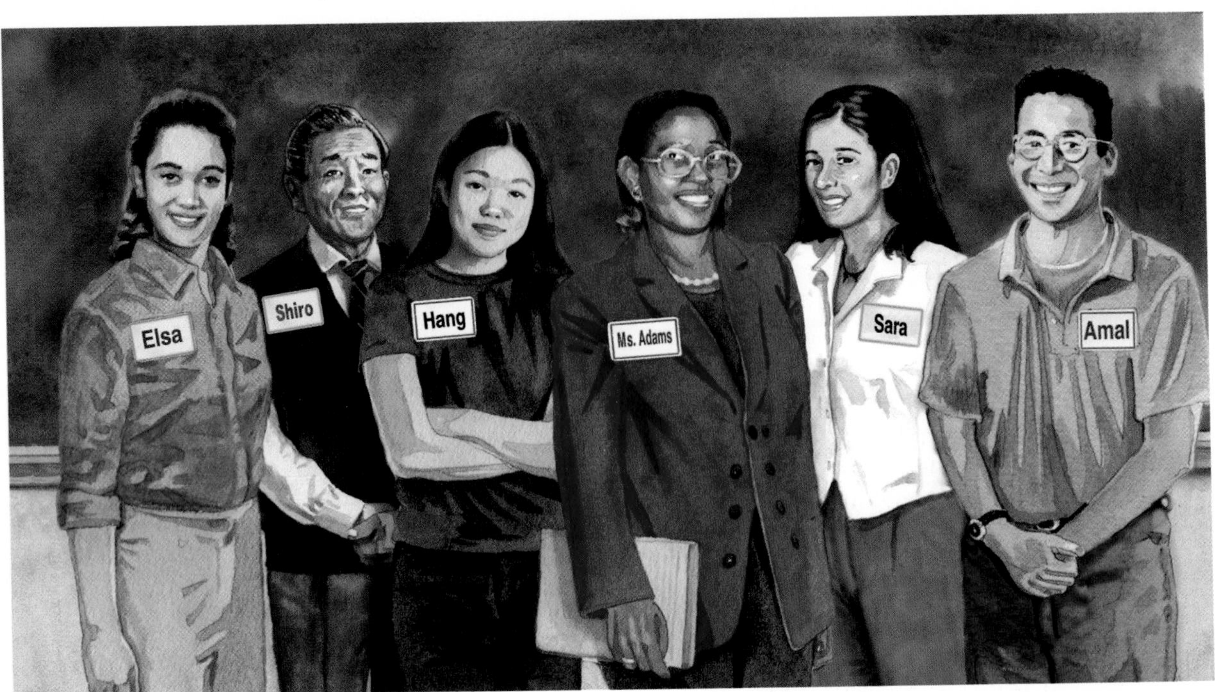

1. Where is Shiro from? ______________________
2. Where is Amal from? ______________________
3. Where is Hang from? ______________________
4. Where is Elsa from? ______________________

F. **Listen and write.**

CD 1
TR 19-23

1. She is from Cuba. _____Sara_____
2. He is from Lebanon. _____Amal_____
3. She is from Vietnam. _____Hang_____
4. She is from Russia. _____Elsa_____
5. He is from Japan. _____Shiro_____

G. **Practice the conversations. Use the information in Exercise F to make new conversations.**

Student A: Where is <u>Sara</u> from?
Student B: She is from <u>Cuba</u>.

Student A: What's her birthplace?
Student B: <u>Cuba</u>.

BIRTHPLACE

Where is he from? He is from Japan.
What's his birthplace? Japan.

Presentation 2

12–15 mins.

E. PREDICT Look at the picture and answer the questions.

Prepare students for listening by asking them simple questions about the picture. Help them to predict where the teacher and students are from. All answers are acceptable at this stage. Make a list on the board.

Discuss focused listening with students.

BEST PRACTICE

Focused listening

There are several different ways that people listen. One important way is to focus on essential information while filtering out what is not important. Students learning another language are often under the misconception that they must understand every word. It is important to teach students how to listen for important information even when they understand very little of the extraneous vocabulary used. They will develop the ability to make educated guesses about the additional information. Future tasks in this book will rely more and more on the students' ability to develop and incorporate this skill.

Go over the vocabulary box. Students need to understand *birthplace* in order to complete application forms and other forms. Review briefly the subject pronouns *he* and *she*, which students have already practiced in Lesson 1 of this unit.

Practice 2

10–15 mins.

F. Listen and write.

Play the recording. Ask students to listen and identify the students being described. Students will need to practice focused listening because several sentences are not related to nationality. You may need to play the recording two or three times.

LISTENING SCRIPT

CD 1 TR 19–23

Conversation 1

Ms. Adams: *Hello, I'm Ms. Adams. What's your name?*
Sara: *My name is Sara. I'm new in the class.*
Ms. Adams: *Nice to meet you. Won't you have a seat?*
Sara: *Thank you.*
Ms. Adams: *Where are you from, Sara?*
Sara: *I'm from Cuba.*

Conversation 2

Ms. Adams: *Are you the new student from Lebanon?*
Amal: *Yes, my name is Amal.*
Ms. Adams: *I hope you enjoy our class.*
Amal: *I will, thank you.*

Conversation 3

Ms. Adams: *Hello, Hang.*
Hang: *Hi, Ms. Adams.*
Ms. Adams: *Hang, where are you from?*
Hang: *I'm from Vietnam.*

Conversation 4

Ms. Adams: *Hello, Elsa. It is so good to see you today.*
Elsa: *Yes, I was sick yesterday, but I feel better today.*
Ms. Adams: *That's good. I thought you might have gone back to Russia.*

Conversation 5

Ms. Adams: *Hello. Welcome to the class. What's your name?*
Shiro: *I'm Shiro. I came to the United States last week.*
Ms. Adams: *Where are you from, Shiro?*
Shiro: *I'm from Japan.*

G. Practice the conversations. Use the information in Exercise F to make new conversations.

Have students practice with a partner. Make sure they substitute information for all the students in the conversations on the CD.

Evaluation 2

5 mins.

Ask students the same questions in Exercise G about themselves. Check for understanding.

Presentation 3

15–20 mins.

H. Read.

Go over the chart with students. At this stage, students are not ready for a lot of grammatical information. For now, it is appropriate to only focus on the first- and third-person singular forms of present-tense verbs. Emphasize that an *s* is only added to the end of a present-tense verb when the subject is in the third person.

> BEST PRACTICE
>
> **Grammar charts**
>
> For students who are used to them, grammar charts are simple and easy to read. But an instructor should never assume students can read a chart. Some students may have very limited education. Walk students through charts carefully. When they can read them without assistance, they will be closer to being independent learners.

Drill the students by saying *he, she,* or *I* and asking them to respond with the correct form of *live*. Ask individual students where they live. Then, have the rest of the class respond: *He (She) lives in* _______.

Work on pronunciation. Students will sometimes "swallow" the final *s*. Make sure students blend the *s* in *lives* and the *i* in *in* so that together they make a /z/ sound.

> BEST PRACTICE
>
> **Drills**
>
> Drills can be a good way to help students become familiar with vocabulary and pronunciation. They also help students gain confidence, especially when performing together with their classmates. However, drills should not be the sole practice or method used to help students learn English. There are several ways to drill (choral repetition, substitution, build-up, backward build-up, etc.). If particular drills are overused, there is a risk of losing meaning for structure.

I. Complete the sentences.

Complete the sentences as a class to confirm that students understand the grammar point.

J. Practice the conversation. Use the information in Exercise I to make new conversations.

Play the recording. Help the students repeat the dialog with proper intonation.

> LISTENING SCRIPT
>
> 
> CD 1 TR 24
>
> *The listening script matches the conversation in Exercise J.*

Show students how to replace Sara with Shiro, Amal, Elsa, and Hang.

Practice 3

5–7 mins.

Ask students to practice the dialog with a partner, substituting the other names.

Evaluation 3

2 mins.

Ask students to demonstrate in front of the classroom.

Refer students to *Stand Out Basic Workbook, Unit 1, Lesson 2* for more practice with first- and third-person singular and the simple present.

Go to the *Activity Bank* online for suggestions on promoting digital literacy and using the Internet to enhance this lesson.

Application

5–7 mins.

K. APPLY Ask four classmates. Make new conversations and complete the table.

Go over the conversation and the table with the students. Have students ask four classmates to make new conversations. Then, ask students to complete the table with information from their conversations.

> MULTILEVEL WORKSHEET
>
> Lesson 2, Worksheet 1: Write about Countries and Cities

H. Read.

Simple Present		
I	live	in Los Angeles.
He	lives	in Irvine.
She		in Chicago.

I. Complete the sentences.

1. Sara is from Cuba. She lives in Irvine.
2. Shiro is from Japan. He lives in Irvine.
3. Amal is from Levanon. He lives in Irvine.
4. Elsa is from Russia. She lives in Irvine.
5. Hang is from Vietnam. She lives in Irvine.
6. I am from Answers will vary. I Answers will vary.

J. Practice the conversation. Use the information in Exercise I to make new conversations.

CD 1 TR 24

Ms. Adams: Hi, Sara. Where are you from?
Sara: I'm from Cuba.
Ms. Adams: Where do you live?
Sara: I live in Irvine.

K. APPLY Ask four classmates. Make new conversations and complete the table.

Answers will vary.

You: Hi, ______. Where are you from?
Classmate: I'm from ______.
You: Where do you live?
Classmate: I live in ______.

Name (What's your name?)	Birthplace (Where are you from?)	Current city (Where do you live?)
1.		
2.		
3.		
4.		

LESSON 3 Are you married?

GOAL ■ Express marital status

A. IDENTIFY Listen and write.

CD 1
TR 25

single married divorced

He is single.

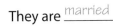

They are divorced.

They are married.

B. With a partner, point at the pictures in Exercise A and say: *He is single, They are married,* or *They are divorced.*

AT-A-GLANCE **PREP**

Goal: Express marital status
Grammar: The verb *Be* and contractions with *Be*
Pronunciation: Rhythm and prominence
Academic Strategies: Focused listening, team work
Vocabulary: *married, divorced, single, marital status*

Agenda

- Learn about marital status.
- Study the verb *Be*.
- Practice the verb *Be*.

Resources

Multilevel Worksheets: Lesson 3, Worksheets 1 and 2
Workbook: Unit 1, Lesson 3
Audio: CD 1, Tracks 25–26
Heinle Picture Dictionary: Family, pages 26–27

Pacing

■ 1.5 hour classes ■ 2.5 hour classes
■ 3+ hour classes

STANDARDS CORRELATIONS

CCRS: SL1, L1, L2, RF3
CASAS: 0.1.2, 0.2.1
SCANS: **Basic Skills** Reading, listening, speaking
Interpersonal Participate as a member of a team
EFF: **Communication** Speak so others can understand, listen actively
Interpersonal Cooperate with others

Warm-up and Review

10–12 mins. ■■■

Ask students to walk around the room and ask six other students where they are from. Ask students to keep a list. Then, ask them to form groups and report to their group.

BEST PRACTICE

Reporting to a group

Reporting in groups gives students more opportunity to speak. Monitoring is easier if students are encouraged to stand up to report.

Introduction

2 mins. ■■■

Write the day of the week, the date, and the agenda on the board. Say the date while pointing to it and have students repeat it. State the goal: *Today, we will learn to speak about marital status.*

Presentation 1

7–10 mins. ■■■

Post signs that say *single* and *married*. Ask students to go to the sign that describes them. Some students will not know the words, but encourage them to ask their classmates.

BEST PRACTICE

"Corners"

Students go to corners or places in the room based on facts or beliefs. Once they get there, they may answer questions or perform a dialog.

While students are standing, write *Marital Status* on the board. Say *I'm* ______ (*single* or *married*). Ask students to say *I'm married*, or *I'm single*. Ask students to be seated.

A. IDENTIFY Listen and write.

Present *divorced* to students. Go over the pictures and do the listening as a class. Prepare students to do Exercise B.

LISTENING SCRIPT

CD 1 TR 25

Adem is a student at Irvine Adult School. He is single. His birth date is July 3rd, 1984. He is from Turkey. Laura is from Estonia. Jeff is from the United States. They are married. They got married two years ago. Mirna and Paul are from Russia. They are divorced. They have three children.

Practice 1

3 mins. ■■■

B. With a partner, point at the pictures in Exercise A and say: *He is single, They are married,* or *They are divorced.*

Allow students to practice. Then, ask them to cover the sentences and keep practicing.

Evaluation 1

2 mins. ■■■

Ask students to demonstrate in front of the class.

Presentation 2

10–15 mins.

C. Read.

Present the information in the table to students by writing the example sentences on the board and underlining the verb *Be*. Explain to students how each pronoun uses a different form of the verb.

Provide practice for students by calling out a pronoun and having them respond with the correct form of the verb *Be*.

BEST PRACTICE

Recycling

At all levels, but especially at the lower levels, recycling is very important. *Recycling* means reintroducing concepts previously taught in different contexts. Don't expect students to learn every concept and always remember it at this level. They will forget some things as they learn new concepts, so it becomes essential to teach them past concepts again.

D. PREDICT Are they married, single, or divorced? Circle *yes* or *no*. Then, listen and write.

Since the vocabulary needed to describe marital status and the verb *Be* is still being presented, this exercise can be done as a class. Refer to the chart in Exercise C after answering each question.

LISTENING SCRIPT

CD 1 TR 26

Hans: *Maria, are you single?*
Maria: *No, I'm married. Hans, are you married?*
Hans: *No, I'm single. Are Mr. and Mrs. Johnson married?*
Maria: *Yes, I think so.*

For shorter classes, ask students to do Exercises E, F, and G for homework.

Practice 2

5–7 mins.

E. Write *am, are,* or *is.*

Help students as necessary.

Evaluation 2

3 mins.

Check students' work in their books.

INSTRUCTOR'S NOTES

C. Read.

The Verb *Be*			
Pronoun	**Be**	**Marital status**	**Example sentence**
I	am	married	I am married.
He She	is	single divorced	He is single. (Amed is single.) She is divorced. (Mirna is divorced.)
We You They	are	divorced married single	We are divorced. You are married. They are single.

D. PREDICT Are they married, single, or divorced? Circle *yes* or *no*. Then, listen and write.

CD 1
TR 26

1.

Maria

Is she married? (Yes) No

She is married.

2.
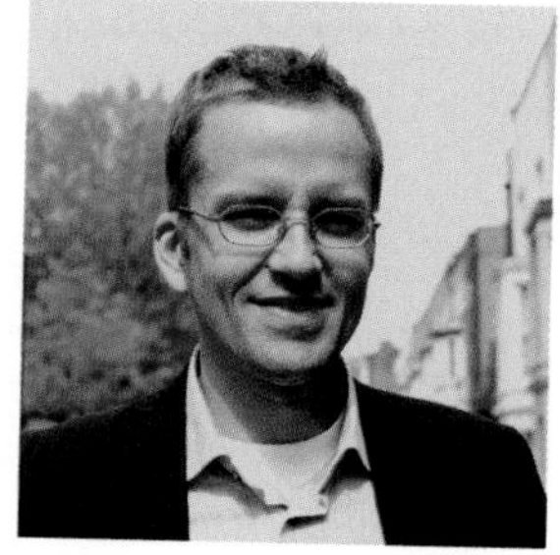

Hans

Is he married? Yes (No)

He is single.

3.

Mr. and Mrs. Johnson

Are they married?  (Yes) No

They are married.

E. Write *am*, *is*, or *are*.

1. Mr. and Mrs. Johnson **are** married.
2. Orlando is divorced.
3. Omar, Natalie, and Doug are single.
4. We are divorced.
5. They are single.
6. She is married.
7. We are single.
8. You are married.

WORKPLACE CONNECTION
Exercise I: Collect and organize information

F. Read and write the contractions.

1. I + am = I'm	I'm married.
2. You + are = You're	You're divorced.
3. He + is = He's	He's single.
4. She + is = She's	She's divorced.
5. We + are = We're	We're married.
6. They + are = They're	They're single.

G. Complete the sentences with the verbs. Rewrite each sentence with a contraction.

1. We are married.	We're married.
2. They are divorced.	They're divorced.
3. I am single.	I'm single.
4. He is divorced.	He's divorced.
5. You are married.	You're married.
6. She is single.	She's single.

H. Read.

A: Hans, are you married?
B: No, I'm single.

A: Lin, are you married?
B: Yes, I'm married.

A: Pam, are you married?
B: No, I'm divorced.

I. CLASSIFY Speak to five classmates. Answers will vary.

Name	Marital status (Are you married?)
Hans	single
1.	
2.	
3.	
4.	
5.	

Presentation 3

10–15 mins.

Introduce the concept of contractions by reminding students of the contraction for *I am* that they learned in the Pre-Unit. Write it on the board.

Contractions are important because native speakers use them a lot. They affect the rhythm of the language and, therefore, students sound more like a native speaker when they use them. Some students will resist using contractions; however, it is imperative to encourage them to use them.

INTONATION

Rhythm and prominence

English sentence rhythm is not a consistent pattern. Various aspects of the language affect it. English has a series of stops and starts based on prominent words and the pauses that sometimes follow. For example, one could pronounce *I am married* in various ways, depending on the information the speaker would like to stress.

If a speaker is saying emphatically that he or she is married, it might be: *I AM (slight pause) married.* If the speaker wants to differentiate between being married and single, he or she might say *I am MARried* in which case the first two words might be rushed through quickly. (*MAR* in this case is more prominent than the final example in this box.)

More often, however, and for this lesson, the statement is a statement of fact. In this case, it would be *I am married* with little or no word prominence. This pronunciation is not very common and comes across a bit stilted.

Changing the phrase to a contraction allows for more dimension and is much more common in everyday speech. The key word is *married* so it receives prominence:
I'm MARried.

F. Read and write contractions.

This exercise can be done as a class.

For shorter classes, ask students to do Exercise G for homework.

Practice 3

5–7 mins.

G. Complete the sentences with the verbs. Rewrite each sentence with a contraction.

Ask students to do the activity alone and then go over the answers as a class.

Evaluation 3

2 mins.

Check students' work in their books.

Refer students to *Stand Out Basic Workbook, Unit 1, Lesson 3* for more practice with contractions and the verb *Be*.

Go to the *Activity Bank* online for suggestions on promoting digital literacy and using the Internet to enhance this lesson.

Application

5–7 mins.

H. Read.

Drill the students briefly on the exchanges. With a few students, model the question: *Are you married?* Ask two students to model the question and appropriate response.

I. CLASSIFY Speak to five classmates.

Show students how to complete the table and then, ask them to talk to five students about their marital status. In this case and others where personal information is requested, give students the option to respond with the phrase *That's personal*. Write the phrase on the board.

MULTILEVEL WORKSHEETS

Lesson 3, Worksheet 1: Marital Status

Lesson 3, Worksheet 2: Be Verb

AT-A-GLANCE **PREP**

Goal: Say and write addresses
Grammar: Review: *he/she/it is*
Academic Strategies: Focused listening
Vocabulary: *street, address, city, state, zip code*

Agenda

- Read addresses.
- Listen for addresses.
- Write addresses.
- Ask for addresses.

Resources

Multilevel Worksheets: Lesson 4, Worksheets 1 and 2
Workbook: Unit 1, Lesson 4
Audio: CD 1, Tracks 27-30
Heinle Picture Dictionary: Post Office, pages 52–53

Pacing

- 1.5 hour classes
- 2.5 hour classes
- 3+ hour classes

STANDARDS CORRELATIONS

CCRS: RI1, SL2, SL4, L1, L2
CASAS: 0.1.2, 0.2.1, 1.1.3, 4.8.7
SCANS: **Basic Skills** Reading, writing, listening, speaking
Information Acquire and evaluate information, organize and maintain information, interpret and communicate information
EFF: **Communication** Speak so others can understand, listen actively

Warm-up and Review 2–5 mins.

Write the following table on the board and ask students to copy it.

What's your name?	Are you married?	Where do you live?	Where are you from?
1.			

Ask students to talk to five students and report to a group.

Introduction 2 mins.

Write the day of the week, the date, and the agenda on the board. Say the date while pointing to it and have students repeat it. State the goal: *Today, you will learn to say and write your address.*

Presentation 1 10–12 mins.

Ask students if they have ID cards. Show students your driver's license if you have one and encourage students to do the same.

A. Read.

Read the ID card with students and ask them questions such as: *Where does Safa live? What's the city, state, and zip code?* Use the proper stress and rhythm. Review numbers 1–10.

Practice 1 3 mins.

B. Write.

Do this as an information-gap activity. Write these questions on the board: *What's the street address? What's the city? What's the state?*

Have students work in pairs. Student A covers Safa's ID card and asks for Safa's information from Student B, who reads from the ID card. Have students reverse roles.

Evaluation 1 3 mins.

Observe students as they work.

C. IDENTIFY Listen and point to the addresses.

Confirm that students are following along with the recording. If time allows, you may produce more examples to give students more practice.

LISTENING SCRIPT

CD 1 TR 27

1. *Write down the following address so you can find the location easily. It is 51 Apple Avenue.*
2. *I need to talk to the resident at 12367 Elm Road. Do you know her?*
3. *Amal's address is not 51 Apple Avenue. It is different.*
4. *Let's go to the new adult school. I think the address is 3259 Lincoln Street.*

LESSON 4 What's your address?

GOAL ■ Say and write addresses

A. Read.

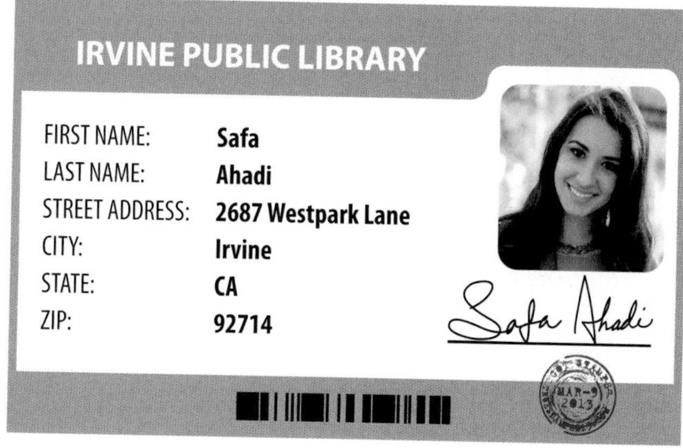
IRVINE PUBLIC LIBRARY

FIRST NAME:	**Safa**
LAST NAME:	**Ahadi**
STREET ADDRESS:	**2687 Westpark Lane**
CITY:	**Irvine**
STATE:	**CA**
ZIP:	**92714**

B. Write.

First name: Safa

Last name: Ahadi

Street address: 2687 Westpark Lane

City: Irvine

State: CA

Zip code: 92714

CD 1 TR 27

C. IDENTIFY Listen and point to the addresses.

3259 Lincoln Street   51 Apple Avenue   12367 Elm Road

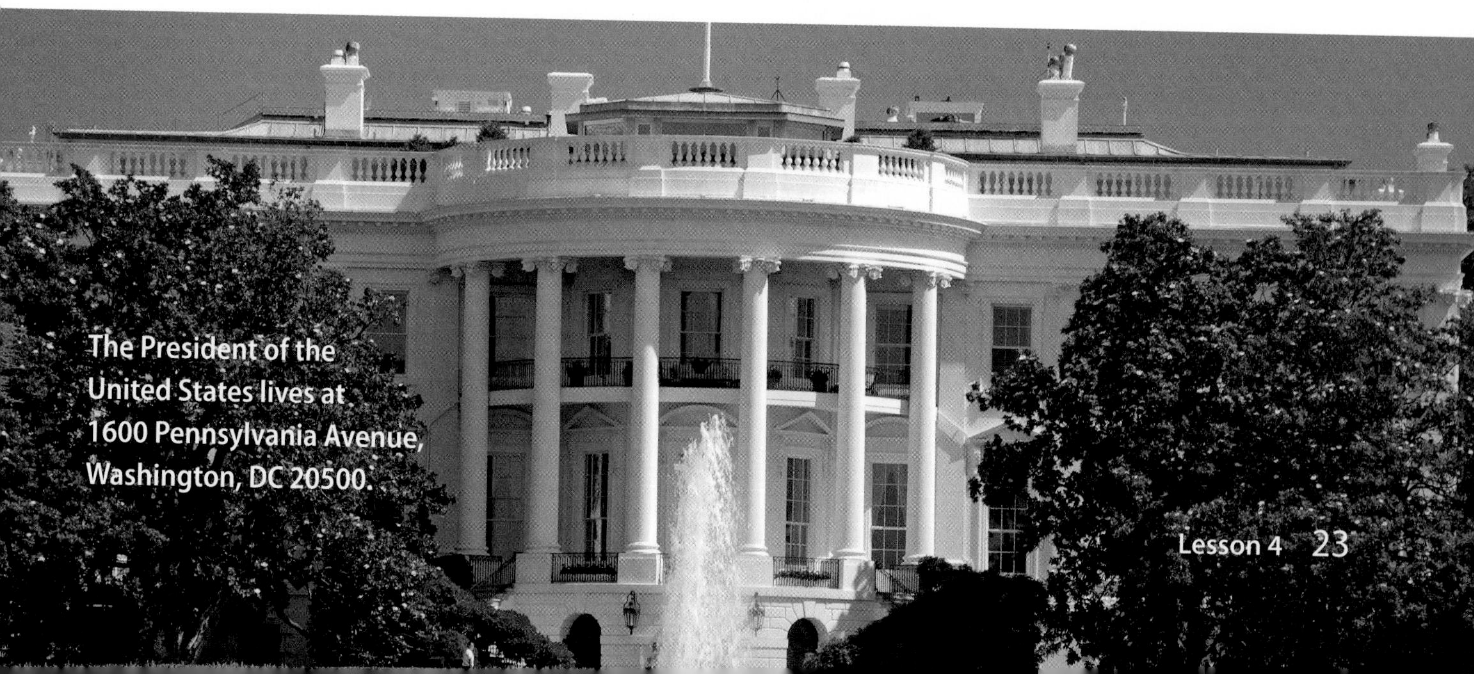
The President of the United States lives at 1600 Pennsylvania Avenue, Washington, DC 20500.

D. Listen to the addresses. Write the numbers only.

CD 1 TR 28

1. 2381 2. 45721 3. 32 4. 4576

E. Listen and write.

CD 1 TR 29

COMMAS
Use commas (,) to separate the different parts of an address.

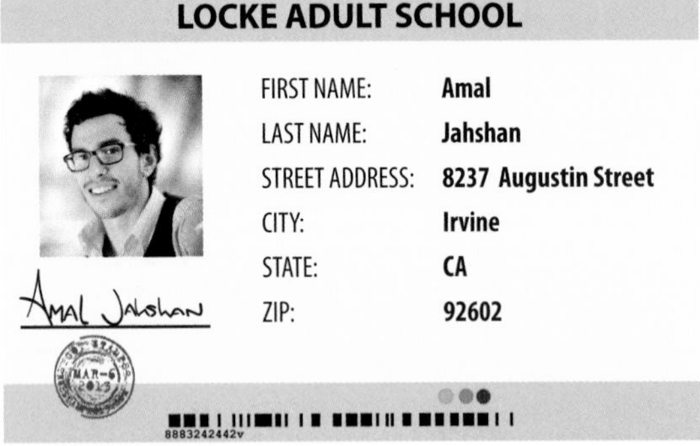

LOCKE ADULT SCHOOL
FIRST NAME: Amal
LAST NAME: Jahshan
STREET ADDRESS: 8237 Augustin Street
CITY: Irvine
STATE: CA
ZIP: 92602

Address:
8237 Augustin Street,
Irvine, CA 92602

IRVINE PUBLIC LIBRARY
FIRST NAME: Hang
LAST NAME: Tran
STREET ADDRESS: ________ Fin Road
CITY: Irvine
STATE: CA
ZIP: 92602

Address:
23905 Fin Road,
Irvine, CA 92602

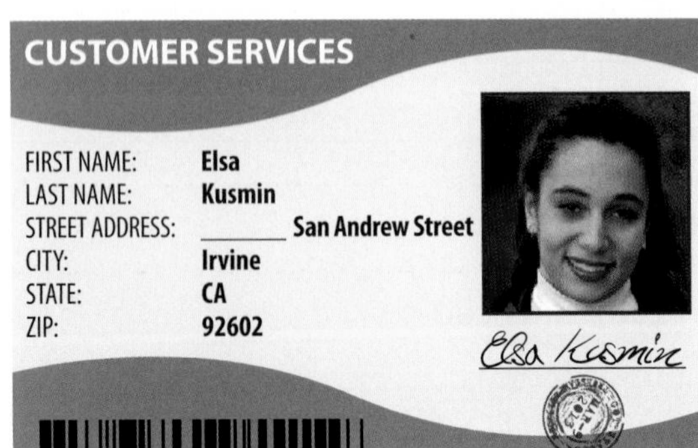

CUSTOMER SERVICES
FIRST NAME: Elsa
LAST NAME: Kusmin
STREET ADDRESS: ______ San Andrew Street
CITY: Irvine
STATE: CA
ZIP: 92602

Address:
23 San Andrew Street,
Irvine, CA 92602

F. RELATE Write the addresses.

Name	Address
Amal	8237 Augustin Street, Irvine, CA 92602
Hang	23905 Fin Road, Irvine, California, 92602
Elsa	23 San Andrew Street, Irvine, California, 92602

Presentation 2

7–10 mins.

Review numbers with students once again. Dictate a few numbers to them that might be street numbers, such as: *2034, 129, 23651,* and *689*. Ask students to compare answers and then, as a class, go over each one.

D. Listen to the addresses. Write the numbers only.

> **LISTENING SCRIPT**
>
> CD 1 TR 28
>
> 1. *She lives at 2381 Olive Avenue.*
> 2. *Their address is 45721 Hampton Street.*
> 3. *My address is 32 West Main Street.*
> 4. *We live in a house at 4576 Hilton Way.*

Practice 2

7–10 mins.

Write your school's address on the board. Help students see what words are capitalized and where commas go. Ask students to copy the address and then, have partners peer-edit for accuracy.

E. Listen and write.

Play the recording a few times until most of the students have gotten the answers. You may wish to have students compare answers with others in a group between listening sessions.

> **LISTENING SCRIPT**
>
> 
>
> CD 1 TR 29
>
> *Amal is a student at Locke Adult School. His address is 8237 Augustin Street, Irvine, California 92602. Hang is also a student at Locke Adult School. She lives at 23905 Fin Road, Irvine, California 92602. Elsa is from Russia. Her address is 23 San Andrew Street, Irvine, California 92602.*

F. RELATE Write the addresses.

Call out the names of the students in Exercise E and encourage students to respond with the correct address. Then, have students complete the exercise by writing the addresses next to the names.

Evaluation 2

7–10 mins.

Check students' work. Help students use commas and capital letters correctly.

INSTRUCTOR'S NOTES

Presentation 3

15–20 mins.

Write a sentence on the board with the school address already there. Write: *The school address is* __________. Remind students once again about capital letters and commas. Show them that on an ID card, the state is usually abbreviated but when speaking, the whole word is uttered.

Explain to students that *is* is a form of *Be* that they have already learned. Refer them to the grammar box at the top of the page to help them visualize it. You may decide to go back to page 21 and look at the chart at the top of the page. It might help here to have students add *it* to the chart and give them a brief explanation. Write on the board:

address = it
dog = it
book = it

G. Listen and read.

Read the dialog with students and teach them about proper rhythm. Here you may wish to stress that usually a native speaker will ask *WHAT'S* (slight pause) *your address?*

Practice the dialog with students. You are preparing them for the information-gap activity that they will do in Exercise H. Prepare students for this activity by modeling it with various students.

LISTENING SCRIPT

CD 1 TR 30

The listening script matches the conversation in Exercise G.

BEST PRACTICE

Information gaps

In an information-gap activity, two students work together. Each student has different pieces of information needed to complete the task. The two students have to ask each other questions in order to get the information they need. In most cases, one student is looking at one page, while the other student is looking at a different page.

Practice 3

5 mins.

H. Practice the conversations. Student A look at this page. Student B look at your answers in Exercise F. Write.

Have students complete the information gap. Student A looks at this page while Student B looks at the answers from Exercise F. Then, they switch.

Evaluation 3

3 mins.

Ask students to demonstrate the dialogs they used to obtain the information in front of the class.

Refer students to *Stand Out Basic Workbook, Unit 1, Lesson 4* for more practice with the verb *Be*.

Go to the *Activity Bank* online for suggestions on promoting digital literacy and using the Internet to enhance this lesson.

Application

5–7 mins.

I. APPLY Ask your partner and write the information. Then, ask two more classmates.

Write these two questions on the board*: What's your name? What's your address?* Show students how to complete this exercise by doing it with a few students on the board.

Teach the students the question *How do you spell that?* They may need to ask this question in order to spell the street and city names correctly.

MULTILEVEL WORKSHEETS

Lesson 4, Worksheet 1: Write Addresses

Lesson 4, Worksheet 2: Personal Information

G. Listen and read.

CD 1
TR 30

Hang: Hi, Amal. What's your address?
Amal: Hello, Hang. My address is 8237 Augustin Street, Irvine, California 92602.
Hang: Thanks.

The Verb *Be*		
Subject	**Be**	**Example Sentence**
He	is	He is a student.
She		She is a student.
It (address)		My address is 8237 Augustin Street, Irvine, California 92602.

H. Practice the conversations. Student A look at this page. Student B look at your answers in Exercise F. Write.

Student A: Hi, Amal. What's your address?
Student B: Hello, Elsa. My address is 8237 Augustin Street, Irvine, California 92602.
Student A: Thanks.

Student A: Hi, Elsa. What's your address?
Student B: Hello, Amal. My address is 23 San Andrew Street, Irvine, California 92602.
Student A: Thanks.

Student A: Hi, Hang. What's your address?
Student B: Hello, Amal. My address is 23905 Fin Road, Irvine, California 92602.
Student A: Thanks.

I. APPLY Ask your partner and write the information. Then, ask two more classmates.

Answers will vary.

Name	Address

LESSON 5 What's your date of birth?

GOAL Say and write dates

A. **Write this year.** Answers will vary.

B. LABEL **Write the month and the year. Circle today's date.** Answers will vary.

		1	2	3	4	5
6	7	8	9	10	11	12
13	14	15	16	17	18	19
20	21	22	23	24	25	26
27	28	29	30	31		

C. **Number the months.**

January	February	March	April
01	02	03	04
May	June	July	August
05	06	07	08
September	October	November	December
09	10	11	12

CD 1 TR 31 **D.** **Listen to the months and say the number. Listen again and write the months on a sheet of paper.**

AT-A-GLANCE **PREP**

Goal: Say and write dates
Grammar: Review contractions
Pronunciation: Final /t/
Academic Strategies: Focused listening
Vocabulary: *birthday, birth date, today, tomorrow,* numbers 1–31, months and days

Agenda

- Learn months and days.
- Practice new vocabulary.
- Complete a calendar.

Resources

Multilevel Worksheets: Lesson 5, Worksheets 1 and 2
Workbook: Unit 1, Lesson 5
Audio: CD 1, Tracks 31–32
Heinle Picture Dictionary: Calendar, pages 6–7

Pacing

- 1.5 hour classes
- 2.5 hour classes
- 3⁺ hour classes

STANDARDS CORRELATIONS

CCRS: RI1, SL1, SL2, L1, L2, RF2, RF3
CASAS: 0.1.2, 0.2.1, 2.3.2
SCANS: **Basic Skills** Writing, listening, speaking
Information Acquire and evaluate information, organize and maintain information
Thinking Skill See things in the mind's eye
EFF: **Communication** Read with understanding, speak so others can understand, listen actively
Interpersonal Cooperate with others

Warm-up and Review

7–10 mins.

Write on the board: *How do you spell that?* Ask students to practice asking for and writing classmates' names.

Introduction

2 mins.

Write the day of the week, the date, and the agenda on the board. Say the date while pointing to it and have students repeat it. State the goal: *Today, we will say and write dates.*

Presentation 1

20–30 mins.

Ask students for the date: month, day, and year. Write the first letter of each month on the board. See if students can identify each month. After they have practiced, complete the names of the months.

A. Write this year.

Ask students to write the current year. Write the current year on the board and help with the pronunciation. Ask students to repeat after you.

B. LABEL Write the month and the year. Circle today's date.

Review numbers 1–31. Practice days of the week if you feel your students are ready. Now ask students to write the month and the year. Then, have them circle today's date. Say the current date and ask students to repeat.

C. Number the months.

Show students how to number the months. Then, show how to point to each month as you say it.

Practice 1

3 mins.

D. Listen to the months and say the number. Listen again and write the months on a sheet of paper.

The months are read three times. The first time students should listen. The second time they should say the number. Then, give them time to write the names of the months. Play the recording again so they can confirm their answers.

LISTENING SCRIPT

CD 1 TR 31

May	*February*	*August*	*June*
March	*November*	*July*	*September*
January	*December*	*April*	*October*

Evaluation 1

3 mins.

Observe students and check their work.

Presentation 2

15–20 mins.

Draw a birthday cake on the board. Sing a happy birthday song to help students identify with the new vocabulary.

Ask students what months their birthdays fall in.

Make a distinction between *birthday* and *date of birth*. This can be done by covering the year with your hand and saying *birthday*. Then, ask students what month their birthdays are in. Ask volunteers to write their birthdays or dates of birth on the board. Then, write your birth date on the board. Under the dates, mark the words and numbers as in Exercise E.

Help students make a distinction between the two terms in their pronunciation by releasing the /t/ in *date of birth* clearly so the /t/ explodes with air as the tongue releases.

INTONATION

Final /t/

Write *date of birth* in the top right-hand corner of the board and *birthday* in the top left-hand corner. Demonstrate to students how they should point to the word when they hear it.

1. Say the words in isolation several times in no particular order, repeating one or the other often.
2. Say the words in the context of sentences.
3. Say the words in the context of a paragraph.

Ask a student to do the first item above with the class.

Ask students what the date is today once again. Write this date on the board with the same notation under it. Write tomorrow's date on the board and say: *Tomorrow is* __________ (tomorrow's date). Make the same notations under that date. Write *21* somewhere arbitrary on the board. Write *September* and *2016* also in the same fashion. Ask a student to come to the board and put the three items together.

Ask students to open their books and review the vocabulary box.

E. Read.

Go over the examples and match them with what you did on the board earlier. Then, add the numbering system.

For shorter classes, ask students to do Exercises F and G for homework.

BEST PRACTICE

Eliciting information

In the *Stand Out* approach, we suggest that instead of merely giving students information, you elicit from them what they may already know in the presentation stage.

This rather lengthy presentation could have been much shorter if students first opened their books and looked at the examples and the vocabulary. However, we recommend the longer approach where students are involved in the presentation and give information themselves because they will remember more of the experience, therefore allowing for better learning.

Practice 2

5–7 mins.

F. IDENTIFY Write the dates with words and numbers (December 5th, 1990).

Help students as necessary.

G. IDENTIFY Write the dates with numbers only (12/05/1990).

Help students as necessary.

Evaluation 2

5 mins.

Check students' work. Look for commas and proper spelling.

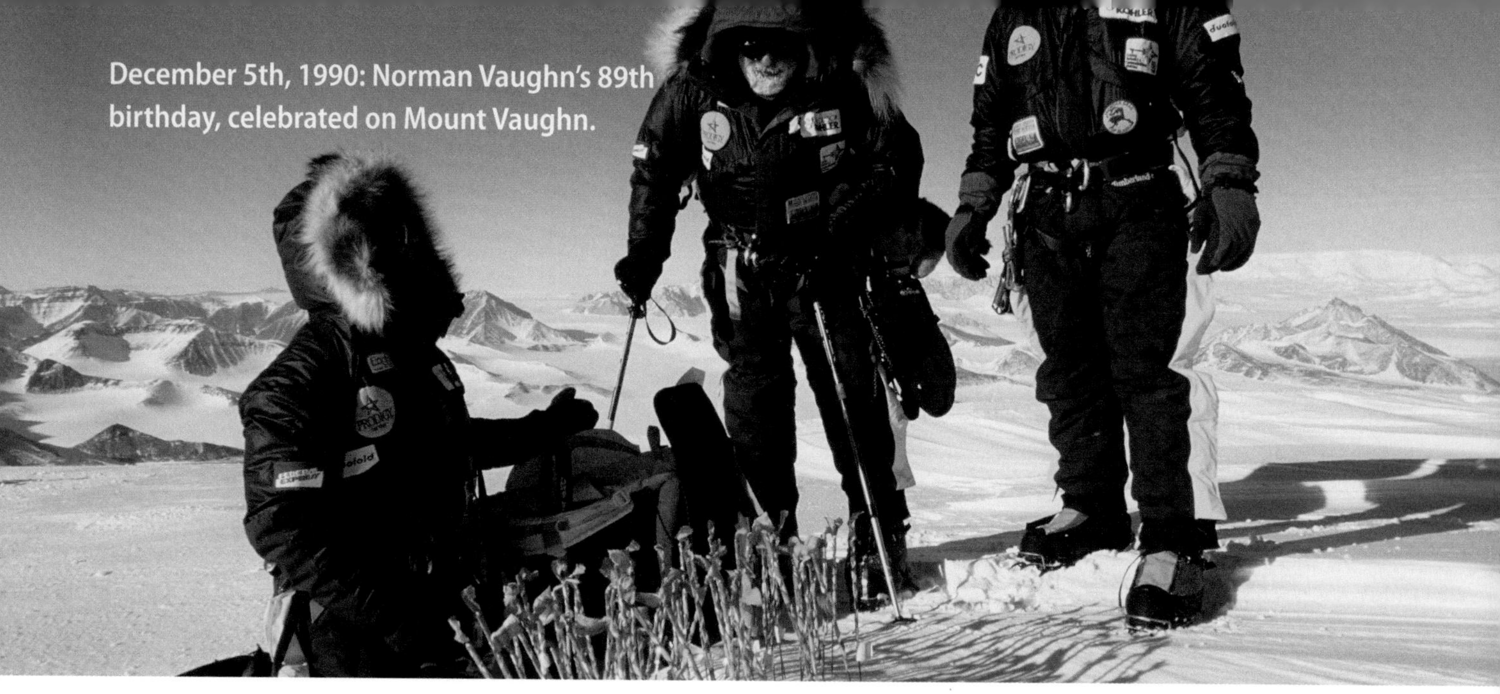

December 5th, 1990: Norman Vaughn's 89th birthday, celebrated on Mount Vaughn.

E. Read.

Month	Day	Year	
September	21	2016	September 21st, 2016 09/21/2016
December	5	1990	December 5th, 1990 12/05/1990
August	2	1974	August 2nd, 1974 08/2/1974

ORDINAL NUMBERS

Notice how to write and say dates with words and numbers.

1st, 2nd, 3rd, 4th, 5th, 6th, 7th, 8th, 9th, 10th

January 1st	January 20th
January 2nd	January 21st
January 3rd	January 22nd
January 4th	January 30th
January 5th	January 31st

F. IDENTIFY Write the dates with words and numbers (December 5th, 1990).

Answers will vary.

1. The date today: ______________________
2. Your date of birth: ______________________
3. The date tomorrow: ______________________
4. Your friend's date of birth: ______________________

G. IDENTIFY Write the dates with numbers only (12/05/1990). *Answers will vary.*

1. The date today: ______________________
2. Your date of birth: ______________________
3. The date tomorrow: ______________________
4. Your friend's date of birth: ______________________

CD 1
TR 32

H. Listen and write the dates.

Today	Date of birth
1. June 25th	July 3rd, 1988
2. January 12th	January 12th, 1990
3. March 2nd	March 14th, 1988

I. APPLY Practice the conversation. Use the information in Exercise H to make new conversations.

Student A: What's the date today?
Student B: It's June 25th.
Student A: Thanks.
Student A: What's your date of birth?
Student B: It's July 3rd, 1988.
Student A: Thanks.

CONTRACTIONS

What is = *What's*
It is = *It's*

J. Develop a list of important class dates. Ask your teacher for help. Answers will vary.

1. Today's date: ____________________
2. First day of school: ____________________
3. Holidays: ____________________
____
____
4. Last day of school: ____________________

July 4th: Independence Day in the United States.

Presentation 3

10–15 mins.

H. Listen and write the dates.

Have students listen as a class and write the answers in the table. Students will hear contractions used again. Go over the contractions and make sure students understand how to form them.

To further expand, write the script on the board. Read it with students, pointing out the contractions as well as the other information.

> LISTENING SCRIPT
>
> CD 1 TR 32
>
> **1.** *My name is Amal. It's June 25th. Next week, July 3rd is my birthday. My date of birth is July 3rd, 1988.*
> **2.** *Elsa is my friend. I see her every day at school. Today is January 12th. It's Elsa's birthday. Her date of birth is January 12th, 1990.*
> **3. Hang:** *What's the date today?*
> **Orlando:** *It's March 2nd.*
> **Hang:** *Thanks. It's almost my birthday.*
> **Orlando:** *When is your birthday?*
> **Hang:** *March 14th*
> **Orlando:** *What year?*
> **Hang:** *1988.*

Prepare students to do Exercise I by going over the conversations. Show students how to substitute new dates for the underlined dates.

Practice 3

10–15 mins.

I. APPLY Practice the conversation. Use the information in Exercise H to make new conversations.

Evaluation 3

5–7 mins.

Ask volunteers to demonstrate their dialogs in front of the class.

Refer students to *Stand Out Basic Workbook, Unit 1, Lesson 5* for more practice with contractions.

Go to the *Activity Bank* online for suggestions on promoting digital literacy and using the Internet to enhance this lesson.

Application

5–7 mins.

J. Develop a list of important class dates. Ask your teacher for help.

Ask students to complete the list with the dates. Review as a class.

> CRITICAL THINKING
>
> **APPLY**
>
> Critical thinking skills are important to help develop students' ability to solve problems and think independently. Teachers can help students develop their critical thinking skills in a number of ways:
>
> 1. **Writing**
> Ask students to write answers to key questions such as, *What information is the most important? What do I think about this subject?* Also ask students to write dialogues or summaries.
>
> 2. **Group Work**
> Better results and understanding often come from group work. Ask students to engage in class discussion, peer reviews, and task-related group work.

> MULTILEVEL WORKSHEETS
>
> Lesson 5, Worksheet 1: Calendars and Dates
>
> Lesson 5, Worksheet 2: Ordinal Numbers

INSTRUCTOR'S NOTES

Nice to Meet You

Before You Watch

- Ask students to look at the title and predict what the video will be about.
- Ask students what they say when they meet someone for the first time. Write any key vocabulary expressions on the board.

A. Look at the picture and answer the questions.

- Go over the questions with students and elicit answers. Write any key vocabulary or ideas on the board.

While You Watch

B. Watch the video and circle the names you hear.

- Ask students to watch the video once so that they can get familiar with the speed and understand the gist.
- Play the video again and ask students to circle the names they hear.

Check Your Understanding

C. Read the statements. Write *T* for true and *F* for false.

- Ask students to discuss the statements with a partner and decide whether they are true or false.
- Have students write their answers and elicit feedback as a class.

BEST PRACTICE

There are many ways to use video in the classroom. Students should rarely watch a video without some kind of task. You might introduce comprehension questions before they watch so they know what they are looking for. Below are a few techniques that you may try for variety beyond the comprehension checks and other ideas already presented in this lesson.

Freeze Frame: Pause the video during viewing and use it like a picture dictionary, identifying and expanding on the vocabulary.

Silent Viewing: Show the video in segments without sound so students can guess at the storyline. This helps them to understand that listening is more than just the words people say.

Prediction Techniques: Show portions of the video and ask students to predict what will come next.

Listening without Viewing: This helps students create their own image of what is happening. After a discussion, allow students to watch the video and the sound together.

Back-to-Back: In pairs, one student faces the video and the other faces away. Play the video without sound and ask the student viewing to report to the student who is facing away what is happening.

Summary Strips: Create strips of sentences that describe the events. Have students watch the video and then put the strips in the correct order, or ask students to predict the story line before watching and then check their answers. The Activity Bank has summary strips for each video in *Stand Out*.

LIFESKILLS  Nice to meet you

Before You Watch

A. Look at the picture and answer the questions.

1. Where are the people?
   They are in a classroom.
2. Who is the person standing at the front?
   The teacher is standing at the front.

While You Watch

B. Watch the video and circle the names you hear.

Roger

Frank

(Mateo)

Edgar

(Mrs. Smith)

James

(Hector)

Linda

(Naomi)

Check Your Understanding

C. Read the statements. Write *T* for true and *F* for false.

1. Mrs. Smith is from California. __F__
2. Hector lives in Boston. __F__
3. Mateo is from Puerto Rico. __T__
4. Naomi is from Pasadena. __T__
5. Naomi works in a diner. __T__

Review

Learner Log

I can say and write dates.

☐ Yes ☐ No ☐ Maybe

A. Read.

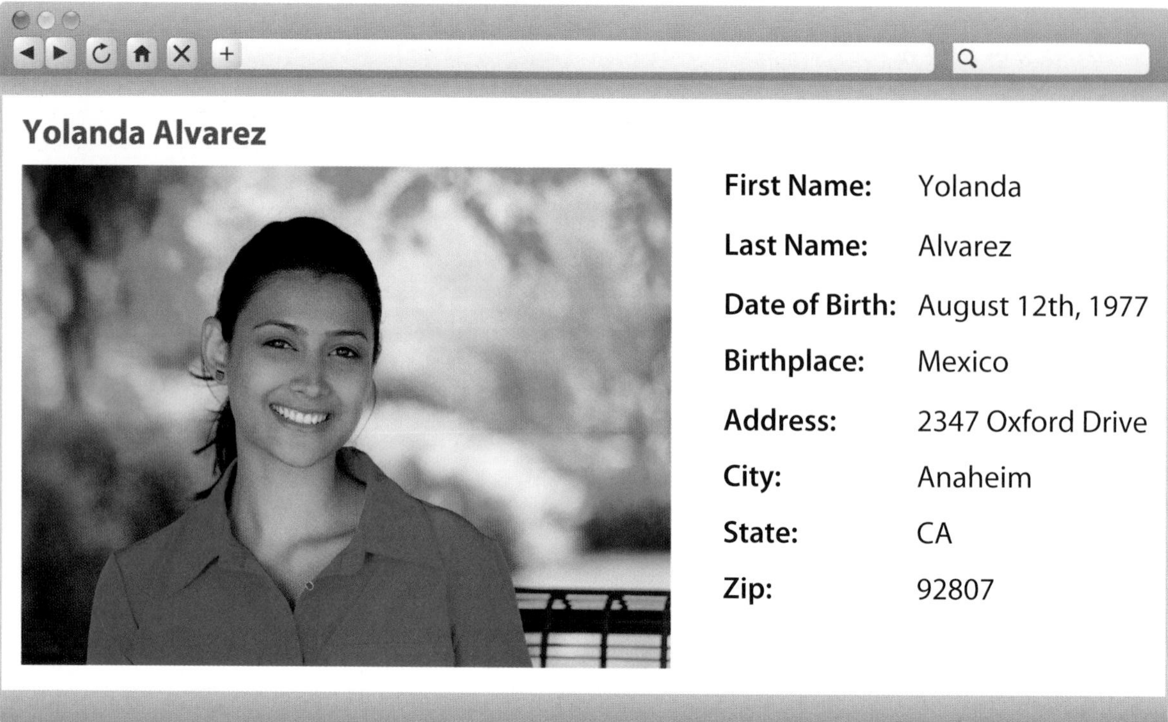

Yolanda Alvarez

First Name:	Yolanda
Last Name:	Alvarez
Date of Birth:	August 12th, 1977
Birthplace:	Mexico
Address:	2347 Oxford Drive
City:	Anaheim
State:	CA
Zip:	92807

B. Write.

1. What's her first name?

   Yolanda

2. What's her last name?

   Alvarez

3. What's her address?

   2347 Oxford Drive, Anaheim, CA 92807

4. What's her date of birth?

   August 12th, 1977

5. What's her birthplace?

   Mexico

AT-A-GLANCE PREP

Goal: All unit objectives
Grammar: All unit grammar
Pronunciation: Rhythm and prominence
Academic Strategies: Focused listening, reviewing, evaluating, developing study skills
Vocabulary: All unit vocabulary

Agenda

- Discuss unit objectives.
- Complete the review.
- Evaluate and reflect on progress.

Pacing

- 1.5 hour classes
- 2.5 hour classes
- 3+ hour classes

STANDARDS CORRELATIONS

CCRS: RI1, SL2, L1
CASAS: 0.1.1, 0.2.1, 7.4.1, 7.4.2, 7.4.3
***SCANS:* Basic Skills** Reading, writing, listening, speaking
Interpersonal Cooperate with others
Information Acquire and evaluate information, organize and maintain information, interpret and communicate information
Thinking Skill See things in the mind's eye
***EFF:* Communication** Speak so others can understand
Lifelong Learning Take responsibility for learning, reflect and evaluate

Warm-up and Review

10–15 mins.

Ask students to write their address and phone number on a 3-by-5 card. Collect the cards and pass them out again to different people. Ask the students to find the author of their cards by asking questions. Write the questions on the board and show them how to do this activity by practicing with a few students.

Introduction

2 mins.

Write all the goals on the board from Unit 1. Show the students the first page of the unit and mention the five goals. Explain that today is review and that they will review the whole unit.

Note: Depending on the length of the term, you may decide to have students do Presentation and Practice 1 for homework and then, review students' work as either the warm-up or another class activity.

Presentation

10–15 mins.

This presentation will cover the first three pages of the review. Quickly go to the first page of each lesson. Discuss the goal of each one. Ask simple questions to remind students of what they have learned.

Practice

15–20 mins. 

A. Read. (Lessons 1–5)

B. Write. (Lessons 1–5)

BEST PRACTICE

Recycling/Review

The review process and the project that follows are part of the recycling/review process. Students at this level need to be reintroduced to concepts to solidify what they have learned. Many concepts are learned and then, forgotten while learning other new concepts. This is because students learn but are not necessarily ready to acquire language concepts.

Therefore, it becomes very important to review and to show students how to review on their own. It is also important to recycle the new concepts in different contexts.

Practice *(continued)*

C. Speak to a partner. Write. (Lessons 1–4)

Monitor students' conversations.

D. Write. (Lesson 3)

Go over the answers as a class.

INSTRUCTOR'S NOTES

C. Speak to a partner. Write. Answers will vary.

What's your first name?
What's your last name?
What's your address?
What's your phone number?

Adult School Application

Student Information>> | Household Information | Essay | Payment | Contact Us

First Name
Last Name
Date of Birth -Date- -Month- -Year-
Birthplace
Street Address
E-mail
City -Select-
State -Select-
Zip Code
Phone Number

Submit

D. Write.

single married divorced

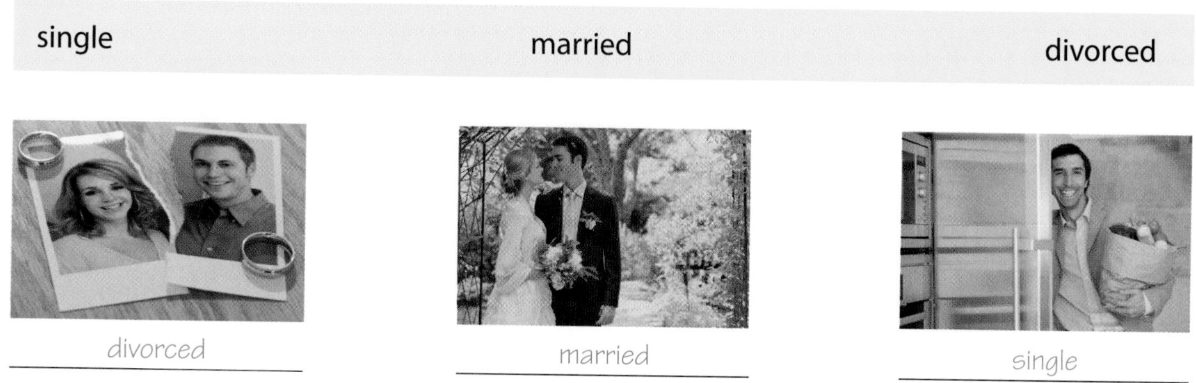

divorced married single

Learner Log

I can identify people.
☐ Yes ☐ No ☐ Maybe

I can express nationalities.
☐ Yes ☐ No ☐ Maybe

E. Circle.

1. 

(She) / He / They is from Germany.

2. 

She / (He) / They is Ron Carter.

3. 

She / He / (They) are in school.

4. 

She / He / (We) live in Irvine.

F. Write the correct form of the verb *Be*. Then, write each sentence with a contraction.

1. She __is__ a student. __She's a student.__
2. She __is__ from Japan. __She's from Japan.__
3. We __are__ students at The Adult School. __We're students at The Adult School.__
4. They __are__ from Honduras. __They're from Honduras.__
5. I __am__ in school. __I'm in school.__

G. Write *live* or *lives*.

1. He __lives__ in Portugal.
2. I __live__ in Chicago.
3. She __lives__ in the United States.

Practice *(continued)*

E. Circle. (Lessons 1 and 2)

Help as necessary.

F. Write the correct form of the verb *Be*. Then, write the sentence with a contraction. (Lesson 3)

Help as necessary.

G. Write *live* or *lives*. (Lesson 2)

Help as necessary.

Evaluation

5 mins.

Go around the room and check on student progress. If you see consistent errors among several students, interrupt the class and give a mini lesson or review to help students feel comfortable with the concept.

BEST PRACTICE

Learner Logs

Learner logs function to help students in many different ways.

1. They serve as part of the review process.
2. They help students to gain confidence and document what they have learned. In this way, students see that they are progressing and want to move forward in learning.
3. They provide students with a tool that they can use over and over to check and recheck their understanding. In this way, students become independent learners.

INSTRUCTOR'S NOTES

WORKPLACE CONNECTION

Combine ideas and information; Make decisions; Exercise leadership roles; Manage time; Complete tasks as assigned; Interact appropriately with team members; Collect and gather information; Interpret and communicate information; Apply technology

STANDARDS CORRELATIONS

CCRS: SL1, L5

CASAS: 0.1.1, 0.2.1, 4.8.1

***SCANS:* Basic Skills** Reading, writing, listening, speaking

Resources Allocate time, allocate money, allocate materials and facility resources, allocate human resources

Information Acquire and evaluate information, organize and maintain information, interpret and communicate information, use computers to process information

Interpersonal: Participate as a member of a team, teach others, serve clients and customers, exercise leadership, negotiate to arrive at a decision, work with cultural diversity

Systems Understand systems, monitor and correct performance, improve and design systems

Thinking Skills Think creatively, make decisions, solve problems, see things in the mind's eye

Personal Qualities Responsibility, sociability, self-management

***EFF:* Communication** Read with understanding, convey ideas in writing, speak so others can understand, listen actively, observe critically

Decision Making Solve problems and make decisions, plan

Interpersonal Cooperate with others, advocate and influence, resolve conflict and negotiate, guide others

Lifelong Learning Take responsibility for learning, reflect and evaluate

Introduction
5 mins.

In this project, students will work in teams to create a book. First, they will make a mini book in teams of four or five. Then, you can bring the mini books together to create a class book. These books can be about real class members, but due to the personal nature of the information to be published, you may opt to have the students create fictitious characters. The teams can complete the project, including a presentation on a second day if necessary.

Stage 1
10–15 mins.

Make a table like the one below.

MULTILEVEL WORKSHEETS

Project 1, Worksheet 1: Student Profile

Project 1, Worksheet 2: Class Phone Book

Complete two or three example profiles with students as a class. Write the position responsibilities on the board as identified on the project page. Simulate a group activity by arbitrarily assigning positions. Help students understand the process.

Next, help students form groups and assign positions within their groups. On the spot, students will have to choose who will be the leader of their group. Review the responsibility of the leader and ask students to write the name of their leader in the books.

Do the same with the remaining positions: writer, artist, and spokesperson. If there are five people in the group, double up on the position of spokesperson. Every member of a group should have a responsibility.

Stage 2
20–30 mins.

Write the information for all the members of your team.

Ask students to complete the worksheet as a team.

Stage 3
10–15 mins.

Draw a picture or add a photo of each member.

Stage 4
10–15 mins.

Make a team book.

Ask teams to decorate the five pages and combine them to make a book.

Stage 5
10–30 mins.

Do a presentation about your team's members.

Ask teams to prepare a presentation. Each student on the team will talk about one page. The presentation can be merely students introducing themselves and reading the information while showing the picture. The activity can be more effective if you videotape the presentations for student review.

Stage 6
20–30 mins.

Make a class book with the other teams.

Collect all the pages and create a class book. As a class, you might suggest putting the pages in alphabetical order by students' last names and creating a table of contents and cover page. (Show examples of this from actual books.) Be sure to display the students' work.

TEAM PROJECT

Make a class book

COLLABORATE Form a team with four or five students. In your team, you need:

Position	Job description	Student name
Student 1: Team Leader	Check that everyone speaks English. Check that everyone participates.	
Student 2: Writer	Write information.	
Student 3: Artist	Draw pictures.	
Students 4/5: Spokespeople	Organize presentation.	

1. Make a table like the one below.
2. Write the information for the members of your team.

What's your first name?	
What's your last name?	
What's your address?	
What's your phone number?	
What's your date of birth?	
What's your marital status?	

3. Draw a picture or add a photo of each member.
4. Make a team book.
5. Do a presentation about your team.
6. Make a class book with the other teams.

About the Explorers

All of the National Geographic explorers featured in this unit appear in later units. Please refer to the unit in which they appear for more information.

- Read more about Jimmy Chin in Unit 5.
- Read more about Sarah Marquis in Unit 4.
- Read more about Diana Nyad in Unit 6.
- Read more about Maritza Morales Casanova in Unit 8.

About the Photos

Jimmy Chin Fellow climber and photographer Mikey Schaeffer took this photo of Jimmy on assignment in Yosemite National Park, California.

Sarah Marquis Sarah takes a seat in the ancient city of Machu Picchu, high in the Andes Mountains of Peru.

Diana Nyad This photo shows Diana mid-stroke during her famous 100-mile swim from Havana, Cuba, to Miami, Florida.

Maritza Morales Casanova This photo shows Maritza with her students at her environmental park where children learn about the world around them.

- Tell students they are going to read about National Geographic explorers. Ask students to tell you what an *explorer* is. *A person who travels to a place no one knows to find new information.* Discuss as a class.
- Ask students to brainstorm and think of examples of famous explorers. *Christopher Columbus, Neil Armstrong, Marco Polo,* etc. Ask where the explorer was born or what country he or she was from.

READING CHALLENGE
Jimmy Chin
Read more about Jimmy in Unit 5.
Sarah Marquis
Read more about Sarah in Unit 4.
Diana Nyad
Read more about Diana in Unit 6.
Maritza Morales Casanova
Read more about Maritza in Unit 8.

A. PREDICT Look at the pictures. Answer the questions. Answers will vary.

1. Who lives in Mexico? ______
2. Who was born in 1973? ______
3. Who lives in Switzerland? ______
4. Who is from New York City? ______

CCRS FOR READING

RI.1.1, RI.2.1, RI.1.5, RI.1.7
RF.2, RF.3

WORKPLACE CONNECTION
Exercise B: Collect and organize information
Exercise E: Combine ideas and information

B. **PREDICT** **Look at the pictures again. Put a check (✓) in the table.** Answers will vary.

	Adventurer	Teacher	Swimmer	Climber
Sarah Marquis				
Jimmy Chin				
Diana Nyad				
Maritza Morales Casanova				

C. **Read about the explorers.**

Sarah Marquis
Sarah Marquis is from Switzerland. She is an adventurer and a National Geographic explorer. Her date of birth is June 20th, 1972.

Jimmy Chin
Jimmy Chin is from Mankato, Minnesota. He is a climber and photographer. He is also a National Geographic explorer. He was born in 1973.

Diana Nyad
Diana Nyad is from New York City. Her birth date is August 22nd, 1949. She is a swimmer and a National Geographic explorer.

Maritza Morales Casanova
Maritza Morales Casanova is a teacher and a National Geographic explorer. She is from Mexico. She was born in 1985.

D. **IDENTIFY** **Underline the date of birth in each paragraph.**

E. **CREATE** **Complete the sentences about the explorers.**

1. Sarah Marquis is an adventurer and a National Geographic explorer.
2. Jimmy Chin is from Mankato, Minnesota.
3. Diana Nyad is from New York City.
4. Maritza Morales Casanova is a teacher and a National Geographic explorer.

READING STRATEGIES

Brainstorming and Group Discussions

Brainstorming and group discussion are two pre-reading strategies that allow students to recall information that they may already know.

- **Brainstorming** requires students to concentrate and recall information they already know.
- **Group discussion** requires students to work together to recall information.

- Introduce the explorers and point to each picture. Say the names aloud and have students repeat.
- Ask students to look at the pictures. Ask them what they can see. Have students guess what each explorer is doing and their location. Discuss as a class.

A. PREDICT Look at the pictures. Answer the questions.

Ask students to look at the pictures and discuss the answer to each question with a partner. Have students look for clues such as clothes, age, and names.

B. PREDICT Look at the pictures again. Put a check (✓) in the table.

Ask students to look at the pictures again and check the word that describes each explorer. Have students share their answers with the class and explain their choices.

C. Read about the explorers.

- Ask students to read the passage to learn about each explorer. Ask students if their guesses in Exercise B were correct.
- Read the passage with students and go over any vocabulary that students do not understand.

D. IDENTIFY Underline the date of birth in each paragraph.

Ask students to underline the date of birth of each explorer in the passage. Ask students if their guesses in Exercise A were correct.

E. CREATE Complete the sentences about the explorers.

Ask students to complete the sentences about each explorer. Have volunteers write their sentences on the board. Discuss as a class and add other personal information.

Our Class

About the Photo

Ed Kashi took this photo. It shows students in a dentistry lab at Kalamoon University—Syria's first private university— practicing dental procedures on specially designed mannequins. These mannequins allow students to learn a whole range of procedures before they start working with real people. Ed Kashi is a photojournalist and filmmaker from New York City. He is known for documenting current social and political issues around the world.

- Introduce the unit. Ask students to look at the picture. Then, ask the questions in the box. Discuss as a class.
- Have students look at the picture again. Ask: *Is your class like this one? What is the same? What is different?* Then, ask students what kind of class they think this is. Discuss as a class.
- Have students guess the ages of the people in the picture. Ask where they think these students are from. Ask what the students are wearing. Discuss as a class.

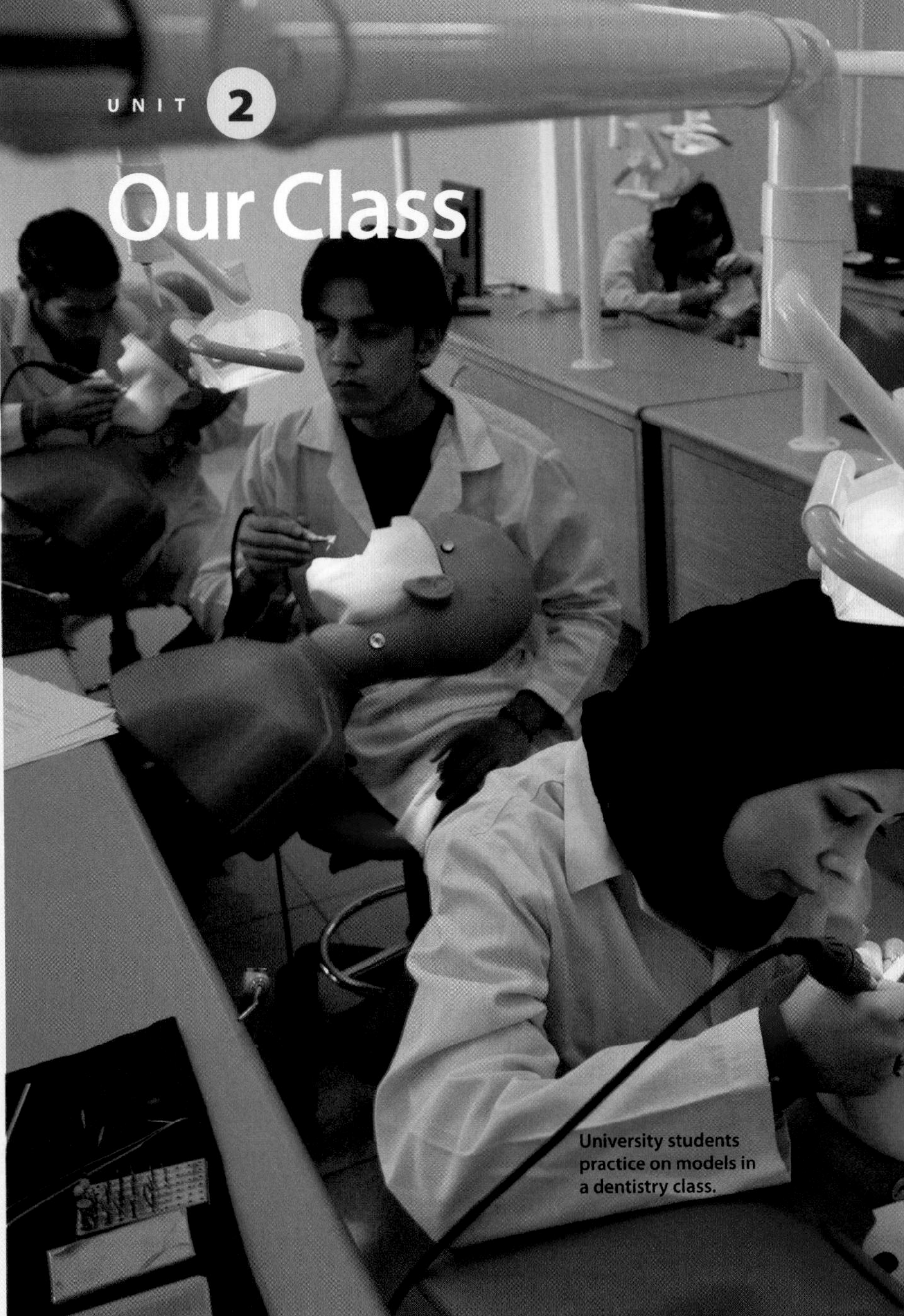

University students practice on models in a dentistry class.

UNIT OUTCOMES	GRAMMAR	VOCABULARY	EL CIVICS
• Introduce yourself and others • Describe your surroundings • Identify common activities • Plan a schedule • Plan for weather	• Possessive adjectives • *This is …* • Prepositions of location • Present continuous • Simple present with *need*	• Weather vocabulary: *foggy, cloudy, rainy, windy, sunny, snowy, hot, cold* • Verbs: *listening, reading, writing, talking, sitting, standing* • Classroom nouns • Clothing	The skills students learn in this unit can be applied to all EL Civics competency areas with a particular focus on the following: • Communication

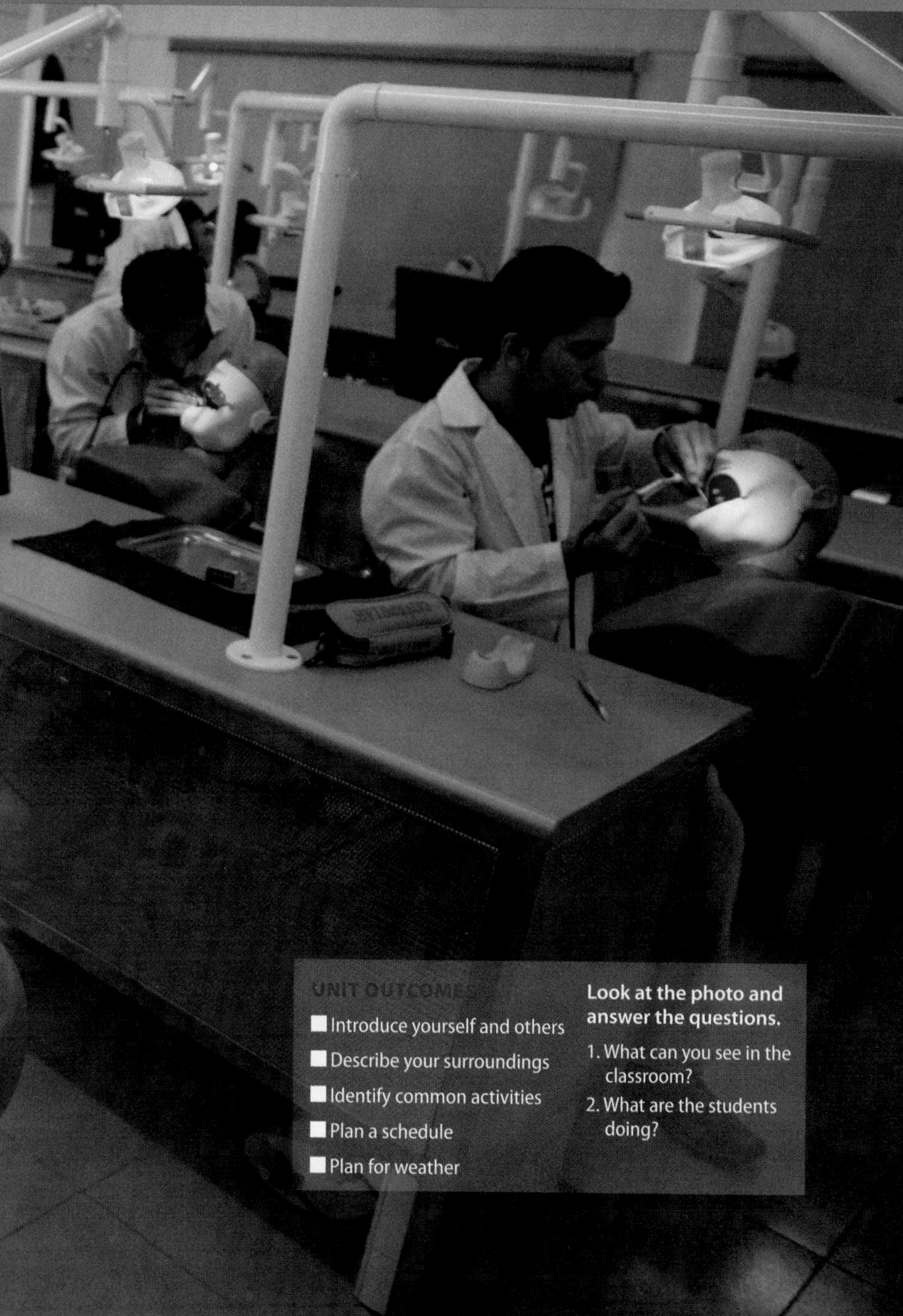

- Read the caption while students read it to themselves. Ask students to underline any words they do not understand.
- Tell students that a dentist cleans and fixes teeth. Tell students that a *dentist* studies *dentistry* in school. Then, explain that students in *dentistry school* practice on *models* and not on real people. Write the vocabulary on the board.
- Discuss the unit outcomes with students. Then, write any key vocabulary on the board.

Life Skills Link

In this unit, students will learn how to interact with others they meet for the first time. They will also learn how to describe their environment and identify common activities and how to schedule them.

Workplace Link

All lessons and units in *Stand Out* include basic communication skills and interpersonal skills important for the workplace. They are not individually identified. Other workplace skills are indicated. They include, collecting and organizing information, making decisions and solving problems, and combining ideas and information.

CASAS	SCANS	CCRS
Lesson 1: 0.1.4 Lesson 2: 0.1.5 Lesson 3: 0.1.5 Lesson 4: 0.2.1, 0.2.4, 2.3.1 Lesson 5: 0.1.2, 0.2.1, 1.1.3, 2.3.3 Review: 0.1.5, 2.3.1, 2.3.2, 2.3.3, 7.4.1, 7.4.2, 7.4.3 Team Project: 0.1.5, 2.3.1, 2.3.2, 2.3.3, 4.8.1	Many SCANs skills are incorporated in the unit with an emphasis on: • Acquiring and evaluating information • Organizing and maintaining information • Interpreting and communicating information • Basic skills • Reflecting and evaluating	RI1, RI7, SL1, SL2, SL4, L1, L2, L5, RF2, RF3

LESSON 1 Meet my friend

WORKPLACE CONNECTION
Exercise C: Collect and organize information

GOAL Introduce yourself and others

A. PREDICT Look at the picture. Where are the students from?

B. Listen and practice.

CD 1
TR 33

I want to introduce two new students today. This is Edgar. He is from Senegal. He lives in Sacramento. His phone number is (916) 555-3765.

Meet Julie. She is also a new student. She is from Canada. She lives in Folsom. Her number is (916) 555-4565.

C. CLASSIFY Write the information about Edgar and Julie.

Name	Phone	City
Edgar	(916) 555-3765	Sacramento
Julie	(916) 555-4565	Folsom

AT-A-GLANCE **PREP**

Goal: Introduce yourself and others
Grammar: Possessive adjectives
Pronunciation: Question intonation
Academic Strategy: Focused listening
Vocabulary: *introduce, lives, address, phone number, this is, meet*

Agenda

- Line up in alphabetical order by first name.
- Learn and practice possessive adjectives.
- Learn different forms of introduction.
- Ask questions.

Resources

Multilevel Worksheets: Lesson 1, Worksheets 1 and 2
Reading and Writing Challenge: Unit 2
Workbook: Unit 2, Lesson 1
Audio: CD 1, Tracks 33–34
Heinle Picture Dictionary: Wave, Greet, Smile, pages 40–41
Stand Out Basic Assessment CD-ROM with ExamView®

Pacing

- 1.5 hour classes
- 2.5 hour classes
- 3+ hour classes

STANDARDS CORRELATIONS

CCRS: RI1, SL2, L1, L2, L5, RF2, RF3
CASAS: 0.1.4
SCANS: **Basic Skills** Reading, writing, listening, speaking
EFF: **Communication** Convey ideas in writing, speak so others can understand, listen actively

Preassessment *(optional)*

Use the Stand Out Basic Assessment CD-ROM with ExamView® to create a pretest for Unit 2.

Warm-up and Review (10–12 mins.)

Write the alphabet across the board. Review each letter by pointing to it and asking students to call out the name of the letter. Then, write a student's name on the board under the letter that corresponds to the student's first name. Show the students, for example, that *Juan* goes under *J*. Next, show students how to form a line in alphabetical order by first name.

Introduction (2 mins.)

Write the day of the week, the date, and the agenda on the board. Say the date while pointing to it and have students repeat it. Introduce yourself to the class. State the goal: *Today we will introduce each other.*

Presentation 1 (12–15 mins.)

Invite three volunteers to the front of the classroom. Ask them: *What's your name? What's your address? What's your phone number?* Teach students that if they don't want to give out this information, they may say, *That's personal.* Write the phrase on the board.

A. PREDICT Look at the picture. Where are the students from?

Ask students to open their books and briefly discuss the picture. Ask students where they think Edgar and Julie are from. Some students may read ahead to the information in Exercise B. This is expected.

B. Listen and practice.

Play the recording. Ask students to follow along as they listen.

LISTENING SCRIPT

CD 1 TR 33

The listening script matches the paragraphs in Exercise B.

Practice 1 (5–7 mins.)

Ask students in groups of three to write a conversation using the students' names as well as the teacher's name, Mr. Jackson, in Exercise B. Ask them to switch roles until all students have played the role of Mr. Jackson.

Evaluation 1 (3–5 mins.)

Ask volunteers to perform their conversation in front of the class.

Presentation 2

7–10 mins.

Write on the board: *My name is* ____ (your name). Ask students to introduce themselves using the phrase. After each student says his or her name in a sentence, ask the class a question: *What's his/her name?* Write the answers on the board. For example, if a student's name is John, write: *His name is John.* Circle *His* or *Her* in each sentence you write on the board. Check for understanding by pointing to the people in Exercise A and asking: *What's his name? What's her name?*

C. CLASSIFY Write the information about Edgar and Julie.

Ask students to use the information from Exercise B to complete the chart.

D. Read the chart.

Ask students to look at the chart at the top of the page. Point out the relationship between the pronouns and the possessive adjectives. Drill students by pointing to a male student in the class and asking them to say: *His name is* ______ (student's name). Then, point to a female student, prompting them to say: *Her name is* ________ (student's name). Do this with groups of students to show all forms. Be careful to always include *name* so students don't confuse *he* and *she* with the possessive adjective.

> BEST PRACTICE
>
> ### Metalanguage
>
> *Metalanguage* in teaching English refers to the labels we give grammatical structures. In this case, we are introducing possessive adjectives.
>
> Students don't need metalanguage to speak English well or to understand grammar. Some English speakers may never know what the *third-person singular* is. However, sometimes when working with adults, some identification of grammar structures can help them to identify things they have learned earlier and to apply them to new structures.

For shorter classes, ask students to do Exercises E and F for homework.

Practice 2

5–7 mins.

E. RELATE Look at the pictures and complete the sentences.

Give students minimal instructions (if any) to do this activity. Allow them time to figure out what to do. Have them work together, if necessary. The instructions don't say to use the possessive adjectives, but students should be able to relate the practice to the presentation.

F. Complete the sentences.

Help as necessary.

Evaluation 2

7–10 mins.

Check students' book work.

> BEST PRACTICE
>
> ### Checking
>
> Important reasons to check students' book work are to focus on lesson objectives, provide immediate feedback, and correct misunderstandings. Keep in mind the following points:
>
> 1. Evaluation can take place during and/or after student book work.
> 2. Accuracy should NOT be expected. Book work is the students' time to practice.
> 3. Evaluation need NOT be teacher-centered. Students may check each other's work in pairs or small groups.

D. Read the chart.

Possessive Adjectives		
Subject	**Possessive adjective**	**Example sentence**
I	My	**My** phone number is 555-3456.
You	Your	**Your** address is 2359 Maple Drive.
He	His	**His** name is Edgar.
She	Her	**Her** name is Julie.
We	Our	**Our** last name is Perez.
They	Their	**Their** teacher is Mr. Jackson.

E. RELATE Look at the pictures and complete the sentences.

This is Mr. Jackson. ____His____ phone number is 555-2813. ____His____ address is 3317 Maple Drive.

Irma and Edgar are married. ____Their____ phone number is 555-3765. ____Their____ address is 1700 Burns Avenue.

F. Complete the sentences.

1. John is single. ____His____ address is 3215 Park Street.
2. You're a student here. ____Your____ phone number is 555-2121, right?
3. We're from Russia. ____Our____ address is 1652 Main Street.
4. I'm a new student. ____My____ name is Julie.

G. Learn the introductions.

This is …	This is Oscar.
Meet …	Meet Julie.
I want to introduce …	I want to introduce Edgar.

H. Listen and circle.

CD 1
TR 34

1. This is … Meet … (I want to introduce …)
2. This is … (Meet …) I want to introduce …
3. (This is …) Meet … I want to introduce …

INTONATION

What's your name?

What's your phone number?

What's your address?

I. SURVEY Talk to four classmates. Answers will vary.

Name (What's your name?)	Phone number (What's your phone number?)	Address (What's your address?)
1.		
2.		
3.		
4.		

J. Introduce a classmate to the class.

Presentation 3

12–15 mins.

Call three volunteers to the front of the class and introduce them using the phrases and words from the vocabulary box. Students should be focused on you at this point, so it is better to have the books closed.

G. Learn the introductions.

Students may resist using *this* because the form isn't common in some other languages. However, it is important that they learn it in preparation for future projects they will do in *Stand Out Basic*.

Show them how *this* is only used when introducing one person and is not used in the plural.

At this point, if you feel your students are ready, you may add other ways to make introductions.

Write the three phrases across the board. Say each one in random order and ask students to point to the one you say. This activity will prepare them for the listening practice that will follow.

Practice 3

5 mins.

H. Listen and circle.

> **LISTENING SCRIPT**
>
> CD 1 TR 34
>
> 1. **Mr. Jackson:** *Hi, Edgar. I want to introduce you to Susan. She is a friend of mine from class.*
>   **Edgar:** *Hello, Susan. Nice to meet you.*
>   **Susan:** *Nice to meet you, too.*
> 2. **Mr. Jackson:** *Class, it is my pleasure to tell you about a new student. Please meet Jonathan. He is from Canada. His address and phone number are available if you want to contact him.*
> 3. **Susan:** *My name is Susan and this is my good friend, Emanuel. Emanuel is from Israel. We live in Sacramento. Our class is next door.*
>   **John:** *Nice to meet you. What's your teacher's name?*
>   **Susan:** *It's Mr. Jackson.*

Evaluation 3

3 mins.

Check students' answers. Play the recording more than once if necessary.

> **BEST PRACTICE**
>
> **Playing recordings multiple times**
>
> It is appropriate to play recordings several times at this level. The speakers speak at an authentic pace so students can transfer their classroom experiences to real-life listening.

Refer students to *Stand Out Basic Workbook, Unit 2, Lesson 1* for more practice with possessive adjectives.

Go to the *Activity Bank* online for suggestions on promoting digital literacy and using the Internet to enhance this lesson.

Application

5–7 mins.

Review the pronunciation box with students. Show them that the emphasis is placed on the first word in this type of question. You may drill students by having them stand when saying the emphasized word and sitting afterwards.

I. SURVEY Talk to four classmates.

Have students complete the chart with the information they gather from four classmates.

J. Introduce a classmate to the class.

Have students present the information about one of the classmates they talked to in Exercise I.

> **MULTILEVEL WORKSHEETS**
>
> Lesson 1, Worksheet 1: Introductions
>
> Lesson 1, Worksheet 2: Possessive Adjectives

> **BEST PRACTICE**
>
> **Books closed**
>
> In the *Stand Out* approach, developing or maintaining the context is as important as the content. In this lesson, students would study the words carefully and perhaps lose sight of the context if the instructor asked them to immediately study the chart in Exercise G. If the information is first practiced or presented in context, students will be more likely to understand the information when they see the chart.

AT-A-GLANCE **PREP**

Goal: Describe your surroundings
Grammar: Prepositions of location
Pronunciation: Question intonation
Academic Strategy: Focused listening
Vocabulary: Classroom objects, prepositions

Agenda

- Learn classroom vocabulary.
- Learn prepositions of location.
- Draw your classroom.
- Write about your classroom.

Resources

Multilevel Worksheet: Lesson 2, Worksheet 1
Workbook: Unit 2, Lesson 2
Audio: CD 1, Tracks 35–36
Heinle Picture Dictionary: Classroom, pages 18–19; In, On, Under, pages 12–13

Pacing

- 1.5 hour classes
- 2.5 hour classes
- 3+ hour classes

STANDARDS CORRELATIONS

CCRS: SL1, SL2, L1, L2, RF2
CASAS: 0.1.5
***SCANS:* Basic Skills** Listening, speaking
Information Acquire and evaluate information, organize and maintain information, interpret and communicate information
Interpersonal Teach others
***EFF:* Communication** Speak so others can understand, listen actively

Warm-up and Review
10–15 mins.

Ask students to get in groups of three and introduce each member to another group.

Introduction
5 mins.

Write the day, the date, and the agenda on the board. Say the date and have students repeat it. Ask students to point to objects in the classroom, for example: *Point to the teacher's desk.* Help them understand by modeling. Next, express where the item is by using a preposition of location. State the goal: *Today we will describe our classroom.*

Presentation 1
15–20 mins.

Go over the new vocabulary in the picture.

A. Listen and repeat. Point to the picture.

LISTENING SCRIPT  CD 1 TR 35

Listening script matches the word list in Exercise A.

B. LOCATE Write: *desk, computer, chair,* and *book.*

To prepare for the next activity, use the new vocabulary in sentences and ask students to point.

C. Listen and point.

Briefly go over the pronunciation box.

LISTENING SCRIPT  CD 1 TR 36

May I have your attention, please? Class, I want to give you a quick tour of the classroom and talk about some class rules. Look around and see if you can find the items I will describe to you. Of course, the board is in the front of the class. Here, I write important information. If you need a pencil sharpener, please use the electric one during group work, and not when I am talking. We can move desks in the classroom when it is necessary to do group work. If you need to borrow a book, go to the bookcase. Please don't leave trash around the room. Use the trash can whenever possible. I hope you know that I don't want you sitting in your chairs all the time. You will have many opportunities to get up and walk around. Also, we will keep the door closed during class, so you can concentrate on your work in the class. Any questions?

Practice 1
5–7 mins.

D. RELATE Ask questions. Use the words in Exercise A.

Ask students to work in pairs.

Evaluation 1
5–7 mins.

Observe students doing the activity.

Where's the pencil sharpener?

GOAL ■ Describe your surroundings

CD 1 TR 35

A. Listen and repeat. Point to the picture.

trash can	file cabinets	board	bookcase	plant	door

B. LOCATE Write: *desk, computer, chair,* and *book.*

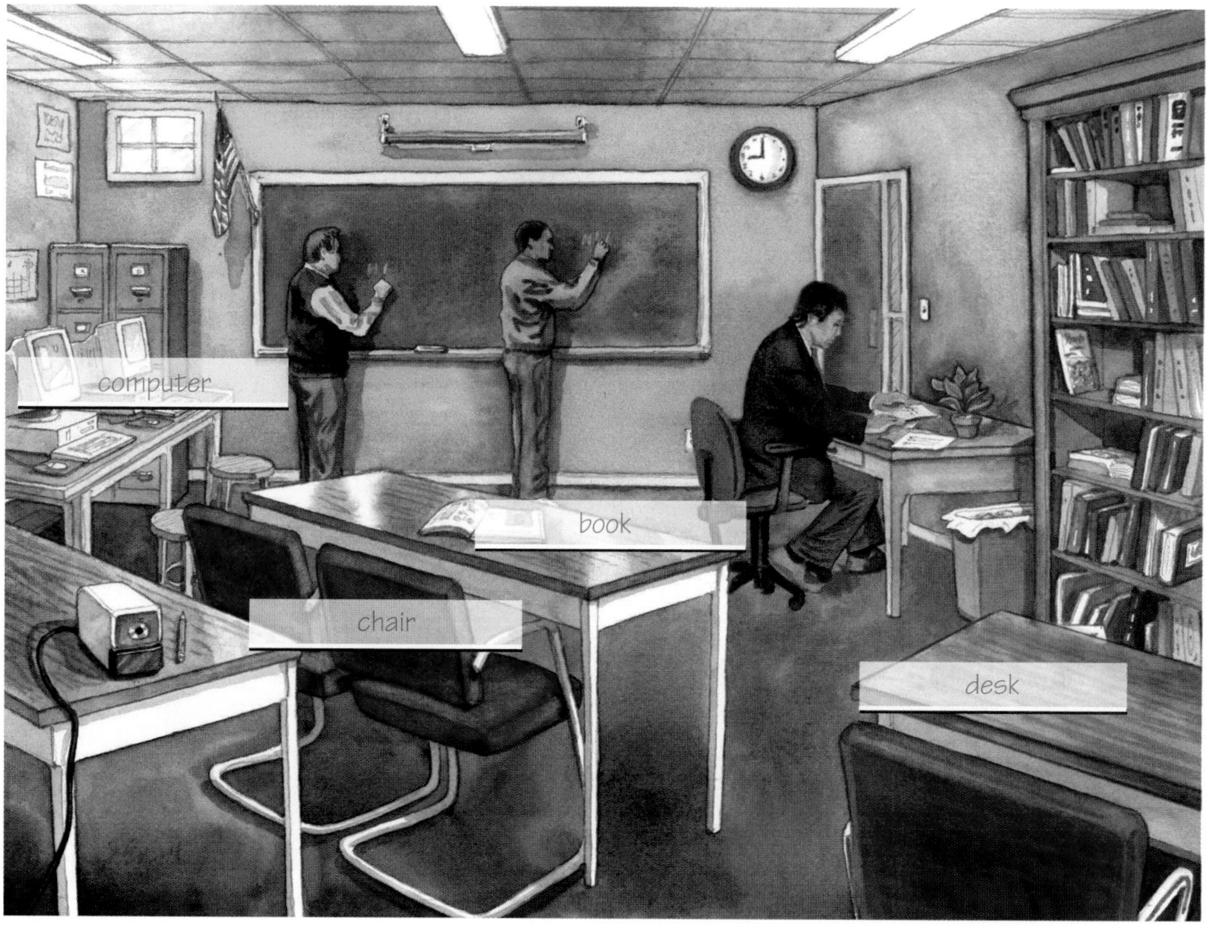

C. Listen and point.

CD 1 TR 36

D. RELATE Ask questions. Use the words in Exercise A.

EXAMPLE: **Where's the trash can?**

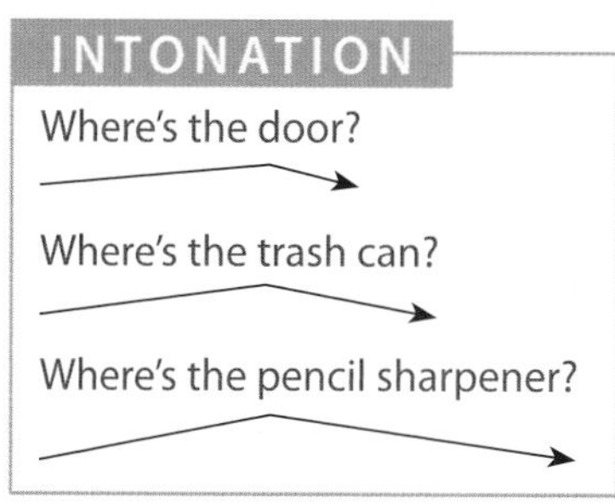

E. Read.

Prepositions of Location	
 Where's the desk? It's **behind** the chair.	 Where's the plant? It's **on** the desk.
 Where's the trash can? It's **between** the desk and the bookcase.	 Where are the file cabinets? They're **next to** the computer.
 Where are the students? They're **in front of** the board.	 Where are the books? They're **in** the bookcase.

F. APPLY Look at the picture in Exercise B. Ask *where is the teacher, plant,* and *trash can.* Ask *where are the file cabinets, students,* and *books.*

Student A: Where is the teacher?
Student B: He is next to the door.

Student A: Where are the file cabinets?
Student B: They are behind the computers.

Presentation 2

12–15 mins.

With books closed, ask students where something is in the classroom. Try to elicit information from students instead of merely giving them prepositions. The conversation with students might go something like this:

Teacher: *Where's the file cabinet?*
[Students point.]
Teacher: *Where?*
[Students point again. One or two students say: *There.*]
Teacher: *Where is it?*
[One or two students might say *next to the desk* or something similar. If they don't, the teacher can cue them.]
Teacher: *Next to*... [Pause for student responses.]

BEST PRACTICE

Eliciting information

The *Stand Out* approach suggests that—as much as possible—instructors elicit information from students first, before giving them the information. This is an important principle in Student-Centered Instruction (SCI). By first eliciting information, the teacher is able to better determine what students already know.

E. Read.

Guide students through the information. Drill students on the new prepositions by looking back at the previous page and asking them where various items are. This might also be a good place to use or create hand signals to identify certain or all the prepositions.

Show students how to do Practice 2. Take plenty of time to set this up for them. Model it with several students until you are confident that they will have success when they do it in pairs.

Practice 2

10–12 mins.

F. APPLY Look at the picture in Exercise B. Ask *where is the teacher, plant,* and *trash can*. Ask *where are the file cabinets, students,* and *books*.

Student A asks the questions from Exercise F. Student B answers while Student A checks to see that Student B is correct. Student B should only look at Exercise B. After completing the activity, students should reverse roles.

Evaluation 2

5 mins.

Ask volunteers to perform their conversations.

INSTRUCTOR'S NOTES

Presentation 3

15–20 mins.

Ask students again where things in the classroom are. When you are confident that students understand that they are to draw the classroom showing where objects are in relation to each other, divide them into groups.

For shorter classes, ask students to do Exercise G for homework.

Practice 3

15–20 mins.

G. CREATE Draw your classroom.

Encourage students to use prepositions of location in their groups. Walk around during this activity and ask students questions using the prepositions.

BEST PRACTICE

Random grouping

Sometimes grouping students randomly without consideration for native language or proficiency is appropriate. A few techniques for random grouping include the following:

Counting off: You want four students in each group. You have 32 students in the class. Have students count off from one to eight. All ones work together, all twos work together, etc.

Birthday months: Students whose birthdays are in the same month work together. The benefit is that students get to know one another better and they recycle learning about months. This method, however, takes a lot of instructor assistance because it is difficult to get even groups. Try having students stand for each month of the year and forming groups from those who are standing.

Playing cards: If you have 28 students in your class, you would use all the playing cards from aces to sevens. Shuffle and pass out the cards to all students. The students with aces work together as do the students with twos, etc.

Evaluation 3

15–20 mins.

Observe students' work.

Refer students to *Stand Out Basic Workbook, Unit 2, Lesson 2* for more practice with prepositions of location.

Go to the *Activity Bank* online for suggestions on promoting digital literacy and using the Internet to enhance this lesson.

Application

5–7 mins.

H. Write.

Have students complete the exercise in groups or in pairs.

MULTILEVEL WORKSHEET

Lesson 2, Worksheet 1: Prepositions of Location

INSTRUCTOR'S NOTES

WORKPLACE CONNECTION
Exercise G: Combine ideas and information

G. CREATE Draw your classroom. Answers will vary.

H. Write. Answers will vary.

1. Where is the teacher's desk? ______________________________
2. Where is the trash can? ______________________________
3. Where is the board? ______________________________
4. Where are the books? ______________________________
5. Where are the file cabinets? ______________________________

LESSON 3 What are you doing?

GOAL ■ Identify common activities

A. Listen and point to the students.

CD 1
TR 37

B. IDENTIFY Write the names of the students.

1. listen ___Shiro___
2. read ___Julie___
3. write ___Edgar___
4. talk ___Sara___

AT-A-GLANCE **PREP**

Goal: Identify common activities
Grammar: Present continuous
Academic Strategies: Focused listening
Vocabulary: Classroom verbs; *pen, pencil, book, notebook, CD, magazine*

Agenda

- Review classroom verbs.
- Match classroom objects and verbs.
- Write actions using the present continuous.

Resources

Multilevel Worksheet: Lesson 3, Worksheet 1
Workbook: Unit 2, Lesson 3
Audio: CD 1, Track 37
Heinle Picture Dictionary: Listen, Read, Write, pages 20–21

Pacing

■ 1.5 hour classes ■ 2.5 hour classes
■ 3+ hour classes

STANDARDS CORRELATIONS

CCRS: S1, S2, L1, L2, L5, RF3
CASAS: 0.1.5
SCANS: **Basic Skills** Listening, speaking
Information Acquire and evaluate information, organize and maintain information, interpret and communicate information
Interpersonal Teach others
EFF: **Communication** Speak so others can understand, listen actively

Warm-up and Review 12–15 mins.

Write these words on the board: *pencil sharpener, board, teacher's desk, trash can, bookcase, door, file cabinet.* Write a sentence describing the location of the trash can, for example: *It's next to the teacher's desk.* Ask students to name the item. Ask students to write sentences about each item using *It's* and quiz a partner. Have a few students report to the class.

Introduction 2 mins.

Write the day of the week and the date on the board. Say the date and have students repeat. Pantomime *reading, talking, listening, sitting, standing,* and *writing*. State the goal: *Today, we will identify common activities.*

Note: In this lesson, students will be introduced to the present continuous. Students are not expected to fully grasp the structure at this time.

Presentation 1 7–10 mins.

Ask students to open their books. Look at the picture with them. Ask them to point to any activities they recognize. Pantomime the actions again and write the words in Exercise B on the board. Ask students to find these actions in the picture. Help students to prepare for the listening task by using the words in sentences and asking them to point to each action.

A. Listen and point to the students.

LISTENING SCRIPT

CD 1
TR 37

All the students work hard in Mr. Jackson's English class. Two students are talking in the back of the room about their homework. One student is writing at his desk. Shiro is at his desk, too. He is listening to a tape. Julie is reading. She is a good student.

Practice 1 3 mins.

B. IDENTIFY Write the names of the students.

Do the first item as a class. After students complete this exercise, have them work in pairs. Student A reads a word and Student B points to the picture. Then they reverse roles. Then, ask them to invert the activity. Student A points to an action and Student B says the word.

Evaluation 1 3 mins.

Observe students as they perform the task.

BEST PRACTICE

Step-by-step

At this level, it is important that you only ask students to do one thing at a time. Carefully model the target behavior. Let students know how much time they have to complete each task, but monitor them to make sure they don't lose interest sooner.

Presentation 2

10–12 mins.

Put examples of the items listed in the vocabulary box on a table in front of the room. Go over the vocabulary and help students with correct pronunciation.

Do a Total Physical Response (TPR) activity. In this activity, students learn the vocabulary by standing up and going through simple motions. Demonstrate the activity and then ask students to do it. Ask different students to stand up, come to the front of class, pick up, and put down a designated item.

Write the four verbs on the board again: *listen, write, read,* and *talk*.

Ask students to do another TPR activity slightly different from the one you have just done. Have a student come to the board and circle one of the four verbs that can best be associated with the item you give them. For example, if you give the student a pencil, he or she should circle the verb *write*.

BEST PRACTICE

Total Physical Response

Total Physical Response, or TPR, was developed by Dr. James J. Asher. The basic idea is that when students engage physically, learning improves. Also, TPR permits students to react to the language without speaking immediately.

For shorter classes, ask students to do Exercises D and E for homework.

Practice 2

5–7 mins.

C. Read the words and find examples in your classroom.

Read the words. Then, ask students to look for examples in the classroom. Once identified, ask volunteers to point to the item and say the word. Have students repeat.

D. IDENTIFY Write the words from Exercise C.

Ask students to look at the pictures. Then, ask students to write the correct word under each picture.

Evaluation 2

5–7 mins.

Drill students by saying one of the nouns and asking students to respond with the corresponding verb. You can check students' understanding better if you assign each verb a number. Instead of responding with the verb, ask students to show the number of fingers that corresponds to the verbs you have numbered.

E. CLASSIFY Complete the table with the objects in Exercise D.

Ask students to complete this activity either in pairs or on their own. Note that the verb *write* has three matches: *pencil, pen,* and *notebook.*

INSTRUCTOR'S NOTES

C. Read the words and find examples in your classroom.

pen   clock   board   ~~pencil~~   book   notebook   CD   magazine   teacher

D. IDENTIFY Write the words from Exercise C.

1. 
pencil

2. 
pen

3. 
book

4. 
notebook

5. 
CD

6. 

magazine

7. 
teacher

8. 

clock

9. 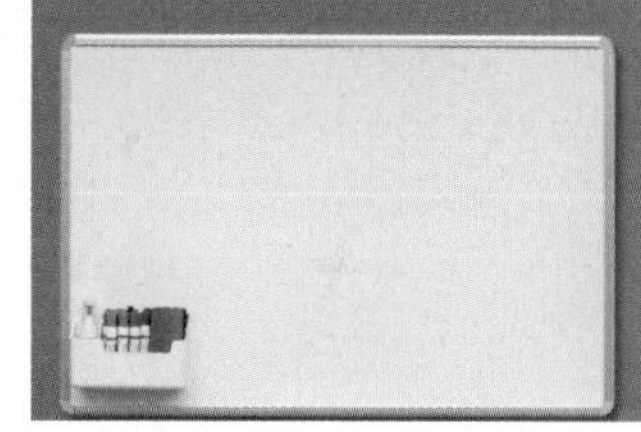
board

E. CLASSIFY Complete the table with the objects in Exercise D.

Write	Listen	Read
pencil	CD	book
pen	teacher	magazine
notebook		clock
		board

F. Read.

Present Continuous				
He	is	read		He is reading. / She is reading.
She		write		He is writing. / She is writing.
		listen	-ing	He is listening. / She is listening.
		talk		He is talking. / She is talking.
		sit		He is sitting. / She is sitting.
		stand		He is standing. / She is standing.

G. Write.

1. She is reading.
2. She is listening.

3. He is standing.
4. He is talking / listening.

5. She is sitting.
6. She is writing.

H. REPORT Write about your classmates. Answers will vary.

1. Juan is sitting.
2. ______
3. ______
4. ______
5. ______

Presentation 3

7–10 mins.

Play the recording from page 44 (CD 1, Track 37) again. Ask students to listen carefully to the verbs. Write on the board: *Julie is reading.* Play the recording one more time and ask students to listen for this sentence.

F. Read.

Read the chart with students. This is their first exposure to the present continuous. It is not separated into morphemes and students are not expected at this point to transfer the information to other verbs. Spelling is also a consideration, but since this structure is only presented for awareness purposes, spelling rules are not introduced. Students will be asked to copy the sentences in the next activity. Point out the spelling issues, but avoid offering rules at this point.

Practice 3

7–10 mins.

G. Write.

Ask students to write the information on the lines provided. Point out that a period is necessary at the end of each sentence they produce.

Evaluation 3

5–7 mins.

Ask students to write their sentences on the board.

Refer students to *Stand Out Basic Workbook, Unit 2, Lesson 3* for more practice with the present continuous.

Go to the *Activity Bank* online for suggestions on promoting digital literacy and using the Internet to enhance this lesson.

Application

5–7 mins.

H. REPORT Write about your classmates.

Help as necessary.

MULTILEVEL WORKSHEET

Lesson 3, Worksheet 1: Classroom Activities

INSTRUCTOR'S NOTES

AT-A-GLANCE **PREP**

Goal: Plan a schedule
Pronunciation: Question intonation
Academic Strategies: Focused listening, scheduling
Vocabulary: *schedule, lunch, work, pronunciation, bed*

Agenda

- Review classroom actions.
- Study a schedule.
- Read clocks.
- Practice talking about time.

Resources

Multilevel Worksheets: Lesson 4, Worksheets 1, 2, and 3
Work book: Unit 2, Lesson 4
Audio: CD 1, Tracks 38–40
Heinle Picture Dictionary: Time, pages 4–5

Pacing

- 1.5 hour classes
- 2.5 hour classes
- 3⁺ hour classes

STANDARDS CORRELATIONS

CCRS: RI1, RI7, SL2, RF2
CASAS: 0.2.1, 0.2.4, 2.3.1
SCANS: **Basic Skills** Writing, listening, speaking
Resources: Allocate time
Information Acquire and evaluate information, organize and maintain information, interpret and communicate information
Systems Understand systems, monitor and correct performance
EFF: **Communication** Speak so others can understand, listen actively

Warm-up and Review

2–5 mins.

Write on the board: *write*. Have students repeat the word a few times. Pantomime *listen, read, talk, sit,* and *stand.* Ask students in groups to choose one person to pantomime the verbs while the rest of the group responds with the action word.

Introduction

10–12 mins.

Write the day of the week and the date on the board. Say the date while pointing to it. Write your daily schedule on the board using the format on page 47. Review your schedule by giving the time for each activity. State the goal: *Today we will learn to plan a schedule.*

Presentation 1

12–15 mins.

A. Read and listen.

Go over the schedule in the book with students and ask them the time of each activity. Be sure to teach *a.m.* and *p.m.*, and practice the pronunciation of *o'clock*. Play the recording.

LISTENING SCRIPT

CD 1 TR 38

Shiro has a busy schedule. He has English class at nine o'clock. At twelve thirty, he eats lunch. He goes to class again at one o'clock. He has pronunciation class. He goes to work at four o'clock.

Review the pronunciation box. Make sure students understand the intonation.

Practice 1

3 mins.

B. IDENTIFY Look at Shiro's schedule.

Ask students to complete the exercise on their own. Then, ask students to practice questions and answers in pairs. Help them use the correct pronunciation. The student asking the questions looks at Exercise B. The student answering looks only at Shiro's schedule in Exercise A. After a few minutes, ask students to reverse roles.

Evaluation 1

3 mins.

Ask students to demonstrate for the class.

INSTRUCTOR'S NOTES

LESSON 4 When's English class?

GOAL ■ Plan a schedule

A. Read and listen.

CD 1
TR 38

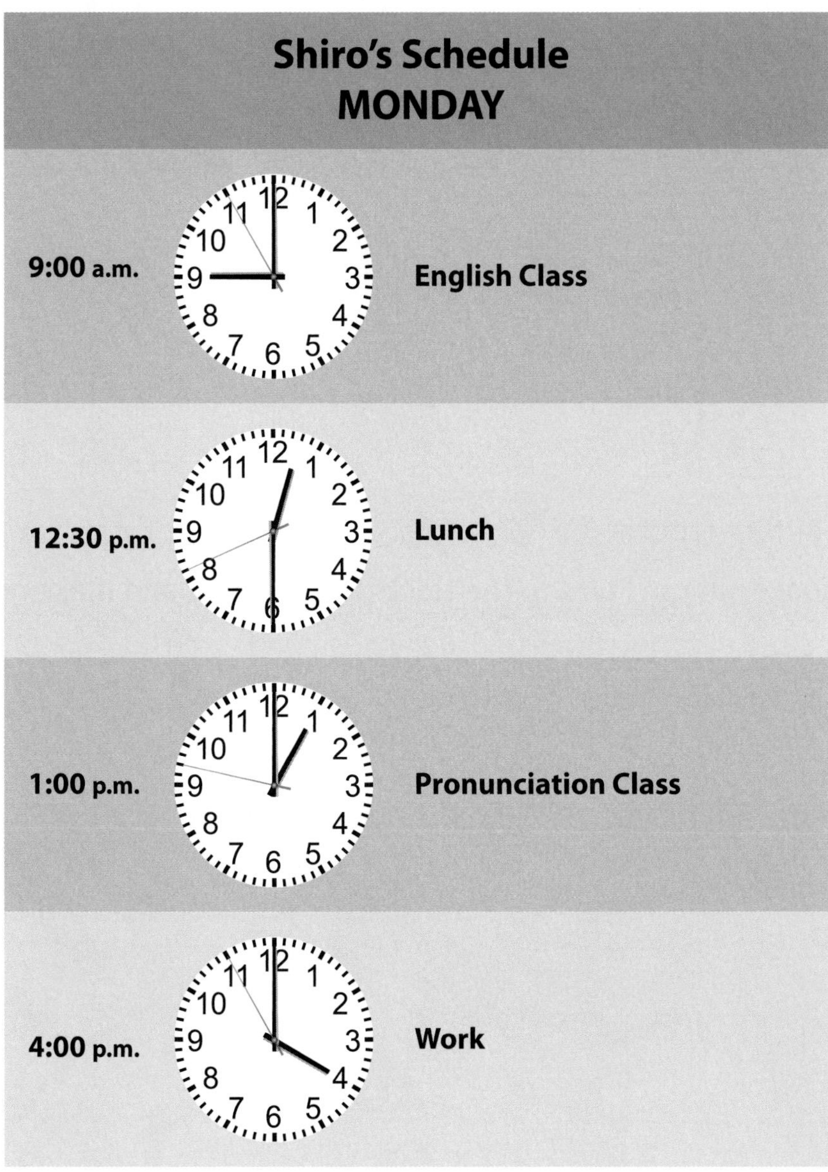

Shiro's Schedule
MONDAY
9:00 a.m.
English Class
12:30 p.m.
Lunch
1:00 p.m.
Pronunciation Class
4:00 p.m.
Work

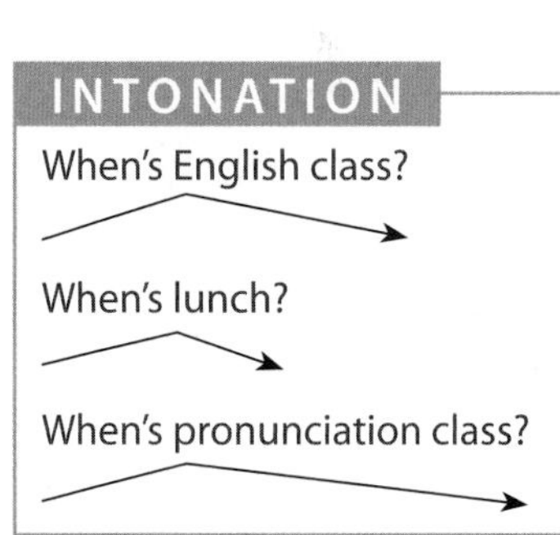

INTONATION
When's English class?
When's lunch?
When's pronunciation class?

B. IDENTIFY Look at Shiro's schedule.

1. When's English class? It's at nine o'clock.
2. When's lunch? It's at twelve thirty.
3. When's pronunciation class? It's at one o'clock.
4. When's work? It's at four o'clock.

C. What time is it? Write.

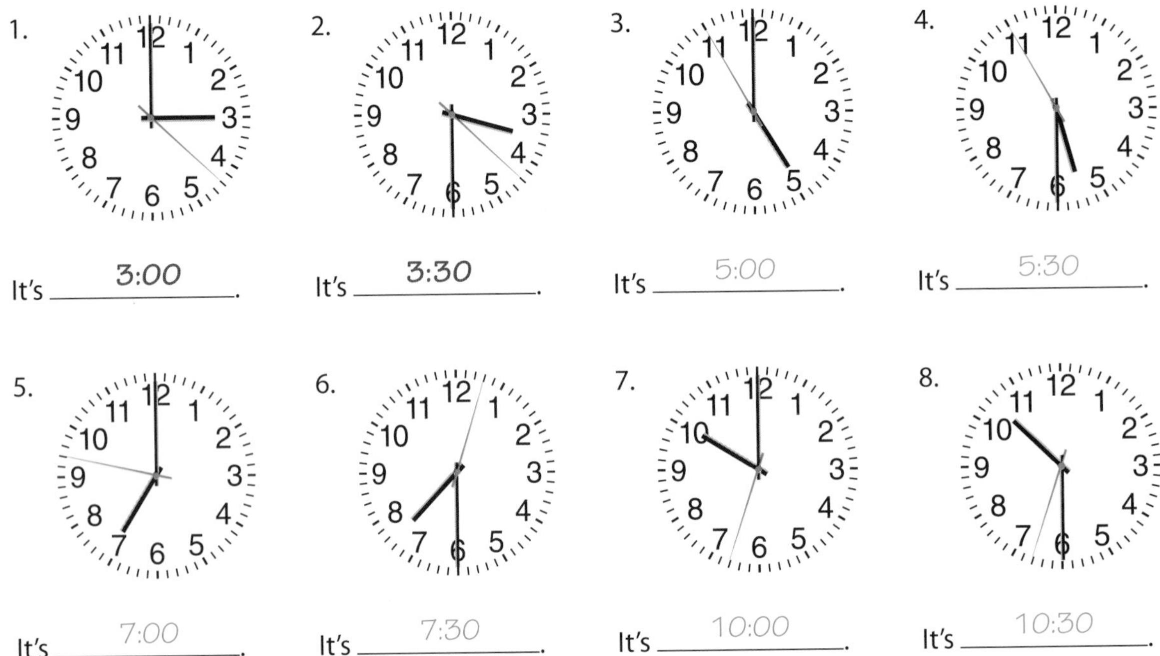

1. It's 3:00.
2. It's 3:30.
3. It's 5:00.
4. It's 5:30.
5. It's 7:00.
6. It's 7:30.
7. It's 10:00.
8. It's 10:30.

D. RELATE Practice the conversation. Point to the clocks in Exercise C and make new conversations.

Student A: What time is it? (Point to number 4 in Exercise C.)

Student B: It's five thirty.

It's one thirty at Grand Central Station in New York City.

Presentation 2

10–15 mins.

C. What time is it? Write.

Ask: *What time is it?* Have students write the correct times. Explain to students that it is not necessary to write *a.m.* or *p.m.* because the time shown in each clock can represent both morning and evening.

Go over each of the clocks in Exercise C. This exercise can be reviewed as a class. Help students to understand that they should only say *o'clock* on the hour.

If you have a clock that you can remove from the wall, write times on the board and have students come up and change the clock to the time given. Ask students when they eat lunch. Change the clock to read this time.

If students are ready, you might also teach them *quarter past* and *quarter to* the hour as well as other ways of giving the time.

BEST PRACTICE

Extending vocabulary

No textbook will give students every vocabulary word they will need. On the other hand, students at times may be overburdened by too many words. If you use the *Heinle Picture Dictionary* or add more vocabulary to a lesson, make sure students know what vocabulary items are a priority. Students with little formal education may get frustrated when given too much vocabulary. These students may only be able to handle six to ten new words a day.

Be aware of student needs. You may choose to use a vocabulary list that students maintain to help them know which words they are responsible for. One possible list is in the appendices of their books. To further remind them of what they absolutely need to learn and to add some accountability, consider giving a weekly spelling test on the words from their lists.

Practice 2

8–12 mins.

D. RELATE Practice the conversation. Point to the clocks in Exercise C and make new conversations.

Ask students to work in pairs.

BEST PRACTICE

Group work

At this level, it is important to model group activities. A variety of grouping strategies are suggested depending on the task.

1. Allow students to self-select groups. Students sometimes perform well with people they feel comfortable with.
2. Arrange groups according to skill level. Proficient students can excel, while less proficient students don't feel intimidated.
3. Arrange cross-ability groups. More proficient students often enjoy helping, and you'll have several mentors in the class instead of just one teacher.
4. Avoid homogeneous language groups to encourage the use of English.

Evaluation 2

7–10 mins.

Observe students as they work together.

BEST PRACTICE

Observing group or pair work

Walking around the classroom allows you to observe students who may be having difficulty with the material. It is important to catch potential problems early on and correct students' misunderstandings.

Remember that this is an opportunity for students to work together, not one-on-one with the teacher. Therefore, try to be present but invisible. Let students know that you are there to help, but do not interrupt their work. Move from group to group or pair to pair as quickly and quietly as possible.

If you would like to verbally check on students' progress, ask: *Is everything OK? How's it going?* Students will eventually get used to observations and they will see the teacher as a possible source for help.

Presentation 3

15–20 mins.

E. Listen and write.

Do this listening activity as a class, starting and stopping the audio several times.

> **LISTENING SCRIPT**
>
> CD 1 TR 39
>
> **Cameron**: *Hi Julie. How are you?*
> **Julie:** *Fine, thanks.*
> **Cameron:** *What is your schedule today?*
> **Julie:** *I have English class at nine o'clock. Then, I work at eleven.*
> **Cameron:** *What about lunch?*
> **Julie:** *I eat lunch at two thirty.*
> **Cameron:** *Wow! That's late. What time do you eat dinner?*
> **Julie:** *Dinner is at eight o'clock, and bedtime is at ten thirty.*
> **Cameron:** *That is a long day.*

F. Listen and read.

Practice the conversation with students. Ask them to practice briefly in pairs. Prepare students for Exercise G by going over the dialog and reviewing the pronunciation, as well as when and when not to use *at*.

> **LISTENING SCRIPT**
>
> 
> CD 1 TR 40
>
> *The listening script matches the conversation in Exercise F.*

Practice 3

5 mins.

G. Practice the conversation in Exercise F. Make new conversations.

Ask students to take on the role of Julie or Mr. Jackson and ask questions about the schedule in Exercise E.

Evaluation 3

3 mins.

Ask students to demonstrate the conversation in front of the class.

> **BEST PRACTICE**
>
> **Demonstrations**
>
> Student demonstrations often help you to evaluate what students have learned. They also provide a model for other students. Sometimes it becomes necessary to correct students in this circumstance to ensure that no faulty learning is occurring. Be careful to only correct where the error directly relates to the lesson objective. If a lot of correction is necessary, this indicates that more practice is needed.

Refer students to *Stand Out Basic Workbook, Unit 2, Lesson 4* for more practice with when and when not to use *at*.

Go to the *Activity Bank* online for suggestions on promoting digital literacy and using the Internet to enhance this lesson.

Application

5–7 mins.

H. PLAN Write your schedule on a separate piece of paper.

Ask students to write their schedules on another piece of paper.

> **MULTILEVEL WORKSHEETS**
>
> Lesson 4, Worksheet 1: Telling Time
> Lesson 4, Worksheet 2: Schedules and Times
> Lesson 4, Worksheet 3: Daily Planner

CD 1 TR 39

E. Listen and write.

Julie's Schedule MONDAY	
9:00 a.m.	English Class
11:00 a.m.	Work
2:30 p.m.	Lunch
8:00 p.m.	Dinner
10:30 p.m.	Bedtime

CD 1 TR 40

F. Listen and read.

Julie: When's English class?
Mr. Jackson: It's at nine o'clock.
Julie: What time is it now?
Mr. Jackson: It's seven thirty.

G. Practice the conversation in Exercise F. Make new conversations. Answers will vary.

A: When's ______________________________?

B: It's ______________________________.

A: What time is it now?

B: It's ______________________________.

H. PLAN Write your schedule on a separate piece of paper. Answers will vary.

LESSON 5 It's cold today

GOAL ■ Plan for weather

CD 1 TR 41 **A. Listen and repeat.**

windy	cloudy	foggy	rainy	snowy	cold	hot	sunny

CD 1 TR 42 **B. IDENTIFY Listen and write the words from Exercise A.**

San Francisco, United States

foggy

Montreal, Canada

cold/snowy

Havana, Cuba

hot/sunny

Patagonia, Chile

windy/cold

Tokyo, Japan

cloudy

New York City, United States

rainy

AT-A-GLANCE **PREP**

Goal: Plan for weather
Grammar: Simple present with *need*
Pronunciation: Question intonation
Academic Strategies: Focused listening
Vocabulary: *windy, cloudy, foggy, sunny, rainy, snowy, cold, hot, weather*

Agenda

- Review schedules.
- Listen about weather.
- Talk about weather.
- Talk about weather and clothes.
- Predict the weather.

Resources

Multilevel Worksheet: Lesson 5, Worksheet 1
Workbook: Unit 2, Lesson 5
Audio: CD 1, Tracks 41–42
Heinle Picture Dictionary: Weather, pages 166–167

Pacing

- 1.5 hour classes
- 2.5 hour classes
- 3⁺ hour classes

STANDARDS CORRELATIONS

CCRS: RI7, SL2, L1, L2, L4, RF2, RF3
CASAS: 0.1.2, 0.2.1, 1.1.3, 2.3.3
***SCANS:* Basic Skills** Reading, writing, listening, speaking
Information Acquire and evaluate information, organize and maintain information, interpret and communicate information
Interpersonal Participate as a member of a team, teach others
***EFF:* Communication** Convey ideas in writing, speak so others can understand, listen actively
Interpersonal Cooperate with others

Warm-up and Review

10–12 mins.

Ask students to work in pairs, ask for their partner's schedule for the day, and write it down. Then, ask them to report to another pair.

Introduction

2 mins.

Write the day of the week and the date on the board. Say the date while pointing to it and have students repeat it. Look outside and ask students if it is cold or hot today. State the goal: *Today we will learn to plan for weather.*

Presentation 1

5 mins.

Draw the sun on the board and label it. If you have a world or U.S. map, ask students where it might be sunny. You might want to cut out a sun and a picture of rain and have students tape the pictures on the map. Draw weather symbols for your city and say: *It's sunny* (*cloudy, rainy, etc.*) *in* _____ (your city) *today.* Ask students to repeat several times. Make gestures like fanning your face to indicate *It's hot!*

A. Listen and repeat.

Discuss the meaning of each word and repeat the activity of finding places on the map that might have that particular weather. Do this for each new word.

LISTENING SCRIPT

CD 1 TR 41

The listening script matches the word list in Exercise A.

Prepare students for Exercise B by saying the words and asking them to point to them. If you think students are ready, try a short dictation of the words in the list.

Practice 1

3 mins.

B. IDENTIFY Listen and write the words from Exercise A.

Students often stop listening when they begin writing. Show them how to write the first letter of the word so that they can go back and complete it after the listening. You might need to play the recording several times.

LISTENING SCRIPT

CD 1 TR 42

This is Express Weather from Miami, Florida. We are happy to bring you the latest weather throughout the world. Let's start with Havana, Cuba. It's hot today in Havana with a temperature of 98 degrees. In Tokyo, Japan, it is cloudy and unusually cold for this time of year. In Patagonia, Chile, be careful when driving. It's very windy today. Be careful driving in San Francisco, too. It's very foggy. Moving along to the north of us in Montreal, Canada, the bitter cold is keeping most people indoors. Yes, it's very cold. Finally, in New York City, it's rainy and the rain will continue for several days.

Evaluation 1

2 mins.

Go over the answers with students.

Presentation 2

12–15 mins.

C. Review the weather.

Ask students how the weather is in Havana, Cuba. Go on to ask them how it is in the other places listed.

Say: *How's the weather?* Place the stress on *How's*.

INTONATION

Information questions

To help students understand where to place the stress on the correct part of the question, you may try several different techniques.

1. Ask most of the students to say *How's* and ask only a few to finish the sentence with *the weather.*
2. Ask students to stand up on emphasized words and to sit on the others.
3. Ask students to repeat the phrase and add an exaggerated pause after *How's*.
4. Ask students to clap every time they say *How's*.

Practice 2

7–10 mins.

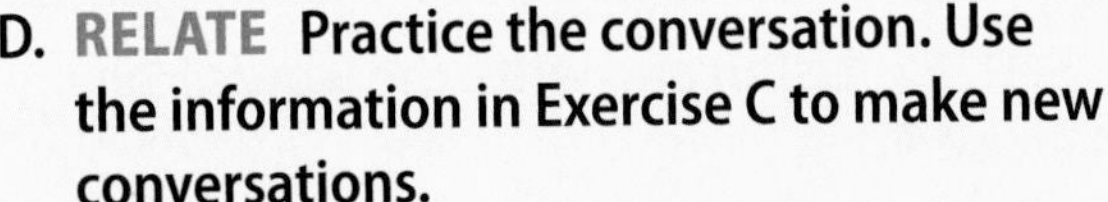

D. RELATE Practice the conversation. Use the information in Exercise C to make new conversations.

Show students how to substitute information about each location as they complete the conversation.

Evaluation 2

5 mins.

Ask for volunteers to demonstrate the questions and answers for different locations in front of the class.

BEST PRACTICE

Realia

Using realia is always effective in the ESL classroom. For example, in this lesson, if you were to bring in an umbrella, a heavy coat, mittens, or a ski mask, students would be able to associate the weather with the objects.

BEST PRACTICE

Asking questions that prompt critical thinking

The key to critical thinking is asking the right questions. Questions determine the information we seek. Teachers can plan to ask students thought-provoking questions that encourage more than just one-word answers:

1. **Knowledge questions** that show students' ability to recall facts, concepts, and answers. *Can you describe the weather in your country?*
2. **Comprehension questions** that show students' understanding of facts by being able to organize, compare, or contrast information. *Can you compare the weather in your country to the weather here?*
3. **Application questions** that show students' ability to use acquired knowledge in order to find answers. *Why do you think the weather is cold today?*
4. **Analysis questions** that show students' ability to classify or categorize. *In what parts of the world is it hot?*
5. **Evaluation questions** that show students' ability to give their opinions based on factual information. *What country has the best weather?*
6. **Creation questions** that show students' ability to put information together to propose different solutions. *What clothes can I take with me to visit Cuba?*

C. Review the weather.

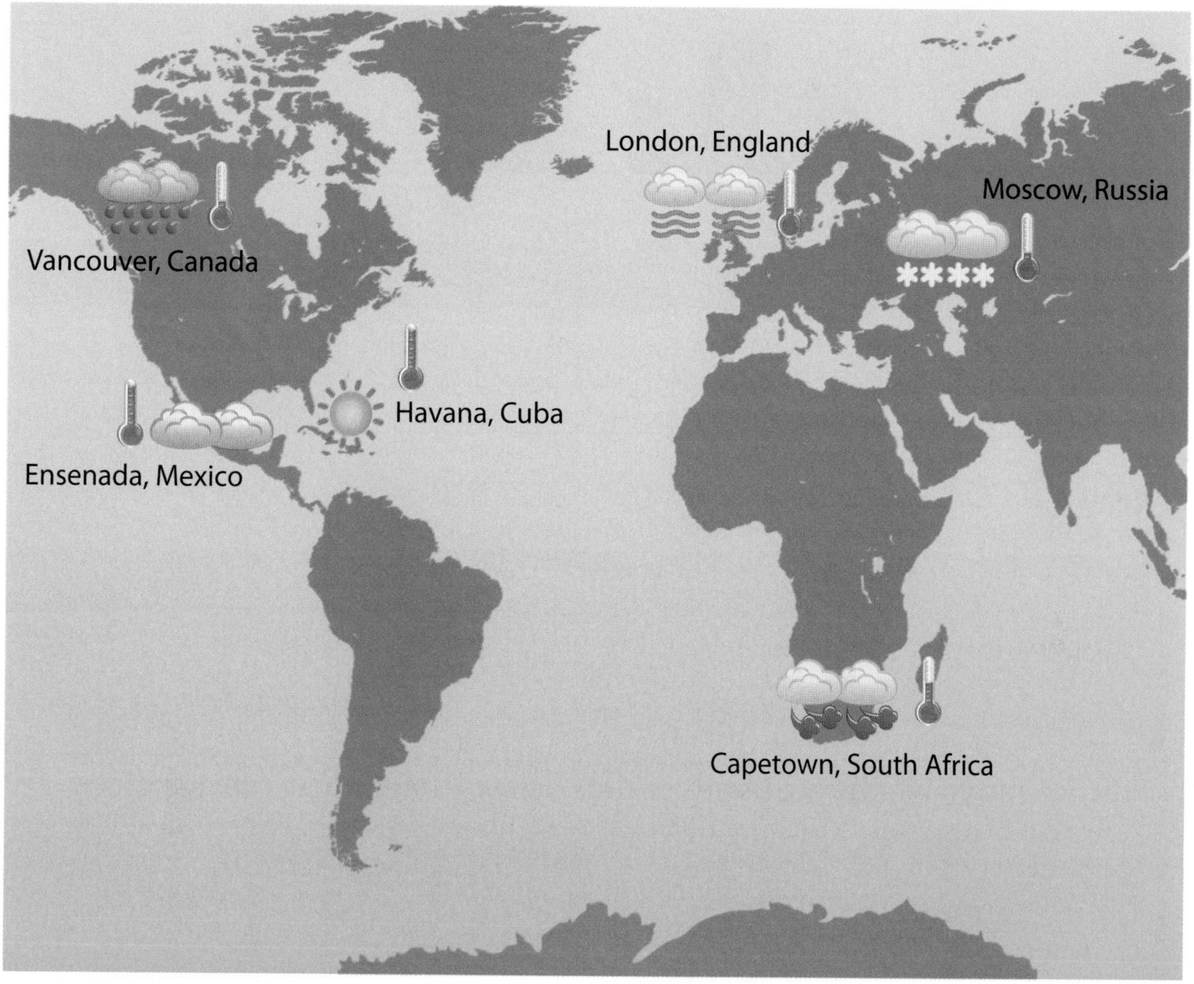

London, England
Moscow, Russia
Vancouver, Canada
Havana, Cuba
Ensenada, Mexico
Capetown, South Africa

rainy
cloudy
sunny
foggy
snowy
windy
hot
warm
cold

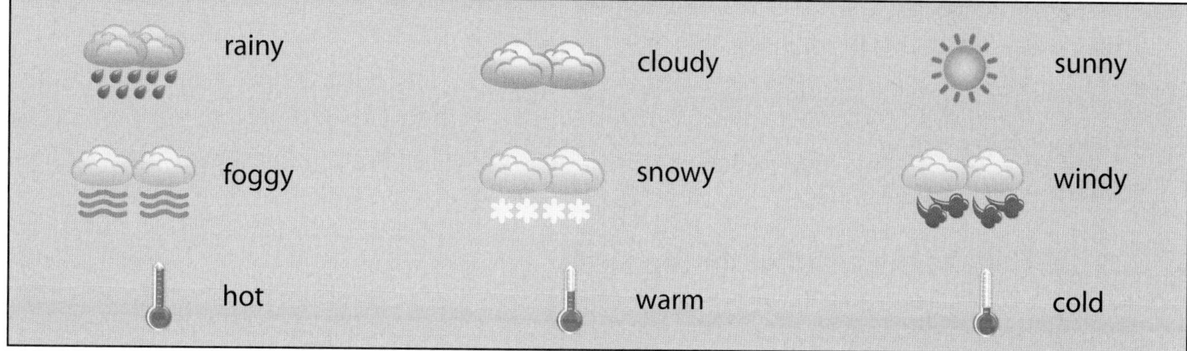

D. RELATE Practice the conversation. Use the information in Exercise C to make new conversations.

A: How's the weather in Havana, Cuba today?
B: It's hot and sunny.

WORKPLACE CONNECTION
Exercises E and H: Collect and organize information
Exercise I: Apply technology to a task

E. **CLASSIFY** **Write the correct clothes for the weather.**

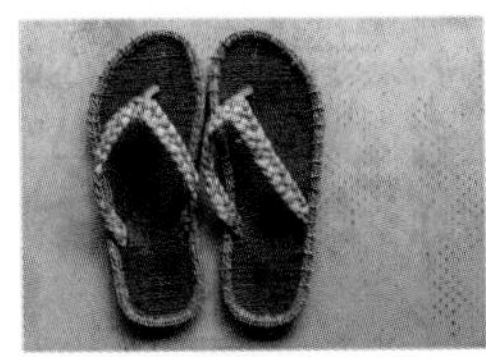
sandals

boots

a t-shirt

an umbrella

Rainy	Sunny
boots	sandals
an umbrella	a t-shirt

F. **Read.**

Simple Present		
I, You, We, They	need	I **need** an umbrella.
He, She	needs	She **needs** an umbrella.

G. **Practice the conversation. Use the words below to make new conversations.**

I	You	He	She	We	They

Student A: How's the weather today?
Student B: It's rainy.
Student A: He needs an umbrella.

Student A: How's the weather today?
Student B: It's sunny.
Student A: I need a t-shirt.

H. **PREDICT** **Write the weather for the week.** Answers will vary.

Monday	Tuesday	Wednesday	Thursday	Friday	Saturday	Sunday

I. **Look on the Internet or in a newspaper. Check the weather for the week and compare it with your predictions in Exercise H.**

Presentation 3

12–15 mins.

The following activities are in preparation for Exercise G. In Exercise G, students will describe their needs when planning to come to class. To do this, they will need some additional vocabulary and possibly the simple present tense. Help students to prepare by going over the new vocabulary and doing Exercises E and F with them.

Use realia when possible with the vocabulary. Act out being very cold and ask students what you can do about it. A few students might know to use the word *coat, sweater,* or *jacket*. Write the words on the board and refer to the vocabulary.

E. CLASSIFY Write the correct clothes for the weather.

F. Read.

This grammar is still being introduced. Help students see that they need an *s* on the third-person singular. There is still no need to transfer this information to other verbs, but students can refer back to other pages in their books where the final *s* has been introduced. Specifically, see page 19, Exercise H.

Practice 3

7–10 mins.

G. Practice the conversation. Use the words below to make new conversations.

Show students how to substitute information.

Evaluation 3

2 mins.

Ask volunteers to demonstrate Exercise G in front of the class.

Refer students to *Stand Out Basic Workbook, Unit 2, Lesson 5* for more practice with the simple present.

Go to the *Activity Bank* online for suggestions on promoting digital literacy and using the Internet to enhance this lesson.

Application

5–7 mins.

H. PREDICT Write the weather for the week.

After groups do this activity, ask them to report to the class and to compare what other groups wrote.

I. Look on the Internet or in a newspaper. Check the weather for the week and compare it with your predictions in Exercise H.

MULTILEVEL WORKSHEET

Lesson 5, Worksheet 1: How's the Weather?

INSTRUCTOR'S NOTES

It's raining hard

Before You Watch

- Ask students to look at the title and predict what the video will be about.
- Ask students: *How's the weather? What clothes do you need in this weather?*
- Write any key vocabulary expressions and words on the board.

A. Look at the picture and answer the questions.

- Ask students to look at the picture. Ask: *What are the people doing?*
- Go over the questions with students to elicit answers.
- Discuss the answers as a class. Ask: *What is the weather like today where we live? How do you know?*
- Write any key vocabulary expressions and words on the board.

While You Watch

B. Watch the video and circle the words you hear.

- Ask students to watch the video once so that they can get familiar with the speed and understand the gist.
- Read the words and ask students to repeat.
- Play the video again and ask students to circle the words they hear.

Check Your Understanding

C. Put the events in order.

- Ask: *What happens in the story?* Have students discuss the video in pairs.
- Ask students to read the sentences and put them in the correct order.
- Ask students to check their answers in pairs. Then, discuss as a class.

BEST PRACTICE

There are many ways to use video in the classroom. Students should rarely watch a video without some kind of task. You might introduce comprehension questions before they watch so they know what they are looking for. Below are a few techniques that you may try for variety beyond the comprehension checks and other ideas already presented in this lesson.

Freeze Frame: Pause the video during viewing and use it like a picture dictionary, identifying and expanding on the vocabulary.

Silent Viewing: Show the video in segments without sound so students can guess at the storyline. This helps them to understand that listening is more than just the words people say.

Prediction Techniques: Show portions of the video and ask students to predict what will come next.

Listening without Viewing: This helps students create their own image of what is happening. After a discussion, allow students to watch the video and the sound together.

Back-to-Back: In pairs, one student faces the video and the other faces away. Play the video without sound and ask the student viewing to report to the student who is facing away what is happening.

Summary Strips: Create strips of sentences that describe the events. Have students watch the video and then put the strips in the correct order, or ask students to predict the story line before watching and then check their answers. The Activity Bank has summary strips for each video in *Stand Out*.

LIFESKILLS

It's raining hard

Before You Watch

A. Look at the picture and answer the questions.

1. Where are Hector, Mateo, and Naomi?
   They are in the classroom.
2. What's the weather like? How do you know? It's rainy. Hector and Naomi are holding umbrellas.

While You Watch

B. Watch the video and circle the words you hear.

boots

umbrella

poncho

snowy

rainy

windy

cold

bad weather

cloudy

Check Your Understanding

C. Put the events in order.

1. 2 Mateo enters.
2. 5 Naomi, Hector, and Mateo run outside.
3. 1 Hector enters.
4. 3 Naomi enters.
5. 4 Naomi, Hector, and Mateo talk about the weather.

Review

Learner Log
I can introduce myself and others.
☐ Yes ☐ No ☐ Maybe

A. Read.

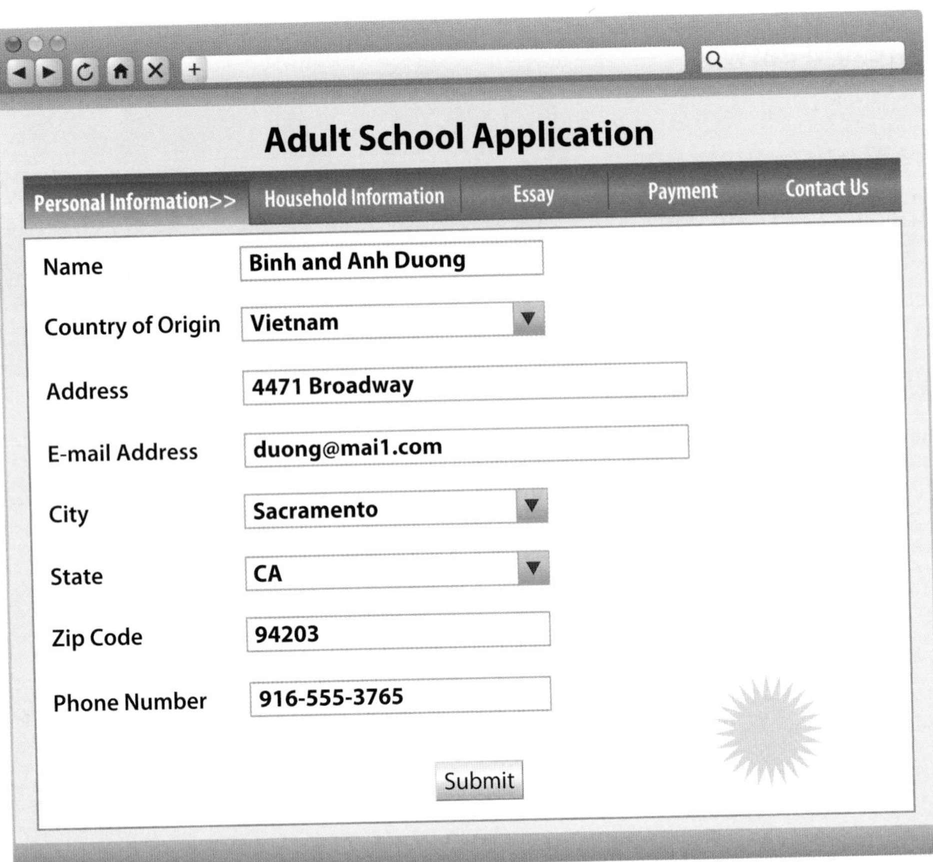

Adult School Application

Personal Information>> | Household Information | Essay | Payment | Contact Us

Name	Binh and Anh Duong
Country of Origin	Vietnam
Address	4471 Broadway
E-mail Address	duong@mai1.com
City	Sacramento
State	CA
Zip Code	94203
Phone Number	916-555-3765

Submit

B. Complete.

I want to introduce ___Binh___ and ___Anh Duong___. They are from ___Vietnam___.
___Their___ address is ___4471 Broadway, Sacramento, CA 94203___.
___Their___ phone number is ___(916) 555-3765___.

C. Ask a classmate for information. Introduce your classmate to another student.

AT-A-GLANCE **PREP**

Goal: All unit objectives
Grammar: All unit grammar
Academic Strategies: Focused listening, reviewing, evaluating, developing study skills
Vocabulary: All unit vocabulary

Agenda

- Discuss unit objectives.
- Complete the review.

Pacing

- 1.5 hour classes
- 2.5 hour classes
- 3+ hour classes

STANDARDS CORRELATIONS

CCRS: RI1, RI7 L1, L2, RF3

CASAS: 0.1.5, 2.3.1, 2.3.2, 2.3.3, 7.4.1, 7.4.2, 7.4.3

***SCANS:* Basic Skills** Reading, writing, listening, speaking

Information Acquire and evaluate information, organize and maintain information, interpret and communicate information

Thinking Skill See things in the mind's eye

***EFF:* Communication** Speak so others can understand, listen actively

Lifelong Learning Take responsibility for learning, reflect and evalute

Warm-up and Review

5–7 mins.

Ask students to go through the unit and find their favorite activity. Ask for volunteers to speak up about what they liked about it.

Introduction

2 mins.

Write all the objectives on the board from Unit 2. Show students the first page of the unit and mention the five objectives. Explain that today is review and that they will review the whole unit.

Note: Depending on the length of the term, you may decide to have students do Exercises A–H for homework and then review student work as the warm-up for another class meeting.

Presentation

10–15 mins.

This presentation will cover the first three pages of the review. Quickly go to the first page of each lesson. Discuss the objective of each. Ask simple questions to remind students what they have learned.

Practice

15–20 mins.

A. Read. (Lesson 1)

Ask students to read the application form silently.

B. Complete. (Lesson 1)

Ask students to complete the personal information using the application form from Exercise A.

C. Ask a classmate for information. Introduce your classmate to another student. (Lesson 1)

BEST PRACTICE

Recycling/Review

The review process and the project that follows are part of the recycling/review process. Students at this level often need to be reintroduced to concepts to solidify what they have learned. Many concepts are learned and forgotten while learning other new concepts. This is because students learn but are not necessarily ready to acquire language concepts.

Therefore, it becomes very important to review and to show students how to review on their own. It is also important to recycle new concepts in different contexts.

INSTRUCTOR'S NOTES

Practice *(continued)*

D. Read. (Lessons 4 and 5)

Ask students to read the information in the exercise silently.

E. Write. (Lessons 4 and 5)

Have students work by themselves to complete the activity using the information from Exercise D.

INSTRUCTOR'S NOTES

D. Read.

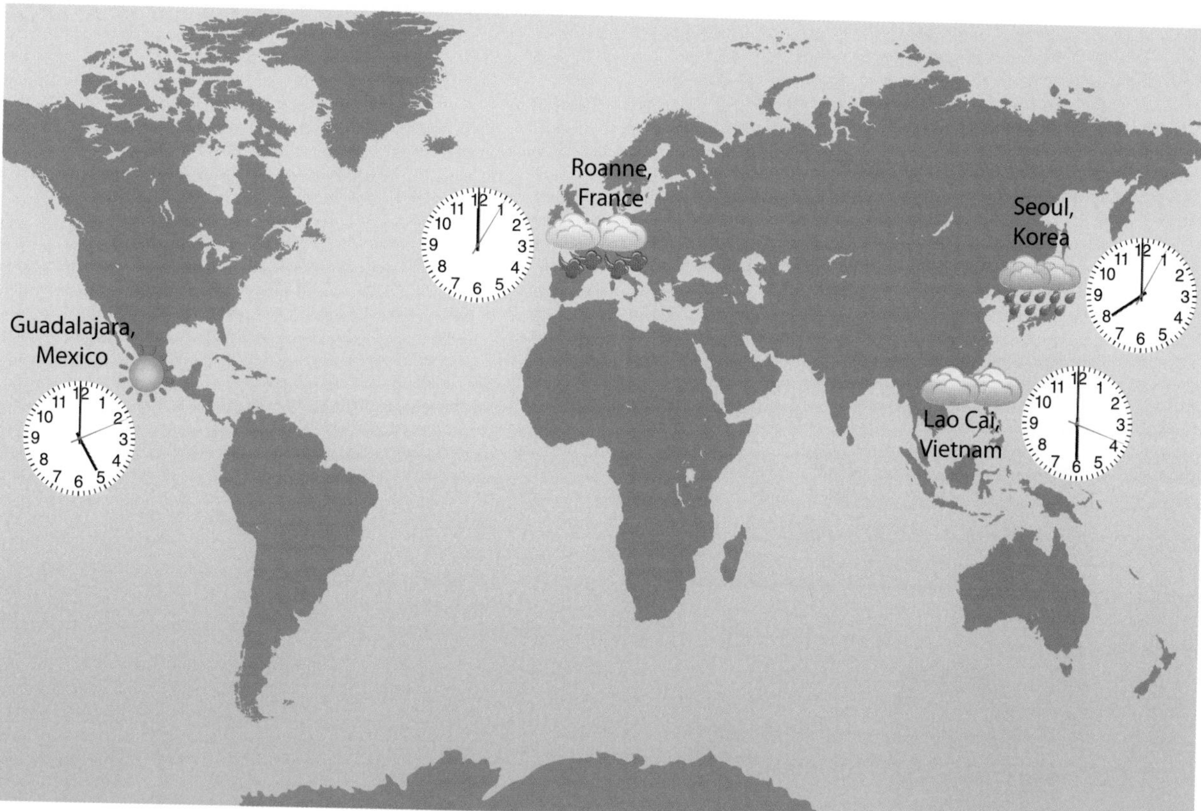

E. Write.

1. How's the weather in Korea? It's rainy in Korea.

   What time is it? It's 8:00.

2. How's the weather in France? It's windy in France.

   What time is it? It's 12:00.

3. How's the weather in Mexico? It's sunny in Mexico.

   What time is it? It's 5:00.

4. How's the weather in Vietnam? It's cloudy in Vietnam.

   What time is it? It's 6:00.

Learner Log

I can identify common activities.
☐ Yes ☐ No ☐ Maybe

I can describe my surroundings.
☐ Yes ☐ No ☐ Maybe

F. Match.

1. 

2. 

3. 

4. 

a. He is listening.

b. He is writing.

c. She is talking.

d. He is reading.

G. Write.

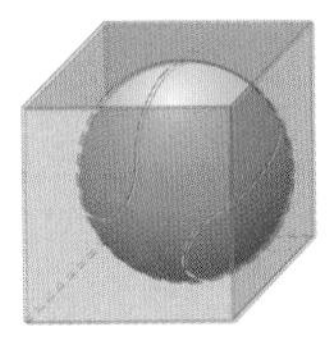

in

next to

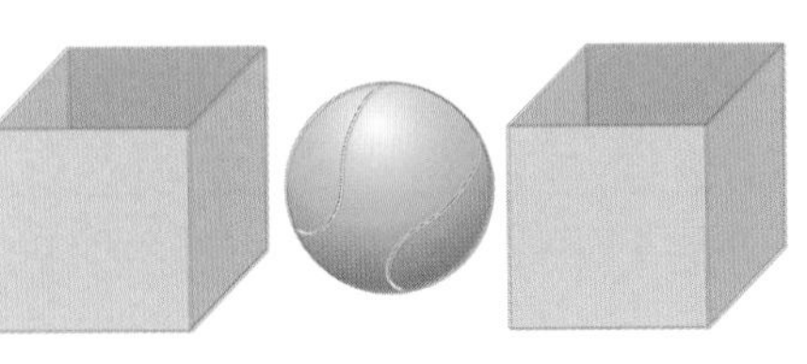

between

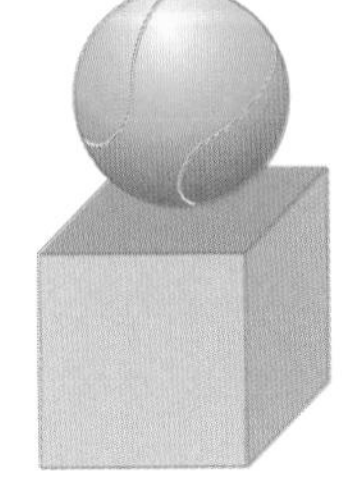

on

Practice *(continued)*

F. Match. (Lesson 3)

Have students work independently to match the pictures with the classroom activity.

G. Write. (Lesson 2)

Have students work independently to write the correct prepositions.

Evaluation

15 mins.

Go around the room and check on students' progress. Help individuals when needed. If you see consistent errors among several students, interrupt the class and give a mini lesson or review to help students feel comfortable with the concept.

INSTRUCTOR'S NOTES

WORKPLACE CONNECTION

Combine ideas and information; Make decisions; Exercise leadership roles; Manage time; Complete tasks as assigned; Interact appropriately with team members; Collect and gather information; Interpret and communicate information; Apply technology

STANDARDS CORRELATIONS

CCRS: RI7, SL1, SL2

CASAS: 0.1.5, 2.3.1, 2.3.2, 2.3.3, 4.8.1

***SCANS:* Basic Skills** Reading, writing, listening, speaking

Resources Allocate time, allocate money, allocate materials and facility resources, allocate human resources

Information Acquire and evaluate information, organize and maintain information, interpret and communicate information, use computers to process information

Interpersonal: Participate as a member of a team, teach others, serve clients and customers, exercise leadership, negotiate to arrive at a decision, work with cultural diversity

Systems Understand systems, monitor and correct performance, improve and design systems

Thinking Skills Think creatively, make decisions, solve problems, see things in the mind's eye

Personal Qualities Responsibility, sociability, self management

***EFF:* Communication** Read with understanding, convey ideas in writing, speak so others can understand, listen actively, observe critically

Decision Making Solve problems and make decisions, plan

Interpersonal Cooperate with others, advocate and influence, resolve conflict and negotiate, guide others

Lifelong Learning Take responsibility for learning, reflect and evaluate

Introduction

5 mins.

In this project, students will work in teams to create a collage showing the diversity of their group. They will section off a large sheet of paper, allowing room in each section for a picture of a group member, a map of the group member's country, and a depiction of the weather that is most common there.

Note: You may decide to bring a map to help students see the outline of your state, province, or region.

Stage 1

10–15 mins.

Form a team with four or five students.

Refer to the *Activity Bank* for a profile template.

Help students form groups and assign positions in their groups. On the spot, students will have to choose who will be the leader of their group. Review the responsibility of the leader and ask students to write the name of their leader in the books.

Do the same with the remaining positions: writer, artist, and spokesperson. If there are five people in the group, double up on the position of spokesperson. Every member of each group should have a responsibility.

Stage 2

40–50 mins.

Draw a picture of yourself. Draw a map of your country. Draw a clock with the time in your country. Draw the weather in your country.

Draw the information on a separate piece of paper.

Stage 3

10–30 mins.

Present each student's work in your group to the class.

Ask teams to prepare a presentation. Each student on the team will talk about one of the other students introducing that student to the class. The activity can be more effective if you videotape the presentations for student review.

BEST PRACTICE

Digital literacy

Projects are a perfect place to allow students opportunities to use other forms of presentations beyond pictures they create. Digital literacy is becoming more necessary as a life skill. Encourage students to create presentations using pictures from the Internet. They might also consider using other digital presentation tools.

TEAM PROJECT

Make a display

COLLABORATE Form a team with four or five students. In your team, you need:

Position	Job description	Student name
Student 1: Team Leader	Check that everyone speaks English. Check that everyone participates.	
Student 2: Writer	Help team members write.	
Student 3: Artist	Arrange a display with help from the team.	
Students 4/5: Spokespeople	Prepare a presentation.	

1. Draw a picture of yourself.
   Draw a map of your country.
   Draw a clock with the time in your country.
   Draw the weather in your country.

2. Present each student's work in your group to the class.

What time is it in your country?

About the Explorer

Joe Riis is a wildlife photojournalist from South Dakota. He has dedicated his life to photographing wild animals not only because he loves the great outdoors, but also because he believes that they deserve a voice in today's changing world. Through photography, Joe hopes to connect people with these changes and inspire them to do something.

About the Photo

This photo was taken in Grand Teton National Park, Wyoming. Moose, deer, elk, and bears are among some of the animals that live in the park that Joe photographs. Grand Teton National Park is a popular destination for people wanting to enjoy outdoor activities such as hiking, camping, and fishing.

- Introduce the explorer. Tell students they are going to read about Joe Riis.
- Ask students to look closely at the picture. Say: *This is Joe Riis. What do you see?*
- Ask students to read the quote on their own. Ask: *Is Joe Riis a very busy man? Why do you think so?* Discuss as a class.
- Direct students' attention back to the quote. Ask: *What do you think the words* ***wildlife*** *and* ***science*** *mean?* Discuss as a class.
- Tell students that *wildlife* means animals and sometimes plants. Tell them that *science* means the study of our natural world or environment.

A. PREDICT Look at the picture. Answer the questions.

- Ask students to look at the picture and discuss the answer to each question with a partner. Have students look for clues such as clothes, location, and weather.

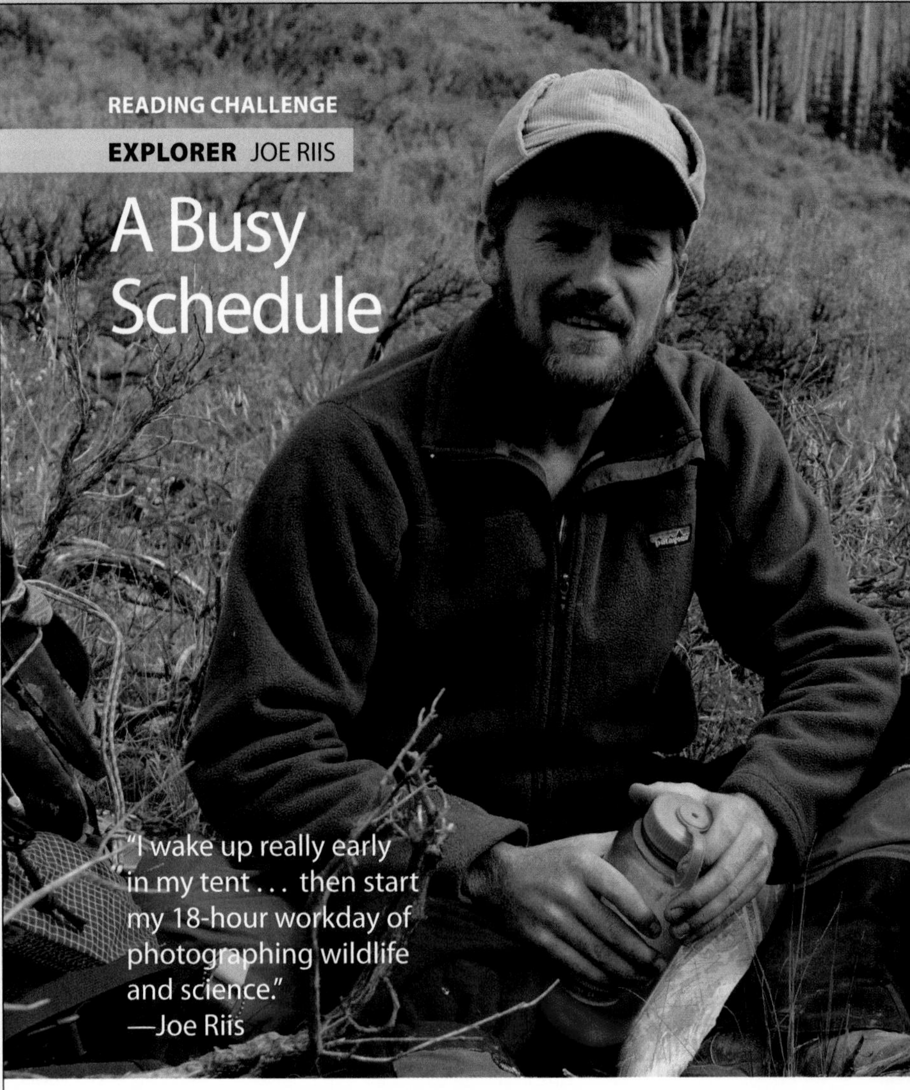

READING CHALLENGE
EXPLORER JOE RIIS
A Busy Schedule
"I wake up really early in my tent . . . then start my 18-hour workday of photographing wildlife and science."
—Joe Riis

A. PREDICT Look at the picture. Answer the questions. Answers will vary.

1. Where is Joe? What is he doing?
2. Look at what Joe is wearing. What's the weather like?

CCRS FOR READING

RI.1.1, RI.2.1, RI.1.5, RI.1.7
RF.2, RF.3

WORKPLACE CONNECTION
Exercise B: Collect and organize information

B. PREDICT What time does Joe do the following activities? Put a check (✓) in the table for each question.

	10:00 p.m.	6:00 a.m.	8:00 a.m.
What time does he wake up?		✓	
What time does he take photos?			✓
What time does he go to bed?	✓		

C. Read the interview with Joe Riis.

Joe Riis is a widlife photojournalist. He takes photos of wild animals and tells stories using his pictures.

Interviewer: Joe, you have a busy schedule, so thank you for your time. Can you tell us what you do?

Joe: Sure. I take photos of wild animals. I share the photos with people so they can connect with the planet.

Interviewer: What time do you wake up?

Joe: I wake up in my tent at 6:00 a.m.

Interviewer: What time do you take photos?

Joe: I take photos all day! I start at 8:00 a.m.

Interviewer: What do you do next?

Joe: I talk with people to get information I need to tell stories with my photos.

Interviewer: What time do you go to bed?

Joe: I go to bed at 10:00 p.m.

D. IDENTIFY Circle the times. Look again at Exercise B. Is your table correct?

E. RELATE Complete the sentences about yourself. Answers will vary.

1. My class is at ______.
2. I eat lunch at ______.
3. My English class is at ______.
4. I ______ at ______.

READING STRATEGIES

Asking Questions

Asking questions is an important reading strategy. Questions are good because they do the following:

- They allow students to check their own understanding.
- They give students a reason to read.
- They encourage students to think while reading.
- They help students relate the reading to what they already know.

B. PREDICT What time does Joe do the following activities? Put a check (✓) in the table for each question.

- Remind students that Joe Riis has a long day. Ask: *How many hours does Joe Riis work every day?* Have students check the quote for the answer.
- Have students guess what time Joe does each activity in the table. Ask students to read the questions on their own and check their answers.

C. Read the interview with Joe Riis.

- Have students read the interview with Joe Riis. Then ask: *What does Joe do with his photos?* Ask students to scan the interview to find the answer.
- Read the interview once again with students and go over any vocabulary students do not understand.

D. IDENTIFY Circle the times. Look again at Exercise B. Is your table correct?

- Ask students to circle the important times that Joe mentions in his interview. Then, ask students to check if their predictions in Exercise B are correct.

E. RELATE Complete the sentences about yourself.

- Ask students to think about their own schedules. Ask them if they are very busy like Joe Riis.
- Have students complete each sentence with what is true about their own schedule. Then, ask students to share their answers in small groups.

Food

About the Photo

Gerd Ludwig, a German-American documentary photographer, took this photo at KCRW's annual Halloween Masquerade Ball in Los Angeles. It shows people enjoying freshly prepared food from a food truck. The annual party organized by KCRW—a local Los Angeles radio station—is a fund-raiser that features bands, ghost stories, costume contests, and food trucks. Food trucks have become more popular in the United States in recent years with their appearance in downtown areas of a lot of major cities. Customers have a wide range of choices when it comes to the food for sale. Food selections range from Vietnamese sandwiches to tacos.

- Introduce the unit. Tell students what your favorite food to eat is when you feel very hungry. Ask them if they like this food, too.
- Ask students what their favorite food is. Write some of the foods on the board. Then, ask students which items they think people like the most.
- Have students look at the board again. Ask where they can find these foods. Then, ask students

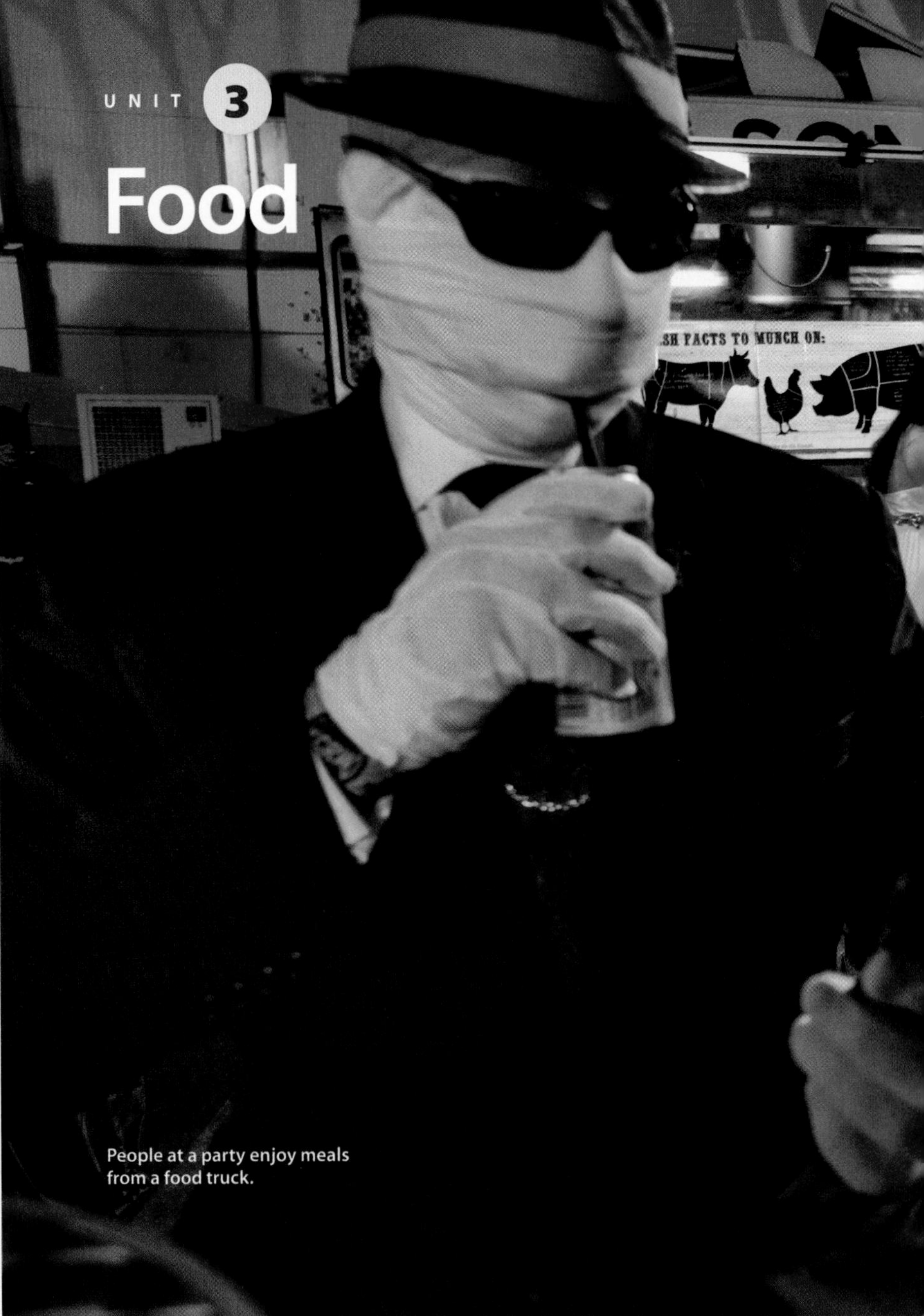

People at a party enjoy meals from a food truck.

UNIT OUTCOMES	GRAMMAR	VOCABULARY	EL CIVICS
• Identify common foods • Express hunger • Plan meals • Make a shopping list • Express preferences	• Prepositions of location • The verb *Be* + adjective • Contractions with *Be* • Negative present tense • Forming singular and plural nouns • Simple present with *want, like, eat*	• Food items: *breakfast, lunch, dinner* • Recipe vocabulary • Supermarket vocabulary • Packaging vocabulary: *bag, pound, can*	The skills students learn in this unit can be applied to the following EL Civics competency areas: • Health and nutrition • Community resources

UNIT OUTCOMES
Identify common foods
Express hunger
Plan meals
Make a shopping list
Express preferences
Look at the photo and answer the questions.
1. What food can you buy from this food truck?
2. What's your favorite food?

if any of the foods are sometimes on their shopping list. *Which ones?*

- Ask students to look at the photo and read the caption. Then, ask if anyone has ever eaten from a food truck. Ask volunteers to explain what a food truck is.
- Have students work with a partner. Ask them to read and share their answers to the questions.
- Point out each unit outcome. Then, have students look at the photo again. Ask: *Do the people look hungry? What are they eating and drinking? Do you sometimes plan food for a party? What do you buy?*

Life Skills Link

In this unit, students will learn how to identify common foods and express their preferences. They will also learn how to locate certain foods within a grocery store or supermarket.

Workplace Link

All lessons and units in *Stand Out* include basic communication skills and interpersonal skills important for the workplace. They are not individually identified. Other workplace skills are indicated. They include, collecting and organizing information, making decisions and solving problems, and combining ideas and information.

CASAS	SCANS	CCRS
Lesson 1: 1.3.8 Lesson 2: 1.3.8 Lesson 3: 1.1.1, 1.3.8 Lesson 4: 1.3.8 Lesson 5: 1.3.8 Review: 1.3.8, 7.4.1, 7.4.2, 7.4.3 Team Project: 1.8.8, 4.8.1	Many SCANs skills are incorporated in the unit with an emphasis on: • Acquiring and evaluating information • Organizing and maintaining information • Interpreting and communicating information • Allocating human resources • Basic skills • Seeing things in the mind's eye	RI1, RI7, RI9, W1, W2, SL1, SL2, SL4, L1, L2, L5, RF2, RF3

LESSON 1 Let's eat!

GOAL ■ Identify common foods

A. Look at the picture. Where are the students? Fair Oaks Adult School Cafeteria

B. RELATE Listen and read the conversation. Use the words below to make new conversations.

CD 1
TR 43

a chicken sandwich	a tuna fish sandwich	a ham sandwich

Andre: The food looks good!
Silvina: Yes, it does.
Andre: What are you eating?
Silvina: A turkey sandwich.

AT-A-GLANCE **PREP**

Goal: Identify common foods
Grammar: Prepositions of location
Academic Strategy: Working in a group
Vocabulary: Common foods, *breakfast, lunch,* and *dinner*

Agenda

- Ask information about a picture.
- Talk about foods in a refrigerator.
- Review prepositions of location.
- Practice prepositions of location.
- Discuss breakfast, lunch, and dinner.

Resources

Multilevel Worksheet: Lesson 1, Worksheet 1
Workbook: Unit 3, Lesson 1
Audio: CD 1, Tracks 43–44
Heinle Picture Dictionary: Inside the Refrigerator, pages 88–89; Fruits and Nuts, pages 82–83; Meat, Poultry, and Seafood, pages 86–87; Vegetables, pages 84–85
Stand Out Basic Assessment CD-ROM with ExamView®

Pacing

- 1.5 hour classes
- 2.5 hour classes
- 3+ hour classes

STANDARDS CORRELATIONS

CCRS: SL2, L1, L2, L5, RF3
CASAS: 1.3.8
SCANS: **Basic Skills** Reading, writing, listening, speaking
Resources Allocate human resources
Information Acquire and evaluate information, organize and maintain information, interpret and communicate information
EFF: **Communication** Speak so others can understand, listen actively
Interpersonal Cooperate with others

Preassessment *(optional)*

Use the Stand Out Basic Assessment CD-ROM with ExamView® to create a pretest for Unit 3.

Warm-up and Review

10–15 mins.

Ask students to look at the picture. Ask them to guess where the two students are from. There is no one correct answer. Next, ask where they think the students are now. Finally, ask what foods they like to eat. Make a list on the board.

A. Look at the picture. Where are the students?

Ask students to listen to the conversation. Ask what Silvina is eating.

Introduction

10 mins.

Write the agenda on the board. Ask a volunteer to write the day of the week and the date above the agenda. Ask students if they like American food. Ask individuals to name one food item from their country. Ask students which of the four sandwiches listed in the picture they like best. Help students with the new vocabulary. State the goal: *Today we will identify common foods.*

Presentation 1

30–45 mins.

B. RELATE Listen and read the conversation. Use the words below to make new conversations.

Play the recording and ask students to read the dialog. Ask students what ingredients you need to make a turkey sandwich. At this level, they may not completely understand. Lead them through different parts of a turkey sandwich, including *bread, mayonnaise, cheese, lettuce,* etc.

Show students how to substitute different sandwiches in the conversation.

LISTENING SCRIPT

CD 1 TR 43

The listening script matches the conversation in Exercise B.

Practice 1

7–10 mins.

Ask students to practice substituting different sandwiches. Then, ask students to reverse roles.

You might want to expand this activity so students ask each other which sandwich they prefer. Ask students to write five student responses and the students' names.

Evaluation 1

3–5 mins.

Ask for volunteers to demonstrate the dialog in front of the class.

Presentation 2

10–15 mins.

C. IDENTIFY Listen and point.

Go over each vocabulary word with students. It is important that students don't work on Exercise D while you are doing Presentation 2. To prevent this from happening, ask students to cover Exercise D with a sheet of paper. There are considerably more words in this lesson than in most other lessons. These are very high-frequency words that your students have undoubtedly heard, so elicit the vocabulary before merely giving them the information. You might do this by asking students questions about the picture such as: *What is your favorite food in the picture? What do you eat for breakfast? What do you have in YOUR refrigerator?*

For shorter classes, ask students to do Exercise D for homework.

LISTENING SCRIPT CD 1 TR 44

a. milk	*b. water*
c. eggs	*d. chicken*
e. bananas	*f. bread*
g. cheese	*h. turkey*
i. tomatoes	*j. lettuce*
k. apples	*l. oranges*
m. potatoes	*n. mayonnaise*
o. butter	

Practice 2

10–15 mins.

D. Match the letters in the picture to the food words. Write the words.

Ask students to complete the exercise in pairs.

Evaluation 2

3 mins.

Ask students to write the information on the board. Check for accuracy in spelling.

BEST PRACTICE

Keeping students' attention

At times, it is appropriate and advisable that higher-level students are given opportunities to work faster or ahead of the rest of the class. Most classes are multilevel in nature and some students may naturally complete an exercise some time before others. The best way to manage these situations is to be prepared to give students who finish an exercise before everyone else additional challenging work as an extension to the practice.

Having said this, it is nevertheless important to keep students from starting the practice before you assign the exercise. In the presentation stage of a lesson, you need the support, attention, and involvement of all students. You also want to be sure that all students have the opportunity to get all the information you provide in the presentation. Finally, if students do the exercises early, they become bored because they often finish before the rest of the students start.

Some strategies for keeping student attention include the following:

1. Asking students to stop writing and tell them that they will have plenty of time to do the assignment.
2. Asking all the students to cover the practice part of the page so they are not tempted to do the work.
3. Getting students who are writing in the book when it isn't time involved in the presentation by asking them questions.

C. IDENTIFY Listen and point.

CD 1
TR 44

apples	butter	eggs	milk	tomatoes
bananas	cheese	lettuce	oranges	turkey
bread	chicken	mayonnaise	potatoes	water

D. Match the letters in the picture to the food words. Write the words.

a. milk
b. water
c. eggs
d. chicken
e. bananas
f. bread
g. cheese
h. turkey
i. tomatoes
j. lettuce
k. apples
l. oranges
m. potatoes
n. mayonnaise
o. butter

WORKPLACE CONNECTION
Exercise F: Collect and organize information

E. Look and read.

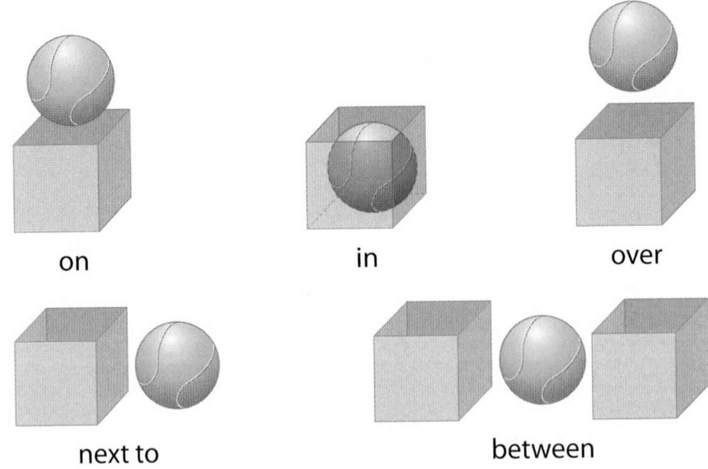

F. CLASSIFY Look at the picture in Exercise C. Write the foods in the table.

on the counter	*in* the refrigerator	*over* the counter
bread	water	bananas
tomatoes	milk	apples
cheese	eggs	oranges
lettuce	chicken	
turkey	mayonnaise	
potatoes	butter	

G. Look at the picture in Exercise C again. Complete the sentences with *next to* or *between*.

1. The water is ___next to___ the milk.
2. The turkey is ___between___ the bread and the cheese.
3. The mayonnaise is ___next to___ the chicken.
4. The cheese is ___between___ the turkey and the tomatoes.

H. Practice the conversation. Use the picture in Exercise C to make new conversations.

A: Where's the bread?
B: It's next to the turkey.

I. APPLY Make a list of foods in your refrigerator on a sheet of paper and share it with a partner.

Presentation 3

10–15 mins.

E. Look and read.

Review prepositions of location with students. You may also wish to go back to page 63. In this lesson, students will be introduced to a new preposition of location: *over*.

Another idea is to teach them the prepositions as if for the first time. Use the picture on the previous page to identify all the objects. Ask: *What is next to the butter?*

Prepare students to do the exercise by modeling it with several students and asking a few pairs to model it for the class. Show students how to substitute important information.

F. CLASSIFY Look at the picture in Exercise C. Write the foods in the table.

Before students begin, ask them to review the prepositions of location: *on, in,* and *over* in Exercise E. Then, have students look at the picture in Exercise C and locate the *refrigerator* and the *counter*. Ask: *Where is the refrigerator? Where is the counter?*

Tell students to look at the foods *in the refrigerator, on the counter,* and *over the counter* in the picture and write them in the correct column in the table. Read the example and ask students to check the food's location in the picture.

Have students work individually. Then, ask them to check their answers in pairs.

G. Look at the picture in Exercise C again. Complete the sentences with *next to* or *between*.

Do this together as a class as part of the review of prepositions of location.

BEST PRACTICE

Recycling

At all levels, but especially at the lower levels, recycling is very important. Recycling means introducing concepts already taught again in different contexts. Don't expect students to learn every concept and always remember it at this level. They will forget some things as they learn new concepts, so it becomes essential to teach them past concepts again. Also, students who may have missed a previous lesson will benefit from the review.

Practice 3

10–15 mins.

H. Practice the conversation. Use the picture in Exercise C to make new conversations.

Ask students to practice this activity in pairs. Make sure they understand that they will be describing the location of all the labeled foods in the picture in Exercise C. Monitor students closely to make sure they are using the correct prepositions.

Evaluation 3

5–7 mins.

Ask for volunteers to demonstrate.

MULTILEVEL WORKSHEET

Lesson 1, Worksheet 1: Food

Application

10–15 mins.

I. APPLY Make a list of foods in your refrigerator on a sheet of paper and share it with a partner.

Ask students to use vocabulary they have learned from this lesson, foods they know, foods they find in a bilingual dictionary or the *Heinle Picture Dictionary*, and foods that are from their country to complete the list. Then, ask them to share their list with other students.

BEST PRACTICE

Categorizing vocabulary

Find different ways to allow students to classify vocabulary so that you meet the needs of different learning styles. Also, students at this level should be introduced to ways to think critically when they are ready and have enough information and resources to do so.

Refer students to *Stand Out Basic Workbook, Unit 3, Lesson 1* for more practice with prepositions of location.

Go to the *Activity Bank* online for suggestions on promoting digital literacy and using the Internet to enhance this lesson.

AT-A-GLANCE **PREP**

Goal: Express hunger
Grammar: The verb *Be* + adjective
Academic Strategy: Focused listening
Vocabulary: Common foods, *hungry, thirsty, snack*

Agenda

- Review fruits and vegetables.
- Learn to express feelings of hunger and thirst.
- Review and practice *Be*.
- Discuss snacks.

Resources

Multilevel Worksheet: Lesson 2, Worksheet 1
Workbook: Unit 3, Lesson 2
Audio: CD 1, Tracks 45–50
Heinle Picture Dictionary: Inside the Refrigerator, pages 88–89; Fruits and Nuts, pages 82–83; Meat, Poultry, and Seafood, pages 86–87; Vegetables, pages 84–85; Feelings, pages 38–39

Pacing

■ 1.5 hour classes ■ 2.5 hour classes
■ 3+ hour classes

STANDARDS CORRELATIONS

CCRS: SL2, L1, RF3
CASAS: 1.3.8
SCANS: **Basic Skills** Reading, writing, listening, speaking
Resources Allocate human resources
Information Acquire and evaluate information, organize and maintain information, interpret and communicate information
EFF: **Communication** Speak so others can understand, listen actively
Interpersonal Cooperate with others

Warm-up and Review 10–15 mins.

Ask students in groups to make lists of all the fruits and vegetables they know. They can include words in their own languages. Ask them to make a table like the one below.

Fruits	Vegetables
apples	*lettuce*

Introduction 2 mins.

Write the day, the date, and the agenda on the board. Say the date and have students repeat. Rub your stomach and say: *I'm hungry! Is there anything to eat?* State the goal: *Today we will learn how to express hunger.*

Presentation 1 30–40 mins.

Ask students what they eat for dinner. They may want to look back at page 63.

A. Look at the picture. Where are Saul and Chen?

Ask questions about the picture to see how much students understand. You may introduce the word *homework* and other words that they may need. Ask students to read the clock. Ask: *What time is it?* Ask if it is night or morning.

B. Listen and read.

Play the recording once and ask students to read along. Next, ask students to practice the exchange a few times with a partner.

LISTENING SCRIPT

CD 1 TR 45

The listening script matches the conversation in Exercise B.

Ask students to do a Corners activity. In this activity, students go to different corners of the room, depending on their preferences. The four preferences in this case are the foods listed in Exercise C. Once in the corners, prepare students to do Practice 1.

Practice 1 15–20 mins.

C. RELATE Practice the conversation in Exercise B. Use the meals below to make new conversations.

Ask students to practice the conversation in Exercise B in their corner. They will then leave their corners and go to the other corners and practice with at least one person. Ask students to use the meals in the pictures in their conversations. Continue this activity until all students have practiced the conversation.

Evaluation 1 15–20 mins.

Observe as students practice the conversation.

LESSON 2 I'm hungry!

GOAL ■ Express hunger

A. Look at the picture. Where are Saul and Chen? Saul and Chen are in the kitchen.

B. Listen and read.

CD 1 TR 45

Saul: I'm hungry.
Chen: Me, too.
Saul: What's for dinner?
Chen: Chicken and vegetables.

C. RELATE Practice the conversation in Exercise B. Use the meals below to make new conversations.

chicken sandwiches

hamburgers and fries

tacos

rice and vegetables

D. Read about Saul and Chen. Then, read the chart.

Saul is hungry. He is not thirsty.

Chen is thirsty. He is not hungry.

The Verb *Be*			
Subject	***Be***		**Example sentence**
I	am (not)	hungry thirsty	I am (I'm) hungry. I am not (I'm not) hungry.
He	is (not)		He is (He's) thirsty. He is not (He's not) thirsty.
She			She is (She's) hungry. She is not (She's not) hungry.
We	are (not)		We are (We're) thirsty. We are not (We're not) thirsty.
You			You are (You're) hungry. You are not (You're not) hungry.
They			They are (They're) thirsty. They are not (They're not) thirsty.

E. RELATE Write. Follow the example sentences in the chart.

1. Edgar ____is____ hungry.
   He's not thirsty.
2. Roselia and Thanh ____are____ thirsty.
   They are not hungry. / They're not hungry.
3. We ____are____ hungry.
   We are not thirsty. / We're not thirsty.
4. She ____is____ not hungry.
   She is thirsty. / She's thirsty.
5. I ____am____ thirsty.
   I am not hungry / I'm not hungry.
6. You ____are____ not hungry.
   You are thirsty. / You're thirsty.

Presentation 2

10–15 mins.

Review the verb *Be* with students. You may want to do this first with the books closed to see how much students remember from Unit 1, Lesson 3, page 21. Recreate the chart from this page on the board, only leave out the forms of the verb *Be*. Ask for volunteers to complete the chart with their books closed.

D. Read about Saul and Chen. Then, read the chart.

Present *hungry* and *thirsty* to students by showing them the pictures and pantomiming. This will be the first time students have been exposed to the negative form of the verb *Be*. Demonstrate many times so that they clearly understand.

Present the grammar table to students and have students repeat the sentences after you. You may want to give them actions to demonstrate what they are saying, such as rubbing their stomach for hungry and shaking their head for negative statements.

For shorter classes, ask students to do Exercise E for homework.

Practice 2

8–10 mins.

E. RELATE Write. Follow the example sentences in the chart.

Do the example as a class. Show students how the second sentence is negative.

Evaluation 2

9–12 mins.

Review students' book work. Ask for volunteers to write the sentences on the board.

CRITICAL THINKING

RELATE

Asking students to *relate to* or *personalize* lessons is a good way to emphasize and test the learning of target items. This is a particularly useful strategy when dealing with sentence completion exercises where students provide correct verb forms.

Ask students to work in small groups and personalize sentences making them true for them and their group members. Have students substitute pronouns with their own names and the names of one or more of their classmates. Ask them to rework the exercise using this new information. For example, students change the sentence, *I am thirsty.* to *Diego and Hussein are thirsty.*

Teachers can expand exercises by asking students to practice negative sentence forms: *Diego and Hussein are not thirsty.* Teachers may also want to have students practice substituting adjectives to further make the sentences more personal: *Diego and Hussein are not hungry.*

When students are finished, ask them to share with the class by writing some of their new sentences on the board.

INSTRUCTOR'S NOTES

Presentation 3

10–15 mins.

Introduce the word *snack* to students. You may choose to do this by drawing three clocks on the board with no hands. Write *breakfast, lunch,* or *dinner* under each clock. Ask students what time to put for each meal and complete the clocks. Now, make a clock with a time between the ones given and ask students what the meal would be. Explain that this is *a snack.* Ask students what they eat for snacks. Get as much information from them as you can before they open their books.

F. Read and listen.

Practice the pronunciation of each word in the pictures with students. Then, have them point to objects and repeat them as you say them.

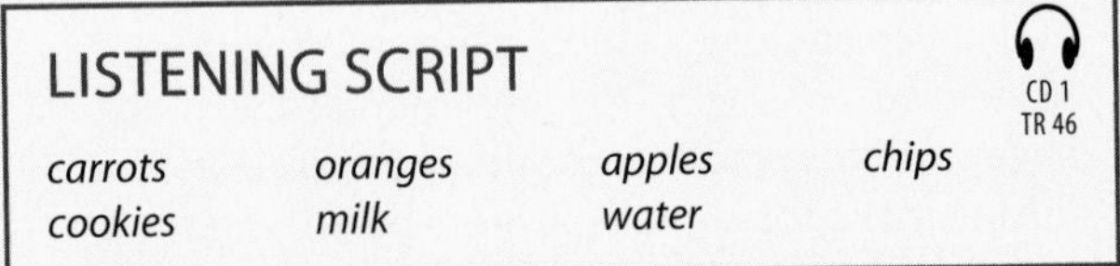

LISTENING SCRIPT

CD 1 TR 46

carrots	*oranges*	*apples*	*chips*
cookies	*milk*	*water*	

Practice 3

10–15 mins.

G. IDENTIFY Listen and write.

Ask students to listen to the four conversations and write the snack they hear.

LISTENING SCRIPT

CD 1 TR 47–50

1. **A:** *I'm hungry.*
   B: *Me, too. I really need something healthy.*
   A: *Carrots are always good and healthy, too.*
2. **A:** *I'm thirsty.*
   B: *Can I get you anything?*
   A: *Maybe some water would help.*
   B: *I'll get it right away.*
3. **A:** *Do you have anything to eat?*
   B: *Sure, but what do you want?*
   A: *I don't know. I'm very hungry.*
   B: *How about an apple?*
   A: *Thanks.*
4. **A:** *My sister is very hungry. She needs to eat.*
   B: *What can I get her?*
   A: *Do you have any oranges?*
   B: *I'll get her one.*

BEST PRACTICE

Repeating audio

It may become necessary with focused listening to repeat the audio. You may ask students to compare answers before you play a recording again.

It is very difficult for students at this level to listen and write at the same time. Teach students the dictation strategy of listening to a recording completely before attempting to write anything. You may wish to pause the recording when necessary to allow students plenty of time to write.

Evaluation 3

3 mins.

Check students' book work.

MULTILEVEL WORKSHEET

Lesson 2, Worksheet 1: I'm Hungry!

Application

10–15 mins.

H. Practice.

Review the dialog with a volunteer. Then, practice a few more times with different students, asking them to insert their own preferences for snacks.

I. SURVEY Ask your classmates about their favorite snacks. Use the conversation in Exercise H.

Have students list the snacks they like. Then, have them practice the conversation in Exercise H again with a few partners, this time inserting the snacks they like.

Refer students to *Stand Out Basic Workbook, Unit 3, Lesson 2* for more practice with using the *be* verb in the affirmative and the negative.

Go to the *Activity Bank* online for suggestions on promoting digital literacy and using the Internet to enhance this lesson.

F. Read and listen.

CD 1
TR 46

carrots

oranges

apples

chips

cookies

milk

water

G. IDENTIFY Listen and write.

CD 1
TR 47-50

1. carrots
2. water
3. apple
4. oranges

H. Practice.

Student A: What's your favorite snack?

Student B: My favorite snack is <u>cookies</u>.

I. SURVEY Ask your classmates about their favorite snacks. Use the conversation in Exercise H.

Answers will vary.

Name	Food

LESSON 3 Let's have spaghetti!

GOAL Plan meals

A. Look at the recipe. Read the ingredients.

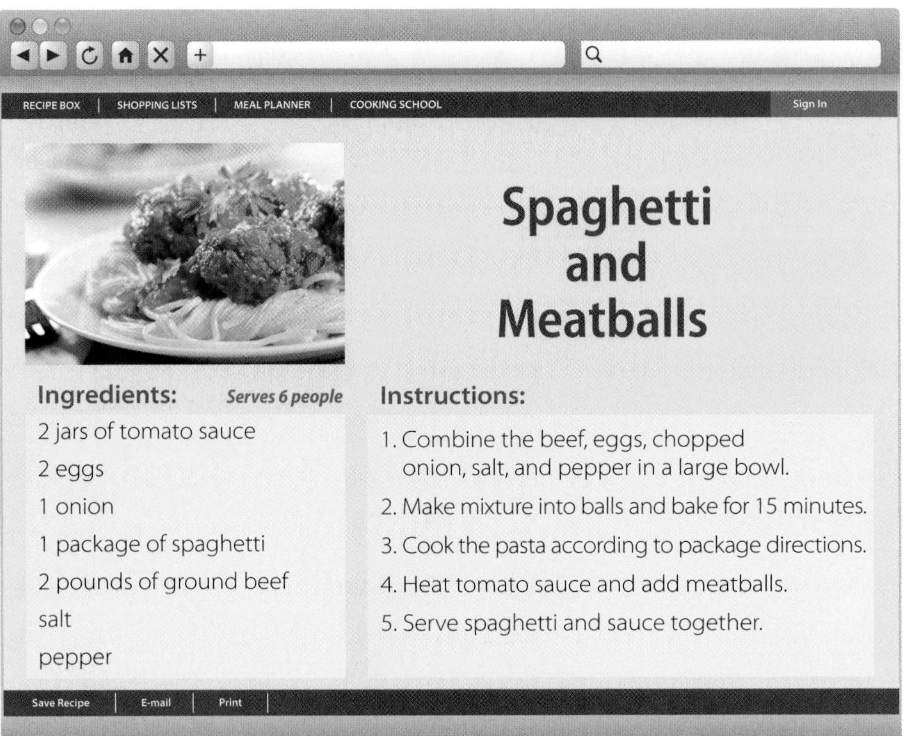

RECIPE BOX | SHOPPING LISTS | MEAL PLANNER | COOKING SCHOOL
Sign In
Spaghetti and Meatballs
Ingredients: Serves 6 people
2 jars of tomato sauce
2 eggs
1 onion
1 package of spaghetti
2 pounds of ground beef
salt
pepper
Instructions:
1. Combine the beef, eggs, chopped onion, salt, and pepper in a large bowl.
2. Make mixture into balls and bake for 15 minutes.
3. Cook the pasta according to package directions.
4. Heat tomato sauce and add meatballs.
5. Serve spaghetti and sauce together.
Save Recipe | E-mail | Print

B. Write.

1. How many jars of tomato sauce do you need? ___two jars___
2. How many eggs do you need? ___two eggs___
3. How many onions do you need? ___one onion___
4. How many packages of spaghetti do you need? ___one package___
5. How many pounds of ground beef do you need? ___two pounds___

C. IDENTIFY Listen and circle.

CD 1 TR 51-54

1. jar (package) pound
2. jar package (pound)
3. jar (package) pound
4. (jar) package pound

AT-A-GLANCE **PREP**

Goal: Plan meals
Grammar: Singular and plural nouns
Pronunciation: Final consonant /s/
Academic Strategies: Focused listening, skimming
Vocabulary: Common foods and ingredients, packaging

Agenda

- Review breakfast, lunch, and dinner.
- Read a recipe.
- Learn about containers and measurements.
- Practice plurals.
- Write a recipe.

Resources

Multilevel Worksheet: Lesson 3, Worksheet 1
Workbook: Unit 3, Lesson 3
Audio: CD 1, Tracks 51–55
Heinle Picture Dictionary: Inside the Refrigerator, pages 88–89; Fruits and Nuts, pages 82–83; Meat, Poultry, and Seafood, pages 86–87; Vegetables, pages 84–85; Measurements and Containers, pages 96–97; Cooking, pages 92–93

Pacing

- 1.5 hour classes
- 2.5 hour classes
- 3+ hour classes

STANDARDS CORRELATIONS

CCRS: RI1, RI7, SL1, SL2, SL4, L1, L2, L5, RF2, RF3
CASAS: 1.1.1, 1.3.8
***SCANS:* Basic Skills** Reading, writing, listening, speaking
Resources Allocate human resources
Information Acquire and evaluate information, organize and maintain information, interpret and communicate information
Interpersonal Participate as a member of a team, teach others
Thinking Skills See things in the mind's eye
***EFF:* Communication** Speak so others can understand, listen actively
Interpersonal Cooperate with others

Warm-up and Review
10–15 mins.

Write this dialog and chart on the board.

A: *What do you eat for <u>dinner</u>?*

B: ______________________

Name	Breakfast	Lunch	Dinner

Ask students to ask five other students what they eat for breakfast, lunch, and dinner and write the answers in the chart. Then, ask individuals to share what they wrote.

Introduction
5–7 mins.

Write the agenda on the board. Ask a volunteer to write the day and the date above the agenda. Then, point to some objects that students have learned. Ask students what they are. Write the words on the board. Choose some plural items and stress the final *s* when you say and write the word. Make a chart on the board with columns for singular and plural. Ask students to help you put the words in the correct column. State the goal: *Today, we will plan meals.*

Presentation 1
30–40 mins.

Write *spaghetti* on the board. Ask students if they like spaghetti.

A. Look at the recipe. Read the ingredients.

Go over the new vocabulary with students. Make sure students understand *jar, pound,* and *package.*

B. Write.

Ask students to answer the questions. Prepare students for the practice by asking them to point at particular packaging as you say it in isolation and in a sentence.

Practice 1
5–7 mins.

C. IDENTIFY Listen and circle.

(See next page for the listening script.)

Evaluation 1
5–7 mins.

Go over students' answers.

LISTENING SCRIPT

CD 1
TR 51–54

1. **Omar:** *There is so much we need at the store.*
   Maria: *What do you mean? What do we need?*
   Omar: *We need a package of spaghetti, for one thing.*
   Maria: *OK, I'll write it on the list. What else?*
2. **Omar:** *Well, let's see . . . We need at least one pound of chicken for dinner tonight.*
   Maria: *Are you sure one pound is enough?*
   Omar: *Yes. We have a pound in the refrigerator.*
   Maria: *I'm adding it to the list. What else?*
3. **Omar:** *We need a package of cheese for sandwiches.*
   Maria: *No, we don't. I have three packages in the refrigerator.*
   Omar: *Oh, I didn't see them.*
   Maria: *What else?*
4. **Omar:** *We need a jar of mayonnaise for the sandwiches.*
   Maria: *I don't like mayonnaise, but I will put it on the list for you.*
   Omar: *Thanks!*

Presentation 2

10–15 mins. 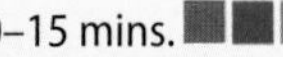

Pantomime making a cake. Crack a few eggs into a bowl and stir them up. Add flour and milk. Say what you are doing throughout: *I'm cracking three eggs and mixing them with flour and milk.* Stop and do it again. Repeat this three times. Then, ask: *How many eggs?* Some students will understand this expression and answer. Write on the board: *How many?*

D. Read the chart. Listen and repeat.

Show students how the plurals of regular nouns are formed. Use some additional examples that are not in the book. This is not a lesson on count and noncount nouns so students don't need to understand that some words are not plural at this point, but if you feel they are ready, you can introduce the concept here.

Also, introduce the various pronunciations of the final *s* here. Sometimes the final *s* is problematic for students because they may not fully pronounce final consonants.

LISTENING SCRIPT

CD 1
TR 55

jar	*jars*
can	*cans*
bag	*bags*
package	*packages*
pound	*pounds*

INTONATION

Final consonant *s*

In many languages, the final consonant of words is de-emphasized and often not completely pronounced. When English is spoken in a natural way, the final consonants blend into the next word; however, at the end of phrases, it becomes important to pronounce the sound and release it. Therefore, it is essential to help students not only say the *s* sound at the end of the word, but to release it so the sound resonates.

It is important to keep in mind that some languages don't mark nouns plural or singular. In other words, they don't distinguish between the plural and singular forms. Make sure that students understand that the *s* is essential to being understood.

Overemphasizing a sound is OK for demonstration as long as you also demonstrate the sound in context with appropriate emphasis.

Practice 2

7–10 mins.

E. CONSTRUCT Practice the conversation. Complete the table and make new conversations.

Show students how to practice this activity with a partner.

Evaluation 2

7–10 mins.

Observe students as they practice.

CD 1 TR 55

D. Read the chart. Listen and repeat.

Singular and Plural Nouns	
Singular	**Plural**
jar	jars
can	cans
bag	bags
package	packages
pound	pounds
Exceptions	
potato	potatoes
tomato	tomatoes
sandwich	sandwiches

E. CONSTRUCT Practice the conversation. Complete the table and make new conversations.

Student A: What do we need?
Student B: We need apples.

PLURALS		
/s/	/z/	/iz/
chip**s**	jar**s**	packag**es**
carrot**s**	can**s**	orang**es**

Fruit		Vegetables	
apple	/z/ apples	carrot	/s/ carrots
orange	/iz/ oranges	tomato	/z/ tomatoes
banana	/z/ bananas	potato	/z/ potatoes
pear	/z/ pears	pepper	/z/ peppers

WORKPLACE CONNECTION

Exercise F: Perform basic computations

Exercise H: Collect and organize information; Make decisions and solve problems

F. Write the food words and the quantities.

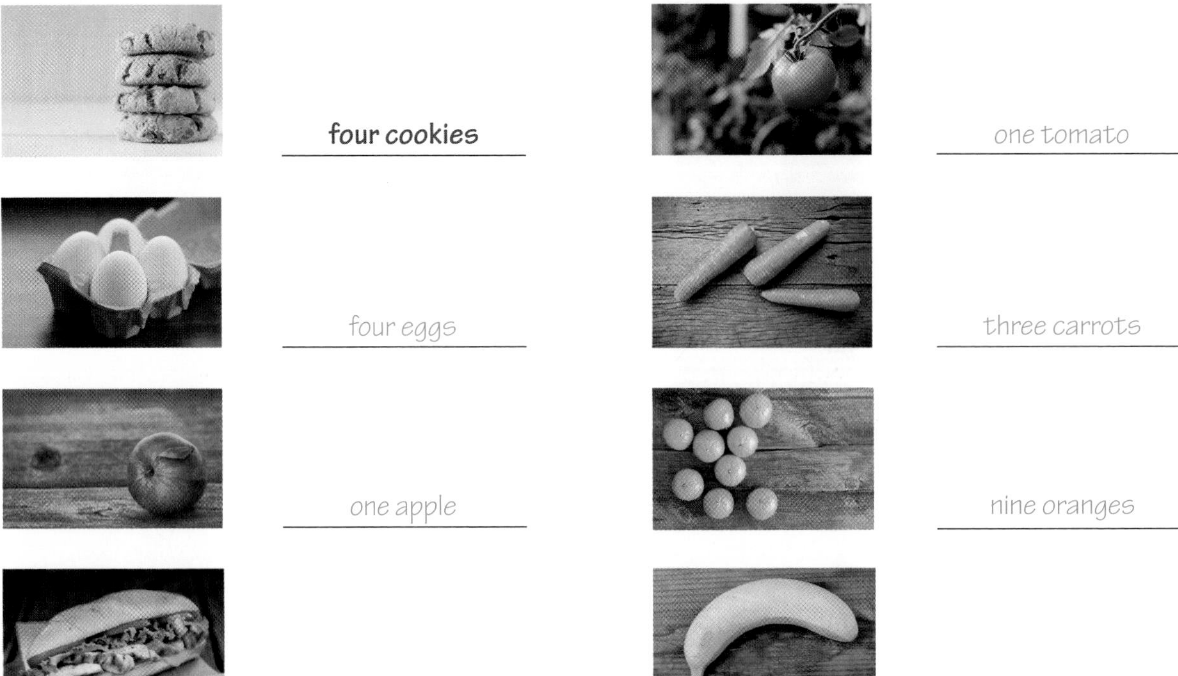

four cookies

one tomato

four eggs

three carrots

one apple

nine oranges

one sandwich

one banana

G. RELATE Practice the conversation. Use the pictures to make new conversations.

Student A: What are the ingredients?

Student B: Two eggs and one onion.

H. PLAN Work in a group. Think of more fruits to make a fruit salad. Answers will vary.

Fruit Salad		
Ingredients ***Serves 6 people***	1 banana	___ ______
	2 apples	___ ______
	___ pear	___ ______
	___ orange	___ ______

Presentation 3

10–15 mins.

Dictate the words in the list below to students. Then, ask for volunteers to write the words on the board. Now, ask students to write the plural form on their paper. Again, ask for volunteers to write the plural forms on the board.

1. apple
2. chip
3. cookie
4. carrot
5. orange

F. Write the food words and the quantities.

Do this activity together as part of the presentation. Repeat the words as many times as necessary.

Prepare students to do the conversation in Exercise G. Practice the short conversation a few times so students are comfortable with it. Demonstrate with a few students.

Practice 3

20–30 mins.

G. RELATE Practice the conversation. Use the pictures to make new conversations.

Evaluation 3

2–3 mins.

Observe students as they practice the conversation.

MULTILEVEL WORKSHEET

Lesson 3, Worksheet 1: Singular and Plural

Application

10–15 mins.

H. PLAN Work in a group. Think of more fruits to make a fruit salad.

Go over the recipe card with students. Help them to see that this salad will serve six people. Ask students in groups to complete the list of ingredients by adding names of fruit and quantities.

Refer students to *Stand Out Basic Workbook, Unit 3, Lesson 3* for more practice with forming plurals.

Go to the *Activity Bank* online for suggestions on promoting digital literacy and using the Internet to enhance this lesson.

INSTRUCTOR'S NOTES

AT-A-GLANCE **PREP**

Goal: Make a shopping list
Grammar: Simple present with *want*
Academic Strategies: Focused listening, teamwork skills, categorizing and organizing information
Vocabulary: Sections in a supermarket and their associated foods

Agenda

- Review and categorize food.
- Read a shopping list.
- Express things you want.
- Complete a Venn diagram.
- Make a shopping list.

Resources

Multilevel Worksheet: Lesson 4, Worksheet 1
Workbook: Unit 3, Lesson 4
Audio: CD 1, Tracks 56–57
Heinle Picture Dictionary: Inside the Refrigerator, pages 88–89; Fruits and Nuts, pages 82–83; Meat, Poultry, and Seafood, pages 86–87; Vegetables, pages 84–85; Supermarket, pages 98–99

Pacing

■ 1.5 hour classes ■ 2.5 hour classes
■ 3+ hour classes

STANDARDS CORRELATIONS

CCRS: R1, R9, L1, L5, RF3
CASAS: 1.3.8
***SCANS:* Basic Skills** Reading, writing, listening, speaking
Resources Allocate human resources
Information Acquire and evaluate information, organize and maintain information, interpret and communicate information
Interpersonal Participate as a member of a team, teach others
Thinking Skills See things in the mind's eye
***EFF:* Communication** Speak so others can understand, listen actively
Interpersonal Cooperate with others

Warm-up and Review 15–20 mins.

On the board, list all the vocabulary used in this unit thus far. Make a four-column chart with the following headers: *fruit*, *vegetables*, *meat*, and *drinks*. Ask students to work in groups to put all the items in the correct columns. Provide one chart per group.

Ask representatives from groups to put the information on the chart on the board. Erase the board and have a dictation with a few words.

Introduction 5 mins.

Write the agenda on the board. Ask a volunteer to write the day and the date. Ask students if they take a shopping list to the store. State the goal: *Today, we will make a shopping list.*

Presentation 1 10–15 mins.

Have students look at the picture.

A. Listen and point.

Have students point at each food item as they hear it. Then, turn the recording off and call out items in a different order. Ask students to point.

LISTENING SCRIPT (CD 1 TR 56)

oranges	*apples*	*pears*	*bananas*
carrots	*tomatoes*	*potatoes*	*broccoli*
strawberries	*lettuce*	*chicken*	*ground beef*
turkey	*fish*	*cheese*	*yogurt*

Practice 1 10–15 mins.

B. CLASSIFY Write the words in the correct shopping lists.

Write the column headings on the board and have students help you write a few items. Then, let them finish their lists by themselves.

C. Complete the shopping lists with your own ideas.

Ask groups to add more words to the lists.

Evaluation 1 7–10 mins.

Ask pairs to share their answers. Then, complete the columns on the board.

LESSON 4 What's for dinner?

WORKPLACE CONNECTION
Exercise B: Collect and organize information

GOAL Make a shopping list

A. Listen and point.

CD 1
TR 56

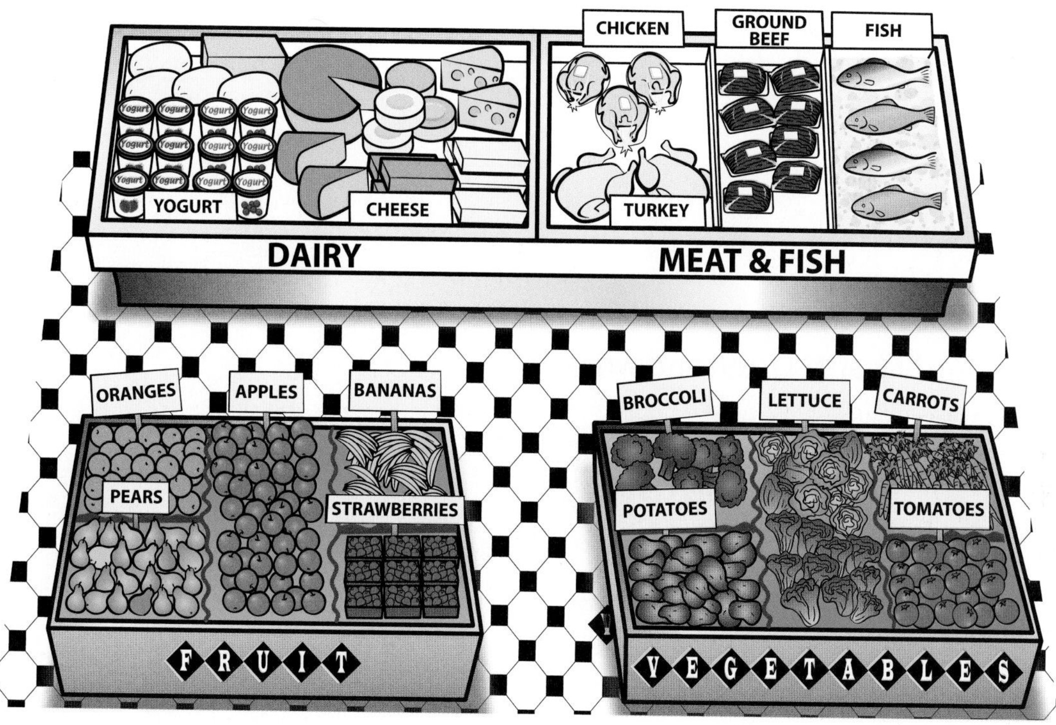

B. CLASSIFY Write the words in the correct shopping lists.

Meat and Fish	Vegetables	Fruit	Dairy
1. ground beef	1. broccoli	1. oranges	1. yogurt
2. chicken	2. lettuce	2. apples	2. cheese
3. fish	3. carrots	3. bananas	
4. turkey	4. potatoes	4. pears	
	5. tomatoes	5. strawberries	

C. Complete the shopping lists with your own ideas. Answers will vary.

D. Read Amadeo's shopping list.

Shopping List

apples	tomatoes
water	chicken
milk	eggs
carrots	chips
cheese	

E. LOCATE What does Amadeo want? Circle the items.

oranges	(apples)	(eggs)
potatoes	(cheese)	broccoli

F. What does Yoshi want? Listen and write.

CD 1 TR 57

Shopping List

oranges	yogurt	potatoes
apples	cheese	fish
strawberries	eggs	water

Farmers markets sell local food products.

Presentation 2

10–15 mins.

D. Read Amadeo's shopping list.

Ask for a volunteer to read the list out loud. Then, go back to Exercise B and ask students to decide in which column each word would go. Ask students to look back at page 63 where the vocabulary was first introduced.

BEST PRACTICE

Text as a tool

Students become independent learners when they realize that they can do their own review. The learner logs at the end of each unit will help them learn this concept.

You will also see in the *Stand Out* approach many opportunities for students to go back to pages they completed days and weeks before. This is an important part of effective review. Doing this makes the book as much a tool for learning English as a day-to-day textbook.

E. LOCATE What does Amadeo want? Circle the items.

Have students circle each of the items on Amadeo's list.

This simple activity introduces students to the skill of scanning for information. Students will get more practice with this important skill throughout the text.

Go over the new vocabulary in Exercise E and prepare students for listening in Exercise F.

Practice 2

7–10 mins.

F. What does Yoshi want? Listen and write.

Prepare students for the listening by talking briefly about the things you personally need to get at the grocery store. Do this until they realize that they only have to listen for the food words. Ask students to tell you what food words they heard.

Play the recording and have students write the words they hear. You may need to play this listening several times. Have students work in groups between sessions to share answers with one another.

LISTENING SCRIPT

CD 1
TR 57

Amadeo: *Yoshi, I'm going to the supermarket. What do you want?*
Yoshi: *Um, I want some oranges, apples, and strawberries.*
Amadeo: *Is that all?*
Yoshi: *No. I think I want some yogurt, cheese, and eggs, too.*
Amadeo: *OK, is that it?*
Yoshi: *No. Get me some potatoes, fish, and water.*
Amadeo: *Anything else?*
Yoshi: *No, that's it.*
Amadeo: *OK, let me read it back to you. You want oranges, apples, strawberries, yogurt, cheese, eggs, potatoes, fish, and water.*
Yoshi: *Yep, that's all!*

Evaluation 2

5–10 mins.

Ask students to share their list with a partner and ask for two or three volunteers to write Yoshi's list on the board.

INSTRUCTOR'S NOTES

Presentation 3

15–20 mins.

G. Read.

Go over the grammar box with students. Show them that the rule for the third-person singular is the same in other places in the book. Ask them to find those places or guide them to pages 19 and 52. In the next lesson, the regular simple present will be completely introduced.

Prepare students to do the Venn diagram by drawing two interlocking circles on the board and asking them to give you one food that both Yoshi and Amadeo want. Write the food item in the space where the circles overlap. Then, ask them to give you one food that only Amadeo wants and one food that only Yoshi wants. Write these items in the appropriate spaces. Make sure they understand the placement of the items before they go on to the practice. Use *he/she wants,* and *they want* while preparing students.

BEST PRACTICE

Graphic organizers

Graphic organizers are a productive way to allow students to think critically, for example, to understand similarities and differences in the vocabulary being studied. Venn diagrams are also an effective means to comprehend and visually categorize vocabulary at all levels of English study.

Practice 3

15–20 mins.

H. COMPARE Look at Amadeo's and Yoshi's shopping lists in Exercises D and F. Complete the diagram.

Help as necessary.

MULTILEVEL WORKSHEET

Lesson 4, Worksheet 1: Simple Present: *Want*

Application

20–30 mins.

I. What do you want? Make a list.

Ask students to write their own shopping lists.

J. What does your partner want? Ask your partner and write.

Pair students up and have them ask each other: *What do you want*? Have them write their partner's list in their books.

K. Share your partner's information with a group.

Arrange students in small groups.

Refer students to *Stand Out Basic Workbook, Unit 3, Lesson 4* for more practice with the simple present.

Go to the *Activity Bank* online for suggestions on promoting digital literacy and using the Internet to enhance this lesson.

INSTRUCTOR'S NOTES

WORKPLACE CONNECTION
Exercise H: Collect and organize information
Exercises I and J: Combine ideas and information

G. Read.

Simple Present		
Subject	**Verb**	**Example sentence**
I, You, We, They	want	They **want** apples.
He, She	wants	She **wants** apples.
		He **wants** apples.

H. COMPARE Look at Amadeo's and Yoshi's shopping lists in exercises D and F. Complete the diagram.

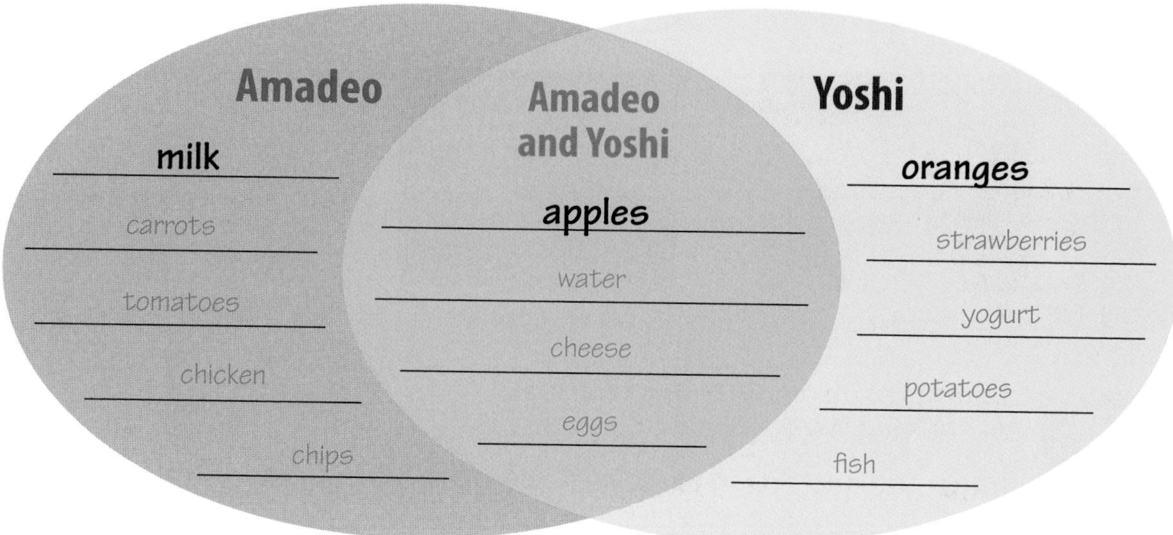

I. What do you want? Make a list.
Answers will vary.

Shopping List

J. What does your partner want? Ask your partner and write. Answers will vary.

Shopping List

K. Share your partner's information with a group.

LESSON 5 What do you like?

GOAL ■ Express preferences

A. Circle the desserts you like to eat. Listen and repeat.

CD 1 TR 58

cake

pie

ice cream

yogurt

cookies

bar of chocolate

bag of candy

B. Listen and point to the desserts in Exercise A.

CD 1 TR 59-61

C. RANK Number the desserts in Exercise A. Number 1 is your favorite. Answers will vary.

cake ____

pie ____

ice cream ____

yogurt ____

cookies ____

chocolate ____

candy ____

D. Listen and take notes. Write what Maria likes.

CD 1 TR 62

1. Maria likes dessert.
2. She likes cake.
3. She likes cookies.

AT-A-GLANCE **PREP**

Goal: Express preferences
Grammar: Simple present
Pronunciation: Final /s/
Academic Strategies: Focused listening, organizing information
Vocabulary: Dessert foods

Agenda

- Review foods you like.
- Listen for foods.
- Write sentences.
- Complete a Venn diagram.

Resources

Multilevel Worksheet: Lesson 5, Worksheet 1
Workbook: Unit 3, Lesson 5
Audio: CD 1, Tracks 58–62
Heinle Picture Dictionary: Restaurant, pages 100–101

Pacing

- 1.5 hour classes
- 2.5 hour classes
- 3+ hour classes

STANDARDS CORRELATIONS

CCRS: W1, SL2, L1, RF2
CASAS: 1.3.8
SCANS: **Basic Skills** Reading, writing, listening, speaking
Resources Allocate human resources
Information Acquire and evaluate information, organize and maintain information, interpret and communicate information
Interpersonal Participate as a member of a team, teach others
Thinking Skills See things in the mind's eye
EFF: **Communication** Speak so others can understand, listen actively
Interpersonal Cooperate with others

Warm-up and Review

5–7 mins.

Make a list of foods included thus far in the unit. Read the list to students. Ask students to stand up when they hear a food item they like and to sit back down when they hear a food they don't like.

Introduction

5–7 mins.

Write the agenda on the board. Ask a student to write the day and the date above the agenda. State the goal: *Today, we will express our preferences.*

Presentation 1

15–20 mins.

A. Circle the desserts you like to eat. Listen and repeat.

Do a quick listening practice where students point to the item you say.

LISTENING SCRIPT

CD 1 TR 58

cake *pie* *ice cream* *yogurt*
cookies *bar of chocolate* *bag of candy*

Practice 1

10–15 mins.

B. Listen and point to the desserts in Exercise A.

LISTENING SCRIPT

CD 1 TR 59–61

1. **Man:** *What dessert would you like?*
   Woman: *Well, I really like chocolate, but the apple pie looks good, too.*
2. **Woman:** *Just wait until you see what's for dessert.*
   Man: *What is it?*
   Woman: *I have cake and cookies. We also have some candy for later.*
3. **Man:** *Let me take you out and buy you a special dessert.*
   Woman: *That sounds great. What dessert?*
   Man: *I don't know. What do you want?*
   Woman: *How about ice cream or pie?*
   Man: *OK. We could also have cookies if you want.*

C. RANK Number the desserts in Exercise A. Number 1 is your favorite.

Model the exercise. Write some of the desserts from the exercise on the board. Then, tell students which is your favorite. Write the number 1 next to the dessert. Continue with your second favorite. Write the number 2.

Ask students to rank the desserts. Then, have them share their answers in groups.

D. Listen and takes notes. Write what Maria likes.

After you play the recording, as a class write the words in the spaces provided.

Evaluation 1

10–15 mins.

Observe students doing this activity.

LISTENING SCRIPT

CD 1 TR 62

Maria likes dessert. She especially likes cake. She also likes cookies. She eats dessert after every meal.

Presentation 2

10–15 mins.

E. Read the chart.

Go over the chart with students and drill them with substitution drills where you change the pronoun or the subject and students say the correct form of the verb. This is the first time students are given various verbs in the simple present to work with. Help them to see the rule for the use of the final *s* with the third person. Don't forget, however, that this is still only exposure to the simple present. Although they can learn it here, students will need to be taught the form many more times before they acquire it.

INTONATION

Emphasize again the final *s* sound in the third-person singular.

Ask a student what he or she likes and write a sentence about it on the board. For example: *Cristina, what do you like?* When Cristina says yogurt, write on the board: *Cristina likes yogurt.* Do a few more examples.

F. Write the verb.

Ask students to complete the sentences. Go over the answers as a class.

Practice 2

10–15 mins.

G. IDENTIFY Write about the pictures.

For shorter classes, ask students to do Exercise G for homework.

Evaluation 2

7–10 mins.

Check students' book work and ask volunteers to write their answers on the board.

BEST PRACTICE

Phonemes

A phoneme is an individual sound. The sound can be a vowel or a consonant. To teach the correct pronunciation of a phoneme, you should demonstrate the sound.

1. Ask students to look closely at your face and mouth as you speak.
2. Show students how to move their own tongues, lips, and teeth.
3. Exaggerate movements so that students clearly see your actions.
4. Ask students to imitate you. Then, have them practice phonemes individually and in pairs.

INSTRUCTOR'S NOTES

E. Read the chart.

Simple Present		
Subject	**Verb**	**Example sentence**
I, You, We, They	like eat want	I **like** ice cream. We **eat** ice cream. They **want** ice cream.
He, She	likes eats wants	She **likes** chocolate. He **eats** chocolate. She **wants** chocolate.

F. Write the verb.

1. I ___want___ (want) apple pie.
2. Maria ___likes___ (like) ice cream.
3. You ___eat___ (eat) pie.
4. They ___eat___ (eat) cookies.
5. We ___like___ (like) fruit.
6. Saul ___likes___ (like) candy.
7. We ___want___ (want) yogurt.
8. I ___like___ (like) ___Answers will vary.___.

G. IDENTIFY Write about the pictures.

1. She wants cookies.

2. She likes / eats cake.

3. She likes / eats ice cream.

H. Read.

Student A: Do you like ice cream for dessert?
Student B: No, I like pie.

I. Practice the conversation in Exercise H. Use the words in Exercise A to make new conversations.

J. COMPARE **What desserts does your partner like? Complete the diagram.**

Answers will vary.

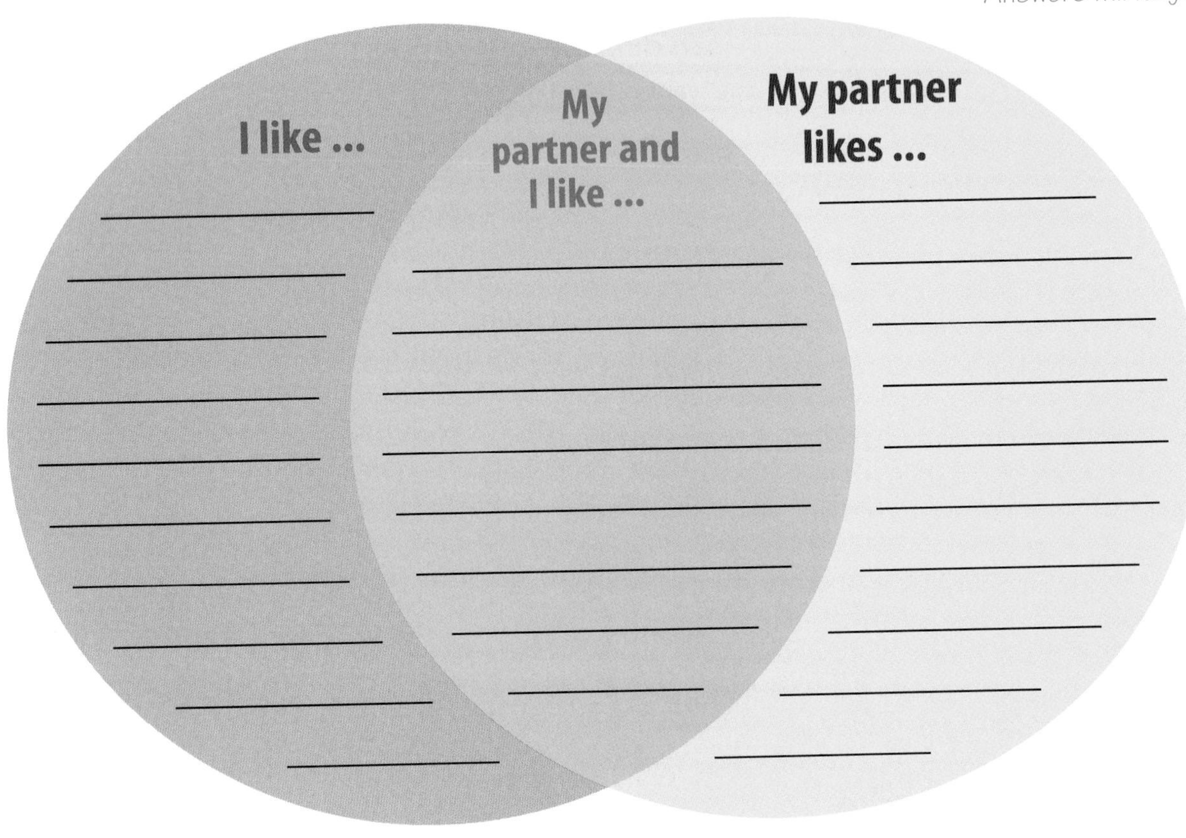

K. Tell your classmates about your partner.

Presentation 3

5–7 mins.

H. Read.

Make sure students are ready to do the practice in Exercise I. Show students how to substitute information.

Draw the chart on the board.

Name	Likes

Practice 3

10–15 mins.

I. Practice the conversation in Exercise H. Use the words in Exercise A to make new conversations.

Ask students to perform the dialog and complete the chart on the board.

BEST PRACTICE

Dialog cards

The use of dialog cards is another way to do pair work when substitution is involved.

1. Pass out 3-by-5 index cards to each student.
2. List the vocabulary on the board.
3. Divide the number of words by the number of students. In other words, if there are thirty-two students and eight vocabulary words, the answer would be four.
4. Instruct every fourth student to write a designated vocabulary word. In other words, when you are finished, you will have four cards for each word.
5. Collect the cards and randomly distribute them.
6. Now, students are to find other students with the same word on their card. They discover who has the same word by doing the conversation. The student recites the information on his or her card.
7. When students find a match, they write the classmate's name on the card. They continue until they find all matches.

Evaluation 3

5–7 mins.

Ask students to report what desserts students they interviewed like. You may want to write an example: *Maria likes chocolate.*

MULTILEVEL WORKSHEET

Lesson 5, Worksheet 1: Simple Present: *Like*

Application

10–15 mins.

J. COMPARE What desserts does your partner like? Complete the diagram.

Students will need to interview their partner to complete the diagram. They should be familiar with the diagram from the previous lesson, but you may need to review it with them.

K. Tell your classmates about your partner.

Ask students and their partners to join other pairs. Ask students in the small groups to talk about what desserts their partners like. Then, have students talk about what they like.

Refer students to *Stand Out Basic Workbook, Unit 3, Lesson 5* for more practice with the simple present.

Go to the *Activity Bank* online for suggestions on promoting digital literacy and using the Internet to enhance this lesson.

INSTRUCTOR'S NOTES

What's for lunch?

Before You Watch

- Ask students: *What's for lunch?* Elicit responses from individual class members.
- Write a few answers that differ on the board. Then, ask students by show of hands which lunch they prefer to eat.

A. Look at the picture and answer the questions.

- Ask the questions. Then, ask students how they know Mateo and Hector are in a diner/restaurant. *They each have a menu.*
- Ask students what things other than food they might see on a menu. *Name, prices, and/or descriptions of food.*
- Ask students who might give them a menu. Ask about fast-food restaurants, food trucks, airplane trips, pizza deliveries, etc. Discuss as a class.

While You Watch

B. Watch the video and circle what Hector and Mateo order.

- Play the video and ask students to watch and listen.
- Read the food items in the table. Explain any unfamiliar vocabulary.
- Play the video again and ask students to circle what Hector and Mateo order.
- Play the video multiple times or use the pause button to check answers.

Check Your Understanding

C. Match the questions to the answers.

- Talk about servers and customers in a restaurant. Ask about how they behave, what they wear, and what they say. Discuss.
- Ask students to look at the things a server and a customer would say in the table. Then, ask them to match the questions to the answers.
- Check answers as a class. Then, ask students to role-play and practice the conversation between the server and the customer. Have students reverse roles.

BEST PRACTICE

There are many ways to use video in the classroom. Students should rarely watch a video without some kind of task. You might introduce comprehension questions before they watch so they know what they are looking for. Below are a few techniques that you may try for variety beyond the comprehension checks and other ideas already presented in this lesson.

Freeze Frame: Pause the video during viewing and use it like a picture dictionary, identifying and expanding on the vocabulary.

Silent Viewing: Show the video in segments without sound so students can guess at the storyline. This helps them to understand that listening is more than just the words people say.

Prediction Techniques: Show portions of the video and ask students to predict what will come next.

Listening without Viewing: This helps students create their own image of what is happening. After a discussion, allow students to watch the video and the sound together.

Back-to-Back: In pairs, one student faces the video and the other faces away. Play the video without sound and ask the student viewing to report to the student who is facing away what is happening.

Summary Strips: Create strips of sentences that describe the events. Have students watch the video and then put the strips in the correct order, or ask students to predict the story line before watching and then check their answers. The Activity Bank has summary strips for each video in *Stand Out*.

What's for lunch?

Before You Watch

A. Look at the picture and answer the questions.

1. Where are Hector and Mateo?
   Hector and Mateo are at a diner.
2. What do you think they are going to eat? Answers will vary.

While You Watch

B. Watch the video and circle what Hector and Mateo order.

Mateo	Hector
1. a. chicken soup (b. chicken salad)	4. a. taco (b. cheeseburger)
2. a. iced coffee (b. iced tea)	5. a. fried rice (b. French fries)
3. a. chocolate pie (b. chocolate cake)	(6. a. onion rings) b. chicken salad

Check Your Understanding

C. Match the questions to the answers.

Server	Customer
1. How are you? d	a. Chocolate cake for me, please.
2. Do you need some more time to look at the menu? b	b. No, I'm ready to order.
3. What would you like? c	c. I'll have the special.
4. Do you want something to drink? e	d. Great. I'm really hungry.
5. Would you like anything for dessert? a	e. Yes, I'll have an iced tea with no sugar.

Review

Learner Log

I can identify common foods.

☐ Yes ☐ No ☐ Maybe

A. Write the food words.

apple

bar of chocolate

yogurt

chips

pie

banana

B. Write the plural food words.

Singular	Plural
apple	apples
orange	oranges
chicken	chickens
banana	bananas
cookie	cookies
egg	eggs
chip	chips
potato	potatoes
tomato	tomatoes
carrot	carrots

AT-A-GLANCE **PREP**

Goal: All unit objectives
Grammar: All unit grammar
Academic Strategies: Focused listening,reviewing, evaluating, developing study skills
Vocabulary: All unit vocabulary

Agenda

- Discuss unit objectives.
- Complete the review.

Pacing

- 1.5 hour classes
- 2.5 hour classes
- 3⁺ hour classes

STANDARDS CORRELATIONS

CCRS: SL2, L1, RF3

CASAS: 1.3.8, 7.4.1, 7.4.2, 7.4.3

SCANS: **Basic Skills** Basic Skills Reading, writing, listening, speaking

Information Acquire and evaluate information, organize and maintain information, interpret and communicate information

Thinking Skills See things in the mind's eye

EFF: **Communication** Speak so others can understand, listen actively

Lifelong Learning Take responsibility for learning, reflect and evaluate

Warm-up and Review

7–10 mins.

Ask individuals what they like to eat. Make a list on the board of all the vocabulary students can come up with from the unit.

Introduction

5 mins.

Write all the objectives on the board from Unit 3. Show students the first page of every lesson so they understand that today will be review. Complete the agenda.

Note: Depending on the length of the term, you may decide to have students do Presentation and Practice for homework and review student work as the warm-up for another class meeting.

Presentation

10–15 mins.

This presentation will cover the first three pages of the review. Quickly go to the first page of each lesson. Discuss the objective of each. Ask simple questions to remind students what they have learned.

Practice

15–20 mins.

A. Write the food words. (Lessons 1–5)

B. Write the plural food words. (Lesson 3)

BEST PRACTICE

Recycling/Review

The review process and the project that follows are part of the recycling/review process. Students at this level often need to be reintroduced to concepts to solidify what they have learned. Many concepts are learned and forgotten while learning other new concepts. This is because students learn but are not necessarily ready to acquire language concepts.

Therefore, it becomes very important to review and to show students how to review on their own. It is also important to recycle the new concepts in different contexts.

INSTRUCTOR'S NOTES

Practice *(continued)*

C. Write ***am, is***, or ***are***. (Lesson 2)

D. Write negative sentences. (Lesson 2)

E. Write the simple present. (Lessons 4–5)

INSTRUCTOR'S NOTES

Learner Log

I can express hunger.
☐ Yes ☐ No ☐ Maybe

I can express preferences.
☐ Yes ☐ No ☐ Maybe

C. Write *am, is,* or *are.*

1. Maria ____is____ thirsty.
2. Kim and David ____are____ not hungry.
3. Lan and Mai ____are____ hungry.
4. Rafael ____is____ not thirsty.
5. Colby ____is____ hungry.
6. Marco and Eva ____are____ thirsty.
7. Lara ____is____ not hungry.
8. I ____am____ thirsty.

D. Write negative sentences.

1. Eric is hungry. He's not thirsty.
2. Maria is thirsty. She's not hungry.
3. Saul and Chen are hungry. They're not thirsty.
4. I am thirsty. I'm not hungry.

E. Write the simple present.

1. Chrissy ____likes____ (like) hamburgers.
2. You ____eat____ (eat) tacos.
3. Laura ____wants____ (want) vegetables.
4. Rosie and Amadeo ____like____ (like) rice.
5. We ____eat____ (eat) fish and chicken.
6. They ____want____ (want) pie.
7. Karl ____likes____ (like) oranges.
8. I ____Answers will vary.____.

I can make a shopping list.
Yes No Maybe

I can plan meals.
Yes No Maybe

F. Talk to two classmates. Ask: *What do you want?* Answers will vary.

Shopping List

Shopping List

G. Read the lists in Exercise F. Write. Answers will vary.

Singular Foods	Plural Foods

Practice *(continued)*

F. Talk to two classmates. Ask: *What do you want?* (Lesson 4)

G. Read the lists in Exercise F. Write. (Lesson 3)

Evaluation 5 mins.

Go around the room and check on students' progress. Help individuals when needed. If you see consistent errors among several students, interrupt the class and give a mini lesson or review to help students feel comfortable with the concept.

BEST PRACTICE

Learner Log

Learner logs function to help students in many different ways.

1. They serve as part of the review process.
2. They help students to gain confidence and document what they have learned. In this way, students see that they are progressing and want to move forward in learning.
3. They provide students with a tool that they can use over and over to check and recheck their understanding. In this way, students become independent learners.

INSTRUCTOR'S NOTES

WORKPLACE CONNECTION

Combine ideas and information; Make decisions; Exercise leadership roles; Manage time; Complete tasks as assigned; Interact appropriately with team members; Collect and gather information; Interpret and communicate information; Apply technology

STANDARDS CORRELATIONS

CCRS: RI7, SL1, SL2

CASAS: 1.8.8, 4.8.1

***SCANS:* Basic Skills** Reading, writing, listening, speaking

Resources Allocate time, allocate money, allocate materials and facility resources, allocate human resources

Information Acquire and evaluate information, organize and maintain information, interpret and communicate information, use computers to process information

Interpersonal: Participate as a member of a team, teach others, serve clients and customers, exercise leadership, negotiate to arrive at a decision, work with cultural diversity

Systems Understand systems, monitor and correct performance, improve and design systems

Thinking Skills See things in the mind's eye

Personal Qualities Responsibility, sociability, self management

***EFF:* Communication** Speak so others can understand, listen actively

Decision Making Solve problems and make decisions, plan

Interpersonal Cooperate with others, advocate and influence, resolve conflict and negotiate, guide others

Lifelong Learning Take responsibility for learning, reflect and evaluate

Introduction
5 mins.

In this project, students will work in teams to create a shopping list for their family, incorporating the vocabulary from this unit. They may choose to use Worksheet 8 from the Multilevel Worksheets.

Stage 1
15–20 mins.

Form a team with four or five members.

Show students examples of the project if you have one. Use Worksheet 8 from the Multilevel Worksheets as a simple example if you don't have samples.

Help students to assign positions by asking all the team leaders to stand. On the spot, students will have to choose who will be the leader of their group. Review the responsibility of a leader and ask students to write the name of their leader in their books. Do the same with all positions.

Stage 2
10–15 mins.

You are a family. What is your last name?

Ask students to form a family and choose a name for themselves. Try to encourage them to be original and not to use a name of someone in their group.

Stage 3
40–50 mins.

Make a shopping list with food from this unit.

The team together creates a shopping list using the vocabulary from the unit. Encourage students to choose items that they like and want so they will use the new vocabulary.

Stage 4
10–30 mins.

Draw pictures of the food on your list.

Ask students to dress up the list with pictures from magazines or sketches they make themselves.

Stage 5
10–30 mins.

Present your list to the class.

Ask groups to present their projects. This can be particularly effective if you videotape the presentations.

BEST PRACTICE

Digital literacy

Projects are a perfect place to allow students opportunities to use other forms of presentations beyond pictures they create. Digital literacy is becoming more necessary as a life skill. Encourage students to create presentations using pictures from the Internet. They might also consider using other digital presentation tools.

TEAM PROJECT ✓ Make a shopping list

1. **COLLABORATE** Form a team with four or five students. In your team, you need:

Position	Job description	Student name
Student 1: Team Leader	Check that everyone speaks English. Check that everyone participates.	
Student 2: Writer	Write food names.	
Student 3: Artist	Draw pictures for the shopping list with help from the team.	
Students 4/5: Spokespeople	Prepare a presentation.	

2. You are a family. What is your last name?

3. Make a shopping list with food from this unit.

4. Draw pictures of the food on your list.

5. Present your list to the class.

Shopping lists are different in other parts of the world.

About the Explorer

Catherine Jaffee is a food anthropologist from Highlands, Colorado. While studying internal migration in Turkey, she encountered groups of female beekeepers producing honey in the northeastern region of the country. She wanted to find a way to encourage economic growth in these rural communities and teach the women there how to become business leaders, so she set up Balyolu—a company that built the world's first honey trekking route.

About the Photo

This photo was taken in a beekeeper's field along the Balyolu honey heritage trail. It shows Catherine and a local beekeeper standing among the bee boxes.

- Ask students what important things a recipe tells them. *Ingredients and number of servings.* Then, ask students how they choose the ingredients for a recipe. Ask: *Where are the best places to shop for different ingredients?* Discuss as a class.
- Introduce the explorer. Tell students they are going to read about Catherine Jaffee. Explain to students that this explorer is very interested in where ingredients come from.
- Ask students to look at Catherine Jaffee in the photo. Then, direct their attention to the quote and read it together.

A. PREDICT Look at the picture. Answer the questions.

Ask students to look at the picture and read the questions. Have students work in pairs to discuss their answers. Then, discuss as a class.

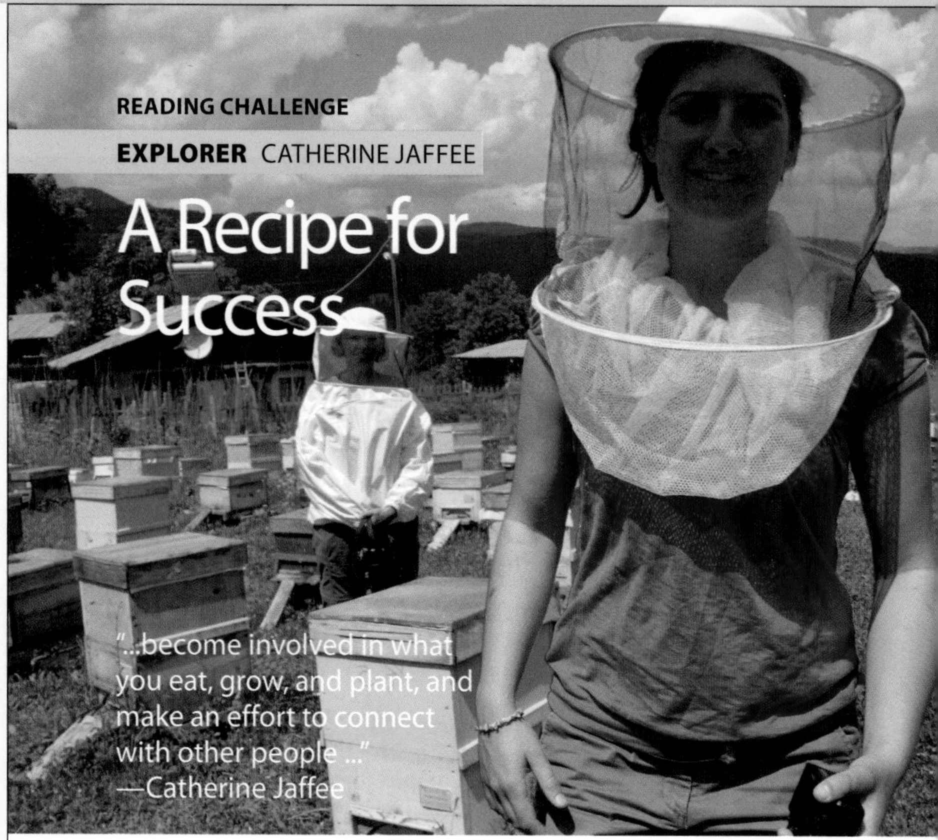

READING CHALLENGE
EXPLORER CATHERINE JAFFEE
A Recipe for Success
"...become involved in what you eat, grow, and plant, and make an effort to connect with other people ..."
—Catherine Jaffee

A. PREDICT Look at the picture. Answer the questions. Answers will vary.

1. What are the people in the picture wearing?
2. What food do you think the article will be about? Why?
3. Do you think Catherine likes her job? Why?

Some kinds of honey bees are disappearing. Balyolu helps the Caucasian honey bee to survive.

82 Unit 3

CCRS FOR READING

RI1, RI2, L1, L5

WORKPLACE CONNECTION
Exercise D: Collect and organize information
Exercise F: Apply technology to a task

B. FIND OUT Circle the correct answers.

1. A *Project* is a . . .
   a. plan of work
   b. vacation
2. A *leader* is a person who . . .
   a. guides others
   b. makes honey
3. *An expert* is a person who . . .
   a. knows a little
   b. knows a lot
4. *Beekeepers* are people who . . .
   a. work with people
   b. work with bees

C. Read about Catherine Jaffee.

Catherine Jaffee is a food *expert*. She has a very important job. She helps communities to be successful through food. Balyolu—one of Catherine's projects—helps *beekeepers* in Turkey to make honey and teaches them how to be business *leaders*. This *project* also helps to care for bees.

Some people put honey in yogurt; some people put it on their toast. However you use honey, Catherine is working to make sure it stays on your shopping list.

D. CLASSIFY Complete the chart about the story.

Person	Food	Insect	Place
Catherine Jaffee	honey yogurt toast	bee	Turkey

E. Read the shopping list.

Summer Salad with Honey
1 package of spinach
1 cup of strawberries
1 small onion
1/2 cup of blueberries
1/4 cup of cheese
honey

F. APPLY Find a meal that contains honey. Write a shopping list. Answers will vary.

Reading Challenge 83

READING STRATEGIES

Summarizing

Summarizing gives students the opportunity to re-tell a story in their own words. When students summarize, they can identify the main idea and remember what is important in the story.

Summarizing clues students in on their own understanding. It also gives students practice in expressing their own ideas.

B. FIND OUT Circle the correct answers.

- Ask students to complete the definition for each word by circling the correct answer.
- Ask students to work with a partner and write one example sentence for each word. Have volunteers share their examples on the board.

C. Read about Catherine Jaffee.

- Ask students to read the article to learn more about Catherine Jaffee.
- Review any vocabulary students may have difficulties understanding. Write the words on the board and elicit definitions from the class.
- Ask volunteers to summarize the article.

D. CLASSIFY Complete the chart about the story.

Ask students to classify information from the article and complete the table. Copy the table on the board. Review answers as a class and write them in the table.

E. Read the shopping list.

Ask students to read the shopping list. Explain any vocabulary that students may not know. Show pictures of strawberries or blueberries if necessary.

F. APPLY Find a meal that contains honey. Write a shopping list.

- Ask students to find a meal that has honey as an ingredient. Allow students time to look for recipes on the Internet for homework.
- Ask students to share their recipes in small groups. Have a few volunteers share their recipes with the class.

Clothing

About the Photo

This photo shows four models from the waist down wearing bright and colorful clothing at a fashion show. Fashion shows occur seasonally and allow fashion designers to showcase their latest line of clothes. The New York Fashion Week and the Paris Fashion Week are probably the most well-known events to influence global fashion trends. During a fashion show, models walk down a catwalk to show the audience—usually made up of buyers—the latest styles from a particular designer. Fashion shows are usually a good opportunity to see some of the more abstract clothing lines from popular designers.

- Introduce the unit. Ask students how important clothing is to them. Ask: *How often do you go shopping for clothes? What is your favorite type of clothing to buy?*
- Ask students to look at the photo. Then, read the questions. Discuss as a class.

Clothing comes in many different styles and colors.

UNIT OUTCOMES	GRAMMAR	VOCABULARY	EL CIVICS
• Identify types of clothing • Ask for and give directions in a store • Describe clothing • Make purchases • Read advertisements	• Simple present with *have* • Forming plural nouns • *Be* verb • Prepositions of location • *How much/How many* • Articles • Adjective/noun order • *Wh-* questions	• Articles of clothing • Colors • *How much …* • Money: bills and coins	The skills students learn in this unit can be applied to the following EL Civics competency areas: • Community resources • Banking systems

UNIT OUTCOMES
Identify types of clothing
Ask for and give directions in a store
Describe clothing
Make purchases
Read advertisements
Look at the photo and answer the questions.
1. What types of clothing can you see?
2. What colors are the clothes?

- Ask a volunteer to read the caption aloud. Then, ask students if they agree with it. Have students think about how different clothing is in their own countries from clothing in the United States. Discuss.
- Go over the unit outcomes with students. Then, ask: *What are you wearing today? What and where is your favorite clothing store? Do you like to buy things on sale? Where do you look for information on sales?*

Life Skills Link

In this unit, students will learn how to identify types of clothing and where they are located within a store. They will also learn how to make purchases based on advertisements.

Workplace Link

All lessons and units in *Stand Out* include basic communication skills and interpersonal skills important for the workplace. They are not individually identified. Other workplace skills are indicated. They include, collecting and organizing information, making decisions and solving problems, and combining ideas and information.

CASAS	SCANS	CCRS
Lesson 1: 1.3.9 Lesson 2: 1.1.9, 1.2.1, 1.3.9 Lesson 3: 1.1.9, 1.2.1, 1.3.9 Lesson 4: 1.1.6, 1.3.9, 4.8.1, 6.1.1 Lesson 5: 1.1.9, 1.2.1, 1.3.9, 4.8.3 Review: 1.1.9, 1.2.1, 1.3.9, 7.4.1, 7.4.2, 7.4.3 Team Project: 1.3.9, 4.8.1	Many SCANs skills are incorporated in the unit with an emphasis on: • Acquiring and evaluating information • Organizing and maintaining information • Interpreting and communicating information • Basic skills • Allocating money • Serving clients and customers	RI1, RI7, SL1, SL2, SL4, L1, L2, L5, RF2, RF3

LESSON 1 What's on sale?

GOAL ■ Identify types of clothing

CD 1 TR 63

A. IDENTIFY **Listen and point to the clothing.**

B. Listen to the conversation and read.

CD 1 TR 64

Salesperson: May I help you?
Maria: Yes, I want a shirt, pants, a sweater, and shoes.

C. Read the conversation in Exercise B again. Write sentences.

1. She wants a shirt.
2. She wants pants.
3. She wants a sweater.
4. She wants shoes.

AT-A-GLANCE PREP

Goal: Identify types of clothing
Grammar: *a*, simple present with *have*
Academic Strategy: Focused listening
Vocabulary: Basic clothing vocabulary, *closet*

Agenda

- Identify types of clothing.
- Talk about a clothing store.
- Describe what people are wearing.
- Write the items of clothing in your closet.

Resources

Multilevel Worksheet: Lesson 1, Worksheet 1
Workbook: Unit 4, Lesson 1
Audio: CD 1, Tracks 63–65
Heinle Picture Dictionary: Clothes, pages 104–105
Stand Out Basic Assessment CD-ROM with ExamView®

Pacing

- 1.5 hour classes
- 2.5 hour classes
- 3+ hour classes

STANDARDS CORRELATIONS

CCRS: SL2, L1, L2, RF3
CASAS: 1.2.1, 1.3.9
SCANS: **Basic Skills** Reading, writing, listening, speaking
Resources Allocate human resources
Information Acquire and evaluate information, organize and maintain information, interpret and communicate information
Interpersonal Participate as a member of a team, teach others
EFF: **Communication** Speak so others can understand, listen actively
Interpersonal Cooperate with others

Preassessment *(optional)*

Use the Stand Out Basic Assessment CD-ROM ExamView® to create a pretest for Unit 4.

Warm-up and Review

10–15 mins.

Pantomime putting on a shirt. Put on shoes.
If students call out items of clothing, write them on the board. Pantomime being cold. Bring a coat or sweater into class and see if a student will suggest that you put it on. Write *coat* or *sweater* on the board. Then, write on the board: *I want a coat. Where can I buy one?* Suggest a few stores.

Introduction

5 mins.

Pantomime other items of clothing. State the goal: *Today, we will identify types of clothing.*

Presentation 1

30–45 mins.

A. IDENTIFY Listen and point to the clothing.

Ask students to look at the picture and think about the different clothing they see. Then, ask students to listen and point to the clothing. Play the audio.

Ask students to work in pairs and take turns saying and pointing to the clothing they see in the picture. Play the recording again if necessary.

LISTENING SCRIPT

CD 1 TR 63

pants, sweaters, t-shirts, coats, shirts, blouses, skirts, hats, socks

B. Listen to the conversation and read.

Play the recording and ask students to read the dialog. Go over the dialog and allow them to practice it in pairs. Point out the use of the simple present in the dialog.

Ask students which words are plural and which are singular. They may be confused about *pants*. Point out that it ends in *s* and that it refers to an article of clothing that has two legs. Help students recognize that singular nouns need an article before them. Make sure they pronounce the indefinite article *a* /uh/.

LISTENING SCRIPT

CD 1 TR 64

The listening script matches the conversation in Exercise B.

Practice 1

5–7 mins.

C. Read the conversation in Exercise B. Write sentences.

If students finish early, encourage them to write other sentences or to use *I*.

Evaluation 1

3 mins.

Ask students to write their sentences on the board. Make sure they use capital letters, periods, and an indefinite article for singular nouns.

Presentation 2

10–15 mins.

D. IDENTIFY What clothes can you see in the ad?

Go over the advertisement with students. Go over the meaning of the word *sale*. Say items in Exercise E in random order and ask students to point to the items. Say the words in sentences and ask them to point again. Finally, use the different words to talk about the pictures and ask students to identify which pictures you are talking about.

For shorter classes, ask students to do Exercise F for homework.

Practice 2

15–20 mins.

E. Listen and write the number of the conversation.

This listening consists of eight short conversations. The object here is not that students understand every word, but that they begin to recognize words they learn in class.

Ask students to listen carefully for each item as it is spoken about. Do the first item as a class.

Unlike previous recordings, the conversations are all on one track with only a short pause between each one. Students are asked to listen and record their answers rapidly. You may play the whole recording more than once, but we suggest that you don't stop in the middle of the recording.

Briefly remind students of the strategy of focused listening.

LISTENING SCRIPT

CD 1 TR 65

Conversation 1
Saleswoman: *Excuse me. Can I help you?*
Customer: *Yes, I need a few things, but I don't see anything here that will fit.*
Saleswoman: *I think this blouse would be perfect for you. The colors go great with your eyes.*
Customer: *Do you really think so? Maybe you're right.*

Conversation 2
Son: *Mom, can you buy some socks when you are out? I need them for basketball practice.*
Mother: *Sure, son, I will buy you three pairs.*

Conversation 3
Man 1: *This shirt is way too big for me. I really need to be more careful when I go shopping.*
Man 2: *That's why I ask my wife to buy shirts for me. She is a much better shopper than me.*

Conversation 4
Wife: *I have three pairs of pants in my closet, but I don't want to wear any of them.*
Husband: *Why don't you wear the blue pair? They look great on you.*

Conversation 5
Woman 1: *It is so cold out. I wish I brought my coat.*
Woman 2: *You're right. Let's get inside as soon as possible.*

Conversation 6
Daughter: *Mom, can I go to the park for a while with Becky?*
Mother: *Yes, dear, but it is getting cold. Please put on a sweater. Then I won't worry.*

Conversation 7
Son: *Dad, will you play basketball with me? I think I need some help.*
Father: *OK, let me get changed. I need to find my shorts.*

Conversation 8
Husband: *Is this a formal dinner we are going to?*
Wife: *I think so. I'm wearing a dress so you should wear something nice.*

Evaluation 2

5–7 mins.

Check students' book work by going over the answers as a class.

F. Write the types of clothing in the picture in Exercise E.

Ask students to write the words under each picture as reinforcement and additional practice. See how many can do it without referring to the words in print.

BEST PRACTICE

Native language in the classroom

In general, avoid speaking the students' first language. Students need to learn to guess at meaning and take risks. In a diverse classroom, students may also perceive you as favoring students who share one native language.

D. IDENTIFY **What clothes can you see in the ad?** sweater, dress, pants, shirt, shorts, coat

E. **Listen and write the number of the conversation.**

CD 1 TR 65

3 shirt

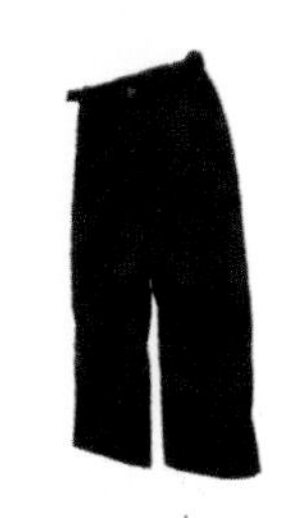

4 pants

A PAIR OF ...

Use *a pair of* with clothes that have two parts (socks, gloves). *A pair of* can also be used with clothes that have two legs (pants, shorts).

8 dress

1 blouse

2 socks

6 sweater

5 coat

7 shorts

F. **Write the types of clothing for each picture in Exercise E.**

~~blouse~~	socks	dress	shirt	pants	sweater	coat	shorts

G. Read.

Simple Present: *Have*		
Subject	***Have***	**Example sentence**
I, You, We, They	have	I **have** two shirts. I **have** a pair of socks.
He, She	has	She **has** a dress. She **has** a pair of shoes.

H. Write.

1. (blouse) She has a blouse.
   (shoes) He has shoes. **or** He has a pair of shoes.
2. (dress) She has a dress.
3. (coats) They have coats.
4. (socks) I have socks. **or** I I have a pair of socks.
5. (sweaters) We have sweaters.
6. (pants) You have pants. **or** You have a pair of pants.

I. What's in Maria's closet? Write.

3 dresses

1 pair of shoes

1 blouse

J. LIST What's in your closet? Write four items. Answers will vary.

Presentation 3

15–20 mins.

Explain to students what a closet is. Tell students what is in your own closet. Make a list on the board of how many pairs of pants, pairs of shoes, shirts, and so on, that you have. Take one of the types of clothing and make a sentence about it. For example, you might write: *I have ten shirts.* Underline *have.* Ask a few students how many shirts they have. Be careful not to make this a competition. Write a sentence about one student. For example: *Maria has five blouses.* Underline *has.* Ask students to open their books.

G. Read.

Go over the chart with students. Make sure they understand how to read it. Also, if you haven't already, introduce students to the phrase *a pair of.* Explain to students that this phrase can be used with *shoes, socks, pants,* and *shorts.*

H. Write.

Do this activity as a class. Make sure that students use the simple present form of *have* correctly.

I. What's in Maria's closet? Write.

Do this activity as a class, or ask students to work in pairs and check the answers as a class.

On the board, write: *What does she have in her closet?* Practice the question several times by asking students to respond. Have students ask each other what Maria has in her closet. Make sure their answers include the correct form of *have.* Also, make sure students are doing the activity with appropriate intonation.

For shorter classes, ask students to do Exercise I for homework.

Practice 3

5–7 mins.

Ask students to practice the question and answers with a partner.

Evaluation 3

5–7 mins.

Observe the activity.

Application

10–15 mins.

J. LIST What's in your closet? Write four items.

Ask students to write the items of clothing in their own closets and to report to a group.

Refer students to *Stand Out Basic Workbook, Unit 4, Lesson 1* for more practice with *have* and the simple present.

Go to the *Activity Bank* online for suggestions on promoting digital literacy and using the Internet to enhance this lesson.

BEST PRACTICE

Inside/Outside circle

At this level, students are asked to do short dialogs often in order to provide fluency practice. Repetition is necessary because students don't have an extensive vocabulary to discuss things yet. It is a good idea to provide different ways to approach pair practice. One approach is called *inside/outside circle.* Here students stand in two circles, one inside the other. There is the same number of students in both circles. Students in the outer circle face students in the inner one. They do the dialog once. Then, you ask one of the circles to rotate so each student repeats the activity with another student. This continues until you feel students have had enough practice.

MULTILEVEL WORKSHEET

Lesson 1, Worksheet 1: Clothing

INSTRUCTOR'S NOTES

AT-A-GLANCE **PREP**

Goal: Ask for and give directions in a store
Grammar: Review prepositions of location
Pronunciation: Minimal pairs, *in/on*
Academic Strategy: Focused listening
Vocabulary: Sections in a clothing store

Agenda

- Review clothes in your closet.
- Talk about clothing stores.
- Describe clothing stores.

Resources

Multilevel Worksheets: Lesson 2, Worksheets 1 and 2
Workbook: Unit 4, Lesson 2
Audio: CD 1, Tracks 66–69
Heinle Picture Dictionary: Buying, Wearing, and Caring for Clothes, pages 114–115; Clothes, pages 104–105

Pacing

- 1.5 hour classes
- 2.5 hour classes
- 3+ hour classes

STANDARDS CORRELATIONS

CCRS: SL1, SL2, L1, L2, L5, RF2, RF3
CASAS: 1.3.9
***SCANS:* Basic Skills** Reading, writing, listening, speaking
Resources Allocate materials and facility resources
Information Acquire and evaluate information, interpret and communicates information
Interpersonal Participate as a member of a team, teach others
Thinking Skills Think creatively, make decisions
***EFF:* Communication** Speak so others can understand, listen actively
Decision Making Solve problems and make decisions, plan
Interpersonal Cooperate with others

Warm-up and Review 10–12 mins.

Remind students how to do a Venn diagram. Refer them to page 76 if necessary. Students can create their own diagram or you can supply them one. Ask students to recall what they have in their closets. They recorded this information in Exercise J in Lesson 1.

Ask students in pairs to do a Venn diagram about what items they have in their closets.

Introduction 7–10 mins.

Point to the back of the classroom. Without saying anything, walk to the back of the room. Then, point to a corner of the room. Again, without saying anything, walk to that corner. Do this for all parts of the classroom. Next, put a coat or another article of clothing in a corner. Walk away, point to that corner, and ask: *What is in the corner of the room?* State the goal: *Today, we will identify and find sections in a store.*

Presentation 1 5 mins.

Describe the classroom as a clothing store. Explain to students that you are in ______ (name of store). Use a popular name of a store so students will recognize the context. Write *Men's Section* on the board. Ask students to help you list clothing in the men's section. Then, ask students to look at the picture.

A. Listen and point.

Play the recording several times and help students with their pronunciation.

Look at the men's section. If there is an item that students didn't mention in Presentation 1, write it on the board. Ask students to write the words in their books in Exercise B in the column for the men's section.

LISTENING SCRIPT CD 1 TR 66

Men's	*Women's*	*Children's*
Teen Boys'	*Teen Girls'*	*Fitting Room*

Practice 1 10–15 mins.

B. CLASSIFY Look at the picture in Exercise A and write the clothes.

Ask students to complete the table.

Evaluation 1 3 mins.

Recreate the table on the board and ask volunteers to complete it.

LESSON 2 Where's the fitting room?

GOAL ■ Ask for and give directions in a store

WORKPLACE CONNECTION
Exercise B: Collect and organize information

A. Listen and point.

CD 1
TR 66

B. CLASSIFY **Look at the picture in Exercise A and write the clothes.**

Men's	Women's	Children's	Teen Boys'	Teen Girls'
socks	shoes	hats	shirts	skirts
hats	blouses	socks	sweaters	dresses
shirts	dresses	shirts	pants	
jackets		pants		
		dresses		

C. **Read.**

Prepositions of Location	
a. It's **in the front of** the store. b. It's **in the corner of** the store. c. It's **in the middle of** the store. d. It's **in the back of** the store. e. It's **on the left side of** the store. f. It's **on the right side of** the store.	d b b e c f b b a

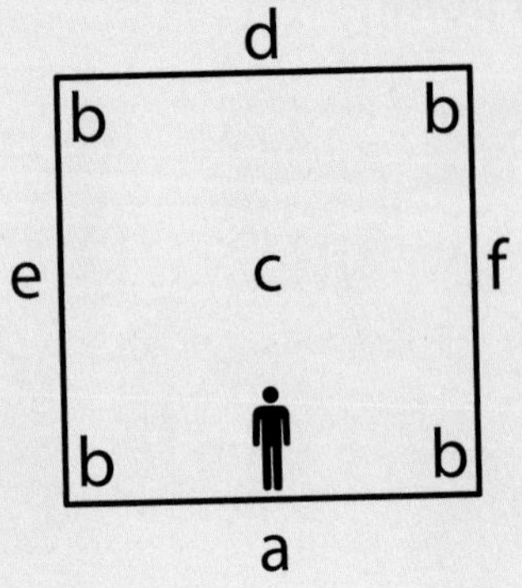

D. **Look at the picture in Exercise A. Answer the questions.**

1. Where's the fitting room? It's in the back of the store.
2. Where's the men's section? It's in the corner of the store.
3. Where's the women's section? It's on the left side of the store.
4. Where's the children's section? It's in the middle of the store.
5. Where's the teen boys' section? It's in the back of the store.
6. Where's the teen girls' section? It's on the right of the store.

CD 1 TR 67

E. **RELATE** **Listen and practice the conversation. Make new conversations. (Student A looks at Exercise D and Student B looks at the picture in Exercise A.)**

Student A: Can you help me?
Student B: Sure. What can I do for you?
Student A: Where's the fitting room?
Student B: It's in the back of the store.
Student A: Thank you.

Presentation 2

15–20 mins.

In the introduction, you put an article of clothing in a corner. Now, ask students where it is. For example, ask: *Where's the sweater?* Several students may know the word *corner*. Help them use it in a complete sentence. On the board, write: *It's in the corner.*

C. Read.

Ask students to open their books and read the grammar box together. Don't assume students will understand the concept of prepositions of location without more explanation. For some students, this concept may be unclear.

D. Look at the picture in Exercise A. Answer the questions.

Make sure students are able to make a distinction between *in* and *on*.

Some students may be ready for more complicated phrases. If your class is ready, you might introduce the sentence: *It's in the front right corner.* Receptive practice with combined forms will be introduced in Presentation 3.

INTONATION

Minimal pairs *in/on*

One form of pronunciation practice that deals with sounds is called minimal pair practice. In this type of practice, students learn to distinguish sounds by contrasting them to other sounds. Usually, the practice involves two words that are almost the same, except for one sound. Sometimes this practice is referred to as the *ship/sheep* method. Drilling students on minimal pairs is good for awareness; however, it should be noted that pronunciation practice in context and using other techniques are important to gain fluency.

Many languages don't make the /I/ sound so a word like *in* /In/ may be pronounced /en/. At this level, such a small distinction is not essential to general comprehension. However, students should be led to understand the distinction between *in* and *on*. Show students how the jaw drops to pronounce *on*. Through minimal pair practice, show them how the two words sound different.

E. RELATE Listen and practice the conversation. Make new conversations. (Student A looks at Exercise D and Student B looks at the picture in Exercise A.)

Prepare students for the practice by listening to dialog. Help them with proper intonation.

LISTENING SCRIPT

The listening script matches the conversation in Exercise E.

CD 1
TR 67

Practice 2

7–10 mins.

Student A asks the questions and Student B answers by looking at the picture in Exercise A. Student A checks Student B's answers by looking at Exercise D.

Evaluation 2

5–7 mins.

Ask for volunteers to present the questions and answers in front of the class.

INSTRUCTOR'S NOTES

Presentation 3

15–20 mins.

At this time, students will review prepositions of location, but they will be used in combinations. Prepare students by doing a few examples in the classroom. Say: *Point at the back left corner.* Be sure you turn your body so students don't confuse *left* and *right*. Once students get the hang of it, play the recording.

Note: Presentation 3, Practice 3, and the Application all use the picture on this page. Monitor students and encourage them to stay on task and not to get ahead of the class.

F. Listen and point.

This exercise is part of the presentation so do it as a class.

LISTENING SCRIPT

CD 1
TR 68

Point to the front right corner of the store.
Point to the middle of the store.
Point to the back left corner of the store.
Point to the right side of the store.
Point to the back of the store.
Point to the front of the store.
Point to the back right corner of the store.
Point to the front left corner of the store.

Practice 3

5 mins.

G. Listen and write the sections in the picture.

Here students write the name of the section where designated. You may need to play the recording several times.

LISTENING SCRIPT

CD 1
TR 69

Conversation 1
A: *Excuse me, where is the teen boy's section?*
B: *It's in the back left corner of the store.*
A: *Thanks!*

Conversation 2
A: *Can I help you?*
B: *I'm looking for the women's section.*
A: *The women's section is in the front right corner of the store.*

Conversation 3
A: *I'm looking for the children's section.*
B: *The children's section is in the middle of the store. Do you need any help?*
A: *No, thank you.*

Conversation 4
A: *Excuse me. Where is the men's section?*
B: *It's in the front left side of the store.*
A: *Thanks.*

Conversation 5
A: *I need help.*
B: *Yes, what can I do for you?*
A: *I need to find my sister. She said she would be in the teen girls' section.*
B: *The teen girls' section is in the back right.*

Evaluation 3

3 mins.

Ask students to peer-edit each others' work.

Application

5–7 mins.

H. CREATE In a group, write clothing in the picture for each section.

Encourage students to use words from the unit as well as any other words they would like to include. Monitor students' work and write new words on the board as needed.

Refer students to *Stand Out Basic Workbook, Unit 4, Lesson 2* for more practice with prepositions of location.

Go to the *Activity Bank* online for suggestions on promoting digital literacy and using the Internet to enhance this lesson.

MULTILEVEL WORKSHEETS

Lesson 2, Worksheet 1: Sections in a Store

Lesson 2, Worksheet 2: Locations

WORKPLACE CONNECTION

Exercise F: Collect and organize information

Exercise H: Make decisions and solve problems; Combine ideas and information

F. Listen and point.

CD 1 TR 68

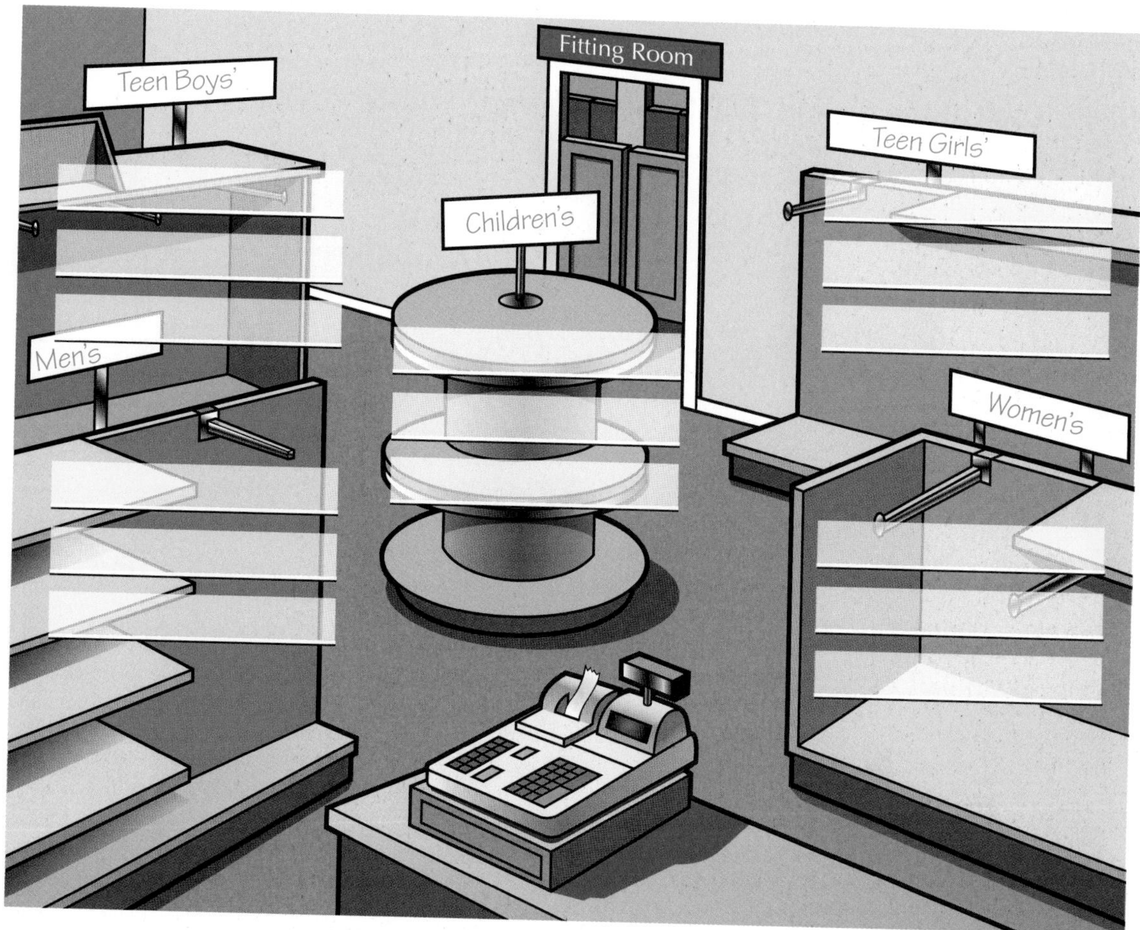

G. Listen and write the sections in the picture.

CD 1 TR 69

H. CREATE In a group, write clothing in the picture for each section. Answers will vary.

The men's section of a clothing store

LESSON 3 What colors do you like?

GOAL Describe clothing

A. INFER Look at the picture. What is Yusuf doing? Answers will vary.

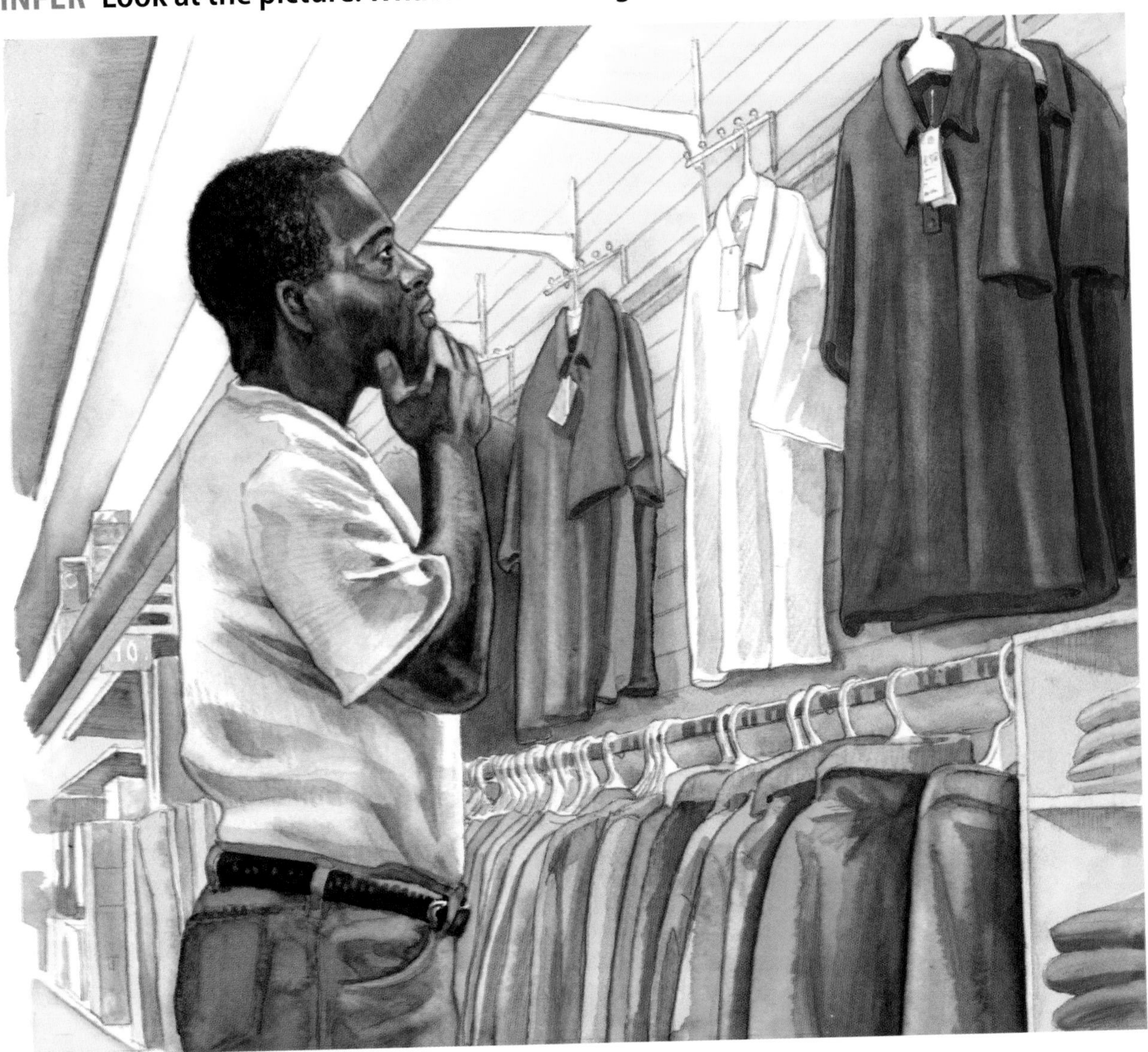

B. Listen and read.

CD 1 TR 70

Salesperson: Can I help you?
Yusuf: Yes, I want a shirt.
Salesperson: What color do you like—white, blue, or red?
Yusuf: I don't know, maybe blue.

YES/NO QUESTIONS

Can I help you?
May I help you?
Do you need help?

AT-A-GLANCE PREP

Goal: Describe clothing
Grammar: *There is, there are*
Pronunciation: *Yes/No* intonation, rhythm, and prominence
Academic Strategies: Focused listening
Vocabulary: Clothing sizes, colors, *inventory, size, item, quantity*

Agenda

- Make a list of articles of clothing.
- Identify colors and clothing.
- Listen for colors and clothing.
- Write a class inventory of classmates' clothing.

Resources

Multilevel Worksheet: Lesson 3, Worksheet 1
Workbook: Unit 4, Lesson 3
Audio: CD 1, Tracks 70–72
Heinle Picture Dictionary: Clothes, pages 104–105; Colors, pages 10–11; Describing Clothes, pages 110–111

Pacing

- 1.5 hour classes
- 2.5 hour classes
- 3+ hour classes

STANDARDS CORRELATIONS

CCRS: SL1, SL2, L1, L2, L5, RF2
CASAS: 1.1.9, 1.2.1, 1.3.9
SCANS: **Basic Skills** Reading, writing, listening, speaking
Resources Allocate materials and facility resources
Information Acquire and evaluate information, interpret and communicate information
Thinking Skills Make decisions
EFF: **Communication** Speak so others can understand, listen actively
Decision Making Solve problems and make decisions

Warm-up and Review

10–15 mins.

Ask groups to list all the types of clothing they see in the classroom. Ask each group to write their list on the board and compare lists.

Introduction

5–7 mins.

Ask students to identify what you are wearing. Ask them *yes/no* questions, for example: *Is my shirt white?* State the goal: *Today, we will identify colors and describe clothing.*

Presentation 1

30–40 mins.

Ask students where they buy clothing. If they don't understand, give some examples of stores.

Ask students to listen to the conversation with their books closed. (CD 1, Track 70) On the board, write: *pants, shirts, socks,* and *shoes.* Ask students to identify what Yusuf is buying: *Is he buying a shirt, a pair of pants, socks, or shoes?*

A. INFER Look at the picture. What is Yusuf doing?

Ask students to point to Yusuf, the shirts, and other details.

B. Listen and read.

Play the recording and ask students to read along. Ask pairs of students to practice the exchange.

LISTENING SCRIPT

The listening script matches the conversation in Exercise B.

Ask students to do a Corners activity. Students go to different corners of the room, depending on their preferences. The preferences are *white, blue, red,* or *I don't like any of the colors.* Help students understand the negative of *like.* Write on the board: *I like blue. I don't like white or red.* Once they are in the corners, ask students to say the color they like and the colors they don't like.

Note: This is only an introduction to the negative form of the simple present. Students are not expected to master the use of this structure.

Practice 1

7–10 mins.

Have students practice this dialog. Have them say the color they chose in the Corners activity.

Student A: *Can I help you?*
Student B: *Yes, I want a shirt.*
Student A: *What color do you like?*
Student B: *I like blue.*

Evaluation 1

3–5 mins.

Ask for volunteers to present the conversation.

Presentation 2

20–30 mins.

C. Listen and repeat. Read the colors in the picture.

Go over the new vocabulary with students. Make sure they understand the word order. Some students will have a difficult time putting the adjective before the noun. They will have an opportunity to practice this in Practice 3.

> **LISTENING SCRIPT** CD 1 TR 71
>
> *green* · *white* · *black* · *purple* · *pink* · *brown*
> *red* · *orange* · *yellow* · *gray* · *blue*

BEST PRACTICE

Error correction

We suggest that you correct students only on the concepts you are teaching or have taught. It is often more desirable to encourage peer-correcting over teacher-correcting because it can be less intimidating. It may also be useful to wait until you hear the error several times and explain the error to the class instead of identifying students who are making the error.

Finally, be careful to limit correcting in application stages and team projects. In these activities, students are taking ownership of their own language, and overcorrecting can inhibit this process.

Look for things in the classroom and identify colors. For example, you may say: *The door is blue.* Also, to practice word order, you may say: *The blue door is over there.* Drill students on the color vocabulary by prompting them to listen and repeat. Then, have them substitute by pointing to an object and asking them to add the color: *The door is* ________.

Discuss the pictures in Exercise D with students. Write *small, medium, large,* and *extra large* on the board. Drill students on the new vocabulary and say the sizes and colors. Have them identify the shirts by pointing to them in their books.

For shorter classes, ask students to do Exercise E for homework.

D. Listen and point to the clothing items.

This recording allows students to practice sifting through a conversation and identifying the new vocabulary. When they hear the color, they point to the item.

> **LISTENING SCRIPT** 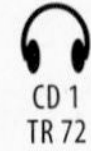 CD 1 TR 72
>
> **Salesperson:** *We have many sizes and colors in our store. For example, in this shirt, we have two extra-large blue shirts.*
> **Yusuf:** *I don't need that size. Do you have any large white shirts?*
> **Salesperson:** *Sure, we have one in the back. I can get it for you.*
> **Yusuf:** *OK, and while you're at it, could you get me a medium green shirt for my brother?*
> **Salesperson:** *OK, but are you sure he might not want a small yellow shirt? We have three of those on sale.*
> **Yusuf:** *Yes, I'm sure.*

Practice 2

7–10 mins.

E. CLASSIFY Look at Exercise D. Complete the inventory.

Help students understand what *inventory* means. Ask them to complete the information.

CRITICAL THINKING

Students at this level are often asked to repeat or to copy. However, students should be introduced to ways of thinking critically when they are ready and given enough information and resources to do so. Activities that force students to complete a puzzle in the context of the given objective are very useful. As students think critically, they become independent learners.

Evaluation 2

3–5 mins.

Ask questions about the chart in Exercise E such as: *How many white shirts are there?*

C. **Listen and repeat. Read the colors in the picture.**

CD 1
TR 71

ADJECTIVE POSITION

A blue tie (correct)

~~A tie blue~~ (not correct)

D. **Listen and point to the clothing items.**

CD 1
TR 72

S = Small	**M = Medium**	**L = Large**	**XL = Extra Large**

E. **CLASSIFY** **Look at Exercise D. Complete the inventory.**

Adel's Inventory List			
Quantity (How many?)	Item	Size	Color
3	shirt	S	yellow
2	shirt	M	green
1	shirt	L	white
2	shirt	XL	blue

Exercise H: Collect and organize information; Combine ideas and information

F. Read.

Singular	Plural
There **is** one green shirt. There**'s** one green shirt.	There **are** two black shirts.

G. Practice the conversation. Use the information in Exercise E to make new conversations.

Student A: How many white shirts are there?
Student B: There's one.

H. CREATE Write an inventory for your class. Write about your classmates' clothing.

Answers will vary.

Class Inventory		
Quantity (How many?)	Item	Color

I. CREATE Write an inventory of the clothes in your closet.

Presentation 3

10–15 mins.

Review singular and plural nouns with students. Ask them the *how many* questions from Exercise E again. Review the verb *Be* with students. You may want to do this first with books closed to see how much students remember from Unit 1, Lesson 3. Re-create the chart from page 21 on the board. Leave out the forms of *Be*. Ask for volunteers to complete the chart.

F. Read.

Teach *there is* and *there are* and prepare students to do Exercise G for practice. Show them how to substitute the underlined information with other information from the inventory on the previous page. Make sure you remind students about adjective order.

Go over the pronunciation of the sentences. Show students that using the contraction is more common than not.

INTONATION

Rhythm and prominence

English sentence rhythm does not follow a consistent pattern. Various aspects of the language affect it. English has a series of stops and starts based on prominent words and the pauses that sometimes follow. In this case, one could pronounce the sentence *There is one white shirt,* in various ways.

If, in the context, a speaker is making a distinction between a white shirt and another color, he might emphasize *one*—making it prominent. In this case, the speaker is answering the question *How many?* Hence, the number is emphasized.

Changing the phrase *there is* to a contraction also changes the rhythm from a steady, even pace to a more natural one. The speaker will generally emphasize the number and follow it with a slight pause.

Practice 3

7–10 mins.

G. Practice the conversation. Use the information in Exercise E to make new conversations.

Help as needed.

Evaluation 3

3 mins.

Ask for volunteers to present the conversation to the class.

Application

15–25 mins.

H. CREATE Write an inventory for your class. Write about your classmates' clothing.

In groups, have students make a class inventory. Put the inventories on the board. Then, in pairs, have students practice the dialog from Exercise G again, using their new class inventory for the information.

I. CREATE Write an inventory of the clothes in your closet.

Refer students to *Stand Out Basic Workbook, Unit 4, Lesson 3* for more practice with *there is* and *there are*.

Go to the *Activity Bank* online for suggestions on promoting digital literacy and using the Internet to enhance this lesson.

MULTILEVEL WORKSHEET

Lesson 3, Worksheet 1: Colors and Clothing

INSTRUCTOR'S NOTES

AT-A-GLANCE PREP

Goal: Make purchases
Grammar: Review *How much is / How much are*
Academic Strategies: Focused listening, test-taking skills
Vocabulary: *dollar, quarter, dime, nickel, penny, receipts, price, cash register*

Agenda

- Review clothing and make a list.
- Read cash register totals.
- Learn about U.S. money.
- Read receipts.
- Write a receipt.

Resources

Multilevel Worksheets: Lesson 4, Worksheets 1 and 2
Workbook: Unit 4, Lesson 4
Audio: CD 1, Tracks 73–80
Heinle Picture Dictionary: Money and Shopping, pages 8–9

Pacing

■ 1.5 hour classes ■ 2.5 hour classes ■ 3⁺ hour classes

STANDARDS CORRELATIONS

CCRS: RI1, SL2, L1, L3, RF3
CASAS: 1.1.6, 1.3.9, 4.8.1, 6.1.1
SCANS: **Basic Skills** Reading, writing, arithmetic, listening, speaking
Resources Allocate money
Information Acquire and evaluate information, organize and maintain information, interpret and communicate information
Systems Understand systems
EFF: **Communication** Read with understanding, convey ideas in writing, speak so others can understand, listen actively
Decision Making Use math to solve problems and communicate

Warm-up and Review 15–20 mins.

Ask groups to list clothing without using a dictionary or their books. Then, ask them to write the words in alphabetical order. Ask each group to write their list on the board. If students introduce new words, acknowledge them and briefly practice their pronunciation.

Introduction 3–5 mins.

Ask students to identify clothes in the classroom by color and name. Ask where they buy clothing. State the goal: *Today, we will learn how to make purchases.*

Presentation 1 15–20 mins.

A. IDENTIFY Listen and point to the cash registers.

Practice saying *cash register*. Play the recording. Ask students to point to which cash register is being talked about. Have them repeat the money amount with you.

LISTENING SCRIPT

CD 1 TR 73

1. **Cashier:** *Let's see. You want this badge. That's $1.00.*
   Tien: *$1.00?*
   Cashier: *That's right.*
   Tien: *OK, here you go.*
2. **Cashier:** *OK, that's one red t-shirt.*
   Tien: *How much is it?*
   Cashier: *That's $6.25 with tax.*
3. **Cashier:** *Let's see. The shorts are $10.41.*
   Tien: *OK, do you have change?*
   Cashier: *Sure.*
   Tien: *Thanks!*

B. Circle the correct number from Exercise A.

Do this exercise with students. Prepare students to do the practice. Show them how to substitute information. Ask students to write the items being purchased in Exercise A next to the cash registers. You may choose to play the recording again (CD 1, Track 73). Item 1 is a badge; Item 2 is a t-shirt; and Item 3 is a pair of shorts.

C. Listen and read with your teacher.

If you have samples of bills and coins, use them. This is also a good place to use "play" money. Put money together in different combinations and see if students can give you the totals.

LISTENING SCRIPT

CD 1 TR 74

The listening script matches the list in Exercise C.

LESSON 4 That's $5.00

WORKPLACE CONNECTION
Exercises A, B, and C: Manage money
Exercise B: Perform basic computations

GOAL ■ Make purchases

CD 1 TR 73

A. IDENTIFY Listen and point to the cash registers.

1. 

2. 

3. 

B. Circle the correct number from Exercise A.

1. one dollar ① 2 3
2. ten dollars and forty-one cents 1 2 ③
3. six dollars and twenty-five cents 1 ② 3

CD 1 TR 74

C. Listen and read with your teacher.

a dollar bill

a dollar coin
$1.00

a quarter
$.25

a dime
$.10

a nickel
$.05

a penny
$.01

Exercise D: Perform basic computations; Manage money

D. RELATE Match the amounts with the money.

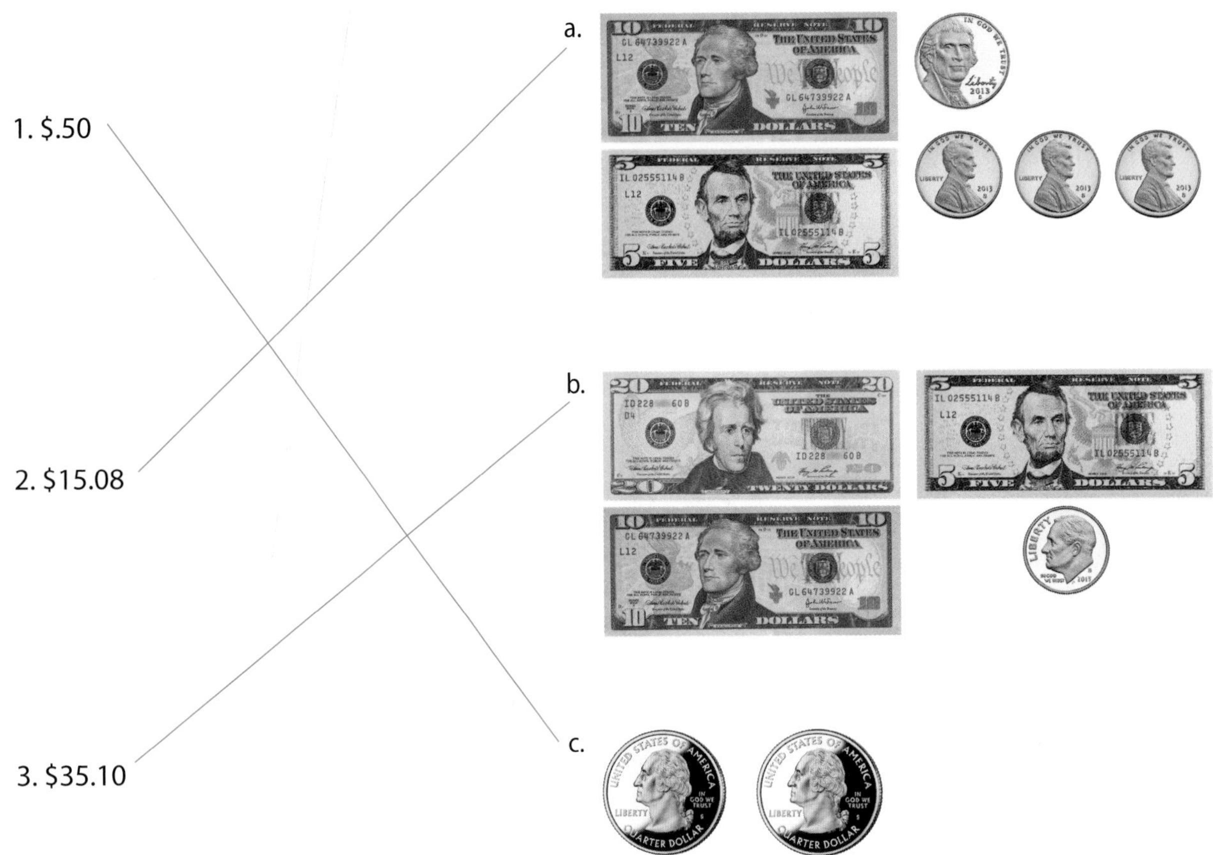

E. Practice the conversations with a partner.

Student A: How much is the shirt?
Student B: It's $15.00.
Student A: Thanks.

Student A: How much are the shorts?
Student B: They're $10.41.
Student A: Thanks.

F. Study the chart.

Singular	Plural
How much **is** the dress?	How much **are** the shoes?

BEST PRACTICE

Playing audio CDs

1. If time permits, walk around while students are listening to the recording.
2. Play the recording multiple times if necessary.
3. Give students the opportunity to follow the text of the audio transcript while or after they listen.

Practice 1

5–7 mins.

D. RELATE Match the amounts with the money.

Ask students when they finish drawing the lines to speak to a partner and recite the type of money (quarter, nickel, etc.) they see in the right column.

Evaluation 1

5–7 mins.

Check students' book work. Practice saying the amounts with students. Make sure they pronounce the *s* in *dollars*. Also, ask students the names of the types of money (quarter, nickel, etc.) in the right column.

Presentation 2

10–15 mins.

Review numbers 1–100 with students.

Practice using *have* and *has* in this presentation as a review. Say: *Kim has $35.00—one 20-dollar bill, one 10-dollar bill, and one 5-dollar bill.* Do a short dictation and give students four amounts. After checking to make sure everyone understood the same number, ask students what bills and coins they might need.

Note: At this level, students need consistency. Insist that they insert *and* between the dollars and cents. They should say *six dollars and twenty-five cents,* not *six dollars, twenty-five cents.* Also, make sure that students do not drop the plural *s* when saying *dollars.*

For shorter classes, ask students to do Exercise D for homework.

Practice 2

5–7 mins.

E. Practice the conversations with a partner.

Ask students to read the conversations. Then, ask: *How much is the shirt? How much are the shorts?* Ask students to practice the conversations in pairs.

Evaluation 2

5–7 mins.

F. Study the chart.

Review the chart with students. Point out the singular and the plural verb forms of the verb *Be*. Add additional examples on the board. *How much is the shirt? How much are the sweaters?*

INSTRUCTOR'S NOTES

Presentation 3

10–15 mins.

G. Listen and write.

Review *How much is?* and *How much are?* Then, play the six brief conversations and ask students to write the prices they hear in their books.

> **LISTENING SCRIPT**
>
> 
>
>
> **Conversation 1**
> **Salesman:** *Can I help you?*
> **Yusuf:** *Yes, I want this pair of pants.*
> **Salesman:** *Great. Step this way.*
> **Yusuf:** *How much are they?*
> **Salesman:** *They're $32.50.*
>
> **Conversation 2**
> **Salesman:** *Can I help you?*
> **Yusuf:** *Yes, I want a shirt. This one looks good.*
> **Salesman:** *That's $24.50.*
>
> **Conversation 3**
> **Salesman:** *Can I help you?*
> **Maria:** *Yes, I need a pair of shoes for work.*
> **Salesman:** *Here is a nice pair.*
> **Maria:** *How much are they?*
> **Salesman:** *They are $44.00.*
>
> **Conversation 4**
> **Salesman:** *Can I help you?*
> **Yusuf:** *Yes, I want a pair of shorts.*
> **Salesman:** *Great. Step this way.*
> **Yusuf:** *How much are they?*
> **Salesman:** *They are $18.00.*
>
> **Conversation 5**
> **Salesman:** *Can I help you?*
> **Maria:** *Yes, I need a dress for a party.*
> **Salesman:** *What color are you looking for?*
> **Maria:** *Something for the summer.*
> **Salesman:** *How about this one?*
> **Maria:** *That's beautiful. How much is it?*
> **Salesman:** *It's $82.50.*
>
> **Conversation 6**
> **Saleswoman:** *Can I help you?*
> **Maria:** *Yes, I'm looking for a blouse.*
> **Saleswoman:** *What color are you looking for?*
> **Maria:** *Maybe white.*
> **Saleswoman:** *How about this one?*
> **Maria:** *That's pretty. How much is it?*
> **Saleswoman:** *It's $22.50.*

Prepare students for the practice by modeling how to do Exercise H. This is an information-gap activity. Student A covers Exercise G and asks: *How much is the shirt?* Student B looks at Exercise G and responds. Student A writes the information on the receipt in Exercise H. Then, students reverse roles.

Practice 3

7–10 mins.

H. CONFIRM Ask a classmate for the prices in Exercise G. Write the receipts.

Evaluation 3

5–7 mins.

Together as a class, add the prices on the receipts. See if everyone gets the same results.

Application

10–15 mins.

I. CREATE Speak to a partner. Ask for three items and complete the receipt.

Have students choose three of the items from Exercise G. A receipt can also be found in the Activity Bank.

Refer students to *Stand Out Basic Workbook, Unit 4, Lesson 4* for more practice with singular and plurals and the verb *Be*.

Go to the *Activity Bank* online for suggestions on promoting digital literacy and using the Internet to enhance this lesson.

MULTILEVEL WORKSHEETS

Lesson 4, Worksheet 1: Money and Totals
Lesson 4, Worksheet 2: Counting Money
Lesson 4, Worksheet 3: Writing Receipts

WORKPLACE CONNECTION
Exercises G, H, and I: Manage money
Exercises H and I: Perform basic computations
Exercise I: Combine ideas and information

CD 1 TR 75-80

G. Listen and write.

1.  $32.50

2.  $24.50

3.  $44.00

4.  $18.00

5. 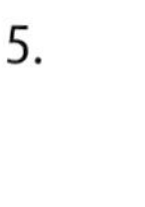  $82.50

6.  $22.50

H. CONFIRM Ask a classmate for the prices in Exercise G. Write the receipts.

Adel's Clothing Emporium

pants $32.50

Total $32.50

Customer Copy

Adel's Clothing Emporium

shirt $24.50
shoes $44.00

Total $68.50

Customer Copy

Adel's Clothing Emporium

dress $82.50
shorts $18.00
blouse $22.50

Total $123.00

Customer Copy

I. CREATE Speak to a partner. Ask for three items and complete the receipt. Answers will vary.

Student A: How can I help you?
Student B: How much are the pants?
Student A: $32.50
Student B: Thanks. I want two pairs.
Student A: Great. Anything else?

Adel's Clothing Emporium

_________ _____
_________ _____
_________ _____

Total .... _____

Customer Copy

LESSON 5 How much are the shoes?

GOAL ■ Read advertisements

WORKPLACE CONNECTION
Exercises A and B: Manage money

A. Read, listen, and write.

CD 1
TR 81

SAVE $5.00
ALL SIZES
$22.50
SAVE $12.00
SIZES 6-12
$33.00
SALE
ALL SIZES
$33.00
SALE
ALL SIZES
$28.00
SAVE $4.00
ALL SIZES
$24.00
SAVE $5.00
ALL SIZES
$18.00
adel's
clothing emporium

B. Write.

1. How much are the shirts? $22.50
2. How much are the dresses? $33.00
3. How much are the shoes? $24.00
4. How much are the pants? $28.00

C. RELATE Ask a classmate the questions in Exercise B.

AT-A-GLANCE **PREP**

Goal: Read advertisements
Grammar: *How much /How many,* subject pronoun *they*
Academic Strategies: Focused listening, asking for information, predict information
Vocabulary: *how much, each, ad, save*

Agenda

- Review writing receipts.
- Read an ad.
- Practice asking for information.
- Take orders.
- Compare stores.
- Create an ad.

Resources

Multilevel Worksheets: Lesson 5, Worksheets 1 and 2
Workbook: Unit 4, Lesson 5
Audio: CD 1, Track 81
Heinle Picture Dictionary: Money and Shopping, pages 8–9

Pacing

- 1.5 hour classes
- 2.5 hour classes
- 3+ hour classes

STANDARDS CORRELATIONS

CCRS: RI1, SL1, SL2, SL4, L1, L2, L5, RF3
CASAS: 1.1.9, 1.2.1, 1.3.9, 4.8.3
SCANS: **Basic Skills** Reading, writing, arithmetic, listening, speaking
Resources Allocate time, allocate money
Information Acquire and evaluate information, organize and maintain information, interpret and communicate information
Interpersonal Participate as a member of a team, teach others, serve clients and customers
Thinking Skills Think creatively, make decisions, solve problems
EFF: **Communication** Read and understand, convey ideas in writing, speak so others can understand, listen actively
Decision Making Use math to solve problems and make decisions, plan
Interpersonal Cooperate with others, guide others

Warm-up and Review — 10–15 mins.

Ask students to turn back to page 94, Exercise G and do the exercise again with a partner.

BEST PRACTICE

Review

Students should be encouraged to do activities over again after a few days or weeks so the book becomes a tool for learning. This activity is a good example. At this level, you will find that students learn and forget readily.

Introduction — 5 mins.

Ask students questions using *what.* For example, you may ask: *What color is your shirt?* State the goal: *Today, we will read advertisements.*

Presentation 1 — 15–20 mins.

Talk a little about clothing stores and where you shop. Ask students where they shop for clothes. Go over the advertisement and review sizes, colors, and prices. Ask questions using *how much.* Remind students what *save* means.

Prepare students for the listening activity by asking them to predict the omitted prices.

Practice 1 — 7–10 mins.

A. Read, listen, and write.

Play the recording and ask students to listen for the omitted prices. Ask them to write what they hear. Then, ask them to do Exercise B.

LISTENING SCRIPT

CD 1 TR 81

Here at Adel's Clothing Emporium, we have great sales. Come in and see for yourself. Men's shirts in all sizes are only $22.50. You will be happy to see women's dresses in sizes 6 to 12 are only $33.00. We have men's sweaters on sale for $33.00. Men's pants are only $28.00 this week. Women's shoes are now only $24.00. Save $4.00! Blouses are a bargain at $18.00! We will be waiting for you. Remember Adel's Clothing Emporium for great savings!

B. Write.

Give students a chance to write the information.

Evaluation 1 — 2–5 mins.

C. RELATE Ask a classmate the questions in Exercise B.

Ask students to read and respond to the information in Exercise B in pairs.

Presentation 2

15–20 mins.

D. Read.

Go over questions carefully with students. Review the verb *Be.*

Show students that when asked in general terms, the questions are always in the plural: *How much are the shirts?* When it is about a specific shirt, the speaker would say: *How much is the shirt?* Don't spend too much time on this point.

> BEST PRACTICE
>
> **Addressing student levels**
>
> Students come to any ESL class at various levels. Formal multilevel classes are very common. In the formal multilevel class, students are designated at different levels within the same classroom.
>
> Even if not formally designated, all classes are multilevel to some extent. Students come to classes with a variety of experience in schooling and in English training or exposure, and they also come with different abilities. Some may be good speakers, but may have trouble writing while others might be just the opposite.
>
> In the *Stand Out* approach, our philosophy is not to hold a student back if he or she is ready for additional information. The instructor should be aware of what individual students can handle. We often suggest limiting exposure to certain concepts in order to avoid overwhelming students with too much information. However, some students might be ready for more. Be aware of this and help those students when appropriate. Use *Stand Out* ancillaries to further challenge these students.

E. Practice the conversation. Use the information in Exercise A to make new conversations.

Go over the dialog with students. Drill them in different ways. Help them to see that *each* means for one item.

> BEST PRACTICE
>
> **Presentation *vs.* practice**
>
> Here, students are preparing to do the practice. Even though in the instruction line we say *practice*, students are not doing anything that requires thinking skills—like getting new or different information from a partner. We say that *presentation* is teacher-centered, *practice* is teacher-guided, and *application* is completely student-centered where students have taken ownership of the task.
>
> Therefore, this task is best categorized as part of a presentation stage in lesson planning.

Prepare students for the practice by showing them how to make the substitutions.

Practice 2

7–10 mins.

F. CLASSIFY Practice the conversation in Exercise E again. Speak to your classmates and take orders. (Use the ad in Exercise A.)

This activity can be extended or made more difficult by asking students to complete the chart without following the dialog in Exercise E.

Evaluation 2

5–7 mins.

Ask volunteers to demonstrate the conversation in front of the class.

WORKPLACE CONNECTION
Exercises E and F: Manage money
Exercise F: Collect and organize information

D. Read.

How much and *How many*		
Question		**Answer**
How much	(money) is the sweater?	$33.00.
How much	is the shirt?	The shirt is $23.00.
How much	are the shoes?	They are / They're $40.00.
How many	coats do you want?	I want three coats.
How many	shirts do you want?	I want two shirts.

E. Practice the conversation. Use the information in Exercise A to make new conversations.

Student A: Can I help you?
Student B: Yes, I want shirts.
Student A: How many shirts do you want?
Student B: I want two shirts. How much are they?
Student A: They are $22.50 each.

F. CLASSIFY Practice the conversation in Exercise E again. Speak to your classmates and take orders. (Use the ad in Exercise A.) Answers will vary.

Name	Quantity (How many?)	Product	Price
Yusuf	two	shirts	$22.50

WORKPLACE CONNECTION
Exercises G and H: Manage money
Exercise I: Combine ideas and information

G. Read.

H. COMPARE Look at the ads for Norma's Fine Clothing and Adel's Clothing Emporium (Exercise A). Write the prices.

	Norma's Fine Clothing	Adel's Clothing Emporium
shirt	$24.00	$22.50
pants	$35.00	$28.00
shoes	$20.00	$24.00
dress	$35.00	$33.00
sweater	$35.00	$33.00

I. CREATE In a group, make an advertisement for a new clothing store. Practice the conversation from Exercise E.

Presentation 3

10–15 mins.

G. Read.

Go over the new advertisement with students. Introduce students to *sale price* and *regular price*. Ask them to help you calculate the regular price of the shirt and the dress. Now, have them look at Exercise A and compare certain items. Ask them which store has a better price for shirts. Students might think Norma's Fine Clothing does because shoppers save more, but Adel's has a cheaper price.

For shorter classes, ask students to do Exercise H for homework.

Practice 3

5–10 mins.

H. COMPARE Look at the ads for Norma's Fine Clothing and Adel's Clothing Emporium (Exercise A). Write the prices.

Have students write the prices for the items at each store in the appropriate column.

Evaluation 3

7–10 mins.

Check students' work and ask which store has better prices. Depending on what items students choose, either store could have better prices. Although there is no clear right answer, note that the prices for men's clothing are cheaper at Adel's while the prices for women's clothing are cheaper at Norma's.

Application

20–30 mins.

I. CREATE In a group, make an advertisement for a new clothing store. Practice the conversation from Exercise E.

In this activity, make sure students form a conversation using the dialog from Exercise E. Monitor each group well. Ask students to share their conversations and ads with the class.

MULTILEVEL WORKSHEETS

Lesson 5, Worksheet 1: Asking Questions
Lesson 5, Worksheet 2: Create an Advertisement

Refer students to *Stand Out Basic Workbook, Unit 4, Lesson 5* for more practice with *How much* and *How many*.

Go to the *Activity Bank* online for suggestions on promoting digital literacy and using the Internet to enhance this lesson.

INSTRUCTOR'S NOTES

That's a good deal

Before You Watch

- Ask students to look at the title and predict what the video will be about.
- Show students an item of clothing that you bought for a good price and say: *This was a good deal.* Then, ask students what clothing they bought for a good price.

A. Look at the picture and answer the questions.

- Ask the questions and elicit answers.
- Ask students what clothing the men are wearing in the picture. Then, have students guess about the prices of the items.

While You Watch

B. Watch the video and fill in the prices.

- Ask students to watch the video.
- Read the items in the table and play the video again. Ask students to fill in the missing prices. Play the video multiple times if necessary.
- Check the answers as a class.

Check Your Understanding

C. Put the sentences in order to make a conversation.

- Ask students to read the sentences and put them in the correct order. Explain that a clerk is a salesperson.
- Ask students to practice the conversation with a partner and take turns with the roles.
- Have volunteers demonstrate the conversation in front of the class.

BEST PRACTICE

There are many ways to use video in the classroom. Students should rarely watch a video without some kind of task. You might introduce comprehension questions before they watch so they know what they are looking for. Below are a few techniques that you may try for variety beyond the comprehension checks and other ideas already presented in this lesson.

Freeze Frame: Pause the video during viewing and use it like a picture dictionary, identifying and expanding on the vocabulary.

Silent Viewing: Show the video in segments without sound so students can guess at the storyline. This helps them to understand that listening is more than just the words people say.

Prediction Techniques: Show portions of the video and ask students to predict what will come next.

Listening without Viewing: This helps students create their own image of what is happening. After a discussion, allow students to watch the video and the sound together.

Back-to-Back: In pairs, one student faces the video and the other faces away. Play the video without sound and ask the student viewing to report to the student who is facing away what is happening.

Summary Strips: Create strips of sentences that describe the events. Have students watch the video and then put the strips in the correct order, or ask students to predict the story line before watching and then check their answers. The Activity Bank has summary strips for each video in *Stand Out*.

LIFESKILLS

That's a good deal

Before You Watch

A. Look at the picture and answer the questions.

1. Where are Hector and Mr. Sanchez?
   They are in a clothing store.
2. What is Hector holding?
   He's holding a suit and tie.

While You Watch

B. Watch the video and fill in the missing prices.

Item	Regular price	Sale price
jacket	$160	$112
coat	$150	$105
pants	$40	$25
tie	$18	$10
shirt	$27.50	$22.50

Check Your Understanding

C. Put the sentences in order to make a conversation.

a. ___3___ Clerk: What color?

b. ___2___ Customer: Yes, I need a new tie.

c. ___6___ Customer: That's nice. I'll take it.

d. ___1___ Clerk: May I help you?

e. ___5___ Clerk: How about this one?

f. ___4___ Customer: Blue. It's for a job interview.

Review

Learner Log

I can identify types of clothing.
■ Yes ■ No ■ Maybe

I can describe clothing.
■ Yes ■ No ■ Maybe

A. Write the types of clothing.

1.  shirt

2.  shoes

3.  socks

4.  pants

5.  shorts

6. dress

7.  blouse

8.  sweater

B. Read and write.

1. We need three blue shirts. They are $18.59 each.
2. We need five green sweaters. They are $22.50 each.
3. We need one pair of black shoes. They are $33.00.
4. We need two red coats. They are $85.00 each.

Adel's Clothing Emporium			
Quantity (How many?)	**Item**	**Color**	**Price**
1. 3	shirt	blue	$55.77
2. 5	sweater	green	$112.50
3. 1	shoes	black	$33.00
4. 2	coat	red	$170.00

AT-A-GLANCE PREP

Goal: All unit objectives
Grammar: All unit grammar
Academic Strategies: Focused listening,reviewing, evaluating, developing study skills
Vocabulary: All unit vocabulary

Agenda

- Discuss unit objectives.
- Complete the review.

Pacing

- 1.5 hour classes
- 2.5 hour classes
- 3+ hour classes

STANDARDS CORRELATIONS

CCRS: R1, SL2, L5, RF3
CASAS: 1.1.9, 1.2.1, 1.3.9, 7.4.1, 7.4.2, 7.4.3
SCANS: **Basic Skills** Reading, writing, listening, speaking
Information Acquire and evaluate information, organize and maintain information, interpret and communicate information
Thinking Skills See things in the mind's eye
EFF: **Communication** Speak so others can understand
Lifelong Learning Take responsibility for learning, reflect and evaluate

Warm-up and Review
7–10 mins.

Ask students what new clothes they want to buy. Make a list on the board of all the vocabulary students can come up with from the unit.

Introduction
5 mins.

Write all the goals on the board from Unit 4. Show students the first page of every lesson so they understand that today will be review. Complete the agenda.

Note: Depending on the length of the term, you may decide to have students do Presentation and Practice for homework and review student work as the warm-up for another class meeting.

Presentation
10–15 mins.

This presentation and practice will cover the first three pages of the review. Quickly go to the first page of each lesson. Discuss the objective of each. Ask simple questions to remind students what they have learned.

Practice
15–20 mins.

A. Write the types of clothing. (Lesson 1)

B. Read and write. (Lessons 3–5)

BEST PRACTICE

Recycling/Review

The review process and the project that follows are part of the recycling/review process. Students at this level often need to be reintroduced to concepts to solidify what they have learned. Many concepts are learned and forgotten while learning other new concepts. This is because students learn but are not necessarily ready to acquire language concepts. Therefore, it becomes very important to review and to show students how to review on their own. It is also important to recycle the new concepts in different contexts.

INSTRUCTOR'S NOTES

Practice *(continued)*

C. Write the locations. (Lesson 2)

D. Which possible bills and coins do you need? Write. (Lesson 4)

INSTRUCTOR'S NOTES

Learner Log

I can ask for and give directions in a store. ☐ Yes ☐ No ☐ Maybe

I can make purchases. ☐ Yes ☐ No ☐ Maybe

C. Write the locations.

a. It's in the corner of the store.

b. It's in the front of the store.

c. It's on the right side of the store.

d. Its at the back of the store.

e. It's in the middle of the store.

f. It's on the left of the store.

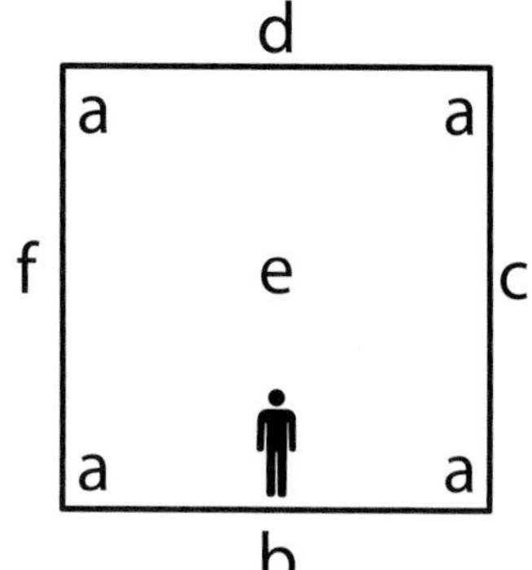

D. Which possible bills and coins do you need? Write. Answers may vary.

Total	\$20 bills	\$10 bills	\$5 bills	\$1 bills	Quarters	Dimes	Nickels	Pennies
\$69.00	3		1	4				
\$22.50	1			2	2			
\$56.90	2	1	1	1	3	1	1	
\$132.00	6	1		2				
\$153.75	7	1		3	3			
\$113.80	5	1		3	3		1	

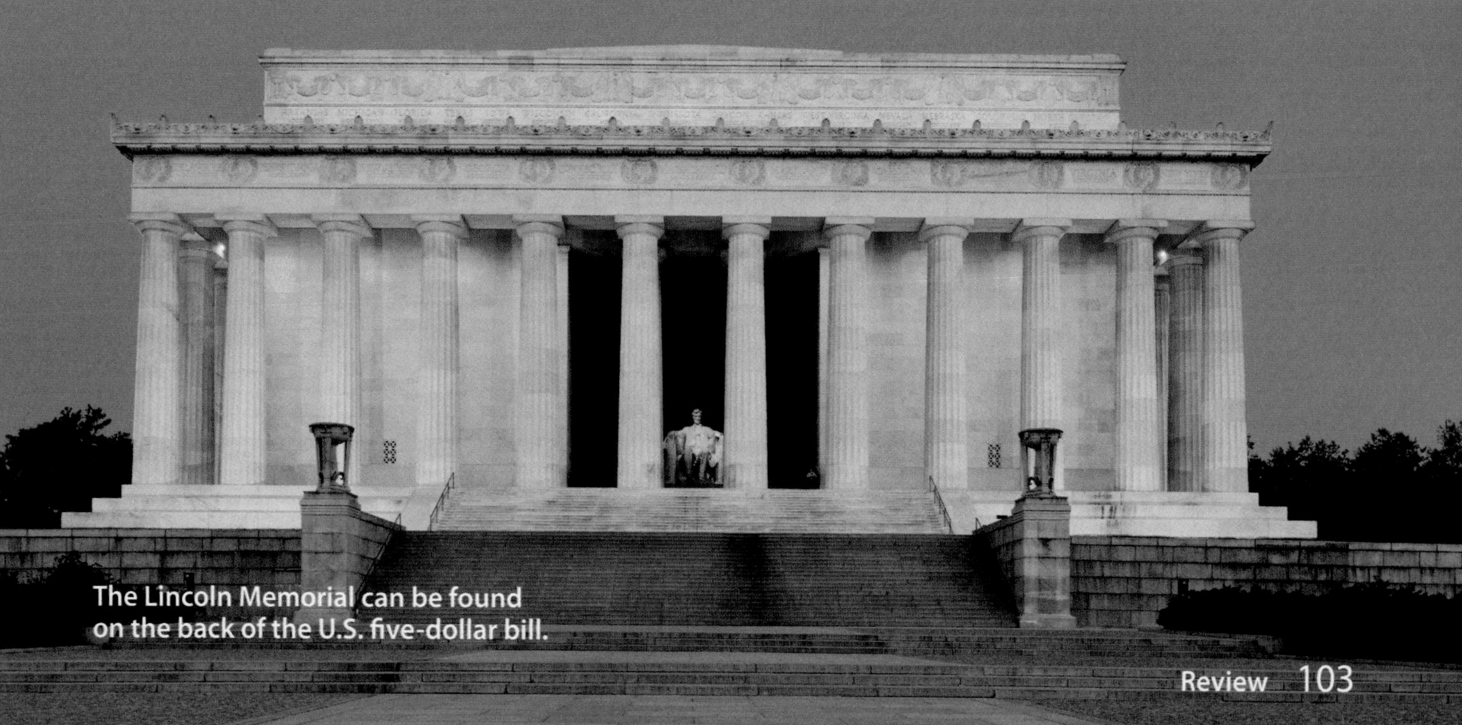

The Lincoln Memorial can be found on the back of the U.S. five-dollar bill.

E. Read the ad.

F. Write the information from the ad.

Item	Price	Savings
gray pants	$28.50	$5.00
jeans	$17.50	$5.00
shirts	$17.50	$2.00
blouses	$23.50	$3.00
socks	$3.50	$1.00
jackets	$44.50	$5.00

Practice *(continued)*

E. Read the ad. (Lesson 5)

F. Write the information from the ad. (Lesson 5)

Evaluation

15–20 mins.

Go around the room and check on students' progress. Help individuals when needed. If you see consistent errors among several students, interrupt the class and give a mini lesson or review to help students feel comfortable with the concept.

BEST PRACTICE

Learner Log

Learner logs function to help students in many different ways.

1. They serve as part of the review process.
2. They help students to gain confidence and document what they have learned. In this way, students see that they are progressing and want to move forward in learning.
3. They provide students with a tool that they can use over and over to check and recheck their understanding. In this way, students become independent learners.

INSTRUCTOR'S NOTES

WORKPLACE CONNECTION

Combine ideas and information; Make decisions; Exercise leadership roles; Manage time; Complete tasks as assigned; Interact appropriately with team members; Collect and gather information; Interpret and communicate information; Apply technology

STANDARDS CORRELATIONS

CCRS: SL1, SL2

CASAS: 1.3.9, 4.8.1

***SCANS:* Basic Skills** Reading, writing, listening, speaking

Resources Allocate time, allocate money, allocate materials and facility resources, allocate human resources

Information Acquire and evaluate information, organize and maintain information, interpret and communicate information, use computers to process information

Interpersonal Participate as a member of a team, teach others, serve clients and customers, exercise leadership, negotiate to arrive at a decision, work with cultural diversity

Systems Understand systems, monitor and correct performance, improve and design systems

Thinking Skills Think creatively, make decisions, solve problems, see things in the mind's eye

Personal Qualities Responsibility, sociability, self-management

***EFF:* Communication** Read with understanding, convey ideas in writing, speak so others can understand, listen actively, observe critically

Decision Making Solve problems and make decisions, plan

Interpersonal Cooperate with others, advocate and influence, resolve conflict and negotiate, guide others

Lifelong Learning Take responsibility for learning, reflect and evaluate

Introduction

5 mins.

In this project, students will work in teams to create a clothing store. They will use the vocabulary from the unit. They may choose to use Worksheets 8 and 9 from the Multilevel Worksheets.

Stage 1

15–20 mins.

Form a team with four or five students.

Set the scene and form teams of four or five. Show students examples of the project if you have one.

Help students to assign positions by asking the leaders to all stand. On the spot, students will have to choose who will be the leader of their group. Review the responsibility of a leader and ask students to write the name of their leader in their books. Do the same with all positions.

Stage 2

40–50 mins.

Make an ad.

The team creates an advertisement. You may bring in magazines for teams to cut up and use in their ads. Another approach would be to have students find pictures on the Internet and use them. Yet another approach would be to have students draw the clothing for their advertisements.

Stage 3

10–15 mins.

Open a store. What is the name? Design the store.

Ask students to create a clothing store and choose a name for it. Try to encourage them to be original and not to use a name of a clothing store they may already know about.

Stage 4

10–30 mins.

Write an inventory list.

Ask students to create the inventory list.

Stage 5

10–30 mins.

Present your store to the class.

Ask groups to present their projects. This can be particularly effective if you videotape the presentations.

BEST PRACTICE

Digital literacy

Projects are a perfect place to allow students opportunities to use other forms of presentations beyond pictures they create. Digital literacy is becoming more necessary as a life skill. Encourage students to create presentations using pictures from the Internet. They might also consider using other digital presentation tools.

TEAM PROJECT Open a clothing store

1. **COLLABORATE** Form a team with four or five students. In your team, you need:

Position	Job description	Student name
Student 1: Team Leader	Check that everyone speaks English. Check that everyone participates.	
Student 2: Writer	Make an inventory list.	
Student 3: Artist	Make an ad for a clothing store.	
Students 4/5: Spokespeople	Prepare a presentation.	

2. Make an ad.

3. Open a store. What is the name? Design the store.

4. Write an inventory list.

5. Present your store to the class.

The grand opening of a new store usually involves cutting a ribbon.

WORKPLACE CONNECTION
Exercise B: Collect and organize information

C. Read about Sarah Marquis.

Sarah Marquis is from Switzerland. She is an explorer who travels around the world *by foot*. In 2014, she was named as one of National Geographic's Adventurers of the Year for her walk from Siberia to Australia. She completed the journey in three years! After each adventure Sarah shares her stories. She walks in places like Siberia, Mongolia, and the Andes mountains in Peru. To explore cold countries like Canada, she has pants, sweaters, and coats. To explore warm countries like Australia, she has t-shirts. No matter where she goes, she always has her most important item of clothing—her shoes!

* *by foot* = to walk

D. IDENTIFY Underline the clothing in the story.

E. Scan the article and write the places Sarah has explored on the map.

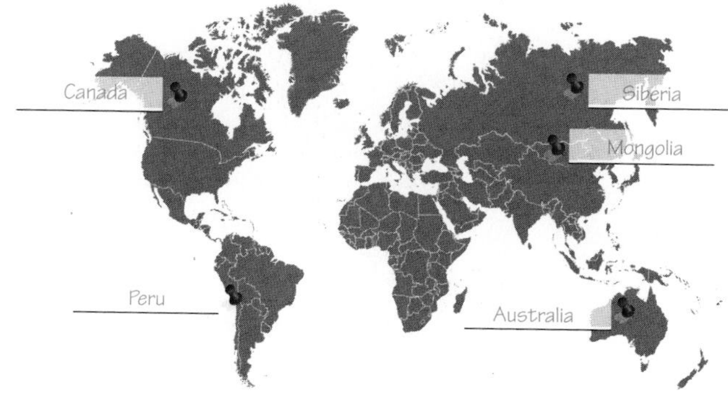

F. Read the article again. Answer the questions.

1. Where is it hot? Australia
2. Where is it cold? Canada

G. APPLY Complete the sentences about you and share with a partner. Answers will vary.

1. I live in ______.
2. It is ______ (cold/warm/hot) most of the time.
3. I wear ______ a lot.
4. My favorite clothes are ______.

B. CLASSIFY Write the clothes people wear when it is hot and cold.

- Remind students that people wear different clothes for hot and cold weather.
- Ask students to think of examples of these different types of clothing.
- Ask students to classify and complete the chart.

C. Read about Sarah Marquis.

Ask students to read the passage to learn more about Sarah Marquis. Ask students if their predictions about Sarah were correct.

D. IDENTIFY Underline the clothing in the story.

Ask students to underline the items of clothing in the story.

E. Scan the article and write the places Sarah has explored on the map.

Ask students to write the places Sarah has explored on the map. Have them refer back to the article to complete the activity.

F. Read the article again. Answer the questions.

Ask students to read the article again and answer the questions. Then, discuss as a class.

G. APPLY Complete the sentences about you and share with a partner.

Ask students to complete the sentences with information that is true for them. Then, have students share their answers with a partner. Have volunteers share with the class.

READING STRATEGIES

Using Maps

Maps can give students valuable information about a story. Maps can help students do the following:

- visualize unfamiliar places
- activate background knowledge
- build interest in the story
- give a story authenticity
- help students memorize key facts

VIDEO CHALLENGE

About the Photo

This photo shows two *gers* in the Gorkhi-Terelj National Park in Mongolia. The National Park—situated in the northeast of the country—is 37 km from the capital city Ulaanbaatar. *Gers*—also called *yurts*—are traditional homes of Mongolian nomads. *Gers* can be assembled and dissembled and moved from place to place. This is a benefit to this particular type of people as they usually travel with livestock that continually needs to find new grazing patches. *Gers* have everything a family could need and some even have modern fixtures, such as satellite TV. Tourists who visit the Gorkhi-Terelj National Park can stay in one during their stay.

VIDEO CHALLENGE

A Mongolian Family

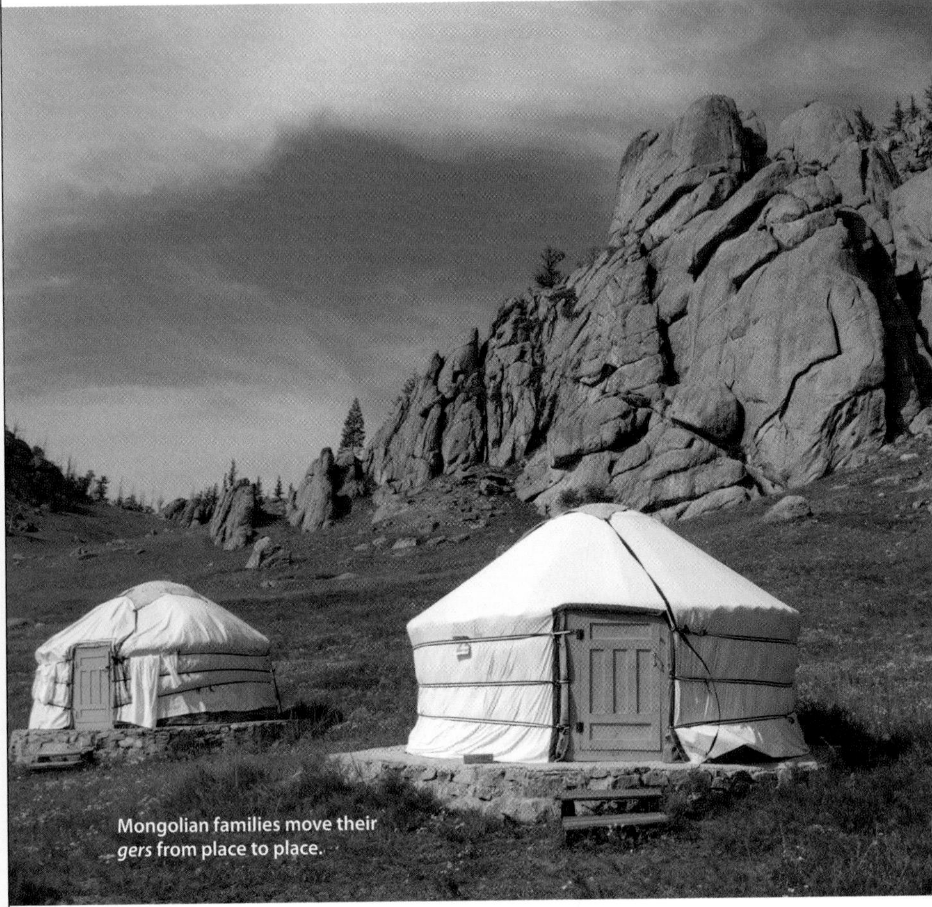
Mongolian families move their *gers* from place to place.

Over the last four units, you have met a lot of new people. You know their names, where they come from, and where they live. You may even know a little bit about their hometowns. Now you will meet a new group of people from Mongolia; however, something is different about these people. They don't always live in the same place.

108 A Mongolian Family

Before You Watch

WORD FOCUS

A *ger* is a large, round tent used as a home by some people in Mongolia.

The *country* is a quiet place where people live outside the city.

A. What do you see in a city? What do you see in the country? Write the words in the table.

taxi	goats	farm	clothing store	farmer
house	cows	horse	bus	apartment

City	Country
taxi	house
clothing store	goats
bus	cows
apartment	farm
	horse
	farmer

B. Complete the table with your own ideas. Answers will vary.

C. How much do you know about country living? Read the sentences and write *T* for true and *F* for false.

1. Families work together to take care of a farm. T
2. Families live together in small apartments. F
3. There are a lot of restaurants in the country. F
4. Cows, goats, and horses live in the country. T
5. It is easy to find a taxi outside the city. F

Before You Watch

- Read the information in the **Word Focus** box. Then, have students look at the picture. Explain that the homes in the picture are *gers* in the *country*.
- Ask students to read the caption under the picture. Then, ask students to brainstorm other examples of homes that people move from place to place like *mobile homes* and *tents*.

A. What do you see in a city? What do you see in the country? Write words in the table.

Read the questions. Then, ask students to complete the table and write the words in the correct columns.

B. Complete the table with your own ideas.

Ask students to complete the tables with anything else they see in the city and the country.

C. How much do you know about country living? Read the sentences and write *T* for true and *F* for false.

Read the question. Then, ask students to read each sentence and answer *T* for true or *F* for false. Have students compare their answers with a partner.

D. You are going to watch a video about Ochkhuu and his family. Read the words and complete the paragraph.

- Discuss the words and their definitions with students. Ask them to complete the paragraph and discuss their answers with a partner.
- Ask individual students to read out their completed paragraphs.

VIDEO CHALLENGE

While You Watch

A. Watch the video. Circle the items you see.

Ask students to watch the video and circle the items they see. Discuss as a class.

B. Watch the video again. Circle the correct clothing.

- Ask students to watch the video again and look at the clothing the people are wearing. Have students make a list of clothing items.
- Play the video again and ask students to read the sentences and circle the clothing that each person wears. Have students check their answers with a partner.

C. Put the events in order. Write the correct number on the line.

Ask students to watch the video again and put the events in order. Discuss what happens in the video as a class.

D. You are going to watch a video about Ochkhuu and his family. Read the words and complete the paragraph.

parents: people who have children
wife: a married woman
daughter: a girl child
mother: a woman who has a child
father: a man who has a child

Ochkhuu is married. He and his ___wife___, Norvoo, have a ___daughter___. Her name is Anuka. She is six years old. Ochkhuu and his family live close to Norvoo's ___parents___ in the country. They all live in large *gers*. Norvoo's ___father___ is a farmer. He is 65 years old. Norvoo's ___mother___ is also 65 years old. Her name is Chantsal.

While You Watch

A. Watch the video. Circle the items you see.

supermarket	(houses)	calendar
school	(cars)	classroom
(ger)	(shops)	clothing store
(TV)	(goats)	(plants)

B. Watch the video again. Circle the correct clothing.

1. Jaya wears a white (hat) / coat on the farm.
2. Anooka is wearing a pink and white (dress) / sweater.
3. Chantsal wears a brown (dress) / shirt.
4. Ochkhuu wears a striped (shirt) / hat in the city.
5. Ochkhuu wears blue (shoes) / pants on the family's farm.

C. Put the events in order. Write the correct number on the line.

___5___ a. Ochkhuu is standing on a city street.
___2___ b. Anuka is sitting on the bed with her family.
___3___ c. Jaya is picking up plants on the farm.
___4___ d. Ochkhuu is cutting plants on the farm.
___1___ e. Ochkhuu is going inside his ger in the city.

110 A Mongolian Family

After You Watch

A. Complete each sentence. Write the correct word on the line.

brother	mother	father	wife	daughter

1. Chantsal is Jaya's _____wife_____.
2. Anuka is Ochkhuu's _____daughter_____.
3. Jaya is Norvoo's _____father_____.
4. Anuka does not have a _____brother_____.
5. Chantsal is Norvoo's _____mother_____.

B. Read the sentences. Circle *T* for true and *F* for false. Correct the false sentences in your notebook.

1. Ochkhuu lives in the city.	(T)	F
2. Mongolian *gers* are in the city and in the country.	(T)	F
3. Anuka is 10 years old.	T	(F)
4. Ulaanbaatar is a city with taxis and many shops.	(T)	F
5. Norvoo and Jaya are 70 years old.	T	(F)

C. Work with a partner. What type of clothing do people wear in the country? Is it different from what people wear in the city? Answers will vary.

EXAMPLE: In the city, men wear suits. In the country, they wear shorts and t-shirts.

Ochkhuu and his daughter, Anuka, watch a video inside a ger.

After You Watch

A. Complete each sentence. Write the correct word on the line.

- Ask students to recall which family members they see in the video including *aunt, uncle, brother, sister,* etc.
- Ask students to complete each sentence with the correct word. Check the answers as a class.

B. Read the sentences. Circle *T* for true and *F* for false. Correct the false sentences in your notebook.

Ask students to read the sentences and circle *T* for true and *F* for false. Have students check their answers with a partner. Then, ask students to make the false sentences true and write them in their notebooks.

C. Work with a partner. What type of clothing do people wear in the country? Is it different from what people wear in the city?

Ask students to discuss with a partner what types of clothing people wear in the country and in the city. Read the example.

VIDEO STRATEGIES

Video repeats

The first viewing introduces students to content. The second and subsequent viewings allow students to watch objectively and focus on specific content.

Our Community

About the Photo

This photo was taken at the Parque de la Reserva (Park of the Reserve) in Lima, Peru. It shows adults and children playing in one of the fountains along the Circuito Mágico del Agua (Magic Water Tour). The park originally opened in 1926, but the Magic Water Tour opened in 2007. The tour holds the world record for being the largest fountain complex. It has 13 fountains—some of which are interactive—that are illuminated at night. The Magic Fountain shoots water 80 meters into the air, the Fountain of Surprises is a 35-meter tunnel of water that people can walk through, and the Fantasia Fountain has a regular laser and picture show.

- Introduce the unit by reading the title, *Our Community*. Then, ask: *What is a community?*
- Ask students to share one interesting fact about their community. Ask students to discuss in small groups and have volunteers share with the class.

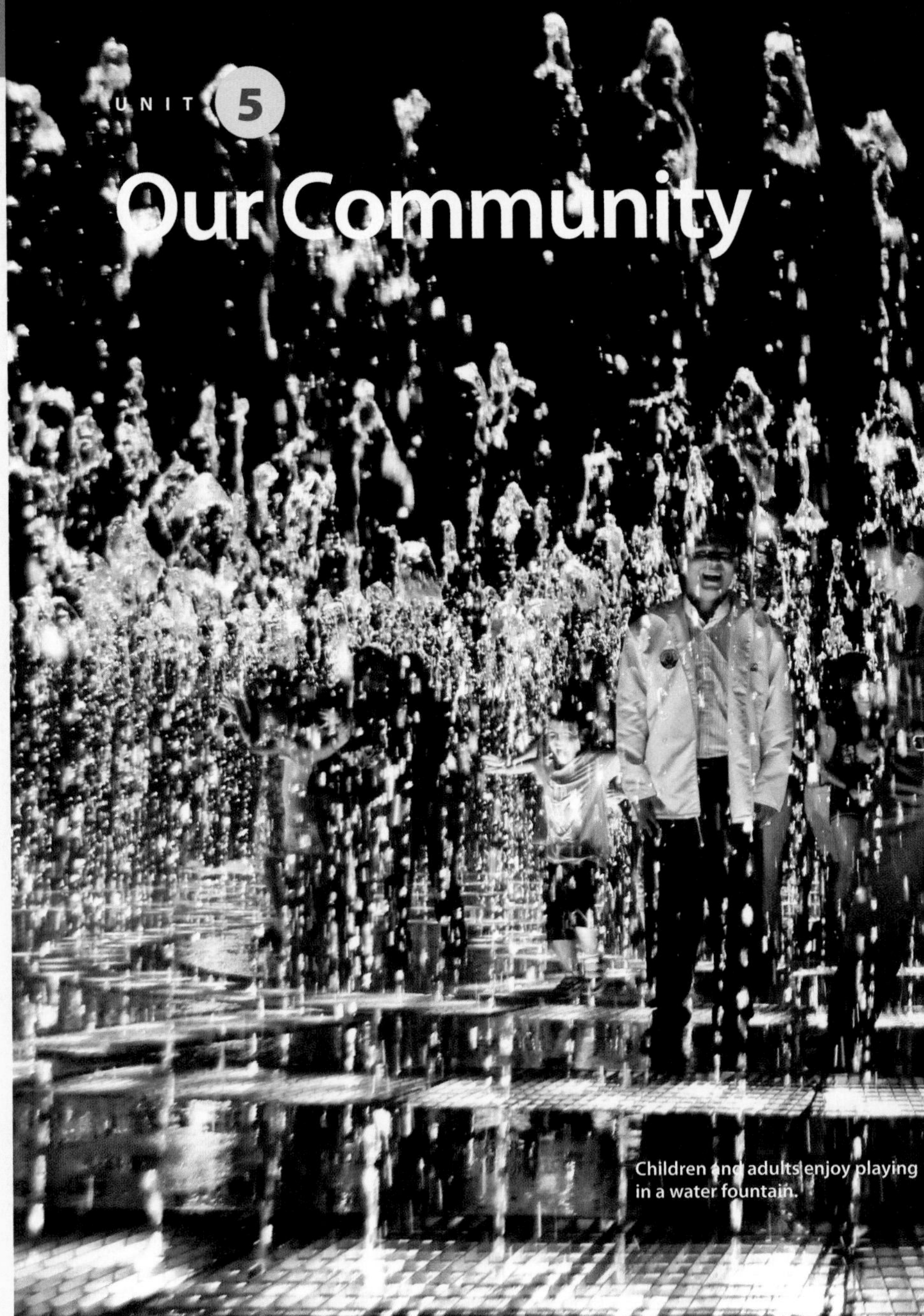

Children and adults enjoy playing in a water fountain.

UNIT OUTCOMES	GRAMMAR	VOCABULARY	EL CIVICS
• Identify and ask about locations • Describe housing • Identify types of transportation • Express personal information • Give and follow directions	• *Yes/No* questions • *on, in* • *a, an* • *come, go, get* • Simple present • The verb *Be* • *Wh-* questions	• Places in the community • Community locations • Housing vocabulary • Transportation nouns • Transportation verbs	The skills students learn in this unit can be applied to the following EL Civics competency areas: • Community resources • Communication

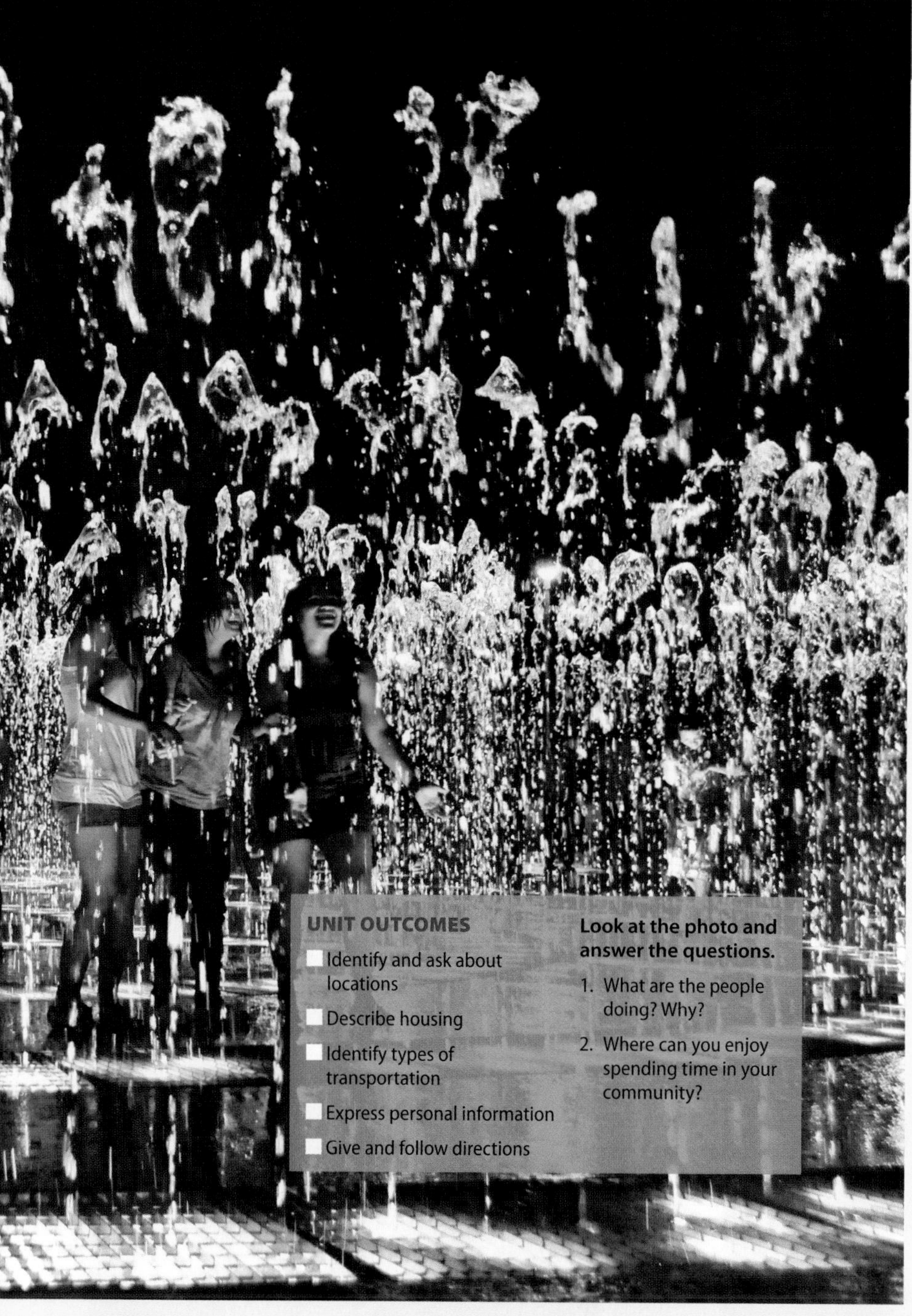
UNIT OUTCOMES
Identify and ask about locations
Describe housing
Identify types of transportation
Express personal information
Give and follow directions
Look at the photo and answer the questions.
1. What are the people doing? Why?
2. Where can you enjoy spending time in your community?

- Ask students to look at the photo and read the caption. Then, ask students to answer the questions. Discuss as a class.
- Go over the unit outcomes. Then, ask discussion questions related to the local community: *Where do you live? Where is a good place to shop or eat? What types of transportation are available in your community?*

Life Skills Link

In this unit, students will learn how to identify resources available to them in their community, how to ask for and give directions to these resources, and how to access them.

Workplace Link

All lessons and units in *Stand Out* include basic communication skills and interpersonal skills important for the workplace. They are not individually identified. Other workplace skills are indicated. They include, collecting and organizing information, making decisions and solving problems, and combining ideas and information.

CASAS	SCANS	CCRS
Lesson 1: 1.3.7, 7.2.3 Lesson 2: 1.4.1, 1.4.2, 1.9.4 Lesson 3: 1.1.3, 2.2.3, 2.2.5, 6.7.2 Lesson 4: 0.1.2, 0.2.4 Lesson 5: 1.1.3, 1.9.1, 1.9.4, 2.2.1, 2.2.2, 2.5.4 Review: 2.2.3, 7.4.1, 7.4.2, 7.4.3 Team Project: 2.2.3, 4.8.1	Many SCANs skills are incorporated in the unit with an emphasis on: • Acquiring and evaluating information • Organizing and maintaining information • Interpreting and communicating information • Basic skills • Creative thinking • Participating as a member of a team	RI1, RI7, SL1, SL2, SL4, L1, L2, L5, RF2, RF3

LESSON 1 Where we live

GOAL ■ Identify and ask about locations

A. Look at the pictures. What types of stores do you see?

1. 

2. 

3. 

4. 

5. 

6. 

B. Listen and point.

CD 2
TR 1

C. Listen and write the number of the conversation.

CD 2
TR 2–5

__1__ supermarket

__4__ pharmacy

__2__ shoe store

__3__ clothing store

AT-A-GLANCE PREP

Goal: Identify and ask about locations
Grammar: *Yes/No* questions and answers, *which*
Pronunciation: Question intonation
Academic Strategy: Focused listening
Vocabulary: Community locations, *which*

Agenda

- Talk about shopping.
- Identify stores.
- Identify places in the community.
- Ask questions about the community.

Resources

Multilevel Worksheet: Lesson 1, Worksheet 1
Workbook: Unit 5, Lesson 1
Audio: CD 2, Tracks 1–6
Heinle Picture Dictionary: Shops and Stores, pages 48–49
Stand Out Basic Assessment CD-ROM with ExamView®

Pacing

■ 1.5 hour classes ■ 2.5 hour classes
■ 3+ hour classes

STANDARDS CORRELATIONS

CCRS: SL2, L1, L2, L5, RF2, RF3
CASAS: 1.3.7, 7.2.3
***SCANS:* Basic Skills** Reading, writing, listening, speaking
Information Acquire and evaluate information, organize and maintain information
***EFF:* Communication** Speak so others can understand, listen actively

Preassessment *(optional)*

Use the Stand Out Basic Assessment CD-ROM ExamView® to create a pretest for Unit 5.

Warm-up and Review 7–10 mins.

Tell students where you shop. List on the board things you need to buy. Include *shoes, food for dinner, a hot dog,* and *medicine*. As a class, list stores where you might buy these items. Use specific store names.

Introduction 7–10 mins.

Draw a map of your school's community. Label cross streets. Ask students to point to locations mentioned in the warm-up. State the goal: *Today, we will identify and ask about locations.*

Presentation 1 30–45 mins.

A. Look at the pictures. What types of stores do you see?

Ask students to look at the pictures. Tell them that these are all stores. Then ask: *What types of stores do you see?*

B. Listen and point.

Play the recording. Help students identify the types of stores with the stores you listed in the warm-up. Drill students by asking questions such as: *Where do I buy a shirt? Where do I buy food?* There may be more than one answer.

LISTENING SCRIPT

1. *clothing store*
2. *supermarket*
3. *shoe store*
4. *electronics store*
5. *pharmacy*
6. *coffee shop*

Use the new vocabulary in context. Ask students to point to the location.

Practice 1 5–7 mins.

C. Listen and write the number of the conversation.

LISTENING SCRIPT

1. **A:** *We need to go to the store.*
   B: *Why? What do we need?*
   A: *We need lots of things. We need milk, apples, and bread.*
   B: *Then we need to go to the supermarket right away.*
   A: *You said it!*

2. **A:** *My feet hurt.*
   B: *It's those shoes you're wearing.*
   A: *These things are old, but I love them.*
   B: *I think if we were to go to a shoe store, you would feel a lot better.*
   A: *OK, let's go.*

3. **A:** *I need a new dress for the party.*
   B: *What size do you wear?*
   A: *I wear a size 9.*
   B: *I think the clothing store on the corner has a good selection.*
   A: *Really? That's great. Let's go.*

4. **A:** *We need some medicine.*
   B: *Yes, I know. We need to buy some aspirin and cough syrup.*
   A: *Sounds like a good idea. Let's get some bandages, too.*
   B: *OK. Let's go to the pharmacy down the street.*

Evaluation 1 3 mins.

Ask students to report their answers.

Presentation 2

10–15 mins.

Ask students to look at the street scene. Ask them to cover Exercise E so they are not tempted to move ahead. Go over the details in the scene.

D. Listen and point to the signs.

LISTENING SCRIPT

1. *Find the hotel.*
2. *Find the restaurant.*
3. *Find the fast-food restaurant.*
4. *Find the clothing store.*
5. *Find the shoe store.*
6. *Find the pharmacy.*
7. *Find the electronics store.*
8. *Find the bus stop.*

For shorter classes, have students do Exercise E for homework.

BEST PRACTICE

Art vs. Photographs

In *Stand Out*, we sometimes choose art, especially at lower levels, to give the instructor more control of the vocabulary. The detail in photographs may provide more information than would be helpful at lower levels. Such detail can overwhelm students, especially if some students begin to ask about each item, detracting from the presentation.

Practice 2

15–20 mins. 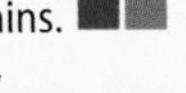

Ask students to drill each other on vocabulary. Student A says a location and Student B points to it in the picture.

E. CLASSIFY Write the places in the table.

Ask students to write and categorize. Students may do this in pairs. Don't prepare students by giving them instructions for this activity. Allow them to figure out what to do.

BEST PRACTICE

Receptive vs. Productive vocabulary

The vocabulary in each lesson is limited to essential words; however, each class is unique and vocabulary needed may vary. A lot of vocabulary may overwhelm students, especially if they are using picture dictionaries. Therefore, it is important to help students know what words they are responsible for. Make sure they are aware of the vocabulary lists in the appendix (pages 212–213). Students will also take more responsibility for their learning if you have regular spelling or vocabulary tests.

Evaluation 2

5–7 mins.

Check students' book work by going over the answers as a class. Reproduce the table on the board and ask students to come up and complete it. Add more items to the list if students come up with places that are not in the picture.

F. What other places can you think of in your community? Talk to your partner.

Have students work in pairs. Ask them to look at Exercise E. Then, ask students to think of other types of places in their community. Discuss with partners and then as a class.

BEST PRACTICE

Preparation for practice and critical thinking

Students at all levels need to begin to think critically and make decisions about what they should be doing in a given activity. One important principle in the presentation stage of a lesson is to prepare students for practice. Occasionally, it is beneficial to allow students the opportunity to think through an activity and discover for themselves what to do. Exercise E is one of those cases. Some students may ask for help. Try to encourage them to take risks and do what makes sense to them.

WORKPLACE CONNECTION
Exercise E: Collect and organize information
Exercise F: Make decisions and solve problems

CD 2
TR 6

D. Listen and point to the signs.

E. CLASSIFY Write the places in the table.

Place to sleep	Places to eat	Places to buy things
hotel	restaurant	clothing store
	fast-food restaurant	shoe store
		pharmacy
		electronics store

F. What other places can you think of in your community? Talk to your partner.

Answers will vary.

G. Read.

Yes/No Questions	
Question	**Answer**
Do you buy clothing at a department store?	Yes, I do. No, I don't.
Do you buy food at a supermarket?	
Do you buy shoes at a shoe store?	

H. Practice the conversations. Use the stores in Exercise A to make new conversations.

Latifa: Chen, do you buy medicine at a pharmacy?
Chen: Yes, I do.
Latifa: Which one?
Chen: Save-A-Lot Pharmacy.

James: Do you work at a shoe store?
Trang: No, I don't. I work at a clothing store.
James: Which one?
Trang: Norma's Fine Clothing.

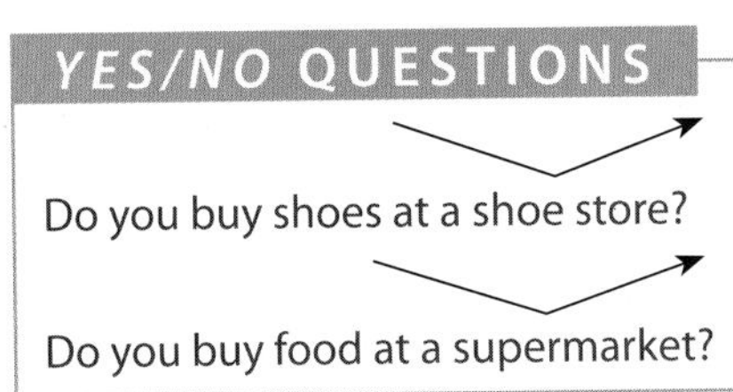
YES/NO QUESTIONS
Do you buy shoes at a shoe store?
Do you buy food at a supermarket?

I. SURVEY Ask classmates where they buy clothes and food. Write. Answers will vary.

Name	Clothes	Food
Peter	Norma's Fine Clothing	El Marco Restaurant

Presentation 3

15–20 mins.

G. Read.

Yes/no questions were introduced in the previous unit. However, students need to review asking and answering these questions with the appropriate intonation. Ask students to see if they can find where they learned this intonation (page 92). In this lesson, we will expand the answer from *no* or *yes* to *No, I don't,* and *Yes, I do.*

In previous lessons, students learned information questions. You may want to help them remember all the information question words they have learned: *how, where, when,* and *what.* As students progress through the book, they will add to the list. Show students how *which* is used when there is a choice between items and how it is followed by a noun. Be careful to avoid spending so much time on the grammar in this lesson that students lose sight of the principal objective.

BEST PRACTICE

Grammar presentations

In the *Stand Out* approach, grammar is introduced many times before students are expected to acquire a structure. At the lower levels, structures are also presented little by little. Students begin to grasp context as more information is added from previous lessons.

It is important that the instructor is mindful of all the information being presented and the objective. The instructor should try to challenge students without overwhelming them. For example, forming questions is an important grammar focus that could have been included in this lesson, but students are not prepared at this level for such a presentation. If the instructor spends time trying to teach the formation of questions at this level, students will become confused and lose confidence.

At this level, it is far better to concentrate on the answers and intonation of the given questions.

Go over the conversations in Exercise H. Show students how they can substitute information from Exercise A. Model the activity with several students.

Practice 3

7–10 mins.

H. Practice the conversations. Use the stores in Exercise A to make new conversations.

Help as needed.

Evaluation 3

5–7 mins.

Ask for volunteers to present the conversation in front of the class.

Application

10–15 mins.

I. SURVEY Ask classmates where they buy clothes and food. Write.

Refer students to *Stand Out Basic Workbook, Unit 5, Lesson 1* for more practice with *yes/no* questions.

Go to the *Activity Bank* online for suggestions on promoting digital literacy and using the Internet to enhance this lesson.

MULTILEVEL WORKSHEET

Lesson 1, Worksheet 1: Locations in the Community

INSTRUCTOR'S NOTES

AT-A-GLANCE **PREP**

Goal: Describe housing
Grammar: *in/on, a/an*
Academic Strategies: Focused listening, test-taking strategies
Vocabulary: housing words, *avenue, park, bedroom, rent*

Agenda

- Review stores and make a list.
- Read a map.
- Read a classified ad.
- Learn about different types of housing.

Resources

Multilevel Worksheet: Lesson 2, Worksheet 1
Workbook: Unit 5, Lesson 2
Audio: CD 2, Tracks 7–9
Heinle Picture Dictionary: Types of Homes, pages 62–63

Pacing

■ 1.5 hour classes ■ 2.5 hour classes
■ 3+ hour classes

STANDARDS CORRELATIONS

CCRS: RI1, SL1, SL2, SL4, L1,L2, L3
CASAS: 1.4.1, 1.4.2, 1.9.4
SCANS: **Basic Skills** Reading, writing, listening, speaking
Information Acquire and evaluate information, organize and maintain information
Interpersonal Participate as a member of a team, teach others
EFF: **Communication** Read with understanding, convey ideas in writing, speak so others can understand, listen actively, observe critically
Interpersonal Cooperate with others

Warm-up and Review 10–12 mins.

Ask groups to list all the places they buy from. Then, ask groups to report to the class.

Introduction 7–10 mins.

Ask individuals where they live. Prompt students to ask you. Respond: *I live in a house/condominium/apartment in* ____ (your city). State the goal: *Today, we will learn how to describe housing.*

Presentation 1 30–40 mins.

Write *apartment, house,* and *mobile home* on the board. Help students understand through pictures what each type of home is like. Ask a few students if they live in a house or an apartment. If students live in condominiums or other kinds of housing, write these on the board.

Write *in* and *on* on the board. Remind students that they are pronounced differently. Help students understand that *in* would mean they live inside a building while *on* literally means that the building rests on top of the street.

Ask questions and encourage students to use the correct words. Teacher: *Do you live in a house or an apartment?* Student: *I live in a house.*

This is the first time students are introduced to *an*. If they are ready, you may expand this explanation beyond *an* with *apartment*. However, most examples will be out of context, so don't spend too much time on it.

A. Look at the map. Write.

Ask students to look for the house, apartment, and mobile home on the map. Ask questions: *Where are the mobile homes?* (They are on Parker Avenue.) Then, ask students to label the pictures with the correct type of housing. Write questions and answers on the board to check answers as a class.

B. Listen and practice.

Ask students to listen to the conversation. Help them hear the rhythm of the language. Have them say the conversation with you a few times.

> **LISTENING SCRIPT** CD 2 TR 7
> *The listening script matches the conversation in Exercise B.*

Practice 1 7–10 mins.

Do a Corners activity. The corners represent *apartment, house, mobile home,* and *other types of housing*. Have students go to corners according to their housing. Ask students to practice the conversation from Exercise B in their corner and answer with their own personal information.

Evaluation 1 3–7 mins.

Ask for volunteers from each group to present the conversation in front of the class.

LESSON 2 Where do you live?

GOAL ■ Describe housing

A. Look at the map. Write.

a house	a mobile home	an apartment

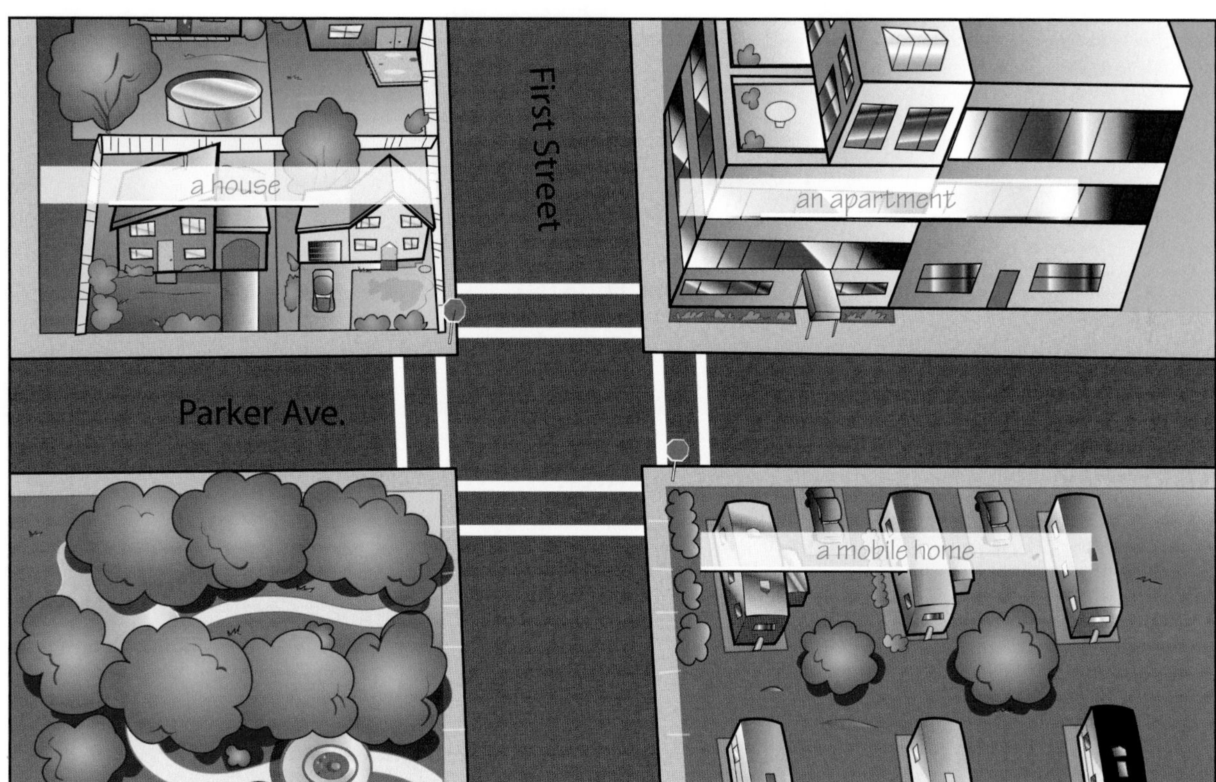

ON / IN

I live **on** First Street. / I live **on** Parker Avenue.

I live **in** a house. / I live **in** an apartment.

B. Listen and practice.

CD 2 TR 7

Student A: Where do you live?

Student B: I live on First Street.

Student A: Do you live in a house or an apartment?

Student B: I live in a house.

C. Read.

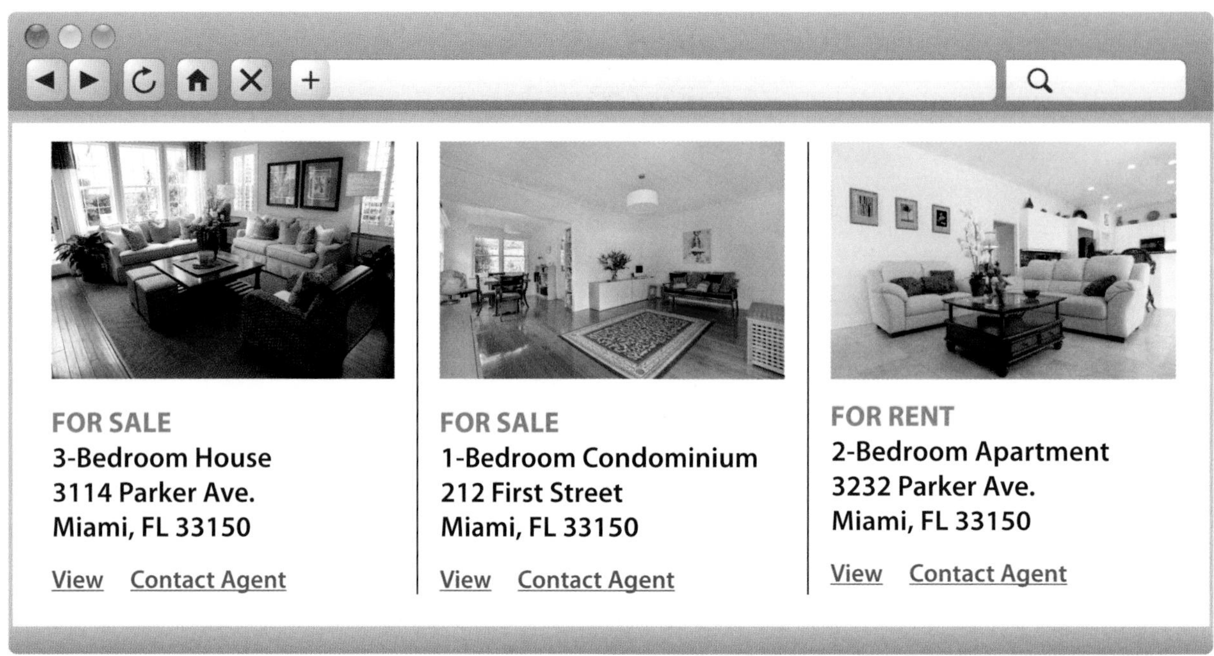

FOR SALE
3-Bedroom House
3114 Parker Ave.
Miami, FL 33150
View Contact Agent
FOR SALE
1-Bedroom Condominium
212 First Street
Miami, FL 33150
View Contact Agent
FOR RENT
2-Bedroom Apartment
3232 Parker Ave.
Miami, FL 33150
View Contact Agent

D. COMPARE Check (✓) the correct answer.

1. Which home is at 3114 Parker Ave.?
   - ☑ the house
   - ☐ the apartment
   - ☐ the condo

2. Which home has only one bedroom?
   - ☐ the apartment
   - ☐ the house
   - ☑ the condominium

3. Which home is for sale?
   - ☐ the apartment
   - ☐ the condominium
   - ☑ the house and the condo

4. Which home is for rent?
   - ☑ the apartment
   - ☐ the house
   - ☐ the house and the apartment

E. Listen and write.

CD 2 TR 8

a house	an apartment	a mobile home

1. a house
2. a mobile home
3. an apartment

Presentation 2

15–20 mins.

C. Read.

Help students with new vocabulary and prepare them for the practice in Exercise D by asking familiar questions about ads. Then, ask students how many bedrooms their home has. Also, be sure you have added *condominium* to the vocabulary for this lesson if students didn't come up with it earlier.

Prepare students for a focused listening activity in Exercise E.

Practice 2

7–10 mins.

D. COMPARE Check (✓) the correct answer.

Ask students to take five minutes and answer the questions on their own without help from other students. After five minutes, go over the answers and check students' work. Walk students through each question and help them find the answers in the classified ads.

E. Listen and write.

Play the recording without pausing it, repeating it in its entirety if necessary.

LISTENING SCRIPT

CD 2
TR 8

1. *I think that you will be very happy with our special this week. This is a fine three-bedroom house with new floors in a beautiful neighborhood. Please come and see it. It's on Parker Street.*
2. *My family and I live in a three-bedroom home in the city. It is on a big lot. We enjoy our mobile home. We have many friends who live in the park.*
3. *There is a great rental on Parker Avenue. I think it is under $1,000 a month. It is a two-bedroom apartment and there is a community pool.*

Evaluation 2

5–7 mins.

Go over the answers students have written in their books.

INSTRUCTOR'S NOTES

Presentation 3

15–20 mins.

F. Listen and read.

Have students listen one time with their books closed or with the information below the pictures covered. Then, ask students to uncover the information and read along as they listen to the recording a second time.

> LISTENING SCRIPT
>
> CD 2 TR 9
>
> *The listening script matches the statements in Exercise F.*

Review the simple present tense. Remind students to use *does* + *live* when asking a question about each person and *lives* in the response. You might ask: *Where does Chen live?* The response should be: *He lives in a house, He lives on First Street,* or *He lives in Alpine City.* Write each answer on the board and show how students can respond.

Do a drill where you ask a student the questions. The student answers and then asks another student. Continue with this drill until all students have responded. You might prompt students to talk about different people on the page. If you want students to respond differently, point to one of the examples on the board.

G. Practice the conversation.

Go over the conversation with students and help them with intonation and rhythm. Ask students to practice in pairs. Make sure students understand every word in the conversation.

For shorter classes, ask students to do Exercise H for homework.

Practice 3

5 mins.

H. Write a conversation. Change the underlined words in the conversation in Exercise G.

This conversation may be very similar to the conversation in Exercise G. Make sure students know to put the information about Natalia into the conversation.

Evaluation 3

3–5 mins.

Ask volunteers to present their conversations in front of the class.

Application

5–7 mins.

I. CREATE On a separate piece of paper, write and practice a conversation about you and a partner.

Show students how they can use previous dialogs for models.

Refer students to *Stand Out Basic Workbook, Unit 5, Lesson 2* for more practice with *on* and *in* and the simple present.

Go to the *Activity Bank* online for suggestions on promoting digital literacy and using the Internet to enhance this lesson.

> MULTILEVEL WORKSHEET
>
> Lesson 2, Worksheet 1: Housing

> BEST PRACTICE
>
> Instructors drill students in order to help them learn vocabulary and produce the language. Drilling is important for this purpose especially at the lower levels, but drilling alone does not create fluency. Students should practice true communication where answers become more spontaneous after they are comfortable producing the sounds or forming grammar structures.

CD 2 TR 9

F. Listen and read.

1. I'm Chen.
   I'm from China.
   I live in a house.
   I live on First Street
   in Alpine City.

2. I'm Latifa.
   I'm from Saudi Arabia.
   I live in an apartment.
   I live in Casper Town
   on Parker Avenue.

3. I'm Natalia.
   I'm from Guatemala.
   I live in a condominium
   in Alpine City on
   First Street.

G. Practice the conversation.

Chen: Hi, I'm Chen.
Latifa: Nice to meet you, Chen. I'm Latifa.
Chen: Where do you live?
Latifa: I live in Casper Town.
Chen: Do you live in an apartment, a condominium, or a house?
Latifa: I live in an apartment.

H. Write a conversation. Change the underlined words in the conversation in Exercise G. Answers will vary.

Latifa: Hi, I'm Latifa.
Natalia: Nice to meet you, Latifa. I'm Natalia.
Latifa: ______
Natalia: ______
Latifa: ______
Natalia: ______

I. CREATE On a separate piece of paper, write and practice a conversation about you and a partner. Answers will vary.

LESSON 3 I take the bus

GOAL ■ Identify types of transportation

~~car~~	bicycle	taxi	train	bus

A. Write the words.

car

train

bus

bicycle

taxi

B. INTERPRET Read the bar graph.

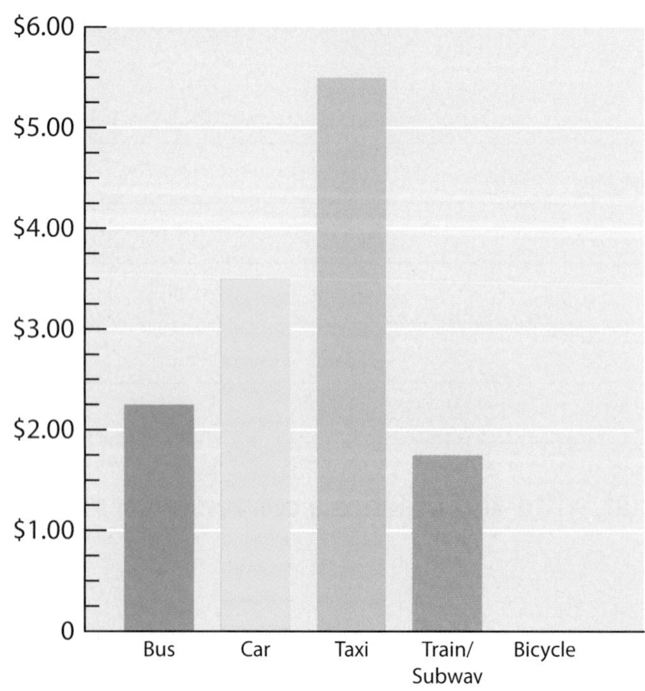

C. Practice the conversation. Use the types of transportation in Exercise A to make new conversations.

Student A: How much is it to go by bus?

Student B: $2.25.

AT-A-GLANCE **PREP**

Goal: Identify types of transportation
Grammar: *come, go,* and *get*
Pronunciation: Information question intonation
Academic Strategies: Focused listening, interpreting graphs
Vocabulary: Types of transportation, *cost, transportation, come, go, drive, take, ride, walk*

Agenda

- Review types of housing.
- Read a map.
- Learn about transportation and calculate cost.
- Talk to other students about their transportation.

Resources

Multilevel Worksheets: Lesson 3, Worksheets 1 and 2
Workbook: Unit 5, Lesson 3
Audio: CD 2, Track 10
Heinle Picture Dictionary: Vehicles and Traffic Signs, pages 118–119; Public Transportation, 128–129

Pacing

- 1.5 hour classes
- 2.5 hour classes
- 3^+ hour classes

STANDARDS CORRELATIONS

CCRS: RI1, RI7, SL2, L1, L2, RF2, RF3
CASAS: 1.1.3, 2.2.3, 2.2.5, 6.7.2
SCANS: **Basic Skills** Reading, writing, arithmetic, listening, speaking
Resources Allocate time, allocate money
Information Acquire and evaluate information, organize and maintain information, interpret and communicate information
Systems Understand systems
Thinking Skills Make decisions, solve problems, see things in the mind's eye
EFF: **Communication** Read with understanding, convey ideas in writing, speak so others can understand, listen actively
Decision Making Use math to solve problems and communicate, solve problems and make decisions, plan

Warm-up and Review

10–15 mins.

Ask students again where they live. Review their conversations from Exercise I on page 119. Have students do the application activity from the previous lesson with different people.

Ask students to have a conversation with four other students and complete a table like the one below.

Name	City	Type of Home

Introduction

5–7 mins.

Tell students about your schedule. Include how you get to work. Describe briefly what transportation you take to school. State the goal: *Today, we will identify types of transportation.*

Presentation 1

20–30 mins.

A. Write the words.

Go over the types of transportation listed in the box. Then, ask students to identify the pictures and write the correct words on the lines.

B. INTERPRET Read the bar graph.

Show students how to read the bar graph. Show them how each white line on the *y* axis is one dollar and each small black line is 25 cents. On the board, write: *How much is it to travel by car?* Substitute other forms of transportation and practice the question. Ask students to follow your lead and ask the questions. *Travel* will be a new word for students, but in context, they should understand it.

Remind students to say *and* between dollars and cents. If you need to, you can refer students to page 95 for review.

BEST PRACTICE

Graphs and critical thinking

Graphs are an excellent way to convey information so that most students with limited vocabulary will understand. Graphs are an especially good strategy when students are at multiple levels of proficiency. The lowest levels can understand the same information as the higher levels.

It is essential that the instructor help students get a feel for how to read and, later, create graphs. Students will use and develop critical thinking skills as they interpret and design graphs. Graphs are especially useful for the visual learner.

See the following page for help with Exercise C.

Practice 1

7–10 mins.

C. Practice the conversation. Use the types of transportation in Exercise A to make new conversations.

Ask students to practice the conversation, substituting the types of transportation in Exercise A.

BEST PRACTICE

Pair work in groups

The instructor cannot possibly be everywhere in the classroom at the same time. Certain students, however, will need special attention. One way to accommodate these students is to group them together in the classroom, as is done in many designated multilevel classes. Then, the instructor can spend extra time with the group that needs more attention.

This strategy will work, but sometimes it will present additional problems:

1. Students in the special group may feel isolated.
2. Students in the larger group may feel neglected.
3. Students in the special group may feel they are not as "good" as the other students.

Another strategy is to use student mentors. Group a stronger student with others who may need additional help.

For example, students will do a drill where Student 1 asks Student 2 a question. Student 2 answers and asks Student 3. Student 3 answers and asks Student 4. Student 4 answers and asks Student 1. This should be modeled several times before students start. Make sure there is one strong student who understands the process and the concepts in each group.

Evaluation 1

7–10 mins.

Observe students doing the activity. Encourage students to continue going around the group until you stop them. If students are getting off task, try asking students to stand when they are asking a question. Then, you can readily see the process at work.

Presentation 2

15–20 mins.

D. Look at the map. What's the distance between Casper Town and Alpine City?

Look at the map with students. Explain the map's scale. *Miles* and other parts of this discussion are mostly receptive vocabulary at this point. Get an idea from students how far they travel to come to school. Pantomime driving and ask: *Who drives to school?*

E. Listen and read.

Go over the dialog with students and help them feel comfortable with the rhythm of the language. Prepare students to do Exercise F.

LISTENING SCRIPT

CD 2 TR 10

The listening script matches the conversation in Exercise E.

Practice 2

7–10 mins.

F. Practice the conversation in Exercise E. Use the phrases below to make new conversations.

Ask students to use the phrases in the box to make new conversations.

D. Look at the map. What's the distance between Casper Town and Alpine City? 5 miles

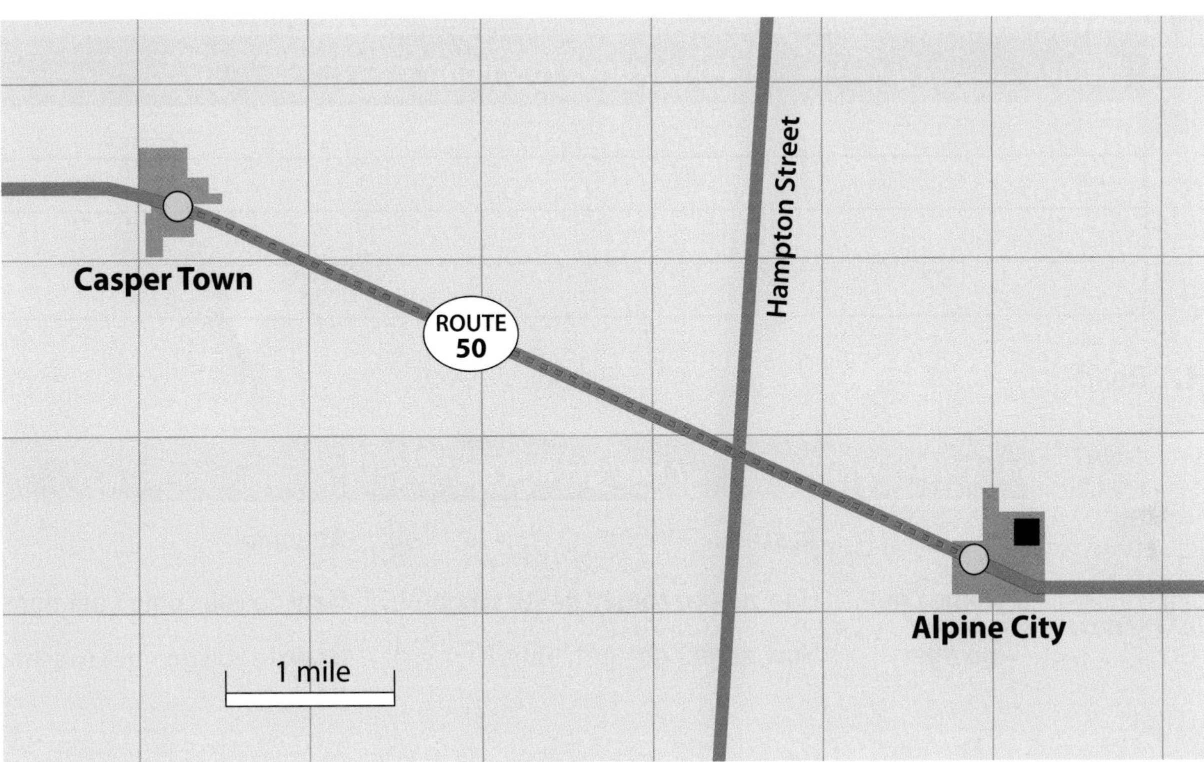

E. Listen and read.

CD 2
TR 10

Chen: Do you drive to school?
Latifa: No, I don't. <u>I take the bus</u>.
Chen: How much is it?
Latifa: It's $3.50.

F. Practice the conversation in Exercise E. Use the phrases below to make new conversations.

drive a car	take a bus
ride a bike	take a train
walk	take a taxi

G. **Complete the table. Ask your classmates.** Answers will vary.

Name	Do you drive to school?

H. **Read.**

come / get and *go / get*			
		At school	At home
How	come / get	How do you **come / get** to school?	How do you **come / get** home?
	go / get	How do you **go / get** home?	How do you **go / get** to school?
When	come / get	**When** do you **come / get** to school?	**When** do you **come / get** home?
	go	**When** do you **go** home?	**When** do you **go** to school?

I. **Practice the conversation. Make new conversations.**

Latifa: How do you get to school?
Natalia: I drive.
Latifa: When do you go home?
Natalia: I go home at 3:00.

J. **SURVEY Ask four classmates.** Answers will vary.

Name	How do you get to school?	When do you go home?
Natalia	drive	3:00

G. Complete the table. Ask your classmates.

Circulate around the classroom and help as needed.

Evaluation 2

3–5 mins.

Take a class poll after students finish the activity. Some students undoubtedly walk or come to school by other means. This is to be expected. Find out what students who don't drive or take the bus use for transportation.

Presentation 3

10–15 mins.

H. Read.

Ask the class to help you make a different pantomime for each vocabulary word in Exercise F. Students can be very creative. Get them started by pantomiming *drive a car* for them. Another way to do this, if there is time, is to play charades. Write each of the phrases on a 3-by-5 index card. Mix the cards up and ask for a volunteer to choose one of them. Ask the volunteer to pantomime the activity and allow the class to guess the phrase.

In this lesson, you will also introduce three new words. Help students understand the difference between *come, go,* and *get*.

Go over the conversation in Exercise I with students. Check for intonation and rhythm. Show them how to substitute and create new conversations using the information on page 120.

Practice 3

7–10 mins.

I. Practice the conversation. Make new conversations.

You might choose to do an alternative pairing activity such as inside/outside circle as described on page 88a, dialog cards on page 76a, or pair work in groups on page 121a.

Evaluation 3

3–7 mins.

Ask for volunteers to present the conversation in front of the class.

Application

10–15 mins.

J. SURVEY Ask four classmates.

Ask students to go around the room and get the information and then ask volunteers to report to the class. Make sure students report using the third-person singular: *Natalia drives to school.*

Refer students to *Stand Out Basic Workbook, Unit 5, Lesson 3* for more practice with *come* and *go* and the simple present.

Go to the *Activity Bank* online for suggestions on promoting digital literacy and using the Internet to enhance this lesson.

MULTILEVEL WORKSHEETS

Lesson 3, Worksheet 1: Transportation Vocabulary

Lesson 3, Worksheet 2: Transportation Prices

INSTRUCTOR'S NOTES

AT-A-GLANCE **PREP**

Goal: Express personal information
Grammar: Simple present
Academic Strategies: Focused listening
Vocabulary: *housing, live, take, walk, drive, ride*

Agenda

- Take a class poll.
- Listen and write about transportation.
- Practice the simple present.
- Write about yourself using the simple present.

Resources

Multilevel Worksheet: Lesson 4, Worksheet 1
Workbook: Unit 5, Lesson 4
Audio: CD 2, Track 11
Heinle Picture Dictionary: Road Trip, pages 122–123

Pacing

- 1.5 hour classes
- 2.5 hour classes
- 3⁺ hour classes

STANDARDS CORRELATIONS

CCRS: RI1, RI7, SL1, SI2, SL4, L1, L2, L5
CASAS: 0.1.2, 0.2.4
***SCANS:* Basic Skills** Reading, writing, listening, speaking
Information Acquire and evaluate information
***EFF:* Communication** Read with understanding, convey ideas in writing, speak so others can understand, listen actively, observe critically

Warm-up and Review
15–20 mins.

Take a class poll. What types of transportation do people take to school? Write the results on the board. Ask students to make a bar graph of the results. If your students are ready and if you have access to computers, you may use spreadsheet software to make graphs.

Introduction
3–5 mins.

Ask students questions about themselves on topics covered thus far. State the goal: *Today, we will express personal information.*

This lesson is primarily review.

BEST PRACTICE

Review

Reviewing and recycling past material are of particular importance at lower levels because students tend to focus so much on new information. On occasion, helping students catch up can be beneficial and give them more confidence. Returning to previously learned material reinforces what students have learned and develops confidence as well.

Presentation 1
15–20 mins.

This presentation is a review of many of the statements students have learned. Review the statements and ask students questions about themselves. If students have trouble, you might want to refer them back to the pages where the concepts were originally taught and ask them to review those pages for homework.

Before introducing Exercise A, ask students to cover Exercise B.

A. Listen and write.

Play the recording and, as a class, listen and write the missing information.

LISTENING SCRIPT

CD 2 TR 11

The listening script matches the statements in Exercise A.

Practice 1
15–20 mins.

B. Write.

Ask students to cover Exercise A. In groups, ask them to see how much they can remember and write. Give them no more than ten minutes. Then, with Exercise A still covered, play the recording again and encourage students to edit their work. Finally, ask students to uncover Exercise A and complete the activity.

Evaluation 1
3–5 mins.

C. COMPARE Look at the information for James and An. Complete the diagram.

LESSON 4 # She takes the train

WORKPLACE CONNECTION
Exercises B and C: Collect and organize information

GOAL Express personal information

A. Listen and write. CD 2 TR 11

1. I'm James.
   I'm from the U.S.
   I live in a house.
   I take the __bus__
   to school.

2. I'm An.
   I'm from Vietnam.
   I live in a house.
   I __ride__ my bike
   to school.

3. I'm Carina.
   I'm from Cuba.
   I live in an
   __apartment__.
   I drive to school.

B. Write.

Name	Country	Housing	Transportation
James	United States	house	bus
An	Vietnam	house	bicycle / bike
Carina	Cuba	apartment	car

C. COMPARE Look at the information for James and An. Complete the diagram.

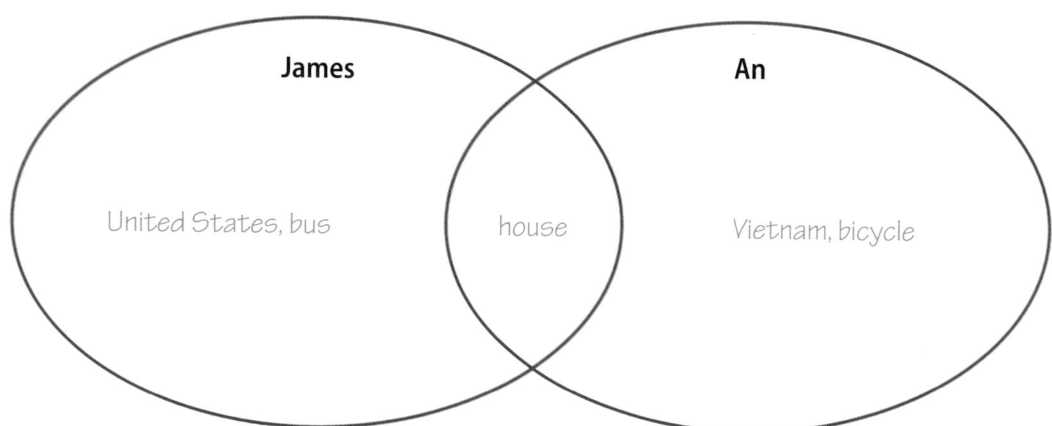

D. Read.

Simple Present		
Subject	**Verb**	**Example sentence**
I, You, We, They	live take ride walk	I **live** in Mexico. We **take** the bus. You **ride** a bicycle. They **walk** to school.
He, She, It	live**s** take**s** ride**s** walk**s**	She **lives** in Mexico. He **takes** the bus. She **rides** a bicycle. She **walks** to school.

E. Write about James, Carina, and An.

1. James **lives** in a house.
2. He takes the bus to school.
3. Carina lives in an apartment.
4. She drives to school.
5. An lives in a house.
6. She rides a bicycle to school.
7. James and An live in a house.

F. Write about Leslie and Briana.

1. Leslie and Briana live in Cambodia.
2. Leslie takes the bus to work every day.
3. Briana drives a car to work.
4. They live in a house.

BEST PRACTICE

Using Venn diagrams and critical thinking

Venn diagrams are a powerful teaching tool and an excellent way to develop critical thinking. The two overlapping circles allow students to list information in three separate categories that show both similarities and differences.

Once students have experience using Venn diagrams, you might continue using them as a tool to make comparisons across multiple lessons. For example, students can compare . . .

* types of housing
* marital status
* weather
* class schedules
* clothing items
* food preferences

Presentation 2

10–15 mins.

D. Read.

Go over the simple present with students. Help them understand that they can use any of the available pronouns in the box on the left to form a sentence. The simple present is being recycled again to reinforce what students have already learned. Help them understand that they will be exposed to it many times before they can say that they have acquired it and that this is a normal part of the process.

Students have previously been introduced to the simple present on pages 19, 52, 73, 75, and 88.

For shorter classes, ask students to do Exercises E and F for homework.

Practice 2

7–10 mins.

E. Write about James, Carina, and An.

Help as needed.

F. Write about Leslie and Briana.

Help as needed.

Evaluation 2

5–7 mins.

Check students' book work.

INSTRUCTOR'S NOTES

Presentation 3

10–15 mins. ■■■

G. Read.

Remind students that the verb *Be* has been introduced in previous lessons. This is the first time in the book that students will have a choice to use the verb *Be* with other verbs.

H. Read the chart.

Show students how the chart is similar to the one they completed on page 123. Ask them questions about the chart. Encourage them to use pronouns.

For shorter classes, ask students to do Exercise I for homework.

Practice 3

10–20 mins. ■

I. Write.

After students have written the correct verbs for the statements, ask them to write the complete sentences in their notebooks.

If you believe your students are ready, you might also give them a dictation of the sentences they have just completed.

Evaluation 3

10 mins. ■

Check students' work.

Application

7–10 mins. ■■■

J. APPLY Answer the questions.

Again, ask students to write the completed sentences in their notebooks.

BEST PRACTICE

Writing sentences in notebooks

Asking students to write sentences in their notebooks reinforces the learning of *syntax* (sentence structure). Students need to practice word order as much as they need to practice grammar forms. Students may translate from their native languages without thinking much about the correct word order. This can be a hard habit to break if not addressed early on.

Having students write classroom exercises in their notebooks allows them to recognize syntax and re-use structures when creating their own sentences. It is important to remember that knowing vocabulary or target grammar forms doesn't mean that students know how to use them in a sentence.

Refer students to *Stand Out Basic Workbook, Unit 5, Lesson 4* for more practice with the simple present.

Go to the *Activity Bank* online for suggestions on promoting digital literacy and using the Internet to enhance this lesson.

MULTILEVEL WORKSHEET

Lesson 4, Worksheet 1: Simple Present

G. Read.

Simple Present: Verb *Be*		
Subject	**Verb *Be***	**Example sentence**
I	am	I **am** An.
He, She, It	is	She **is** from China.
We, You, They	are	They **are** married.

H. Read the chart.

Name	Country	Housing	Transportation to school
James	United States	house	bus
Latifa	Saudi Arabia	apartment	bus

I. Write.

1. James ______is______ from the United States.
2. James ______lives______ in a house.
3. He ______takes______ the bus.
4. Latifa ______is______ from Saudi Arabia.
5. She ______lives______ in an apartment.
6. James and Latifa ______take______ the bus.

J. APPLY Answer the questions. Answers will vary.

1. What's your name?

   My name ____________________.

2. Where are you from?

   I ____________________ from ____________________.

3. Do you live in a house?

   I ____________________ in a(n) ____________________.

4. How do you get to school?

   I ____________________ to school.

LESSON 5 Where's the store?

GOAL ■ Give and follow directions

A. Point to the bank, the post office, and the hospital.

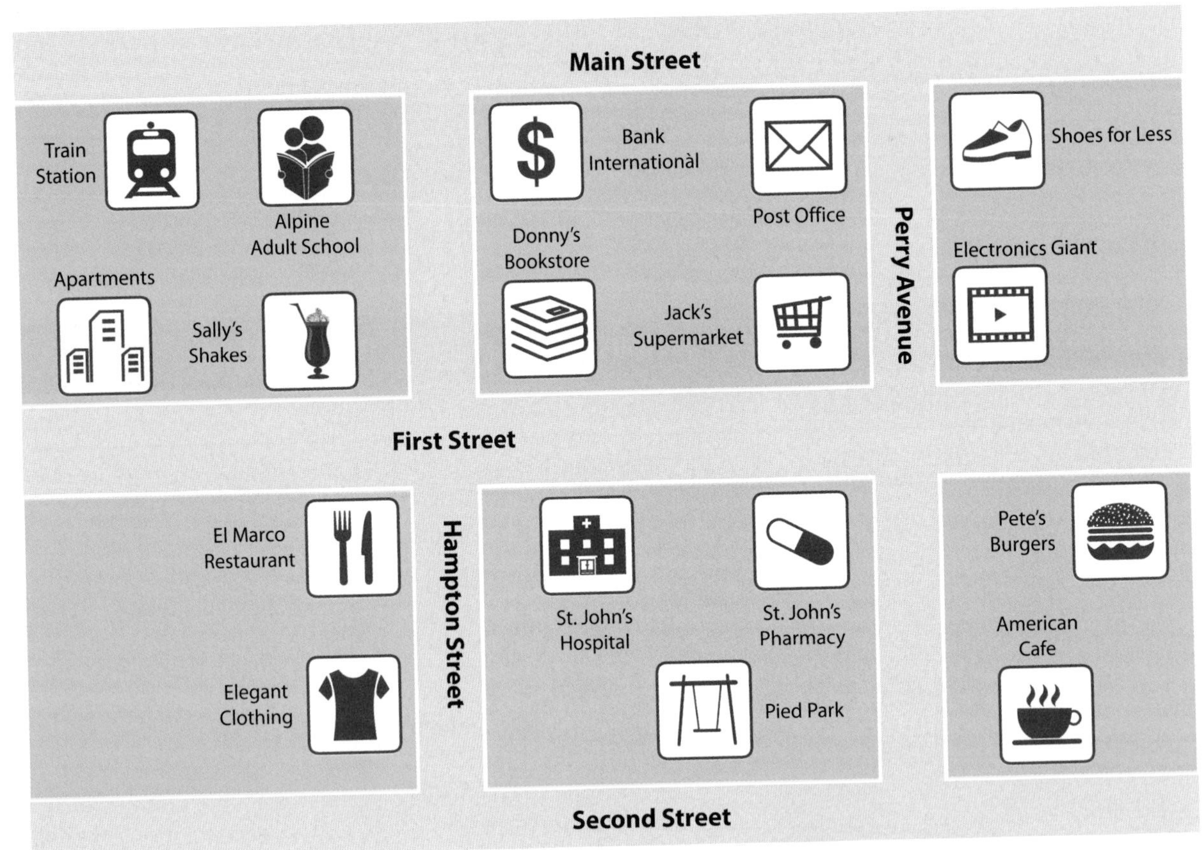

THE

the post office = Alpine City Post Office
the supermarket = Jack's Supermarket

B. Match. Draw a line.

1. Where is the adult school?
2. Where is the electronics store?
3. Where is the bookstore?
4. Where is the post office?

a. It's on Perry Avenue next to Shoes for Less.
b. It's on First Street next to the supermarket.
c. It's on Main Street next to the bank.
d. It's on Hampton Street next to Sally's Shakes.

AT-A-GLANCE **PREP**

Goal: Give and follow directions
Grammar: *the*, imperatives, review prepositions of location
Academic Strategies: Dictation
Vocabulary: *stop, turn, right, left, go straight, bank, post office, hospital*

Agenda

- In groups, make a list.
- Talk about a map.
- Learn and practice giving directions.
- Write directions to a location from school.

Resources

Multilevel Worksheet: Lesson 5, Worksheet 1
Workbook: Unit 5, Lesson 5
Audio: CD 2, Tracks 12–14
Heinle Picture Dictionary: Road Trip, pages 122–123

Pacing

■ 1.5 hour classes ■ 2.5 hour classes
■ 3+ hour classes

STANDARDS CORRELATIONS

CCRS: RI1, RI7, SL2, SL3, SI4, L1, L2, RF2, RF3
CASAS: 1.1.3, 1.9.1, 1.9.4, 2.2.1, 2.2.2, 2.5.4
***SCANS:* Basic Skills** Reading, writing, listening, speaking
Information Acquire and evaluate information
Thinking Skills Think creatively, solve problems, see things in the mind's eye
***EFF:* Communication** Read with understanding, convey ideas in writing, speak so others can understand, listen actively, observe critically

Warm-up and Review 10–15 mins.

In groups, ask students to list all the locations (stores, schools, streets, etc.) they can think of in their community. Ask them to write their lists on the board and go over them briefly. Ask them to point in the direction of where each location is. For example, ask: *Where's the post office?*

Introduction 5 mins.

Remind students what *next to* means. You may use a person who is sitting next to another as an example. You may also want to use some locations students mentioned in the warm-up. For example, say: *The post office is next to...*, allowing them to complete the sentence. State the goal: *Today, we will give and follow directions.*

Presentation 1 15–20 mins.

A. Point to the bank, the post office, and the hospital.

There is a lot of vocabulary in this lesson. Most of the locations are review from Lesson 1 of this unit. Practice using *next to* and ask students questions about the map. Introduce new vocabulary when it is appropriate.

Go over the new vocabulary carefully with students. Then, ask them to point to locations when you identify them. Start by using the names of the places. Then, change to sentences that describe the locations. For example, you might say: *This is a place where people go when they are sick.* Write important words on the board, such as *sick*. Ask more questions and see if students can identify the places by their description. Do the same drill again. This time, identify locations by what they are next to.

Go over the grammar box with students. There are some exceptions to this rule, but following the rule will help students avoid many common errors. Some students might incorrectly say: *I live on the First Street.* Use the definite article *the* with most general words for places, but don't use *the* with proper nouns. Names of streets would not use *the*. There is no need to discuss the exceptions with students at this time.

Practice 1 7–10 mins.

B. Match. Draw a line.

After students complete this activity, have them ask each other the questions in pairs. Students answering should cover Exercise B.

Evaluation 1 5–7 mins.

Ask all students to cover Exercise B and ask individuals or the class the same questions.

Presentation 2

15–25 mins.

C. Listen and repeat.

Play the recording several times.

LISTENING SCRIPT

CD 2
TR 12

The listening script matches the words in the box in Exercise C.

D. Write the correct words.

After going over the road signs and the new vocabulary, ask a student to come to the front of the class. Ask the student to follow the directions you give him or her. The student will walk around the room. Try to do the same thing with other students. Finally, see if the whole class can do it.

E. Use the map in Exercise A to complete the directions. Start on First Street in front of Jack's Supermarket.

Do this activity as a class. Point out that they will use the vocabulary in Exercise C. If you have time, ask students to close their books and do a dictation of the three sentences.

For shorter classes, ask students to do Exercise F for homework.

Practice 2

7–10 mins. 

F. Write directions to the train station.

This activity might be difficult for students. Here they are asked to string more than one sentence together. Have them work in pairs or groups to complete the sentences. During the activity, interrupt them occasionally to remind them to start with capital letters and to end with periods.

Evaluation 2

5–7 mins.

Ask volunteers to write their directions on the board.

BEST PRACTICE

Dictation

There are several ways to do dictation. In higher levels, it is very productive to give dictation where students haven't been exposed to the exact sentences you will be giving. At this level, students don't have a lot of experience so a dictation can be one-word or very short sentences that they have already seen. The objective of this kind of dictation is not to check student ability, but rather to allow students more opportunities to practice what they are learning.

Because this type of dictation is not for evaluative purposes, you may decide in some cases, such as in Exercise F, to read a sentence out loud two or three times and then to ask students to compare what they have written with one another, allowing for a type of peer-editing. Afterwards, read the sentence a final time.

Remember that at the beginning and intermediate levels, students tend to try to write while the instructor is speaking. They need to be taught to listen first, repeat the sentence in their heads, and then write. To help them learn this strategy, you should avoid giving sentence dictation one word at a time.

Finally, some dictation includes words that are intimidating or difficult for students, especially when proper nouns are given. Students tend to focus on these words, which may affect their performance. To avoid this problem, it is wise to write difficult words and names on the board in preparation for the dictation.

CD 2 TR 12

C. Listen and repeat.

stop	go straight	turn right	~~turn left~~

D. Write the correct words.

turn left

go straight

turn right

stop

E. Use the map in Exercise A to complete the directions. Start on First Street in front of Jack's Supermarket.

Give directions to the adult school.

1. Go straight on First Street.
2. Turn right on Hampton Street.

Give directions to the post office.

1. Go straight on First Street.
2. Turn right on Hampton Street.
3. Turn right on Main Street.

F. Write directions to the train station.

Go straight on First Street. Turn right on Hampton Street. Turn left on Main Street.

WORKPLACE CONNECTION

Exercise J: Make decisions and solve problems; Combine ideas and information

G. Listen and read.

CD 2 TR 13

Latifa: Excuse me, where's American Café?

An: It's on Perry Avenue.

Latifa: Can you give me directions?

An: Yes. Go straight on First Street. Turn right on Perry Avenue. It's next to Pete's Burgers.

H. Listen and follow the directions. Number the locations 1–4.

CD 2 TR 14

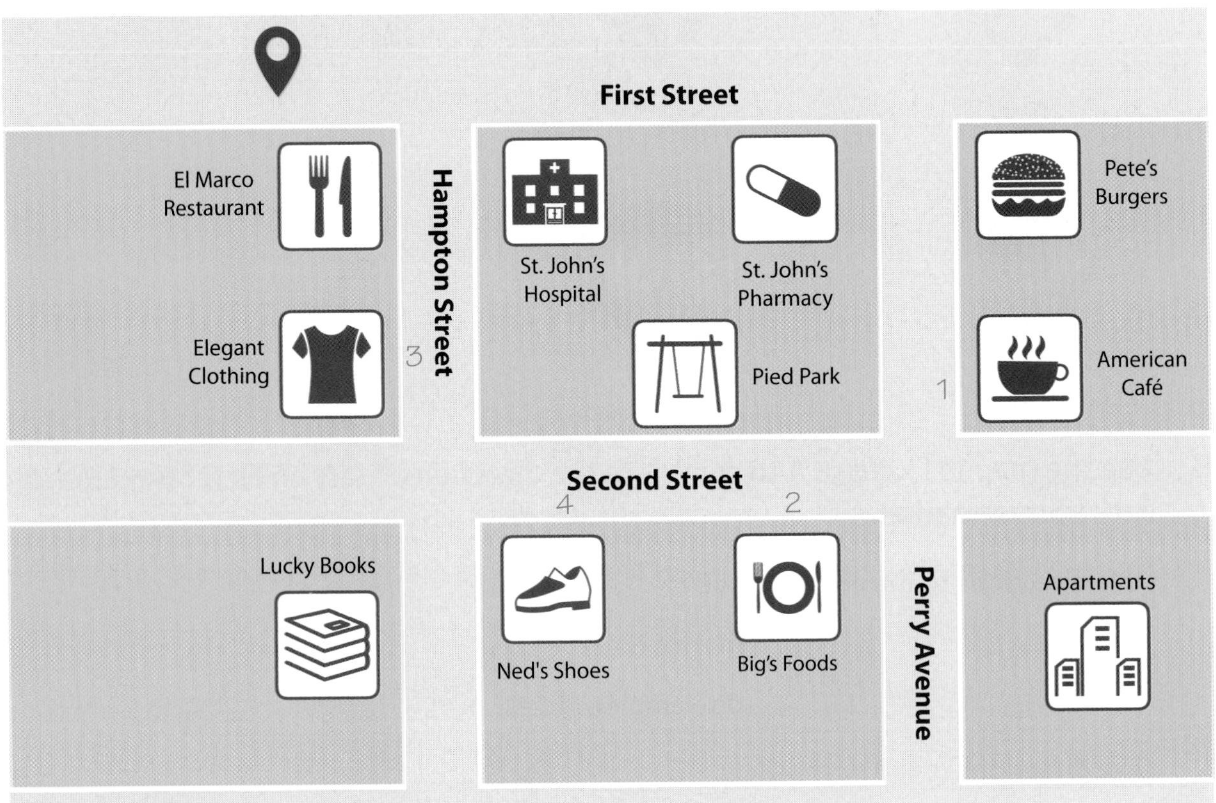

I. Write three stores in your community. Answers will vary.

1. ______________ 2. ______________ 3. ______________

J. CREATE In a group, write directions to a store from your school. Answers will vary.

____

____

____

____

Presentation 3

7–10 mins.

G. Listen and read.

Have students practice the dialog in pairs. Help them to hear the intonation and the rhythm. Ask students to trace the route with their fingers on the map.

> **LISTENING SCRIPT** CD 2 TR 13
>
> *The listening script matches the conversation in Exercise G.*

Practice 3

5–10 mins.

H. Listen and follow the directions. Number the locations 1–4.

The directions on the recording are numbered 1–4. Ask students to write the corresponding number on each final location.

> **LISTENING SCRIPT**  CD 2 TR 14
>
> 1. *Go straight. Turn right on Perry Avenue. It's next to Pete's Burgers.*
> 2. *Turn right on Hampton Street. Turn left on Second Street. It's next to Ned's Shoes.*
> 3. *Turn right on Hampton Street. It's next to El Marco Restaurant.*
> 4. *Go straight. Turn right on Perry Avenue. Turn right on Second Street. It's next to Big's Foods.*

Evaluation 3

5–7 mins.

Go over the answers with students.

Application

20–30 mins.

I. Write three stores in your community.

Help as needed.

J. CREATE In a group, write directions to a store from your school.

Ask students to use the phrases on page 127. You may choose to give students a starting point such as the school itself.

MULTILEVEL WORKSHEET

Lesson 5, Worksheet 1: Following Directions

Refer students to *Stand Out Basic Workbook, Unit 5, Lesson 5* for more practice with imperatives.

Go to the *Activity Bank* online for suggestions on promoting digital literacy and using the Internet to enhance this lesson.

INSTRUCTOR'S NOTES

Do you live around here?

Before You Watch

- Have students work in small groups and share facts about their individual neighborhoods. Write questions on the board to guide discussions:
  1. *What is your address? What are some streets near your home?*
  2. *Is there a shopping center or a hospital? Where are they located?*
  3. *How do you get to school from your house? Which way do you come?*

A. Look at the picture and answer the questions.

- Ask the questions and elicit answers.
- Ask students to plan a route between the school and a well-known destination (library, hospital, park, or bookstore) with a partner.

While You Watch

B. Watch the video and complete the dialog. Use the words in the box.

- Ask students to watch the video and complete the conversation between Naomi and Hector.
- Read the words in the box. Then, play the video at least three times. Use the pause button if necessary.

Check Your Understanding

C. Put the sentences in order to make a conversation.

- Ask students to read the sentences and put them in the correct order.
- Play the video before and after the activity.

BEST PRACTICE

There are many ways to use video in the classroom. Students should rarely watch a video without some kind of task. You might introduce comprehension questions before they watch so they know what they are looking for. Below are a few techniques that you may try for variety beyond the comprehension checks and other ideas already presented in this lesson.

Freeze Frame: Pause the video during viewing and use it like a picture dictionary, identifying and expanding on the vocabulary.

Silent Viewing: Show the video in segments without sound so students can guess at the storyline. This helps them to understand that listening is more than just the words people say.

Prediction Techniques: Show portions of the video and ask students to predict what will come next.

Listening without Viewing: This helps students create their own image of what is happening. After a discussion, allow students to watch the video and the sound together.

Back-to-Back: In pairs, one student faces the video and the other faces away. Play the video without sound and ask the student viewing to report to the student who is facing away what is happening.

Summary Strips: Create strips of sentences that describe the events. Have students watch the video and then put the strips in the correct order, or ask students to predict the story line before watching and then check their answers. The Activity Bank has summary strips for each video in *Stand Out*.

LIFESKILLS

Do you live around here?

Before You Watch

A. Look at the picture and answer the questions.

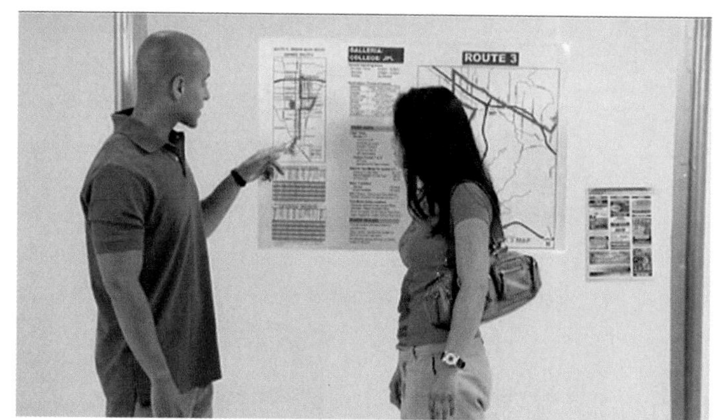

1. Where are Naomi and Hector?
   They are at the bus stop.
2. What is Hector doing?
   He is explaining directions.

While You Watch

B. Watch the video and complete the dialog. Use the words in the box.

bus	town	near	streets	~~live~~	going

Naomi: I (1) ___live___ on Maple Street.

Hector: Maple Street. That's (2) ___near___ Chestnut Street, isn't it?

Naomi: I think so. I'm still learning the names of all the (3) ___streets___. I just moved here.

Mateo: Glendale's a small (4) ___town___. You'll get used to it pretty soon.

Naomi: I hope so. Where are you (5) ___going___?

Hector: I'm taking the (6) ___bus___ to school.

Check Your Understanding

C. Put the sentences in order to make a conversation.

a. __4__ It comes at 11:30.

b. __6__ You're welcome.

c. __2__ Take the Number 2.

d. __1__ Excuse me, how do I get to the mall?

e. __5__ Thank you.

f. __3__ What time does it come?

Review

Learner Log

I can identify and ask about locations.
☐ Yes ☐ No ☐ Maybe

I can identify types of transportation.
☐ Yes ☐ No ☐ Maybe

A. Write the correct letter.

a.

b.

c.

d.

e.

f.

g.

h.

i.
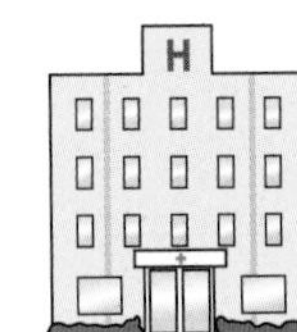

j.

k.

l.

1. d apartments
2. e bank
3. k bus
4. a car
5. i hospital
6. g house
7. f pharmacy
8. b stop sign
9. l supermarket
10. h taxi
11. c train
12. j left turn sign

B. Practice asking and answering the questions with a partner.

1. Where do you live?
2. Where do you buy clothing?
3. Where do you buy shoes?
4. Where do you eat?

READING CHALLENGE

About the Explorer

Sarah Marquis is an adventurer known for her extreme walks. Her walk from Siberia to Australia from 2010 to 2013 earned her the title National Geographic Adventurer of the Year in 2014. Sarah is from northern Switzerland and has been traveling from a young age. In 2000, she walked across the United States in four months and from 2002 to 2003, she walked across Australia. She also spent eight months hiking in the Andes Mountains. Sarah has written books about her adventures in which she explains her journeys and the highs and lows associated with them.

About the Photo

This photo was taken at Machu Picchu in the Andes Mountains of Peru. Machu Picchu is an ancient Incan site that sits almost 8,000 feet above sea level.

- Tell students they are going to read about an explorer. Introduce Sarah Marquis and read the title.
- Ask students what they think the title means. Then, have students read the quote on their own for clues.
- Ask students where they think Sarah Marquis travels. Ask what type of clothing they think Sarah needs to wear. Then, discuss as a class.

A. PREDICT Look at the picture. Answer the questions.

- Ask students to look at the picture and discuss the answers.
- Ask students if they ever wear any of the clothing they see in the picture. *Where and why?*

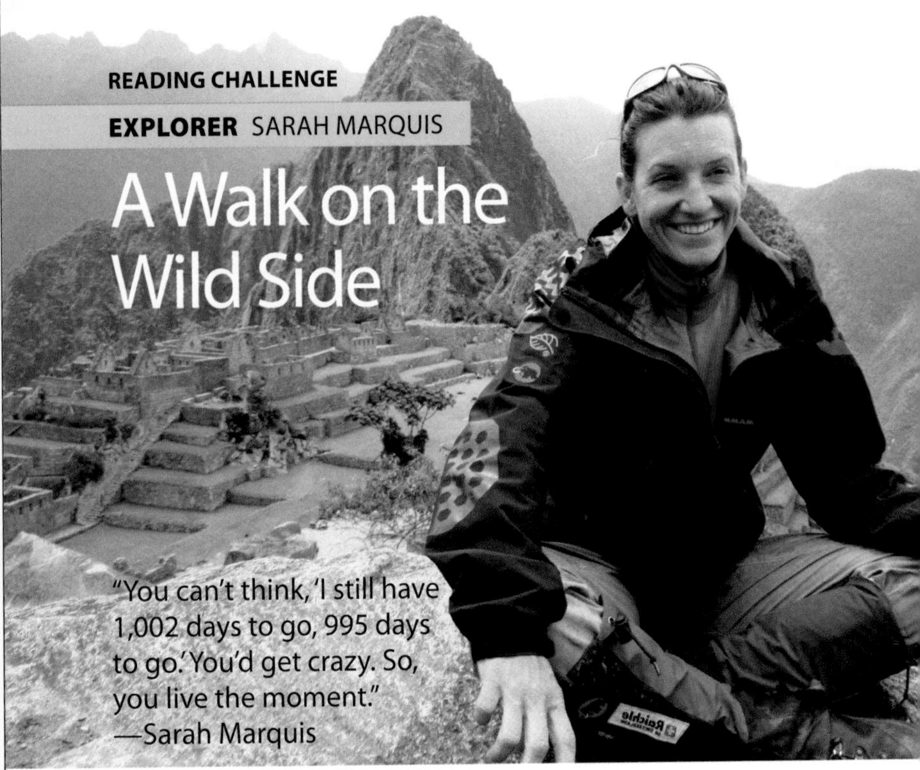

READING CHALLENGE
EXPLORER SARAH MARQUIS
A Walk on the Wild Side
"You can't think, 'I still have 1,002 days to go, 995 days to go.' You'd get crazy. So, you live the moment."
—Sarah Marquis

A. PREDICT Look at the picture. Answer the questions. Answers will vary.

1. Where is Sarah Marquis in the picture? What is she doing?
2. What clothes is she wearing? Why?

B. CLASSIFY Write the clothes people wear when it is hot and cold. Answers will vary.

Hot	Cold

106 Unit 4

CCRS FOR READING

RI1, RI2, SL2, L4

AT-A-GLANCE **PREP**

Goal: All unit objectives
Grammar: All unit grammar
Academic Strategies: Focused listening,reviewing, evaluating, developing study skills
Vocabulary: All unit vocabulary

Agenda

- Discuss unit objectives.
- Complete the review.

Pacing

- 1.5 hour classes
- 2.5 hour classes
- 3+ hour classes

STANDARDS CORRELATIONS

CCRS: RI1, RI7, SL2, SL4, L2, RF3
CASAS: 2.2.3, 7.4.1, 7.4.2, 7.4.3
SCANS: **Basic Skills** Reading, writing, listening, speaking
Information Acquire and evaluate information, organize and maintain information, interpret and communicate information
Thinking Skills See things in the mind's eye
EFF: **Communication** Speak so others can understand
Lifelong Learning Take responsibility for learning, reflect and evaluate

Warm-up and Review

7–10 mins.

With their books closed, ask students to help you make a list on the board of all the vocabulary they can come up with from the unit. Then, have a competition where students in groups look through the unit and write the page numbers for each item on the list. The first group to have the correct page number for each item wins.

Introduction

5 mins.

Write all the goals on the board from Unit 5. Show students the first page of every lesson so they understand that today will be review. Complete the agenda.

Note: Depending on the length of the term, you may decide to have students do Presentation and Practice for homework and then review student work as the warm-up for another class meeting.

Presentation

10–15 mins.

This presentation and practice will cover the first three pages of the review. Quickly go to the first page of each lesson. Discuss the objective of each. Ask simple questions to remind students what they have learned.

Practice

15–20 mins.

A. Write the correct letter. (Lessons 1–5)

B. Practice asking and answering the questions with a partner. (Lesson 1)

BEST PRACTICE

Recycling/Review

The review process and the project that follows are part of the recycling/review process. Students at this level often need to be reintroduced to concepts to solidify what they have learned. Many concepts are learned and forgotten while learning other new concepts. This is because students learn but are not necessarily ready to acquire language concepts.

Therefore, it becomes very important to review and to show students how to review on their own. It is also important to recycle the new concepts in different contexts.

Practice *(continued)*

C. Look at the information about Aki and Adriano. Write and practice a conversation. (Lessons 2 and 4)

D. Write. (Lesson 4)

INSTRUCTOR'S NOTES

Learner Log

I can describe housing.
☐ Yes ☐ No ☐ Maybe

I can express personal information.
☐ Yes ☐ No ☐ Maybe

C. Look at the information about Aki and Adriano. Write and practice a conversation.

Answers will vary.

1. I'm Aki.
   I'm from Japan.
   I live in an apartment.
   I live in New York on Second Street.
   I drive to school.

2. I'm Adriano.
   I'm from Brazil.
   I live in a house.
   I live in New York on East 5th Street.
   I take the subway to school.

Aki: *Hi, Adriano. Where do you live?*

Adriano: ______________________

Aki: ______________________

Adriano: ______________________

Aki: ______________________

Adriano: ______________________

D. Write.

1. Aki ___drives___ to school.
2. Adriano ___takes the subway___ to school.
3. They ___live___ in New York.

Learner Log

I can give and follow directions.

- Yes
- No
- Maybe

E. Read the map.

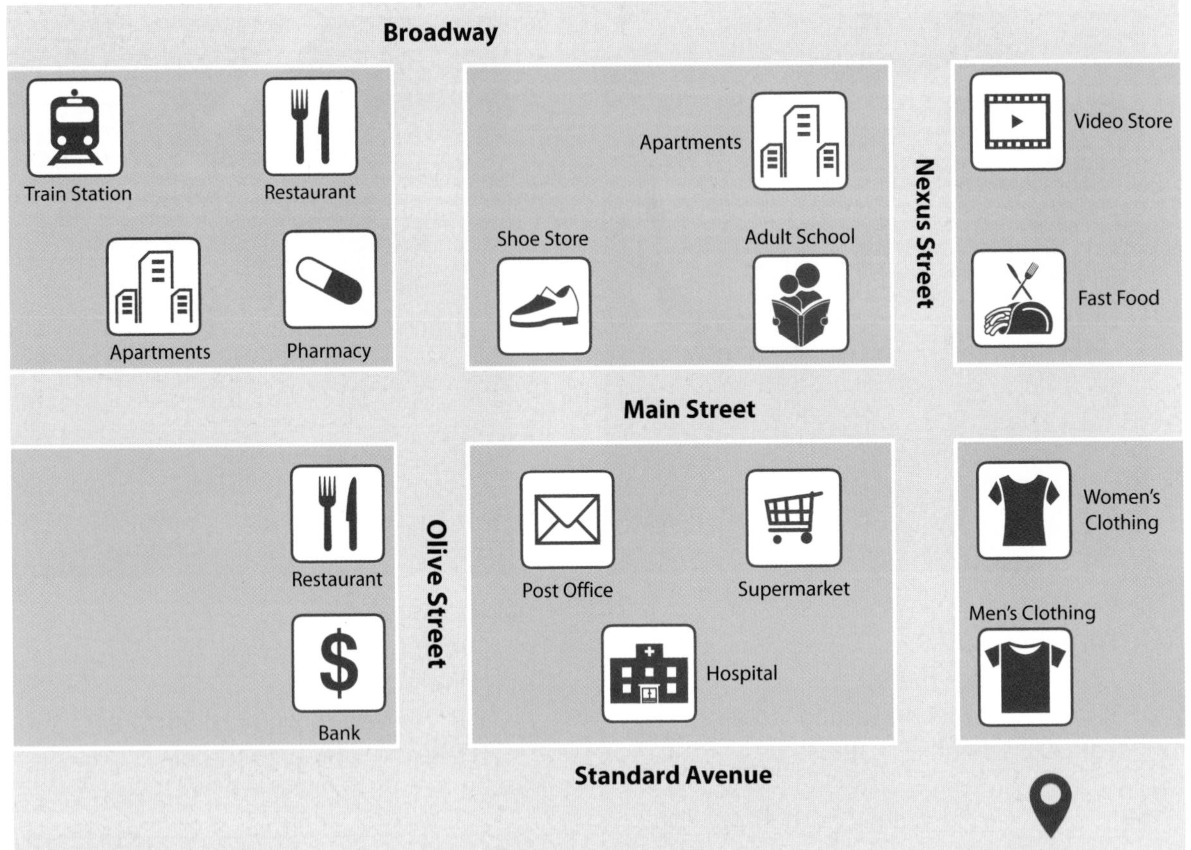

F. Write the place.

Place	Directions
the post office	Turn right on Nexus. Turn left on Main. It's next to the supermarket.
the bank	Go straight. Turn right on Olive Street. It's next to the restaurant.
the shoe store	Go straight. Turn right on Olive Street. Turn right on Main Street. It's next to the adult school.
the train station	Turn right on Nexus. Turn left on Broadway. Go straight. It's next to the restaurant.

Practice *(continued)*

E. Read the map. (Lesson 5)

F. Write the place. (Lesson 5)

Evaluation

15 mins.

Go around the room and check on student progress. Help individuals when needed. If you see consistent errors among several students, interrupt the class and give a mini lesson or review to help students feel comfortable with the concept.

BEST PRACTICE

Learner Log

Learner logs function to help students in many different ways.

1. They serve as part of the review process.
2. They help students to gain confidence and document what they have learned. In this way, students see that they are progressing and want to move forward in learning.
3. They provide students with a tool that they can use over and over to check and recheck their understanding. In this way, students become independent learners.

INSTRUCTOR'S NOTES

WORKPLACE CONNECTION

Combine ideas and information; Make decisions; Exercise leadership roles; Manage time; Complete tasks as assigned; Interact appropriately with team members; Collect and gather information; Interpret and communicate information; Apply technology

STANDARDS CORRELATIONS

CCRS: RI7, SL1, SL2

CASAS: 2.2.3, 4.8.1

***SCANS:* Basic Skills** Reading, writing, listening, speaking

Resources Allocate time, allocate money, allocate materials and facility resources, allocate human resources

Information Acquire and evaluate information, organize and maintain information, interpret and communicate information, use computers to process information

Interpersonal Participate as a member of a team, teach others, serve clients and customers, exercise leadership, negotiate to arrive at a decision, work with cultural diversity

Systems Understand systems, monitor and correct performance, improve and design systems

Thinking Skills Think creatively, make decisions, solve problems, see things in the mind's eye

Personal Qualities Responsibility, sociability, self-management

***EFF:* Communication** Read with understanding, convey ideas in writing, speak so others can understand, listen actively, observe critically

Decision Making Solve problems and make decisions, plan

Interpersonal Cooperate with others, advocate and influence, resolve conflict and negotiate, guide others

Lifelong Learning Take responsibility for learning, reflect and evaluate

Introduction 5 mins.

For this project, tell students they will work in teams to create a map of the community surrounding their school, incorporating the vocabulary from this unit. They may choose to use templates from the Activity Bank to help them.

Stage 1 15–20 mins.

COLLABORATE Form a team with four or five students.

Show students examples of the project, if you have some, or discuss the art on the student book page.

Help students to assign positions by asking the leaders to stand. On the spot, students will have to choose who will be the leader of their group. Review the responsibility of a leader and ask students to write the name of their leader in their books. Do the same with all positions.

Stage 2 10–15 mins.

Make a list of types of transportation in your community.

Ask students to make a list of types of transportation. Ask them to draw pictures of the means of transportation they listed or to use magazine, newspaper, or Internet pictures.

Stage 3 10–30 mins.

Make a map of your community with the school in the middle. Write the names of stores and other places near your school.

Ask students to work together and to be as accurate as possible.

Stage 4 10–30 mins.

Write directions from your school to three places in your community.

Ask students to write out directions to three places in their communities. Ask them to create dialogs that demonstrate in what situations they could be asked to give these directions. This can be part of the group presentation if they decide to use them.

Stage 5 10–30 mins.

Present your project to the class.

Ask groups to present their projects. This can be particularly effective if you videotape the presentations.

BEST PRACTICE

Digital literacy

Projects are a perfect place to allow students opportunities to use other forms of presentations beyond pictures they create. Digital literacy is becoming more necessary as a life skill. Encourage students to create presentations using pictures from the Internet. They might also consider using other digital presentation tools.

TEAM PROJECT Describe your community

1. **COLLABORATE** Form a team with four or five students. In your team, you need:

Position	Job description	Student name
Student 1: Team Leader	Check that everyone speaks English. Check that everyone participates.	
Student 2: Writer	Write directions.	
Student 3: Artist	Make a map.	
Students 4/5: Spokesperson	Prepare a presentation.	

2. Make a list of types of transportation in your community.
3. Make a map of your community with the school in the middle. Write the names of stores and other places near your school.
4. Write directions from your school to three places in your community.
5. Present your project to the class.

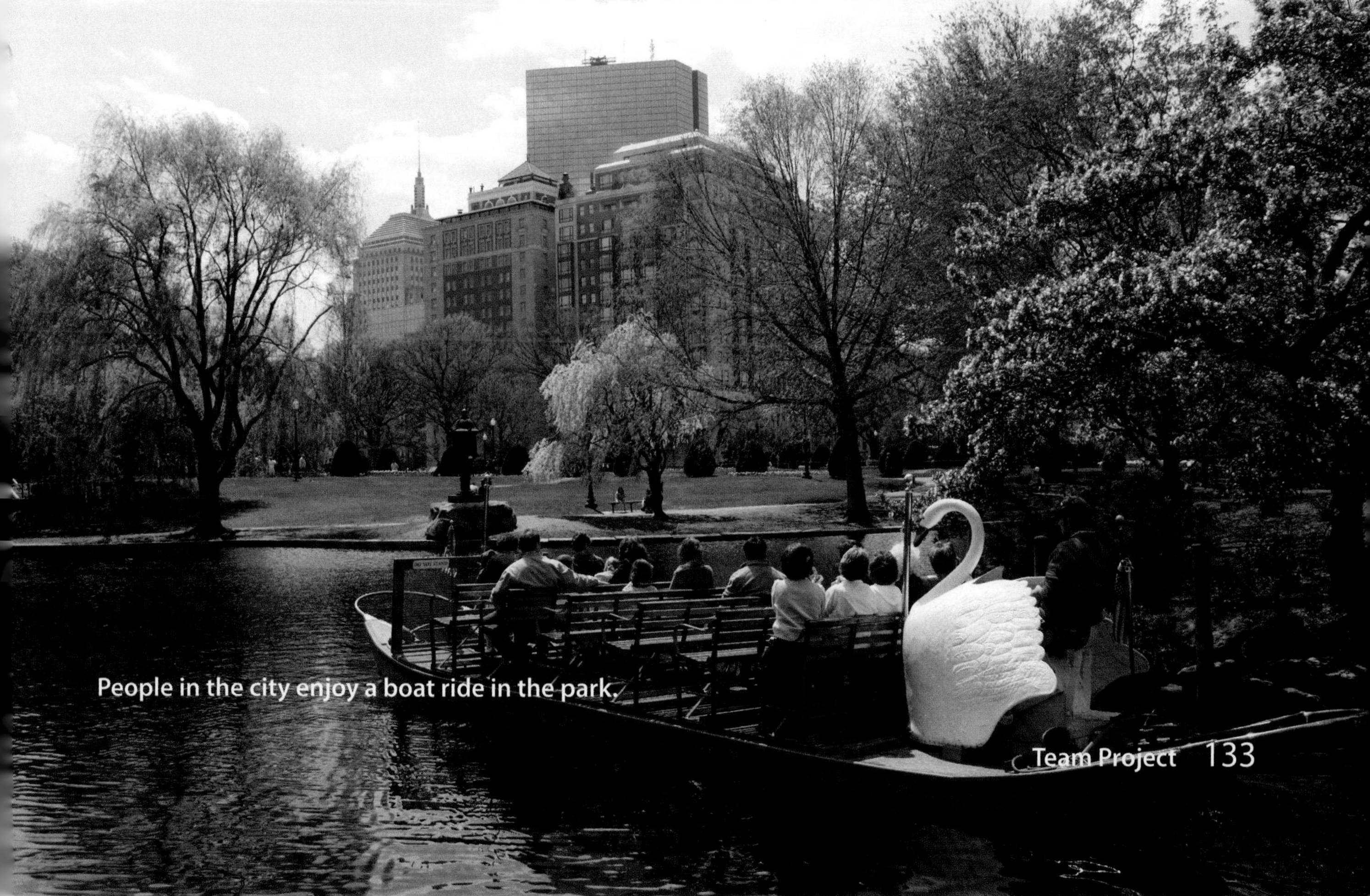

People in the city enjoy a boat ride in the park.

About the Explorer

Jimmy Chin is a professional climber and expedition photographer. As a professional athlete himself, he has photographed and filmed some of the world's most extreme athletes in some of the most dangerous situations. He has climbed Mount Everest numerous times and even skied down from the summit on one occasion. His photographs have appeared in numerous magazines, including *National Geographic Magazine,* and he has won various awards for his cinematography. Jimmy spends a lot of time in Yosemite National Park, where he has documented the climbing culture.

About the Photo

Mikey Schaefer took this photo of Jimmy while they were on assignment in Yosemite National Park, California. Jimmy has spent time documenting the climbing culture in Yosemite and working with professional climbers. In 2014, Tommy Caldwell and Kevin Jorgeson completed the first free-climb ascent of the famous Dawn Wall of El Capitan. During their time spent practicing for the climb, Jimmy joined them to take photos of how they lived on the side of the vertical rock face. Through his photos, he was able to show the world how these elite climbers set up tents on a vertical cliff face and attempted to complete their climb without the use of ropes.

- Introduce the explorer. Tell students they are going to read about an interesting adventurer named Jimmy Chin.
- Read the title and ask students to describe their own commutes to school. Talk about different types of transportation they use.

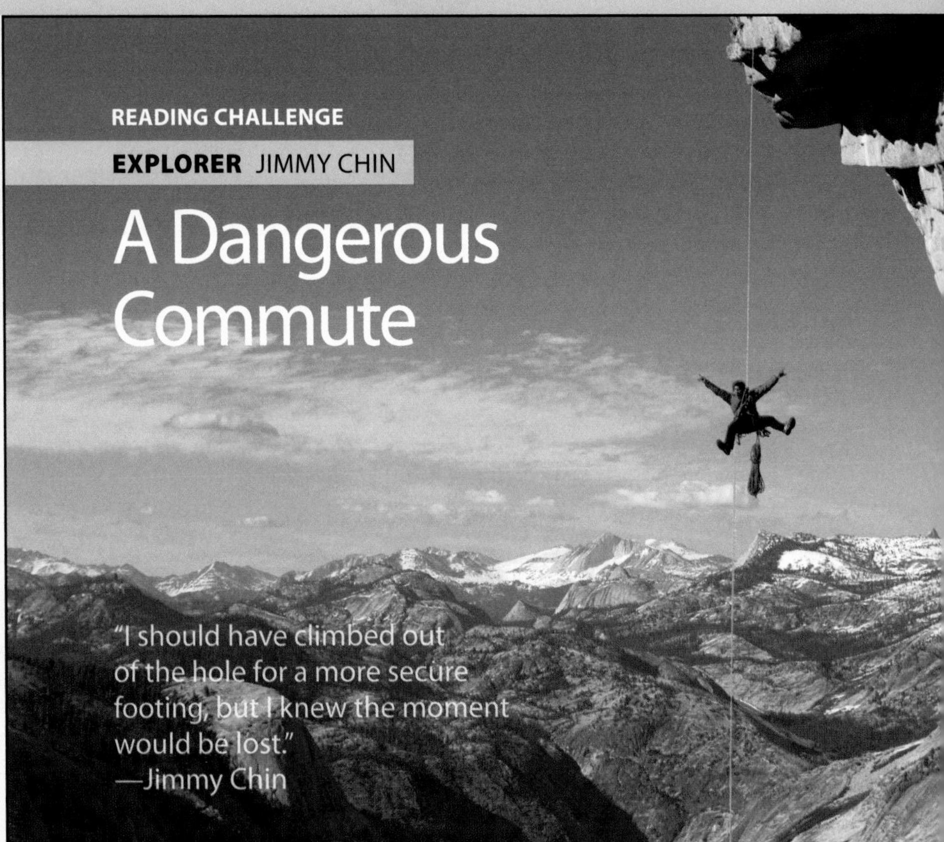

READING CHALLENGE
EXPLORER JIMMY CHIN
A Dangerous Commute
"I should have climbed out of the hole for a more secure footing, but I knew the moment would be lost."
—Jimmy Chin

A. PREDICT Look at the picture and answer the questions. Answers will vary.

1. Where is Jimmy in the picture?
2. What is his job?
3. How do you think he gets to work?

B. BRAINSTORM In a group, make a list of transportation words. Answers will vary.

Type of transportation		Ways to travel	
car	______	drive	______
bicycle	______	walk	______
______	______	______	______

CCRS FOR READING
RI1, RI2, S1, S2, L5

C. Read about Jimmy Chin.

Jimmy Chin is from Mankato, Minnesota. He has a very dangerous job: He's a photographer. But is that a dangerous job? Jimmy takes photos of adventurers in some of the world's most interesting places, like Mount Everest. When Jimmy takes photos of climbers, he doesn't take a bus or a train to work; he doesn't walk to work. He climbs to work!

D. **COMPARE** How does Jimmy get to work? How do you get to school?

Jimmy Chin

Jimmy ___climbs___ to work.

Jimmy doesn't ___take a bus or train___ to work.

Me Answers will vary.

I ______ to work.

I don't ______ to work.

E. **APPLY** Write about you. Answers will vary.

Name	1.
Birthplace	2.
City	3.
Street	4.
Home (apartment / house / mobile home)	5.
Transportation	6.

1. My name is ______.
2. I am from ______.
3. I live in ______.
4. I live on ______.
5. I live in ______.
6. I ______.

F. Tell a group your story. Repeat the sentences in Exercise E.

READING STRATEGIES

Locating Key Words

Tell students that locating key words in a reading passage can provide the correct information to answer important questions. Teachers can use the following approach to practice this strategy:

1. write the questions on the board
2. underline key words in the question
3. have students find and underline these words in the passage
4. ask students to circle the answers

A. PREDICT Look at the picture and answer the questions.

- Ask students to look at the picture and then answer the questions.
- Read the quote and have students look at the picture again. Then, ask them what makes them believe Jimmy Chin's job is dangerous.

B. BRAINSTORM In a group, make a list of transportation words.

Ask groups to think of different types of transportation and ways to travel to complete the table.

C. Read about Jimmy Chin.

- Tell students to read the passage and underline the type(s) of transportation Jimmy uses.
- Ask students to circle interesting facts about Jimmy and his job.
- Read the passage one more time and give information on the different geographical locations.

D. COMPARE How does Jimmy get to work? How do you get to school?

Ask students to compare how Jimmy gets to work with how they get to school.

E. APPLY Write about you.

Ask students to provide information about themselves to complete the table.

F. Tell a group your story. Repeat the sentences in Exercise E.

Have students work in groups to share their information from Exercise E with their classmates.

Healthy Living

About the Photo

Corneliu Cazacu took this photo. It shows people wearing mud masks and bathing in the waters of the Blue Lagoon in Grindavík, Iceland. The Blue Lagoon is a geothermal spa. The water—rich in minerals—is heated naturally by a nearby lava flow and is cooled before entering the lagoon. The minerals give the water its sky blue color and have been known to help people suffering from skin diseases like psoriasis. The Blue Lagoon is a major tourist attraction for visitors to the small country of Iceland where temperatures fall well below freezing in the winter months.

- Introduce the unit. Then, ask students: *What does healthy living mean to you?* Ask students to share their opinions.
- Ask students to look at the photo as you read the caption. Then, have them read and answer the questions.

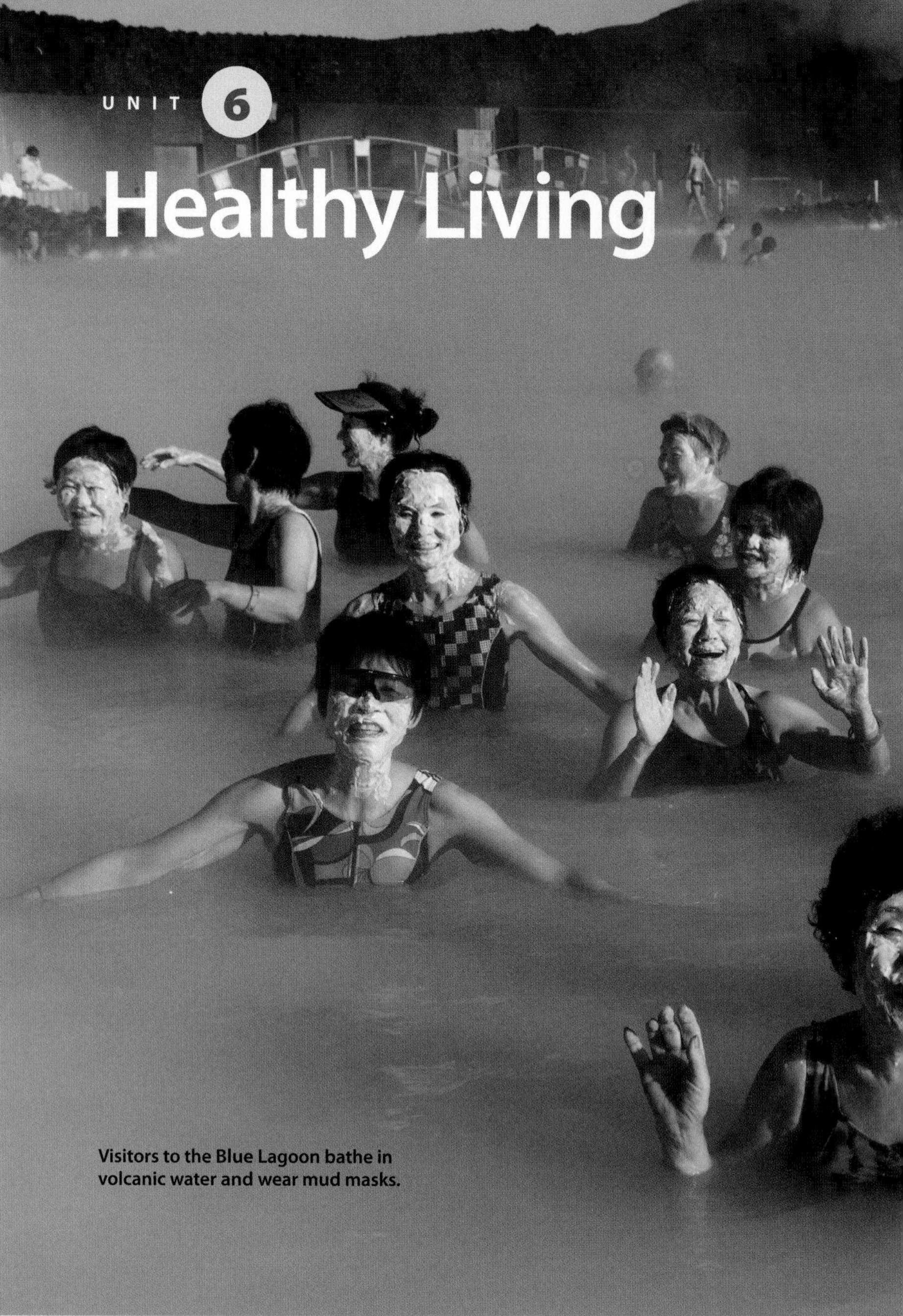

Visitors to the Blue Lagoon bathe in volcanic water and wear mud masks.

UNIT OUTCOMES	GRAMMAR	VOCABULARY	EL CIVICS
• Identify body parts • Describe symptoms and illnesses • Identify medications • Describe healthy habits • Identify actions in a waiting room	• Imperatives • Simple present • Simple present with *be* • Simple present with *have* • Simple present with *need* • Negative simple present • Present continuous	• Body parts • Ailments • Waiting room actions • Health vocabulary	The skills students learn in this unit can be applied to the following EL Civics competency areas: • Medical systems • Health and nutrition

UNIT OUTCOMES
Identify body parts
Describe symptoms and illnesses
Identify medications
Describe healthy habits
Identify actions in a waiting room
Look at the photo and answer the questions.
1. What are the people doing? How does it benefit their health?
2. What other ways can you keep healthy?

- Ask students if they think the Blue Lagoon is a relaxing place. Then, ask them to describe what they think volcanic water and mud masks feel like.
- Go over the unit outcomes. Ask: *When were you last sick? Did you take any medicine? Have you ever been in a hospital waiting room? Do you think you have healthy habits?* Discuss as a class.

Life Skills Link

In this unit, students will learn how to communicate symptoms to a doctor and demonstrate where the symptoms are occurring. They will also learn how to remedy symptoms and stay healthy.

Workplace Link

All lessons and units in *Stand Out* include basic communication skills and interpersonal skills important for the workplace. They are not individually identified. Other workplace skills are indicated. They include, collecting and organizing information, making decisions and solving problems, and combining ideas and information.

CASAS	SCANS	CCRS
Lesson 1: 3.1.1, 3.1.3 Lesson 2: 0.1.2, 0.2.1, 3.1.1 Lesson 3: 2.3.1, 3.1.2, 3.3.1 Lesson 4: 3.1.1 Lesson 5: 3.1.3 Review: 3.1.1, 3.1.2, 3.1.3, 3.3.1 Team Project: 1.3.9, 4.8.1	Many SCANs skills are incorporated in the unit with an emphasis on: • Acquiring and evaluating information • Organizing and maintaining information • Interpreting and communicating information • Basic skills • Self-management • Repsonsibility	RI1, RI2, RI7, W1, SL1, SL2, SL4, L1, L2, L5, RF2, RF3

LESSON 1 I need a checkup

GOAL ■ Identify body parts

A. Where is the man in the picture? Who is he talking to?

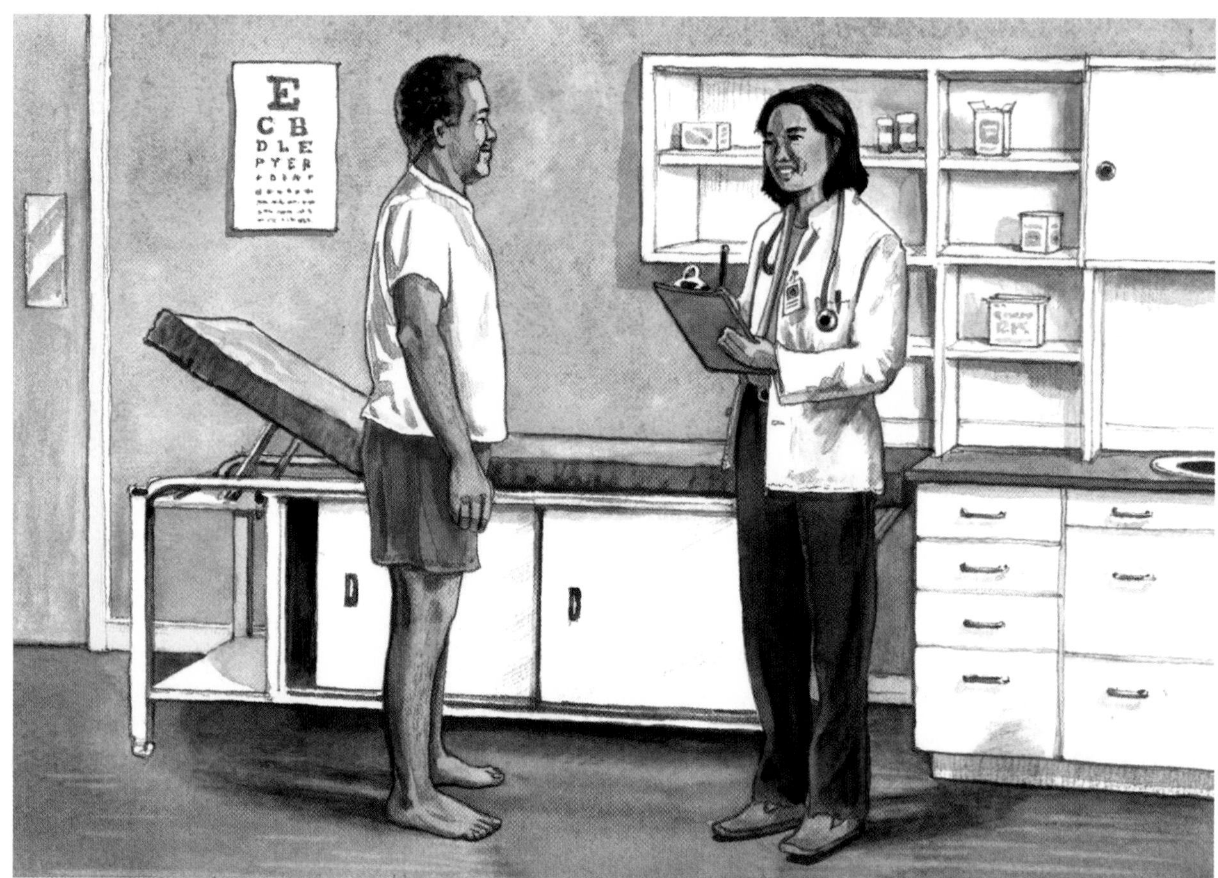

FREQUENCY EXPRESSIONS
once a year = one time a year
twice a year = two times a year

CD 2 TR 15

B. Listen and write.

My name is Guillermo. _____I_____ live in Chicago. I _____am_____ 61 years old.

I _____see_____ the doctor once a year for a checkup. I'm very healthy.

C. Complete the paragraph about yourself. Use Exercise B to help you. Answers will vary.

My name is __________. I am from __________. I __________ years old.

I __________ the doctor __________ a year for a checkup.

AT-A-GLANCE **PREP**

Goal: Identify body parts
Grammar: Imperatives
Pronunciation: Voiced and voiceless consonants
Academic Strategy: Focused listening
Vocabulary: Basic body parts

Agenda

- Draw a map to the hospital.
- Learn about the doctor's office and body parts.
- Follow directions in the doctor's office.

Resources

Multilevel Worksheet: Lesson 1, Worksheet 1
Workbook: Unit 6, Lesson 1
Audio: CD 2, Tracks 15–16
Heinle Picture Dictionary: The Human Body, pages 132–133
Stand Out Basic Assessment CD-ROM with ExamView®

Pacing

■ 1.5 hour classes ■ 2.5 hour classes
■ 3+ hour classes

STANDARDS CORRELATIONS

CCRS: W2, SL2, L1, L2, RF2, RF3
CASAS: 3.1.1, 3.1.3
***SCANS:* Basic Skills** Reading, writing, listening, speaking
Information Acquire and evaluate information, organize and maintain information, interpret and communicate information
***EFF:* Communication** Read with understanding, convey ideas in writing, speak so others can understand, listen actively

Preassessment *(optional)*

Use the Stand Out Basic Assessment CD-ROM with ExamView® to create a pretest for Unit 6.

Warm-up and Review

10–15 mins. ■■■

Ask students where the nearest hospital is. Have groups draw a map from the school to the hospital. See if all groups chose the same route.

Introduction

10–15 mins. ■■■

Write *health* on the board. See if students can figure out what it means. Pantomime minor symptoms such as coughing and sneezing. Say: *Right now my health is bad.* Point to the word when you say it. Demonstrate some exercises and say: *Exercise is good for your health.*

State the goal: *Today, we will identify body parts.*

Presentation 1

20–25 mins. ■■■

A. Where is the man in the picture? Who is he talking to?

Ask students the questions. Ask them to identify things they see. Write *checkup* on the board. Ask: *How many times do you get a checkup every year?* They may not understand, but if you say *I go one time a year,* they may begin to.

Review the Frequency Expressions as a class. Have students practice answering *How many times do you get a checkup every year?,* alternating expressions.

B. Listen and write.

Ask students to close their books and listen to the paragraph. Then, ask students to open their books and listen while reading along. Have students complete the paragraph by filling in the missing words. Tell students that they will do a dictation of the paragraph.

LISTENING SCRIPT

CD 2
TR 15

The listening script matches the paragraph in Exercise B.

To prepare for the dictation, write *Chicago* and *Guillermo* on the board for students to refer to. Ask students to underline any difficult or new words. Go over the words, discuss their meaning, and ask students to write each word several times in their notebooks.

Practice 1

7–10 mins. ■■■

Give a dictation of the paragraph.

C. Complete the paragraph about yourself. Use Exercise B to help you.

Have students read their completed paragraphs in Exercise B. Then, ask them to write a similar paragraph about themselves, completing the paragraph here.

Ask students to read their new paragraphs to a partner.

Evaluation 1

3–5 mins. ■■■

Go over the dictations carefully and allow students to self-correct.

BEST PRACTICE

Multilevel dictation

To give a dictation to a multilevel class, provide students who will struggle the most a handout of the paragraph with key words missing. Another level might have most words missing, and another blank paper.

Presentation 2

10–15 mins.

D. Read the new words.

Go over each word and the pronunciation with students. Make sure students pronounce the final consonants and release them when they say the words in isolation. With *head, hand,* and *foot,* the tongue releases and there is a very brief and quiet *ah* with the release after the articulation of the final sound. Try exaggerating at first so students understand. With *back, neck,* and *leg,* the throat closes to pronounce the sound and then relaxes. Again, there is a very brief and quiet *ah.* With *arm,* the mouth opens after the /m/ is produced, and with *nose,* the /z/ is produced followed by the mouth opening slightly.

This is also a good opportunity to ask what other body-part vocabulary students would like to learn. Possibilities include the following: *shoulders, elbows, knees, wrists,* and *waist.*

For shorter classes, ask students to do Exercise E for homework.

Practice 2

7–10 mins.

E. Write the new words in the picture.

Have students write the parts of the body.

Evaluation 2

5–7 mins.

F. Practice the conversation. Use the words from Exercise D to make new conversations.

Observe students doing this activity.

INTONATION

Voiced and voiceless consonants

Many pronunciation features, like grammar structures, are learned over time and not immediately acquired. Students, for the most part, can be understood without understanding the difference between voiced and voiceless consonants. The following practice might be done as a way to help students become aware of different sounds.

Ask students to put two fingers on their throats, that is, on their voice boxes. Ask students to pronounce an /m/ for an extended period of time. Demonstrate what you want them to do. Ask them what they feel. They may make a fluttering motion with their hands. Then, ask students to sing a melody using only this sound. Choose a song they all know.

Next, ask them to do the same with /d/ and /g/. Now, ask them to pronounce *head, hand, arm,* and *leg.* Show them how each word ends and how the voice box flutters or vibrates.

Do the same with /t/ and /k/. Show them how with these sounds they can't sing a melody because the voice box doesn't vibrate. Contrast the /k/ and the /g/ sounds. Then, contrast the /t/ and the /d/ sounds. Have students then pronounce *back, neck,* and *foot.* Finally, have them contrast the endings by practicing the following:

hand—foot
head—foot
neck—leg

Don't expect students to immediately incorporate this concept into their speech. Review it occasionally to help students pronounce sounds correctly.

D. **Read the new words.**

head	back	hand	foot
neck	arm	leg	nose

E. **Write the new words in the picture.**

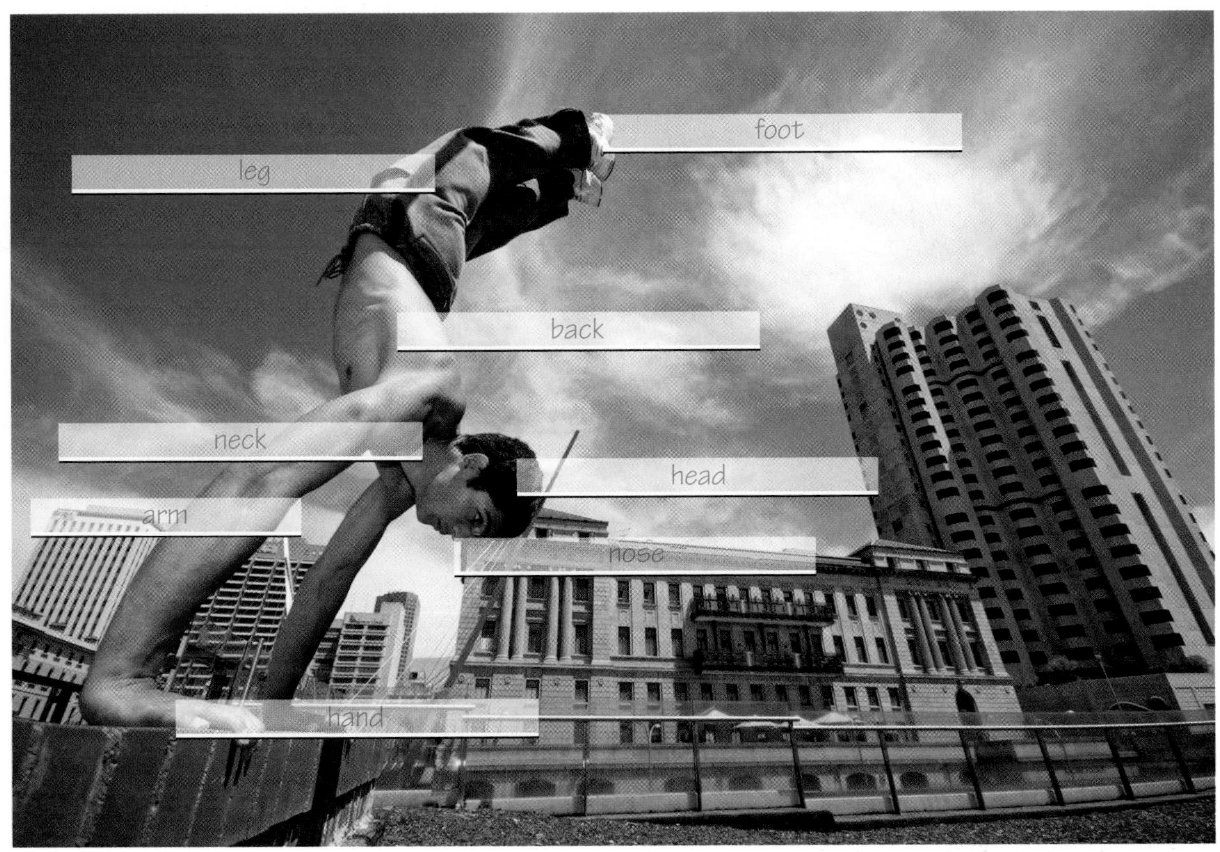

F. **Practice the conversation. Use the words in Exercise D to make new conversations.**

Student A: Where's the nose?
Student B: It's here. (points to own nose)

G. Read.

Imperatives			
	Subject	**Verb**	**Example sentence**
Please	~~you~~	read open let me (look) sit down stand up	Please read the chart. Please open your mouth. Please let me look in your ear. Please sit down. Please stand up.

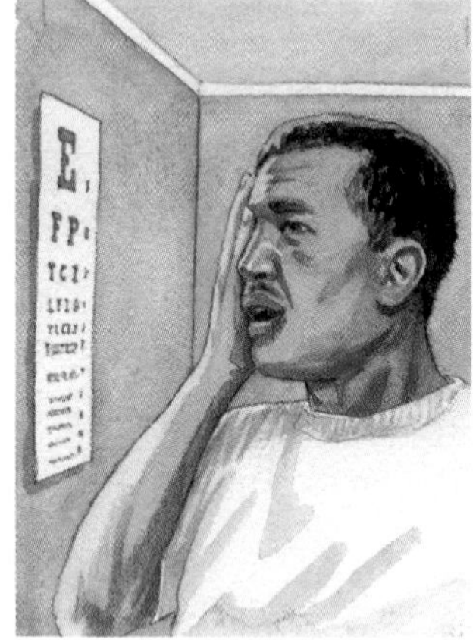

Please read the chart.

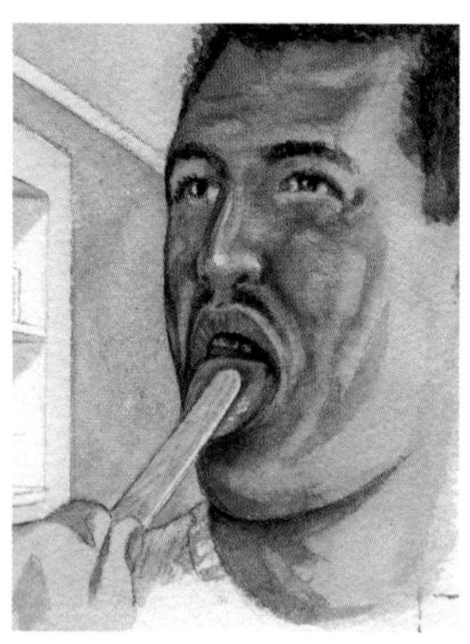
Please open your mouth and say "Ah."

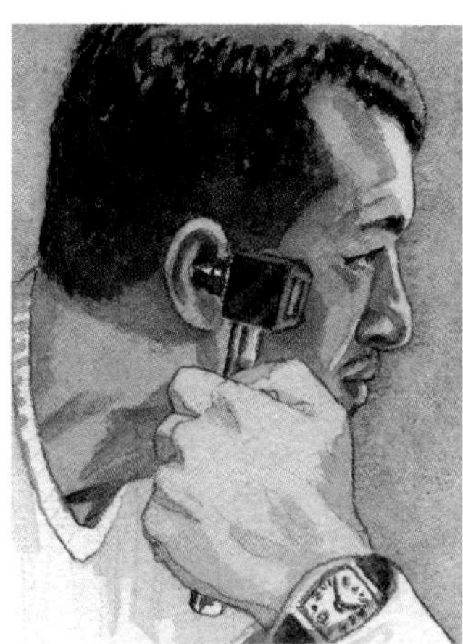
Let me look in your ear.

H. Listen and practice the conversation. Make new conversations.

CD 2 TR 16

Doctor: Please sit down.
Guillermo: OK.
Doctor: Please open your mouth and say, "Ah."
Guillermo: Ah.

I. APPLY Which body parts does the doctor examine during a checkup? Make a list.

Answers will vary.

1. ______________________
2. ______________________
3. ______________________
4. ______________________

Presentation 3

10–15 mins.

G. Read.

Go over the grammar chart with students. Help them to see how imperatives (or commands) imply the subject pronoun *you,* but the pronoun is not used. Take this opportunity to go over the new vocabulary with students as well. Say the statements and see if they can point to the body part each statement implies. Ask students to close their books and say the statements again. Point to your eyes, ears, and mouth and ask students to call out the vocabulary.

Ask students to open their books and say the statements when you say the body part. Then, ask them to close their books and do the same.

Practice 3

7–10 mins.

H. Listen and practice the conversation. Make new conversations.

Go over the conversation with students and help them use proper intonation and rhythm. Show them how to use the other statements in the conversation from Exercise G.

LISTENING SCRIPT

CD 2 TR 16

The listening script matches the conversation in Exercise H.

Ask students to make new conversations. Have them substitute the underlined actions with new ones from Exercise G. Then, ask students to practice the conversation with a partner.

Have students walk around and switch partners often. Have them substitute different actions with each partner. Remind them to do the actions.

Evaluation 3

2–7 mins.

Ask volunteers to present the conversation in front of the class.

BEST PRACTICE

Benefits of role-playing

- Students generally speak more freely when they are acting out a role.
- Students have fun when role-playing conversations.
- Students can correct each other's mistakes in a positive way.
- Students learn and retain lesson goals by bringing situations to life.

Application

7–10 mins.

I. APPLY Which body parts does the doctor examine during a checkup? Make a list.

Ask students to complete the list. Tell them to refer back to the vocabulary words in Exercises D and G.

Refer students to *Stand Out Basic Workbook, Unit 6, Lesson 1* for more practice with imperatives.

Go to the *Activity Bank* online for suggestions on promoting digital literacy and using the Internet to enhance this lesson.

MULTILEVEL WORKSHEET

Lesson 1, Worksheet 1: Body Parts

INSTRUCTOR'S NOTES

AT-A-GLANCE **PREP**

Goal: Describe symptoms and illnesses
Grammar: Simple present
Academic Strategies: Focused listening, test-taking skills
Vocabulary: *headache, backache, stomachache, fever, cold, runny nose, sick, illness, lasts*

Agenda

- Practice identifying body parts.
- Identify symptoms and illnesses.
- Practice stating symptoms.
- Use the simple present to describe illnesses and symptoms.
- Listen to people talking about illnesses.

Resources

Multilevel Worksheets: Lesson 2, Worksheets 1 and 2
Workbook: Unit 6, Lesson 2
Audio: CD 2, Tracks 17–27
Heinle Picture Dictionary: Illnesses, Injuries, Symptoms, and Disabilities, pages 134–135

Pacing

■ 1.5 hour classes ■ 2.5 hour classes
■ 3+ hour classes

STANDARDS CORRELATIONS

CCRS: RI1, RI2, R7, SL1, SL2, L2, RF3
CASAS: 0.1.2, 0.2.1, 3.1.1
SCANS: **Basic Skills** Reading, writing, listening, speaking
Information Acquire and evaluate information, organize and maintain information, interpret and communicate information
EFF: **Communication** Read with understanding, convey ideas in writing, speak so others can understand, listen actively

Warm-up and Review
7–10 mins. ■■■

Ask students to do Exercise F from Lesson 1.

Introduction
5–7 mins. ■■■

Pantomime a stomachache. Write on the board: *What's the matter?* Pantomime again and point to the question. When students ask, say: *I have a stomachache.* State the goal: *Today, we will describe symptoms and illnesses.*

Presentation 1
15–20 mins. ■■■

Present the symptoms by pantomiming.

A. Listen and repeat.

Go over each picture with students. Ask them to identify each illness as you describe it.

LISTENING SCRIPT

CD 2 TR 17

The listening script matches the list of words in Exercise A.

B. Listen and point.

LISTENING SCRIPT

CD 2 TR 18–23

1. **Doctor:** *It is good to see you.*
   Man: *It's good to see you, too.*
   Doctor: *What's the matter today?*
   Man: *I have a terrible stomachache. Maybe I ate something bad yesterday.*
2. **Doctor:** *You look like you are in a lot of pain today.*
   Man: *I sure am. Every day I get these terrible headaches. What can I do about it?*
   Doctor: *For headaches, we usually prescribe pain relievers, but maybe we should check this out with some tests.*
   Man: *Thanks, Doctor.*
3. **Doctor:** *How can I help you?*
   Woman: *I think I have a high fever.*
   Doctor: *Let's check it out.*
   Woman: *Thanks, Doctor. I hope I'm not too sick.*
4. **Doctor:** *You must be feeling terrible.*
   Woman: *I sure am. I think I've only got a cold, but it is causing so many problems.*
   Doctor: *I know you want to go to work, but sometimes, even with a cold, you need to take it easy for a few days.*
   Woman: *I guess you're right. I just hate staying home!*
5. **Doctor:** *Can I help you?*
   Woman: *Yes, I can hardly move.*
   Doctor: *What seems to be the trouble?*
   Woman: *I have a terrible backache.*
6. **Doctor:** *How are you feeling today?*
   Man: *Not very well. I think I have a cold. I have a bad cough and a sore throat.*
   Doctor: *Let me take a look.*
   Man: *Thanks, Doctor.*

LESSON 2 I'm sick!

GOAL Describe symptoms and illnesses

A. Listen and repeat.

CD 2 TR 17

headache

backache

stomachache

cold and runny nose

cough and sore throat

fever

B. Listen and point.

CD 2 TR 18–23

C. Listen and check (✓) the correct answer.

CD 2 TR 24–27

1. Maritza has ___________
   - ☐ a cold.
   - ☑ a headache.
   - ☐ a fever.

2. Shan has ___________
   - ☐ a backache.
   - ☑ a fever.
   - ☐ a cold.

3. John has ___________
   - ☑ a runny nose.
   - ☐ a fever.
   - ☐ a headache.

4. Anakiya has ___________
   - ☑ a fever.
   - ☐ a runny nose.
   - ☐ a backache.

D. Read about colds and make a list of symptoms.

The Common Cold

A cold is an illness that usually lasts for up to ten days. There are many symptoms. For example, many people have a runny nose and a sore throat. Others have a low fever. Some people have a cough, too.

1. runny nose
2. sore throat
3. fever/low fever
4. cough

E. Complete the table. Answers will vary.

Symptom	Duration (how long)	Do you see the doctor?	
		Yes ✔	No ✔
runny nose	1 day		
sore throat	1 month		
cough	2 weeks		
low fever	2 days		
high fever	2 days		
headache	3 hours		
stomachache	1 week		

F. Discuss your table in a group.

A cold is an illness that usually lasts up to ten days.

Practice 1

7–10 mins.

C. Listen and check (✓) the correct answer.

You may need to play the recording a few times. In this case, don't stop between conversations. This technique will help students think quickly and is a precursor to note taking.

Evaluation 1

Ask students to check each other's work and then review the answers as a class.

LISTENING SCRIPT

CD 2 TR 24–27

1. *Maritza is a good student. She can't come to school today because she has a headache. I hope she comes back tomorrow.*
2. *Shan works all day and comes to school at night. He isn't at school today. He called me and told me he would be out because he had a fever of around 102 degrees. I hope he is all right and will get better soon.*
3. *Hi, John! This is your teacher, Rob. I hear you are having a hard time with a cold and a runny nose. It's no fun to be sick. Get well soon! Bye.*
4. *Anakiya is new in the United States. She arrived Tuesday. I hope she will be OK. She is already sick. She has a fever.*

BEST PRACTICE

Focused listening

Focused listening has been discussed throughout the book. The recordings are at an authentic speed and are filled with language students may not understand. The purpose of the task is to help students develop the ability to pull meaning out of complex and natural conversations by identifying key words.

It's important to remind students of this every time you do a focused listening activity so they don't become frustrated and stop listening altogether.

Presentation 2

10–15 mins.

With books closed, write *symptoms* on the board and ask students to help you make a list. Then, write *cold* on the board. Ask students what they think the symptoms might be. Circle them or add them to your list as students mention them.

D. Read about colds and make a list of symptoms.

Ask students to quickly read the paragraph. Then, ask them to circle the symptoms they find in the paragraph. Finally, ask students to write the symptoms in the space provided. This activity is done mostly as a class to help students learn to scan for specific information.

Practice 2

7–10 mins.

E. Complete the table.

Ask students to do this activity on their own.

F. Discuss your table in a group.

Ask students to attempt to come to a consensus in their groups.

Evaluation 2

3–5 mins.

Ask groups to share their completed charts with the class.

BEST PRACTICE

Pantomiming vocabulary

Pantomiming is a good way to teach vocabulary connected with symptoms and illnesses. It is fun and students enjoy it. It is also memorable and good for kinaesthetic learners who appreciate active lessons. Pantomiming can be used in both individual and pair or group situations.

1. Individual - Teachers may first choose to model pantomimes alone in order to introduce new vocabulary or to test students on previously acquired vocabulary.
2. Pair or Group - Students can imitate pantomimes as a class to demonstrate knowledge. Student pairs may also test classmates' knowledge by having them guess vocabulary words from pantomimes.

Presentation 3

10–15 mins.

G. Read the charts.

Lesson 5 introduces the present continuous. This lesson includes a recap of the simple present. Most students have learned the simple present throughout the book, but probably have not acquired it yet. It is important to reinforce and review it from time to time so students don't confuse the two structures once the present continuous has been introduced.

For shorter classes, ask students to do Exercise H for homework.

Practice 3

10–15 mins.

H. Write.

Go over the first item with students and ask them to complete the exercise by themselves. When they have finished, ask them to share their answers with a partner and peer-edit their work.

Evaluation 3

3–5 mins.

Check students' book work and ask for volunteers to write the answers on the board.

Application

5–7 mins.

I. Practice the conversation. Use the symptoms in Exercise A to make new conversations.

Ask students to work in pairs and practice the conversation. Tell them to pay attention to the underlined symptom.

Then, ask students to use the symptoms in Exercise A to make new conversations. First, have students substitute the underlined symptom for another.

When students feel comfortable, encourage them to try substituting other lines in the conversation with new ones.

Ask volunteers to present their new conversations to the class.

BEST PRACTICE

Grammar presentation

There are many ways to present grammar. In this case, the structure has already been covered so it will be a student-centered review. It is important to stay within the context. Students, especially at lower levels, are working with new vocabulary, new structures, and all the other skills they need to develop to learn English. If you stray from the context to give grammar explanations, you ask students to deal with new or different vocabulary while learning the structures. It is advisable to teach and review the same structures later in future lessons in different contexts. In this way, students learn to transfer the structure to new contexts.

In this case, with books closed, you might write the verbs from the chart: *be* and *have*. Ask students what the words have to do with the lesson. Guide them to the sentences in the chart. You might recreate the chart on the board and put in some information including one sample sentence.

Encourage students to come to the board and complete the chart. Then, compare the chart to what is in the book.

Refer students to *Stand Out Basic Workbook, Unit 6, Lesson 2* for more practice with the simple present.

Go to the *Activity Bank* online for suggestions on promoting digital literacy and using the Internet to enhance this lesson.

MULTILEVEL WORKSHEETS

Lesson 2, Worksheet 1: Symptoms and Illnesses

Lesson 2, Worksheet 2: *How often?*

G. Read the charts.

Simple Present with *Be* (Irregular)		
Subject	***Be***	**Example sentence**
I	am	I **am** sick.
You, We, They	are	We **are** sick.
He, She, It	is	He **is** sick.

Simple Present with *Have* (Irregular)		
Subject	***Have***	**Example sentence**
I, You, We, They	have	I **have** a headache.
He, She, It	has	She **has** a runny nose.

H. Write.

1. He ______has______ (have) a headache.
2. She ______is______ (be) very sick.
3. I ______am______ (be) sick.
4. You ______have______ (have) a cold.
5. Oscar ______has______ (have) a stomachache.
6. You ______are______ (be) sick.

I. Practice the conversation. Use the symptoms in Exercise A to make new conversations.

Maritza: How are you?
Shan: I'm sick!
Maritza: What's the matter?
Shan: I have a headache.

LESSON 3 You need aspirin

WORKPLACE CONNECTION
Exercise A: Collect and organize information

GOAL Identify medications

A. Read, listen, and write the missing words.

CD 2 TR 28

Calendar | New | Import Share

February 18 View: Day

	NAME	PROBLEM	PHONE
3:30	Julio Rodriguez	headache	(777) 555-1395
4:00	Huong Pham	fever	(777) 555-3311
4:30	Richard Price	stomachache	(777) 555-2323
5:00	Mele Ikahihifo	sore throat	(777) 555-5511
5:30	Fred Wharton	cold	(777) 555-9764
6:00	Ayumi Tanaka	backache	(777) 555-8765

B. Look at the schedule in Exercise A and write the problems.

fever

sore throat

stomachache

backache

headache

cold

HAVE	
I, You, We, They	*have*
He, She	*has*

C. Write sentences.

1. Julio has a headache.
2. Richard has a stomachache.
3. Ayumi has a backache.

AT-A-GLANCE **PREP**

Goal: Identify medications
Grammar: Simple present
Academic Strategy: Focused listening
Vocabulary: *medicine, sore throat, cough, aspirin, antacid, pain relievers, cough syrup, illness, caution*

Agenda

- Review time.
- Read an appointment book.
- Talk about medicine and illnesses.
- Discuss what medicine you have at home.

Resources

Multilevel Worksheets: Lesson 3, Worksheets 1 and 2
Workbook: Unit 6, Lesson 3
Audio: CD 2, Track 28
Heinle Picture Dictionary: Pharmacy, pages 142–143

Pacing

- 1.5 hour classes
- 2.5 hour classes
- 3+ hour classes

STANDARDS CORRELATIONS

CCRS: RI1, SL1, SL2, SL4, L1, L2, RF3
CASAS: 2.3.1, 3.1.2, 3.3.1
SCANS: **Basic Skills** Reading, writing, listening, speaking
Resources Allocate time
Information Acquire and evaluate information, organize and maintain information, interpret and communicate information
Interpersonal Participate as a member of a team, teach others
Systems Understand systems
EFF: **Communication** Read with understanding, speak so others can understand, listen actively
Decision Making Solve problems and make decisions
Interpersonal Cooperate with others

Warm-up and Review

10–15 mins.

Ask students what time it is. Write this dialog on the board and ask students to practice it in pairs.

A: *What time do you eat lunch?*
B: *I eat lunch at 12:00.*
A: *What time do you eat dinner?*
B: *I eat dinner at 6:00.*

Ask students to do the dialog with four students and complete this table.

Name	Dinner	Lunch

Introduction

10–15 mins.

Pantomime having a headache. Students may remember to ask, *What's the matter?* Ask students what you should do. Ask them if you should take medicine. Write the word *medicine* on the board. State the goal: *Today, we will identify medications.*

Presentation 1

40–50 mins.

A. Read, listen, and write the missing words.

Go over the appointment book carefully. Review phone numbers. Tell students that they will listen to a recording to get the missing information. Play the recording.

LISTENING SCRIPT

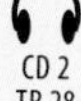
CD 2 TR 28

Doctor: *I'm a little late. I will be there soon. What patients do we have today? Oh, and can you give me their numbers, too? I might want to call a few before I get to the office.*
Nurse: *No problem, Doctor. Let's see. Julio Rodriguez has an appointment at 3:30. He has a headache. His number is 555-1395. Huong Pham is coming in at 4:00. He has a high fever. His phone is 555-3311. Richard Price has an appointment at 4:30. He has a stomachache. His number is 555-2323. Mele Ikahihifo has a sore throat. She's coming in at 5:00. You can reach her at 555-5511. Fred Wharton's number is 555-9764. He has a cold. Ayumi Tanaka is coming in at 6:00 with a backache. Her number is 555-8765.*
Doctor: *Thanks.*

Practice 1

10–15 mins.

B. Look at the schedule in Exercise A and write the problems.

Ask students to look at the schedule in Exercise A and then write the problems under the correct times indicated on the clocks.

C. Write sentences.

Before you help them, see if students can use the correct form of *have*.

Evaluation 1

5–7 mins.

Ask students to write their sentences on the board.

Presentation 2

10–12 mins.

D. ANALYZE Look at the medicine bottles. In a group, write the illnesses each medicine is for.

Go over the medicines and make sure students understand the vocabulary.

BEST PRACTICE

Group work

Students should be getting more comfortable working in groups. It may be a good idea to have the groups choose a leader whose job it is to make sure all group members speak English. Also, they should have a secretary who writes down the information. Some students may want to work on their own. Tell the groups that you will only accept answers if all members of the group agree and have discussed their answers.

Try to avoid managing the teams yourself. Encourage group interaction and monitor progress by asking questions as you walk from group to group.

Practice 2

15–20 mins.

E. APPLY Write other types of medicine you take.

Help students with the vocabulary words needed to describe the types of medicine they take. To avoid students feeling uneasy with listing very personal medications, tell them to list medications for common symptoms and illnesses mentioned so far: *headaches, backaches, colds* or *flu, coughs, runny noses, sore throats,* etc. Write a list on the board to guide students.

Evaluation 2

5–7 mins.

Ask the groups to report to the class.

INSTRUCTOR'S NOTES

Exercise D: Collect and organize information; Make decisions and solve problems

D. ANALYZE Look at the medicine bottles. In a group, write the illnesses each medicine is for. Answers will vary.

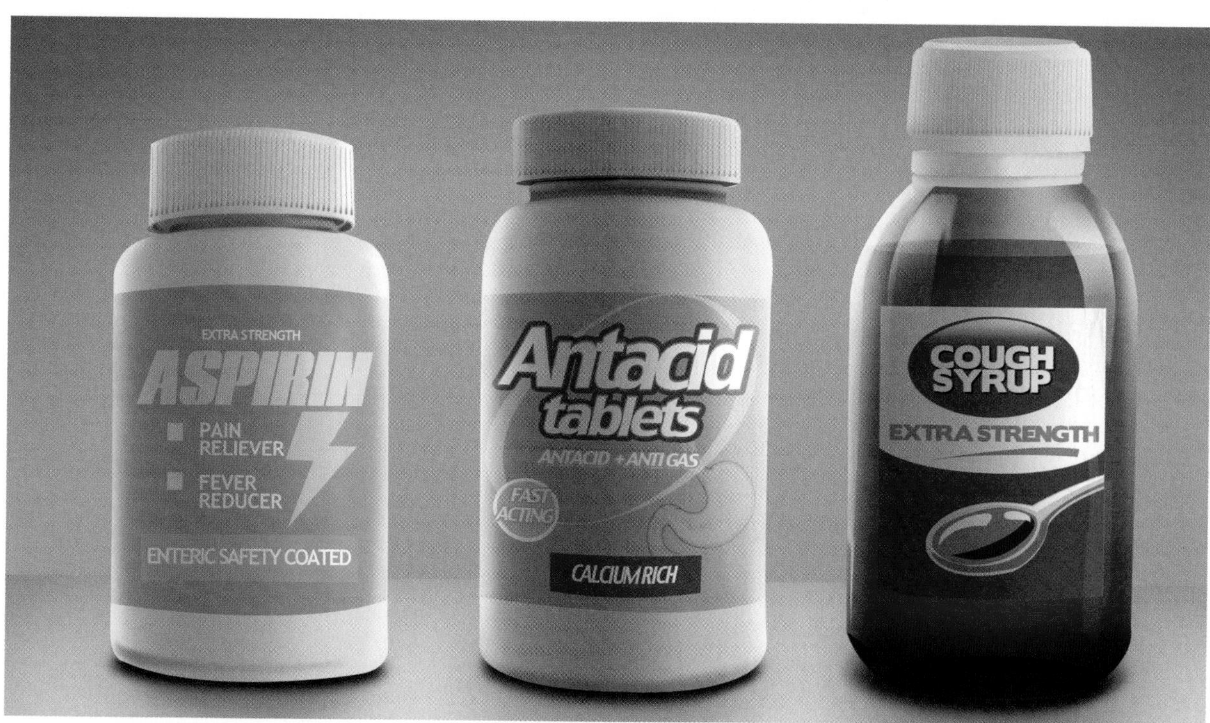

Aspirin	Antacid	Cough Syrup
fever		

E. APPLY Write other types of medicine you take. Answers will vary.

____

____

____

____

____

F. Read.

Simple Present		
I, You, We, They	need	aspirin
He, She, It	needs	antacid

G. Write sentences. Use *need*.

1. Julio has a headache. He needs aspirin.
2. Huong has a fever. He needs aspirin.
3. Richard has a stomachache. He needs antacid.
4. Mele has a sore throat and cough. She needs cough syrup.
5. Fred has a cold. He needs aspirin.
6. Ayumi and Sue have backaches. They need aspirin.
7. Tami and I have stomachaches. We need antacid.
8. Shiuli and Sang have sore throats. They need cough syrup.

H. What types of medicine do you have at home? Write. Answers will vary.

____

____

____

____

____

____

____

____

I. Speak to family members. What home remedies do you or your family use? Tell them to the class. Answers will vary.

Presentation 3

10–15 mins.

F. Read.

Students will once again review the simple present. It is important to avoid making the mistake of thinking that most students have acquired the simple present tense at this point. You may also choose to review earlier presentations of the structure or ask students to find those presentations in their books.

Go over the chart with students. You are now introducing the verb *need* for the first time; however, many students will already understand it because of the contexts they have heard or seen it used in.

For shorter classes, ask students to do Exercise G for homework.

BEST PRACTICE

Earlier pages in the book

The technique of showing students where they learned something earlier will help reinforce your teaching. It will also help them to identify the book as a tool that they can refer to during class and even after they advance to a higher level.

Practice 3

15–20 mins.

G. Write sentences. Use *need*.

Ask students to complete the sentences.

If students are ready, you may also choose to give them a dictation of the same sentences once they have completed them.

Evaluation 3

7–10 mins.

Ask students to write their sentences on the board.

Application

15–20 mins.

H. What types of medicine do you have at home? Write.

After students write the information, ask them to share their work with a group.

I. Speak to family members. What home remedies do you or your family use? Tell them to the class.

Refer students to *Stand Out Basic Workbook, Unit 6, Lesson 3* for more practice with the simple present.

Go to the *Activity Bank* online for suggestions on promoting digital literacy and using the Internet to enhance this lesson.

MULTILEVEL WORKSHEETS

Lesson 3, Worksheet 1: Medicine

Lesson 3, Worksheet 2: Medicine for Ailments

INSTRUCTOR'S NOTES

AT-A-GLANCE **PREP**

Goal: Describe healthy habits
Grammar: Negative simple present
Academic Strategies: Focused listening, interpreting graphs
Vocabulary: *tip, exercise, see, smoke, meal, healthy, per day, per month, per year*

Agenda

- Review illnesses.
- Read about healthy practices.
- Write about healthy habits.

Resources

Multilevel Worksheets: Lesson 4, Worksheets 1 and 2
Workbook: Unit 6, Lesson 4
Audio: CD 2, Tracks 29–30
Heinle Picture Dictionary: Daily Activities, pages 34–35

Pacing

■ 1.5 hour classes ■ 2.5 hour classes
■ 3+ hour classes

STANDARDS CORRELATIONS

CCRS: RI1, RI7, W2, SL1, SL2, L1, L5
CASAS: 3.1.1
***SCANS:* Basic Skills** Reading, writing, listening, speaking
Resources Allocate time, allocate materials and facility resources
Information Acquire and evaluate information, organize and maintain information, interpret and communicate information
Personal Qualities Responsibility, sociability, self-management
***EFF:* Communication** Read with understanding, convey ideas in writing, speak so others can understand, listen actively, observe critically
Lifelong Learning Take responsibility for learning, reflect and evaluate

Warm-up and Review 10–15 mins.

Ask students what medicine they take for various illnesses and symptoms. List them on the board. Write the following conversation on the board and ask students to practice it:

Doctor: *What's the matter?*
Julio: *I have a headache.*
Doctor: *You need aspirin.*

Ask students to write their own information and complete this table about four classmates.

Name:	
Illness	**Medicine**
Headache	
Stomachache	
Backache	
Cold	
Sore throat	
Fever	

Introduction 15–20 mins.

Ask how many hours each student sleeps every night. Make a bar graph as a class. State the goal: *Today, we will describe healthy habits.*

Presentation 1 15–20 mins.

A. INTERPRET Read and listen.

Help students learn the new vocabulary by asking them questions about the brochure. Teach them that *every day* and *a day* mean almost the same thing. Play the recording one time and ask them to read along as they listen.

LISTENING SCRIPT
The listening script matches the brochure in Exercise A.

CD 2 TR 29

As a class, decide on things for each category on the brochure that would not be healthy. Show students how to use this information in the conversation in Exercise B.

Practice 1 5–7 mins.

B. Practice with a partner.

Ask students to practice the conversation with a partner, substituting information.

Evaluation 1 5–7 mins.

Ask volunteers to present the conversation.

LESSON 4 Exercise every day!

GOAL ■ Describe healthy habits

A. INTERPRET Read and listen.

CD 2 TR 29

MAIN STREET HEALTH CENTER

We are happy you are a patient of Dr. Ramsey. Our goal is to help you stay healthy. Follow these suggestions and you will be healthier.

DO'S

Sleep:
Sleep 7-8 hours a night.

Exercise:
Walk, run, or do some other form of exercise 30 minutes a day.

Eat:
Eat three good meals a day.

See the Doctor:
See the doctor once a year for a checkup,

DONT'S

Don't smoke!

B. Practice with a partner.

Dr. Ramsey: How many hours do you sleep a night?
Hasna: I sleep four hours a night.
Dr. Ramsey: That is not healthy. You need to sleep seven to eight hours.

CD 2
TR 30

C. Listen and read Huong's story. Why is Huong healthy?

I'm healthy. I exercise one hour every day. I eat breakfast, lunch, and dinner. I don't eat a lot of candy. I don't smoke. I sleep seven hours every night.

D. What does Huong do? Fill in the table.

What does Huong do?	What doesn't Huong do?
exercise	eat a lot of candy
eat breakfast, lunch, and dinner	smoke
sleep seven hours every night	

E. Read the charts.

Simple Present		
Subject	**Verb**	**Example sentence**
I, You, We, They	eat	I **eat** three meals a day.
He, She, It	sleeps	She **sleeps** seven hours a night.

Negative Simple Present			
Subject	**Verb**		**Example sentence**
I, You, We, They	**don't**	eat	We **don't eat** three meals a day.
He, She, It	**doesn't**	sleeps	He **doesn't sleep** seven hours a day.

F. Write about Huong.

1. Huong ___exercises___ (exercise) one hour every day.
2. Huong ___sleeps___ (sleep) seven hours every night.
3. Huong ___eats___ (eat) breakfast, lunch, and dinner.
4. Huong ___doesn't smoke___ (smoke).
5. Huong ___doesn't eat___ (eat) a lot of candy.

Presentation 2

15–20 mins.

C. Listen and read Huong's story. Why is Huong healthy?

Ask students to first listen to Huong's story with their books closed. Write the four categories on the board. Ask students to see if they can hear the information that goes with each one.

Sleep	
Eat	
Exercise	
Smoke	

LISTENING SCRIPT

CD 2 TR 30

The listening script matches the paragraph in Exercise C.

D. What does Huong do? Fill in the table.

Ask students to open their books, read Exercise C, and complete the table with little if any explanation from you. Encourage students to try to figure out what to do on their own, but be careful not to allow students to get frustrated.

E. Read the charts.

Read the charts with students. Review the third-person singular and then help them to see that the verb in the negative is the base form.

Review the second chart carefully where the *s* is deleted. Point out the use of *don't* and *doesn't*.

Work with students by doing some choral, substitution, and transformational drills.

BEST PRACTICE

Choral drills

Choral drills can be a very enjoyable method that helps student participate more. It is also excellent for modeling correct pronunciation since students repeat immediately after you.

Choral drills are highly flexible as the approach to using it can be easily changed to suit the teacher or students. Varying the speed or volume of the drills tests students' listening and pronunciation skills. Dividing the classroom into sections where different groups alternate gives more practice on the target feature and also helps to develop skills.

BEST PRACTICE

Metalanguage

Students don't need metalanguage to speak English well or to understand grammar. Some English speakers may never know what the *third-person singular* is. However, sometimes when working with adults, some labeling of grammar structures can help them to identify things they have learned earlier and apply them to new structures.

The chart in the book does not identify the base (*simple* or *root*) form of the verb by name. It merely shows that it no longer carries the *s* in the negative. You may choose to introduce the term *base* and/or *root* at this time if you feel students will understand the concept. (*Base* is the term used in *Stand Out* Levels 1–5.)

Practice 2

7–10 mins.

F. Write about Huong.

Make sure that students refer to Exercise C so that they know when to use the negative. Then, show students how to group the sentences into a paragraph.

Evaluation 2

5 mins.

Check students' sentences. Ask students to write their sentences on the board in paragraph form.

INSTRUCTOR'S NOTES

Presentation 3

10–15 mins.

G. Look at the pictures and read the information in the table.

Go over the pictures with students. Ask questions and ask them to answer. Practice the negative when appropriate.

For shorter classes, ask students to do Exercise H for homework.

Practice 3

10–15 mins.

H. Write.

After students finish doing the exercise, have them write the entire sentences on another sheet of paper.

If you have time, you may consider using these sentences as a modified multilevel dictation as described on page 139a.

Evaluation 3

5–7 mins.

Ask students to write the complete sentences on the board.

Application

20–30 mins.

I. Write.

After students put in their personal information, ask them to share their information with a group. They might say: *I exercise one hour every day.*

MULTILEVEL WORKSHEETS

Lesson 4, Worksheet 1: Personal Inventory

Lesson 4, Worksheet 2: Negative Simple Present

Refer students to *Stand Out Basic Workbook, Unit 6, Lesson 4* for more practice with the negative simple present.

Go to the *Activity Bank* online for suggestions on promoting digital literacy and using the Internet to enhance this lesson.

INSTRUCTOR'S NOTES

G. **Look at the pictures and read the information in the table.**

Julia

Hasna

Dalmar

Name	Julia	Hasna	Dalmar
Sleep	8 hours	5 hours	8 hours
Meals	breakfast, lunch, dinner	lunch, dinner	breakfast, lunch, dinner
Exercise	30 minutes a day	0 minutes a day	20 minutes a day
Checkup	once a year	once a year	0 times a year
Smoke	no	no	yes

H. **Write.**

1. Julia and Hasna ___don't smoke___ (smoke).
2. Hasna ___doesn't eat___ (eat) breakfast.
3. Dalmar and Julia ___sleep___ (sleep) eight hours every day.
4. Hasna ___doesn't exercise___ (exercise).
5. Julia and Hasna ___see___ (see) the doctor for a checkup.
6. Dalmar ___doesn't see___ (see) the doctor for a checkup.

I. **Write.** Answers will vary.

Your name: ______________ **Exercise:** ______________

Sleep: ______________ **Checkup:** ______________

Meals: ______________ **Smoke:** ______________

LESSON 5 I have an appointment

GOAL ■ Identify actions in a waiting room

A. Use the words in the box to talk about the picture.

talk	wait	read	answer	sleep

B. Listen to the conversation and put the actions in order. Write 1–5.

CD 2 TR 31

__2__ talk (are talking)

__1__ wait (are waiting)

__3__ read (is reading)

__5__ answer (am answering)

__4__ sleep (is sleeping)

AT-A-GLANCE **PREP**

Goal: Identify actions in a waiting room
Grammar: Present continuous
Pronunciation: /g/
Academic Strategy: Focused listening
Vocabulary: *wait, read, answer, talk, sleep, reception, magazine*

Agenda

- Review illnesses.
- Talk about waiting rooms.
- Describe waiting rooms.

Resources

Multilevel Worksheet: Lesson 5, Worksheet 1
Workbook: Unit 6, Lesson 5
Audio: CD 2, Track 31–32
Heinle Picture Dictionary: Medical Center, pages 140–141

Pacing

- 1.5 hour classes
- 2.5 hour classes
- 3+ hour classes

STANDARDS CORRELATIONS

CCRS: RI1, SL2, L2, L3, RF2, RF3
CASAS: 3.1.3
***SCANS:* Basic Skills** Reading, writing, listening, speaking
Resources Allocate materials and facility resources
Information Acquire and evaluate information
Interpersonal Participate as a member of a team, teach others
***EFF:* Communication** Read and write, convey ideas in writing, speak so others can understand, listen actively, observe critically
Interpersonal Cooperate with others, guide others

Warm-up and Review

7–10 mins.

Divide the class into two. One half will pretend that they are sick. Ask students who are not "sick" to look for students pantomiming an illness and ask them: *What's the matter?* Students continue this activity with several partners.

Introduction

3–5 mins.

Ask students if they go to the hospital or the doctor's office when they are sick. Go through the ailments on page 141. Ask students where they think is the best place to go for each symptom. Ask students if they wait at the doctor's office or hospital. Pantomime *waiting* impatiently. State the goal: *Today, we will discuss actions in a waiting room.*

Presentation 1

20–30 mins.

Ask students to open their books. Point to the picture and say: *She has a doctor's appointment.* Point again and say: *She is waiting.* Point to people in the picture and ask questions: *Where is she? What are they doing?* Help students hear the *-ing* sound when you say it. Don't expect students to use the present continuous yet.

A. Use the words in the box to talk about the picture.

Make sure students know what each word means. Write many of the sentences students say on the board. Don't overcorrect individuals, but always write the sentences correctly.

Go over the words in Exercise B. Explain that verbs can take different forms. Ask students to repeat the words in parentheses. Emphasize *-ing.* Prepare students for focused listening.

Practice 1

5–7 mins.

B. Listen to the conversation and put the actions in order. Write 1–5.

LISTENING SCRIPT

CD 2
TR 31

Doctor: *I'm a little late. I will be there in ten minutes. How many patients are there?*
Receptionist: *There are four. They are all waiting. Mrs. Hill and Mrs. Johnson are talking, and Guillermo Espinosa is reading a magazine. Mr. Masters is sleeping in a chair.*
Doctor: *What are you doing?*
Receptionist: *I'm answering the phone and writing patient information in their files.*
Doctor: *OK, I'll see you in a few minutes.*

Evaluation 1

7–10 mins.

Check answers as a class.

Presentation 2

20–30 mins.

C. Read the chart.

As you go over the chart, remind students that these structures, like the others learned in this book (with the exception of the imperative), can have other subjects besides the pronouns. Substitute other names and words in place of the pronouns.

Students may also be confused about *people, men,* and *women.* Show them how the plural works with these words.

> **INTONATION**
>
> **/ing/**
>
> The present continuous is used a great deal in English. Students will tend to hear the /ing/ as it runs together with other words in discourse. The /g/ is sometimes difficult to hear if it is present at all in native speech.
>
> There is a relationship between what students hear, what they say, and what they write. Some students, after learning the structure, may leave off the *g* when writing the word, much like students often leave off the *s* when writing the plural. Therefore, it is to students' advantage to stress the /ing/ in practice.

D. Listen and repeat.

Tell students that they will now hear some of the present continuous verb forms from the table in Exercise C. Ask students to look again at the previous exercise to see how the present continuous is formed.

> **LISTENING SCRIPT**
>
> 
> CD 2 TR 32
>
> *The listening script matches the words in Exercise D.*

E. Look at the picture in Exercise A. Write.

Since this is the first real exposure to the present continuous, do this activity as a class as part of the presentation. Show students the role *now* plays with the present continuous.

Prepare students for the practice.

Practice 2

7–10 mins.

F. With a partner, ask and answer the questions about the picture in Exercise A.

Exercise E contains the answers to the questions in Exercise F. Ask students who might be ready to do this activity with Exercise E covered.

Evaluation 2

5–7 mins.

Observe the activity.

INSTRUCTOR'S NOTES

C. Read the chart.

Present Continuous (right now)			
Subject	***Be***	**Base + *ing***	**Example sentence**
I	am	talking	I **am talking.**
He, She, It	is	sleeping	He **is sleeping.**
We, You, They	are	waiting	They **are waiting.**

D. Listen and repeat.

CD 2
TR 32

talking
waiting
reading
sleeping

E. Look at the picture in Exercise A. Write.

1. The receptionist is answering (answer) the phone now.
2. The man in the white shirt is sleeping (sleep) in the chair now.
3. The people are waiting (wait) for the doctor now.
4. The women are talking (talk) about their children now.
5. Guillermo is reading (read) a magazine now.

F. With a partner, ask and answer the questions about the picture in Exercise A.

What is the receptionist doing now?
What is the man in the white shirt doing now?
What are the people doing now?
What are the women doing now?
What is Guillermo doing now?

G. Look at the picture.

H. Talk about the picture with a partner.

I. Imagine you are in a waiting room. Write sentences. Answers will vary.

1. ______________________________

2. ______________________________

3. ______________________________

4. ______________________________

Presentation 3

8–10 mins.

G. Look at the picture.

Look at the picture with students and discuss all the verbs that might be used with the picture. Write the verbs in the base form on the board. Refer students to page 150 to remind them of what verbs might be used.

Review again using the present continuous. Write one appropriate sentence using the present continuous on the board.

Practice 3

10–15 mins.

H. Talk about the picture with a partner.

Ask one student to point to an action in the picture while the other responds with a sentence in the present continuous.

After they have talked about the picture for a sufficient amount of time, ask them to write sentences.

Evaluation 3

3 mins.

Ask for volunteers to write their sentences on the board.

Application

10–15 mins.

I. Imagine you are in a waiting room. Write sentences.

You will have to convey to students the meaning of *imagine* before they can do this exercise.

Refer students to *Stand Out Basic Workbook, Unit 6, Lesson 5* for more practice with the present continuous.

Go to the *Activity Bank* online for suggestions on promoting digital literacy and using the Internet to enhance this lesson.

MULTILEVEL WORKSHEET

Lesson 5, Worksheet 1: Present Continuous

INSTRUCTOR'S NOTES

LIFESKILLS I've got a lot of stress

Before You Watch

- Ask students if they have ever been stressed. Then, ask: *What were you stressed about? Did you see a doctor? Do you think stress can make you sick?*

A. Look at the picture and answer the questions.

- Ask the questions and elicit answers.
- Ask students if they can tell what type of doctor the man is in the picture. Then, ask students what doctors usually wear.

While You Watch

B. Watch the video and complete the dialog. Use the words in the box.

- Ask students to watch the video and complete the conversation between Victor and the doctor.
- Read the words in the box and then play the video. Use the pause button if necessary.
- Review any vocabulary that might be unfamiliar to students.

Check Your Understanding

C. Put the sentences in order to make a conversation.

- Ask students to read the sentences and put them in the correct order.
- Play the video again. Then, play the video once more so that students can check their answers.

BEST PRACTICE

There are many ways to use video in the classroom. Students should rarely watch a video without some kind of task. You might introduce comprehension questions before they watch so they know what they are looking for. Below are a few techniques that you may try for variety beyond the comprehension checks and other ideas already presented in this lesson.

Freeze Frame: Pause the video during viewing and use it like a picture dictionary, identifying and expanding on the vocabulary.

Silent Viewing: Show the video in segments without sound so students can guess at the storyline. This helps them to understand that listening is more than just the words people say.

Prediction Techniques: Show portions of the video and ask students to predict what will come next.

Listening without Viewing: This helps students create their own image of what is happening. After a discussion, allow students to watch the video and the sound together.

Back-to-Back: In pairs, one student faces the video and the other faces away. Play the video without sound and ask the student viewing to report to the student who is facing away what is happening.

Summary Strips: Create strips of sentences that describe the events. Have students watch the video and then put the strips in the correct order, or ask students to predict the story line before watching and then check their answers. The Activity Bank has summary strips for each video in *Stand Out*.

LIFESKILLS

I've got a lot of stress

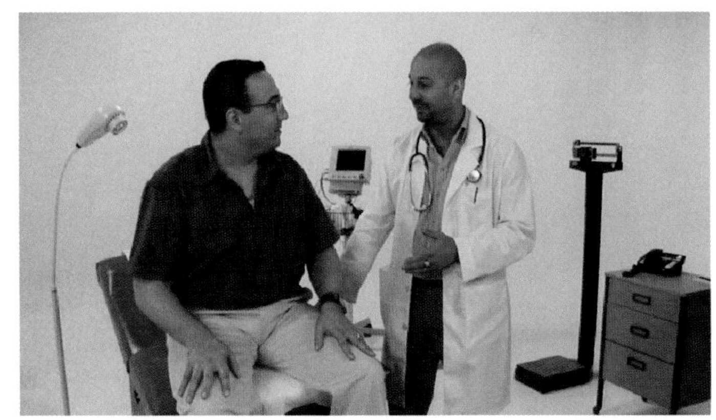

Before You Watch

A. Look at the picture and answer the questions.

1. What is wrong with Mr. Sanchez?
   He has a lot of stress.
2. Who is the man in the white coat?
   He is a doctor.

While You Watch

B. Watch the video and complete the dialog. Use the words in the box.

do	don't	ear	normal	~~mouth~~	sleep

Doctor: Your heart rate is normal. Can you open your (1) ____mouth____ and go "Ah."

Victor: Ah.

Doctor: Good. Now let me see inside your (2) ____ear____.

Victor: What (3) ____do____ you see?

Doctor: Everything looks fine. All your vital signs are (4) ____normal____. Tell me, what brings you in today?

Victor: Well, I'm very tired all the time. I (5) ____don't____ have any energy.

Doctor: Do you get enough (6) ____sleep____?

Check Your Understanding

C. Put the sentences in order to make a conversation.

a. __4__ **Patient:** About five hours a night.

b. __1__ **Doctor:** How are you feeling?

c. __6__ **Patient:** I think you're right. Thanks for the advice, Doctor.

d. __3__ **Doctor:** How much sleep do you get?

e. __2__ **Patient:** Not well. I'm tired all the time.

f. __5__ **Doctor:** That's not enough. You should get at least seven hours a night.

Review

Learner Log

I can identify body parts.
■ Yes ■ No ■ Maybe

I can describe symptoms and illnesses.
■ Yes ■ No ■ Maybe

A. Write the body parts.

head	stomach	hand	foot
neck	arm	leg	nose

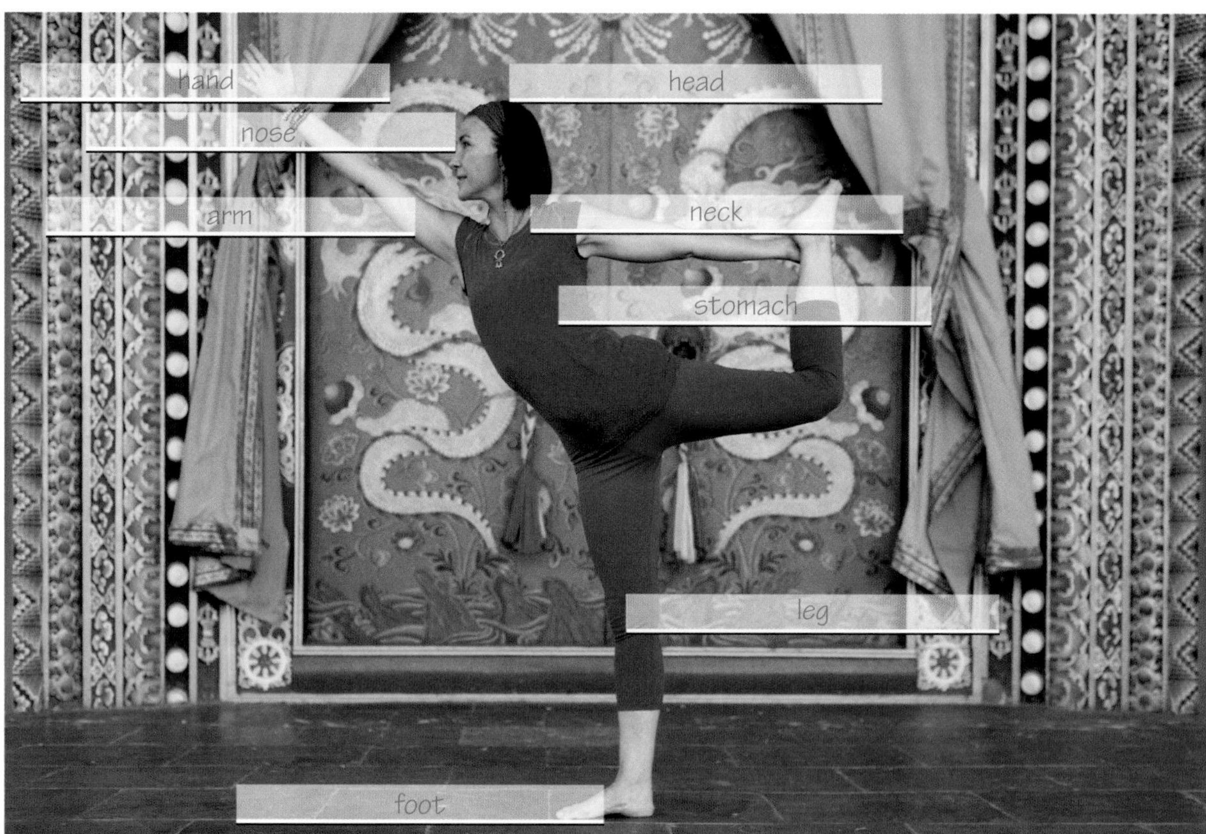

B. Write the symptom or illness.

stomach ___stomachache___

head ___headache___

back ___backache___

throat ___sore throat___

nose ___runny nose___

AT-A-GLANCE **PREP**

Goal: All unit objectives
Grammar: All unit grammar
Academic Strategies: Focused listening, reviewing, evaluating, developing study skills
Vocabulary: All unit vocabulary

Agenda

- Discuss unit objectives.
- Complete the review.

Pacing

- 1.5 hour classes
- 2.5 hour classes
- 3+ hour classes

STANDARDS CORRELATIONS

CCRS: RI1, L1, L2, L5, RF3
CASAS: 3.1.1, 3.1.2, 3.1.3, 3.3.1
***SCANS:* Basic Skills** Reading, writing, listening, speaking
Information Acquire and evaluate information, organize and maintain information, interpret and communicate information
Thinking Skills See things in the mind's eye
***EFF:* Communication** Speak so others can understand
Lifelong Learning Take responsibility for learning, reflect and evaluate

Warm-up and Review

7–10 mins.

With their books closed, ask students to help you make a list on the board of all the vocabulary they can come up with from the unit. Then, have a competition where students in groups will find and write page numbers for each item on the list. The first group to have the correct page number for each item wins.

Introduction

5 mins.

Write all the objectives on the board from Unit 6. Show students the first page of every lesson so they understand that today will be review. Complete the agenda.

Note: Depending on the length of the term, you may decide to have students do Presentation and Practice for homework and then review student work as the warm-up for another class meeting.

Presentation

10–15 mins.

This presentation and practice will cover the first three pages of the review. Quickly, go to the first page of each lesson. Discuss the goal of each. Ask simple questions to remind students what they have learned.

Practice

15–20 mins.

A. Write the body parts. (Lesson 1)

B. Write the symptom or illness. (Lesson 2)

BEST PRACTICE

Recycling/Review

The review process and the project that follows are part of the recycling/review process. Students at this level often need to be reintroduced to concepts to solidify what they have learned. Many concepts are learned and forgotten while learning other new concepts. This is because students learn but are not necessarily ready to acquire language concepts.

Therefore, it becomes very important to review and to show students how to review on their own. It is also important to recycle the new concepts in different contexts.

Practice *(continued)*

C. **Complete the sentences with the present continuous. (Lesson 5)**

D. **Write the medicines. (Lesson 3)**

E. **Read and write in the chart. (Lesson 5)**

INSTRUCTOR'S NOTES

Learner Log

I can identify medications. ■ Yes ■ No ■ Maybe

I can describe actions in a waiting room. ■ Yes ■ No ■ Maybe

C. Complete the sentences with the present continuous.

1. The receptionist ___is___ ___talking___ (talk) on the phone.
2. The patient ___is___ ___sleeping___ (sleep).
3. The people ___are___ ___waiting___ (wait) for the doctor.
4. The women ___are___ ___asking___ (ask) about their children.
5. Hector ___is___ ___reading___ (read) a magazine.

D. Write the medicines.

1. Richard has a headache. What does he need?

   Medicine: ___aspirin___

2. Orlando has a stomachache. What does he need?

   Medicine: ___antacid___

3. Hue has a fever. What does she need?

   Medicine: ___aspirin___

4. Chan has a sore throat. What does he need?

   Medicine: ___cough syrup___

E. Read and write in the chart.

Jeremiah is not very healthy. He smokes ten cigarettes a day. He doesn't exercise. He eats one meal a day. He doesn't sleep eight hours a night. He doesn't drink water. He sees the doctor once a year.

What does Jeremiah do?	What doesn't Jeremiah do?
smoke	exercise
eat one meal a day	sleep eight hours a night
see the doctor once a year	drink water

Learner Log

I can describe healthy habits.

Yes No Maybe

F. Complete the sentences with the simple present.

1. She ___has___ (have) a headache.
2. They ___need___ (need) medicine.
3. We ___are___ (be) sick.
4. I ___am___ (be) healthy.
5. You ___exercise___ (exercise) every day.
6. Mario and Maria ___visit___ (visit) the doctor.
7. He ___sleeps___ (sleep) eight hours a day.
8. Alfonso ___smokes___ (smoke) cigarettes.

G. Complete the sentences with the negative simple present.

1. He ___doesn't smoke___ (smoke) every day.
2. They ___don't eat___ (eat) breakfast.
3. We ___don't need___ (need) medicine.
4. They ___don't exercise___ (exercise).
5. Nga ___doesn't have___ (have) a headache.
6. She ___doesn't visit___ (visit) the doctor.
7. I ___don't want___ (want) lunch.
8. You ___don't exercise___ (exercise).

Practice *(continued)*

F. Complete the sentences with the simple present. (Lessons 2 and 4)

G. Complete the sentences with the negative simple present. (Lesson 4)

Evaluation

15 mins.

Go around the room and check on students' progress. Help individuals when needed. If you see consistent errors among several students, interrupt the class and give a mini lesson or review to help students feel comfortable with the concept.

BEST PRACTICE

Learner Logs

Learner Logs function to help students in many different ways.

1. They serve as part of the review process.
2. They help students to gain confidence and document what they have learned. In this way, students see that they are progressing and want to move forward in learning.
3. They provide students with a tool that they can use over and over to check and recheck their understanding. In this way, students become independent learners.

INSTRUCTOR'S NOTES

WORKPLACE CONNECTION

Combine ideas and information; Make decisions; Exercise leadership roles; Manage time; Complete tasks as assigned; Interact appropriately with team members; Collect and gather information; Interpret and communicate information; Apply technology

STANDARDS CORRELATIONS

CCRS: RI7, SL1, SL2

CASAS: 1.3.9, 4.8.1

***SCANS:* Basic Skills** Reading, writing, listening, speaking

Resources Allocate time, allocate money, allocate materials and facility resources, allocate human resources

Information Acquire and evaluate information, organize and maintain information, interpret and communicate information, use computers to process information

Interpersonal Participate as a member of a team, teach others, serve clients and customers, exercise leadership, negotiate to arrive at a decision, work with cultural diversity

Systems Understand systems, monitor and correct performance, improve and design systems

Thinking Skills Think creatively, make decisions, solve problems, see things in the mind's eye

Personal Qualities Responsibility, sociability, self-management

***EFF:* Communication** Read with understanding, convey ideas in writing, speak so others can understand, listen actively, observe critically

Decision Making Solve problems and make decisions, plan

Interpersonal Cooperate with others, advocate and influence, resolve conflict and negotiate, guide others

Lifelong Learning Take responsibility for learning, reflect and evaluate

Introduction

In this project, students will work in teams to create a role play about two patients visiting the doctor's office. The role play should incorporate the vocabulary and some of the conversations they have learned in this unit.

Stage 1

15–20 mins.

COLLABORATE Form a team with four or five students.

Show students examples of the project if you have one or discuss the art on the student book page.

Help students to assign positions in their groups. On the spot, students will have to choose who will be the leader of their group. Review the responsibility of a leader and ask students to write the name of their leader in their books. Do the same with all positions: writer, artist, and spokesperson.

Stage 2

10–15 mins.

Prepare your roles.

Help students understand that all of them will be part of the conversations. They should write their role assignments in their books.

Stage 3

40–50 mins.

Make an appointment book page.

Together, team members write the conversations between doctor, patient, and receptionist. They may use their books as a resource. The artist will also make an appointment book page as a prop with everyone's assistance.

Stage 4

10–30 mins.

Write conversations for Patient 2.

Ask students to prepare a set of conversations.

Stage 5

10–30 mins.

Present your conversations and appointment book page to the class.

Ask teams to practice their presentations before they give them. Videotaping can greatly enhance the learning experience.

BEST PRACTICE

Digital literacy

Projects are a perfect place to allow students opportunities to use other forms of presentations beyond pictures they create. Digital literacy is becoming more necessary as a life skill. Encourage students to create presentations using pictures from the Internet. They might also consider using other digital presentation tools.

TEAM PROJECT At the doctor's office

1. **COLLABORATE** Form a team with four or five students. In your team, you need:

Position	Job description	Student name
Student 1: Team Leader	Check that everyone speaks English. Check that everyone participates.	
Student 2: Writer	Write conversations to act out.	
Student 3: Artist	Make an appointment book page.	
Students 4/5: Spokespeople	Prepare a presentation.	

2. Prepare your roles.

   Who is the doctor? ______________________

   Who is Patient 1? ______________________

   Who is Patient 2? ______________________

   Who is the receptionist? ______________________

3. Make an appointment book page.

   What is Patient 1's name?
   When is the appointment?
   What is the problem?
   Write a conversation between the receptionist and Patient 1.
   Write a conversation between the doctor and Patient 1.

4. Write conversations for Patient 2.

5. Present your conversations and appointment book page to the class.

About the Explorer

Diana Nyad is a long-distance swimmer from New York City. In 1975, she swam 28 miles around Manhattan. In 1979, she swam 102 miles from North Bimini in the Bahamas to Juno Beach in Florida. In 2013, she successfully swam 110 miles from Havana, Cuba, to Key West, Florida, without a shark cage—the first person to do so. Diana's 110-mile swim took five attempts. Bad weather and jellyfish stings had previously stopped her from reaching her goal, but she persevered and succeeded 35 years after attempting this incredible feat the first time.

About the Photo

This photo was taken during Diana's successful fifth swim from Havana, Cuba, to Key West, Florida. She was the first person to make the crossing without the use of a shark cage. While she avoided shark attacks, she still encountered jellyfish stings and had to wear a protective mask so that the Portuguese men o' war would not sting her face like in previous attempts.

- Introduce the explorer. Tell students they are going to read about a different kind of explorer, Diana Nyad.

A. PREDICT Look at the picture and circle the answers you think are correct.

- Ask students to look at the picture and then answer the questions.
- Read the title and ask students if they know how to swim. Then, ask: *How far do you think you can swim? How many miles?*
- Read the quote and ask students what they think Diana means.

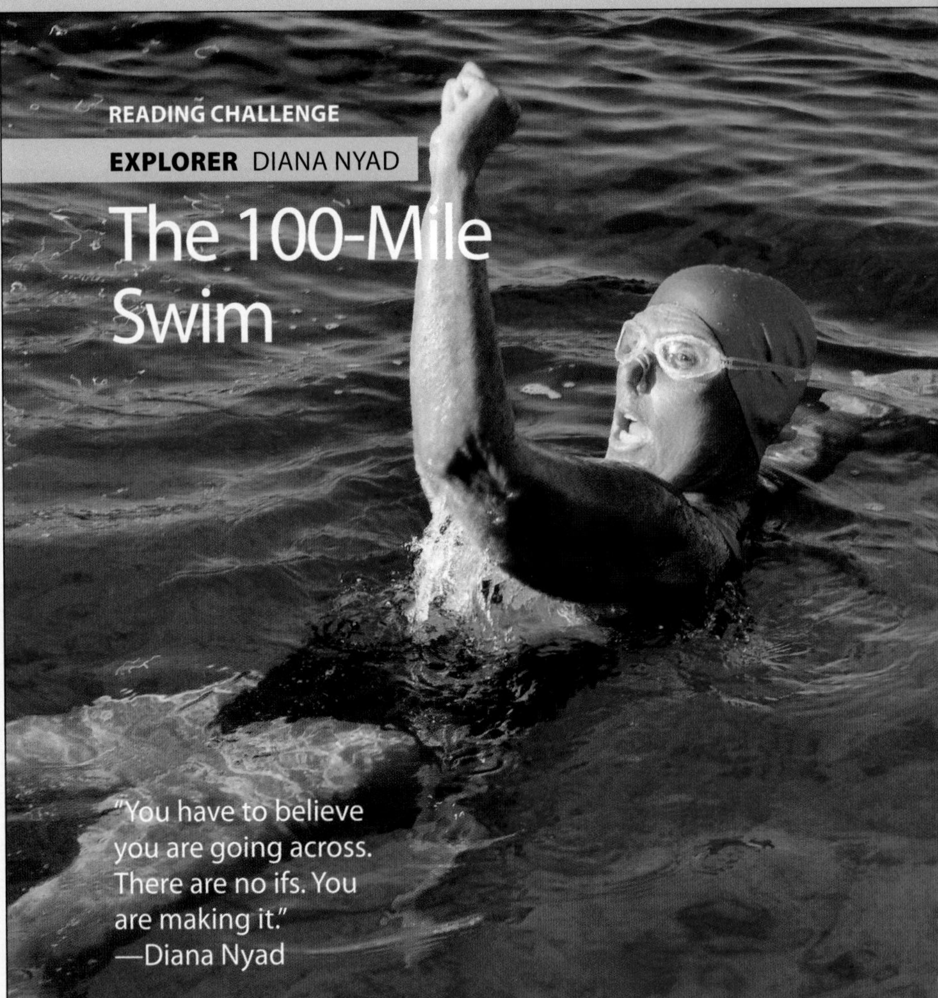

READING CHALLENGE
EXPLORER DIANA NYAD
The 100-Mile Swim
"You have to believe you are going across. There are no ifs. You are making it."
—Diana Nyad

A. PREDICT Look at the picture and circle the answers you think are correct.

1. **Where is Diana Nyad?**
   a. in a pool b. in a lake c. in the ocean d. in a river
2. **What do you think the article is about?**
   a. the ocean b. swimming c. sports d. healthy foods

B. In a group, take turns talking about your favorite sport.

158 Unit 6

CCRS FOR READING
RI1, RI2

WORKPLACE CONNECTION
Exercise E: Collect and organize information
Exercise F: Combine ideas and information

C. Read about Diana Nyad.

It's 2012; Diana Nyad wants to swim from Havana, Cuba to Florida in the United States. The distance between the two countries is over 100 miles, and there are sharks and jellyfish in the water! But, Diana is a professional swimmer. For a long time, she exercises, eats healthy food, and trains to get ready. It's now 2013, and on her fifth attempt, Diana successfully makes it all the way—110.86 miles—from Cuba to the United States.

D. Check your answers in Exercise A. Ask and answer with a partner.

1. Where is Diana Nyad? c. in the ocean
2. What is the story about? b. swimming

E. Answer the questions about the article and complete the table.

1. What does Diana do to get ready?

She exercises, eats healthy foods, and trains.

2. What dangers are in the water?

Sharks and jellyfish are in the water.

Everyday activities	Dangers in the water
exercises	sharks
eats	jellyfish
trains	

F. CREATE What healthy things do you do every day? Make a list. Answers will vary.

READING STRATEGIES

Making Lists

Creating lists is a good strategy to help students summarize readings, note details, key points, or main ideas. It is a valuable tool for recalling both general and specific information. A good list is also useful as a study tool that enables students to review their notes in a well-organized manner.

B. In a group, take turns talking about your favorite sport.

- Ask students to work in small groups and take turns talking about their favorite sports.
- Have students make a list of the sports mentioned in their group discussion and ask them to compare with another group.
- Ask the class: *What are the most unusual sports mentioned?* Discuss as a class.

C. Read about Diana Nyad.

Ask students to read the passage about Diana Nyad.

D. Check your answers in Exercise A. Ask and answer with a partner.

Have students check their predictions about Diana from Exercise A by answering the questions with a partner.

E. Answer the questions about the article and complete the table.

- Ask students to read each question and complete the statement.
- Then, ask students to complete the table with the correct information.
- Copy the table on the board and have volunteers write the correct answers.

F. CREATE What healthy things do you do every day? Make a list.

- Ask students to make a list of their own healthy habits that they do daily.
- Have students share their lists in small groups.
- Write your own list on the board and share it with the class. Then, discuss common and uncommon daily habits everyone does to stay healthy.

UNIT 7

Work

About the Photo

Abner Kingman took this photo. He is a photographer who specializes in marine subjects. He attends events such as the America's Cup to photograph the fast-paced action, and he also spends time aboard fishing vessels in different parts of the world. This photograph was taken aboard a vessel in the San Francisco Bay area. It shows a group of fisherman working hard to haul in their fishing nets full of anchovies. Surrounding the boat are flocks of seagulls that like to eat the anchovies. The anchovies collected by the fishermen will be sold as bait to sport fishermen.

- Introduce the unit. Then, ask students: *Do you work? What do you do?* Ask students to share their experiences.
- Ask students to read and answer the questions. Have volunteers write the job duties on the board.
- Read the caption. Then, ask: *What else do fishermen fish for?*
- Go over the unit outcomes. Ask: *What are some of your job duties? Have you ever been given a work evaluation? Do you follow directions well?* Discuss as a class.

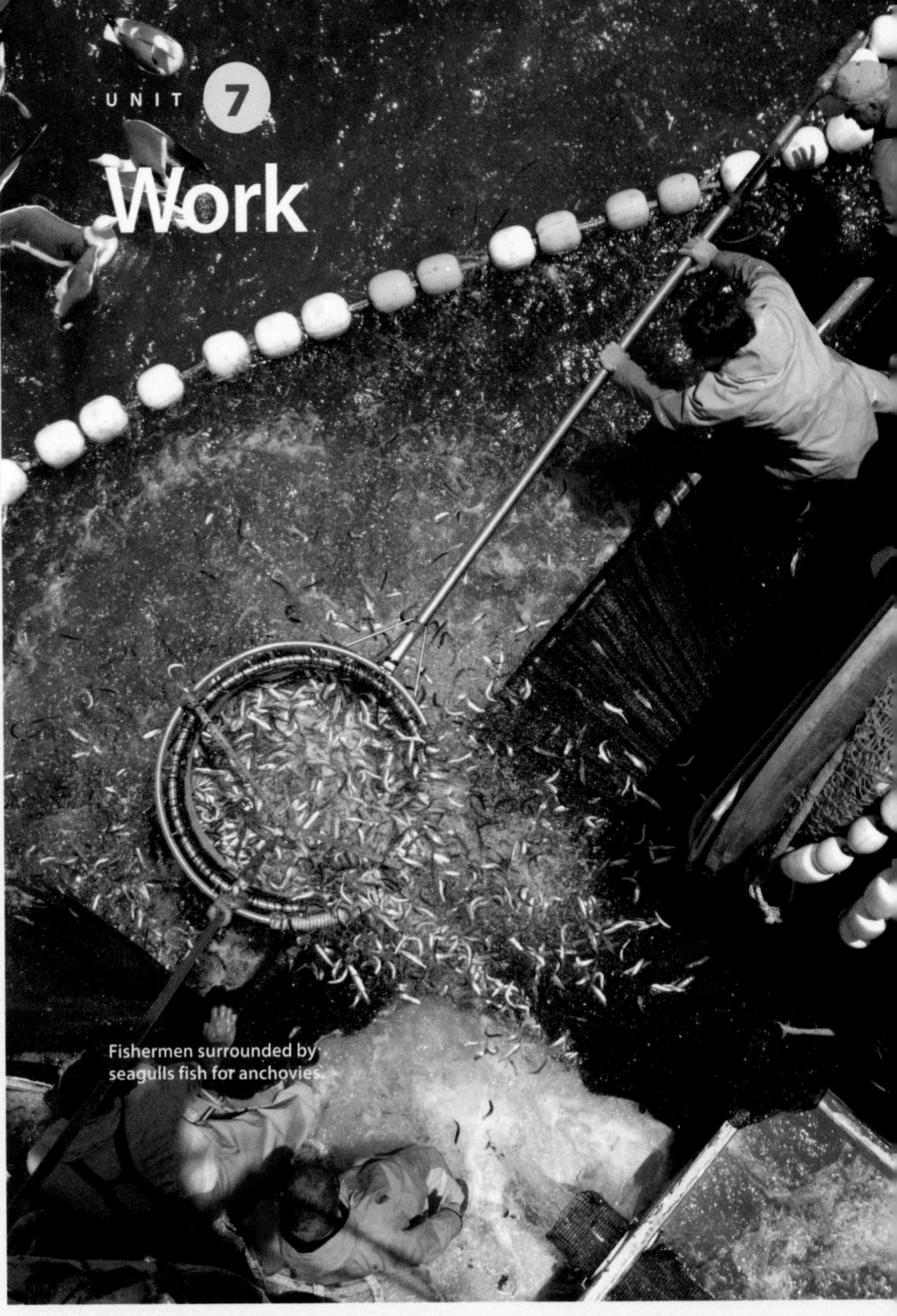

Fishermen surrounded by seagulls fish for anchovies.

UNIT OUTCOMES	GRAMMAR	VOCABULARY	EL CIVICS
• Identify occupations • Give information about work • Identify job duties • Read evaluations • Follow directions	• Information questions: *when, where, what, who* • Modal: *can* and *can't* • Simple present • Negative simple present • Affirmative and negative commands	See scope and sequence on pages viii-xiii for a detailed list of vocabulary related to the following topics: • Occupations • Workplace • Character adjectives	The skills students learn in this unit can be applied to the following EL Civics competency areas: • Employment • Communication

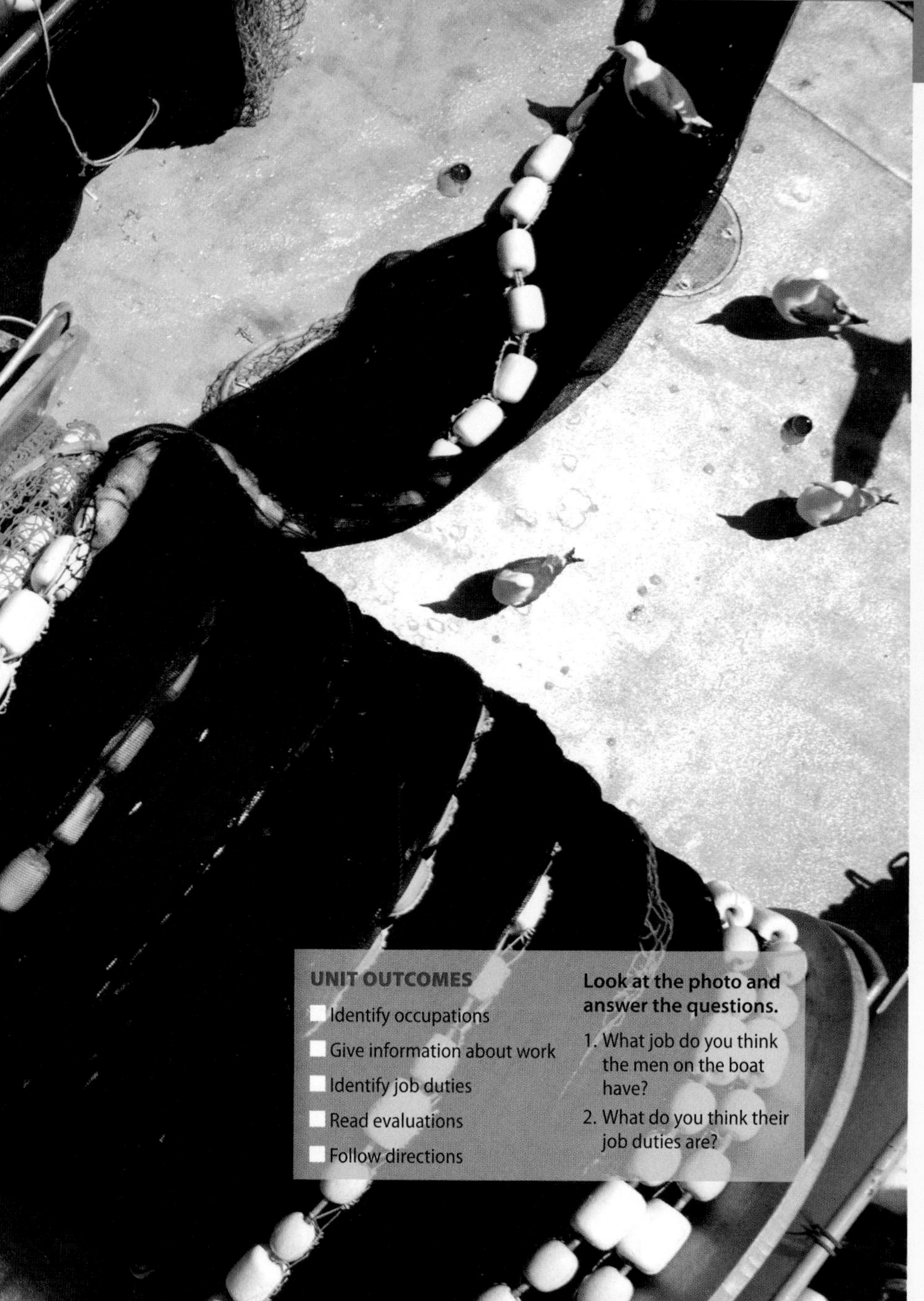

UNIT OUTCOMES

- Identify occupations
- Give information about work
- Identify job duties
- Read evaluations
- Follow directions

Look at the photo and answer the questions.

1. What job do you think the men on the boat have?
2. What do you think their job duties are?

Life Skills Link

In this unit, students will learn how to identify different occupations and what is required within different positions. They will also learn how their efforts are evaluated and assessed in the workplace.

Workplace Link

All lessons and units in *Stand Out* include basic communication skills and interpersonal skills important for the workplace. They are not individually identified. Other workplace skills are indicated. They include, collecting and organizing information, making decisions and solving problems, and combining ideas and information.

CASAS	SCANS	CCRS
Lesson 1: 0.2.1, 4.1.8 Lesson 2: 0.1.6, 4.8.1 Lesson 3: 4.1.3, 4.1.8, 4.4.4 Lesson 4: 4.4.4 Lesson 5: 4.4.4, 4.8.1, 4.8.3 Review: 4.1.3, 4.1.8, 4.4.1, 4.8.1, 4.8.3, 7.4.1, 7.4.2, 7.4.3 Team Project: 2.2.3, 4.8.1	Many SCANs skills are incorporated in the unit with an emphasis on: • Acquiring and evaluating information • Organizing and maintaining information • Interpreting and communicating information • Basic skills • Self-management	RI1, RI7, SL1, SL2, SL4, L1, L2, L5, RF2, RF3

LESSON 1 Do you work?

GOAL ■ Identify occupations

A. PREDICT **Look at the picture. What are the people talking about?**

B. Listen and read.

CD 2
TR 33

My name is Emilio. I live in Dallas, Texas. I have a new job. I'm a cashier at Ultra Supermarket on Broadway! This is a picture of my class.

C. Write. What does Emilio do?

He's a student; he's also a cashier.

AT-A-GLANCE **PREP**

Goal: Identify occupations
Grammar: Simple present
Pronunciation: /r/
Academic Strategy: Focused listening
Vocabulary: *job, student, occupations*

Agenda

- Interview classmates.
- Talk about Emilio's job.
- Learn about jobs.
- Practice writing about jobs.
- Ask a classmate about jobs.

Resources

Multilevel Worksheet: Lesson 1, Worksheet 1
Workbook: Unit 7, Lesson 1
Audio: CD 2, Tracks 33–34
Heinle Picture Dictionary: Jobs 1, pages 146–147; Jobs 2, pages 148–149
Stand Out Basic Assessment CD-ROM with ExamView®

Pacing

- 1.5 hour classes
- 2.5 hour classes
- 3⁺ hour classes

STANDARDS CORRELATIONS

CCRS: RI1, W2, SL2, L1, L2, L5, RF2, RF3
CASAS: 0.2.1, 4.1.8
SCANS: **Basic Skills** Reading, writing, listening, speaking
Information Acquire and evaluate information
EFF: **Communication** Read with understanding, speak so others can understand, listen actively

Preassessment *(optional)*

Use the Stand Out Basic Assessment CD-ROM with ExamView® to create a pretest for Unit 7.

Warm-up and Review

15–20 mins.

Ask students their names, addresses, and phone numbers. Write the three questions and any others you would like on the board and ask students to interview one another.

Introduction

3–7 mins.

Write *teach* on the board. Ask: *What do I do?* Lead students to the response *teach* and say: *I teach. I'm a teacher.* Add *-er* to *teach*. State the goal: *Today, we will identify occupations.*

Presentation 1

40–50 mins.

A. PREDICT Look at the picture. What are the people talking about?

Ask students questions and pull out as many nouns as you can.

B. Listen and read.

Have students close their books and listen. Then, have them open their books and read along.

LISTENING SCRIPT

CD 2 TR 33

The listening script matches the paragraph in Exercise B.

C. Write. What does Emilio do?

Teach that *What do you do?* is often asked to find out one's job. Ask students what they do. Make sure they understand that they can answer *student, homemaker*, or a paid job.

Practice 1

15–20 mins.

Ask students to copy the paragraph in Exercise B. Show them how it is indented.

Write on the board the following two sentences: *I have a job. I don't have a job.* Ask students to write a paragraph about themselves based on the model in Exercise B. If students don't finish in class, ask them to finish their paragraphs for homework.

In this unit, students will be introduced to several paragraphs. This activity will prepare them for this exposure.

A paragraph for a student who doesn't have a job might look like the following:

My name is Lidia. I live in Sacramento, California. I don't have a job. I'm a student at Oak Haven Adult School.

Evaluation 1

3–5 mins.

Check students' writing. Focus on indenting, capital letters, periods, and the comma before the state. Make sure students understand that state names are usually not abbreviated in paragraphs.

Presentation 2

10–15 mins.

Ask students to close their books. Play charades by using 3-by-5 index cards with the six occupations in Exercise D on them. Give six student volunteers each a card and have them act out the occupation on that card.

D. Listen and repeat the words. What do these people do?

Ask students to point as you say: *He's a cashier. She's a doctor.*

LISTENING SCRIPT

CD 2 TR 34

cashier	*student*
doctor	*salesperson*
bus driver	*teacher*

Prepare students to do the practice by going over the dialog as a class. Show them how to substitute information.

BEST PRACTICE

Practicing dialogs

1. Ask students to read the dialog individually.
2. Ask students to note any words or expressions that they do not understand.
3. Discuss the dialog as a class. Ask students if they have ever had a similar conversation.
4. Have students learn the correct pronunciation. Read the dialog aloud or play the recording while students listen. Ask students to repeat as a group and in pairs. Check pronunciation.
5. Ask students to create their own dialog based on the vocabulary and expressions used in the dialog presented.

INTONATION

/r/

The /r/ sound in English is problematic for many students. Many languages don't pronounce the /r/ like Americans do. When they see it, students will often tend to try to pronounce it as they would in their own language.

Help students to see that the /r/ in *doctor, driver, cashier*, and *teacher* is pronounced with little if any tongue movement and the lips are rounded. Exaggeration can help students see how it is done.

In this presentation, you may choose to expand the lesson and in turn, the pronunciation portion, by showing students how adding *-er* to most any verb will change it to a noun indicating someone who performs this verb. Use the following examples:

teach-teacher
drive-driver
clean-cleaner
walk-walker
talk-talker
drink-drinker
run-runner
play-player

Practice 2

7–10 mins.

E. Practice the conversation with a partner. Use the words in Exercise D.

Evaluation 2

7–10 mins.

F. Write sentences about the people in Exercise D.

Check students' work.

D. Listen and repeat the words. What do these people do?

CD 2
TR 34

Emilio
cashier

Hue
doctor

Chan
bus driver

Carolina
student

Davit
salesperson

Pete
teacher

E. Practice the conversation with a partner. Use the words in Exercise D.

Student A: What does Emilio do?
Student B: He's a cashier.

F. Write sentences about the people in Exercise D.

1. Emilio is a cashier.
2. Hue is a doctor.
3. Chan is a bus driver.
4. Carolina is a student.
5. Davit is a salesperson.
6. Pete is a teacher.

WORKPLACE CONNECTION

Exercises G and J: Collect and organize information

G. CLASSIFY Write the jobs in the table. Answers will vary.

cook custodian mail carrier manager nurse

School	Restaurant	Clothing store	Community	Doctor's office
teacher	cashier	salesperson	bus driver	doctor
custodian	cook	manager	mail carrier	nurse

H. Practice the conversation. Use the information in Exercise G to make new conversations.

Student A: Where does a teacher work?
Student B: A teacher works in a school.

SIMPLE PRESENT	
I work.	I don't work.
He works.	He doesn't work.
She works.	She doesn't work.

I. Read the conversation.

Student A: Do you work?
Student B: Yes, I work. I'm a cashier. How about you? Do you work?
Student A: No, I don't work. I'm a student.

Answers will vary.

J. Practice the conversation in Exercise I with four classmates and complete the table.

Name	Occupation

K. What do your friends and family do? Make a list.

Presentation 3

10–15 mins.

Go over the vocabulary with students. Help them with pronunciation. Pay particular attention to the final consonants. Make sure they release on the /n/ of *custodian*, the /k/ in *cook*, and the /s/ in *nurse*. Also, make sure they round their lips with the /r/ in *manager* and *carrier*.

G. CLASSIFY Write the jobs in the table.

Write *where* on the board. Show students how the information they write in Exercise G will help them do the practice, Exercise H. Do Exercise G as a class. The first words in the chart are from Exercise D. The second entries can be the new words in the box above. See if students can come up with one more word for each category. Notice that the categories relate to the topics covered in Units 1–6. Show students how they can go back in their books and discover more job titles.

Prepare students for the practice by going over the dialog in Exercise H. Remind students how to use the simple present in the affirmative and in the negative.

Practice 3

7–10 mins.

H. Practice the conversation. Use the information in Exercise G to make new conversations.

Evaluation 3

2–7 mins.

Ask volunteers to present their new conversations in front of the class.

Application

7–10 mins.

I. Read the conversation.

Go over the conversation and show students how they will change it to do Exercise J.

J. Practice the conversation in Exercise I with four classmates and complete the table.

K. What do your friends and family do? Make a list.

Refer students to *Stand Out Basic Workbook, Unit 7, Lesson 1* for more practice with the simple present.

Go to the *Activity Bank* online for suggestions on promoting digital literacy and using the Internet to enhance this lesson.

MULTILEVEL WORKSHEET

Lesson 1, Worksheet 1: Occupations

INSTRUCTOR'S NOTES

AT-A-GLANCE **PREP**

Goal: Give information about work
Grammar: Information questions
Academic Strategies: Focused listening, making graphs
Vocabulary: *receptionist, custodian, manager, nurse, supervisor, when, where, what, who*

Agenda

- Review occupations.
- Listen to information about jobs.
- Ask *what, when, where,* and *who*.
- Read about a nurse.
- Answer questions about your job or school.

Resources

Multilevel Worksheet: Lesson 2, Worksheet 1
Workbook: Unit 7, Lesson 2
Audio: CD 2, Tracks 35–39
Heinle Picture Dictionary: Working, pages 150–151

Pacing

■ 1.5 hour classes ■ 2.5 hour classes
■ 3+ hour classes

STANDARDS CORRELATIONS

CCRS: RI1, SL1, SL2, L1, L2, RF3
CASAS: 0.1.6, 4.8.1
SCANS: **Basic Skills** Reading, writing, listening, speaking
Information Acquire and evaluate information, organize and maintain information, interpret and communicate information
EFF: **Communication** Read with understanding, speak so others can understand, listen actively, observe critically

Warm-up and Review 15–20 mins.

Take a class poll of jobs, including *students* and *homemakers*. Make a bar graph of the results.

Introduction 5–7 mins.

Write *when* and *where* on the board. Use these words to ask about work. State the goal: *Today, we will learn to give information about work.*

Presentation 1 15–20 mins.

Help students to understand the information next to the pictures. Ask questions about it.

A. PREDICT Write the jobs from the box. Then, listen to check your answers.

Play the recording. Ask students to follow along.

LISTENING SCRIPT

CD 2 TR 35

1. *Hello, I'm Isabel. I have a great job. I am a receptionist. I work for the Johnson Company and my supervisor's name is Martin. I work from 9:00 a.m. to 6:00 p.m., Monday through Friday. I take a one-hour lunch break at 12:00.*
2. *My name is Cory. I am the manager of Freedman's Foods. My supervisor is Amelia. I work Wednesday through Sunday from 2:00 p.m. to 10:00 p.m. I take a one-hour break at 6:00.*
3. *I'm Fred. My friends call me Freddy. I work late at night. I work from 10:00 p.m. to 7:00 a.m., Sunday to Friday. I'm a custodian at America Bank. My supervisor's name is Mary.*

Practice 1 15–20 mins.

B. Listen and write the names of the people from Exercise A.

The people in these conversations are the same ones as in Exercise A. Students will write *Isabel, Cory,* or *Fred* in the blanks.

LISTENING SCRIPT

CD 2 TR 36

1. **Manager:** *Please take care of the customer over there.*
Employee: *OK. You are the boss.*
Manager: *Oh, and please write down any problems she is having.*
Employee: *I can do that.*
Manager: *You can go home after you take care of those two things.*
Employee: *Thanks!*

2. **Custodian:** *Excuse me, I need to mop under your desk.*
Coworker: *OK, I'll move for a few minutes.*
Custodian: *Thanks. I need to mop the whole bank every day.*

3. **Manager:** *My name is Martin. I am your new supervisor.*
Receptionist: *Nice to meet you, Martin.*
Manager: *Nice to meet you, too. When do you come to work?*
Receptionist: *I work from 9:00 a.m. to 6:00 p.m. every weekday.*

Evaluation 1 3–5 mins.

Check students' work.

LESSON 2 When do you go to work?

GOAL ■ Give information about work

A. PREDICT Write the jobs from the box. Then, listen to check your answers.

CD 2 TR 35

manager	receptionist	custodian

1\. 

Name: Isabel
Title: receptionist
Company: Johnson Company
Supervisor: Martin
Hours: 9 a.m. to 6 p.m.
Break: 12 p.m. to 1 p.m.
Days: Monday to Friday

2\. 

Name: Cory
Title: manager
Company: Freedman's Foods
Supervisor: Amelia
Hours: 2 p.m. to 10 p.m.
Break: 6 p.m. to 7 p.m.
Days: Wednesday to Sunday

3\. 

Name: Fred
Title: custodian
Company: America Bank
Supervisor: Mary
Hours: 10 p.m. to 7 a.m.
Break: 1 a.m. to 2 a.m.
Days: Sunday to Friday

B. Listen and write the names of the people from Exercise A.

CD 2 TR 36

1\. Cory 2. Fred 3. Isabel

C. Read.

Question word	Type of answer	Example sentence with *be*	Example sentence with *do*
What	Asking for information	What **is your** name? What **is his** name?	What **do you** do? What **does** he do?
Where	Asking about a place or position	Where **is your** office? Where **is her** office?	Where **do you** work? Where **does she** work?
When	Asking about time	When **is your** break? When **is his** break?	When **do you** work? When **does he** work?
Who	Asking about a person	Who **is your** supervisor? Who **is her** supervisor?	Who **do you** like? Who **does she** like?

D. Match the questions and answers about Cory.

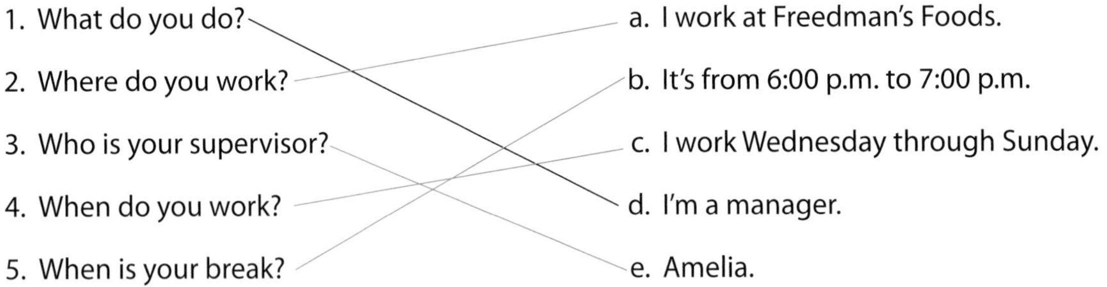

1. What do you do?
2. Where do you work?
3. Who is your supervisor?
4. When do you work?
5. When is your break?

a. I work at Freedman's Foods.
b. It's from 6:00 p.m. to 7:00 p.m.
c. I work Wednesday through Sunday.
d. I'm a manager.
e. Amelia.

E. With a partner, ask and answer the questions in Exercise D. Take turns being Isabel, Cory, and Fred from Exercise A.

F. Read.

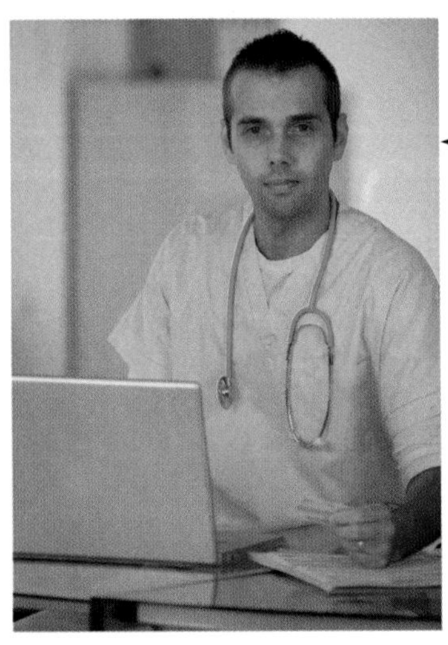

My name is Ben. I'm a nurse. I work at a hospital from 7:00 a.m. to 7:00 p.m. I work Monday through Thursday. I help the doctors and talk to patients. My supervisor is Dr. O'Malley.

Presentation 2

10–15 mins.

C. Read.

Go over the uses of *what, where, when,* and *who*. The first three words have been previously introduced. You may ask some questions such as: *Where do you live? When do you come to school? What do you do?* Remind students of questions they have been exposed to throughout *Stand Out Basic*. Show them the difference between each word by identifying what kind of information is being asked for. Note that forming questions will be complicated for students at this level. They are exposed here to the structure, but it should not be assumed that they will acquire the structure at this stage in their language learning.

D. Match the questions and answers about Cory.

This is still at the presentation stage, so do the exercise as a class. After you finish, ask the same questions about Isabel.

Practice 2

7–10 mins.

E. With a partner, ask and answer the questions in Exercise D. Take turns being Isabel, Cory, and Fred from Exercise A.

Ask students in pairs to imagine one of them is Fred. Student A uses the questions in Exercise D. Student B, or Fred, answers by looking at the information on page 165. Have students reverse roles.

Evaluation 2

3–5 mins.

Ask for volunteers to demonstrate the questions and answers in front of the class.

BEST PRACTICE

Stages in grammar acquisition

It is important at this level that students don't get overwhelmed with too much information. Learning one objective well is often more important than having a weak grasp of many things.

Teaching grammar becomes problematic when instructors expect students to acquire the structure after introducing it to them only a few times. Consider the order of the following:

1. Exposure
2. Instruction
3. Application outside of the classroom
4. Acquisition

A lot of what students see in *Stand Out Basic* is exposure and instruction. Students do receive instruction at various times on the same structures in different contexts and are given the opportunity to apply what they have learned, but few students at this level will use the structures outside of the classroom. This is because they don't have the other necessary tools (vocabulary, competencies, etc.) to be able to use them regularly. This is why we repeat and recycle the structures so often in *Stand Out Basic*. Acquisition will come as students take the language they are using in the classroom outside of the classroom. *Stand Out 1* and *2* review most of these same structures while adding more in preparation for language acquisition.

In this lesson, students are not ready to form questions. This process is somewhat complicated. They are, however, ready to answer questions. The formation of questions, therefore, is merely necessary exposure.

Presentation 3

10–15 mins.

F. Read.

Allow students time to read the paragraph about Ben silently. After 30 seconds, have students close their books. Ask students the questions in Exercise G. See how much students remember. Then, ask students to open their books again.

G. Answer the questions.

Do this activity as a class. Remind students about the differences between the question words, especially *when* and *where*. Sometimes, students have a problem distinguishing between these two words.

Prepare students for the listening practice in Exercise H. Remind them of the principles of focused listening. This activity is much harder than the previous focused listening activities because students are listening for three pieces of information for each person.

Practice 3

7–10 mins.

H. Listen. Complete the chart about Tan, Maria, and Alfredo.

Play the recording four times. Allow students to discuss among themselves between tracks.

LISTENING SCRIPT

CD 2
TR 37–39

My name is Tan. I have a great job. I work late at night and sleep during the day. I'm a custodian. I start work at 3:00 p.m. I work at a school.

My name is Maria. I'm a manager at a restaurant. I work Monday through Friday. I work with customers and all the employees.

My name is Alfredo. I'm a nurse. I work at a hospital. I take care of patients and help the doctors on the fifth floor. I start work at 6:00 p.m.

Evaluation 3

5–7 mins.

Check students' answers as a class. Play the recording again if necessary.

Application

10–15 mins.

I. Practice the conversation. Use the information in Exercise H to make new conversations. Ask and answer questions about Tan, Maria, and Alfredo.

Ask students to practice the conversation. Have them use the information from Exercise H to make new conversations. Ask students to substitute the names and the questions words: *what, when,* and *where*.

J. APPLY Answer the questions.

Ask students to answer the questions and report to a group. One student in each group will stand and give his or her answers. Then, a new student stands and does the same.

Refer students to *Stand Out Basic Workbook, Unit 7, Lesson 2* for more practice with answering information questions.

Go to the *Activity Bank* online for suggestions on promoting digital literacy and using the Internet to enhance this lesson.

MULTILEVEL WORKSHEET

Lesson 2, Worksheet 1: *When, Where,* and *What*

INSTRUCTOR'S NOTES

G. Answer the questions.

1. What does Ben do? He's a nurse.
2. When does he start work? He starts work at 7:00 a.m.
3. Where does he work? He works at a hospital.
4. Who is Ben's supervisor? His supervisor is Dr. O'Malley.

H. Listen. Complete the chart about Tan, Maria, and Alfredo.

CD 2
TR 37–39

	What	When	Where
Tan	custodian	3:00 p.m	school
Maria	manager	Monday-Friday	restaurant
Alfredo	nurse	6:00 p.m.	hospital

I. Practice the conversation. Use the information in Exercise H to make new conversations. Ask and answer questions about Tan, Maria, and Alfredo.

Student A: What does Tan do?
Student B: He's a custodian.

J. APPLY Answer the questions. Answers will vary.

1. What do you do? ______
2. Where do you work or go to school? ______
3. Who is your supervisor or teacher? ______
4. When do you work or go to school? ______

LESSON 3 What do you do?

WORKPLACE CONNECTION
Exercise B: Collect and organize information

GOAL ■ Identify job duties

CD 2 TR 40

A. Listen and write.

answer phones	talk to customers	send memos	change light bulbs

1. 

answer phones

2. 

send memos

3. 

talk to customers

4. 

change light bulbs

CD 2 TR 41

B. What do they do? Listen and write.

supervises employees   helps doctors   makes change
answers phones   talks to customers   ~~sends memos~~   mops floors

Occupation	Job description
1. administrative assistant	sends memos
2. custodian	mops floors
3. receptionist	answers phones
4. salesperson	talks to customers
5. cashier	makes change
6. manager	supervises employees
7. nurse	helps doctors

AT-A-GLANCE **PREP**

Goal: Identify job duties
Grammar: *Can*
Academic Strategy: Focused listening
Vocabulary: *worker, salesperson, administrative assistant, floor, schedule, memo, customer, on time*

Agenda

- Talk about jobs.
- Learn about job actions.
- Listen and answer *yes/no* questions.
- Use *can* to describe what you are able to do.

Resources

Multilevel Worksheets: Lesson 3, Worksheets 1 and 2
Workbook: Unit 7, Lesson 3
Audio: CD 2, Tracks 40–41
Heinle Picture Dictionary: Working, pages 150–151

Pacing

■ 1.5 hour classes ■ 2.5 hour classes
■ 3⁺ hour classes

STANDARDS CORRELATIONS

CCRS: RI1, SL1, SL2, L1, L2, RF3
CASAS: 4.1.3, 4.1.8, 4.4.4
SCANS: **Basic Skills** Reading, writing, listening, speaking
Resources Allocate human resources
Information Acquire and evaluate information, interpret and communicate information
EFF: **Communication** Read with understanding, convey ideas in writing, speak so others can understand, listen actively, observe critically
Lifelong Learning Reflect and evaluate

Warm-up and Review 7–10 mins. ■■■

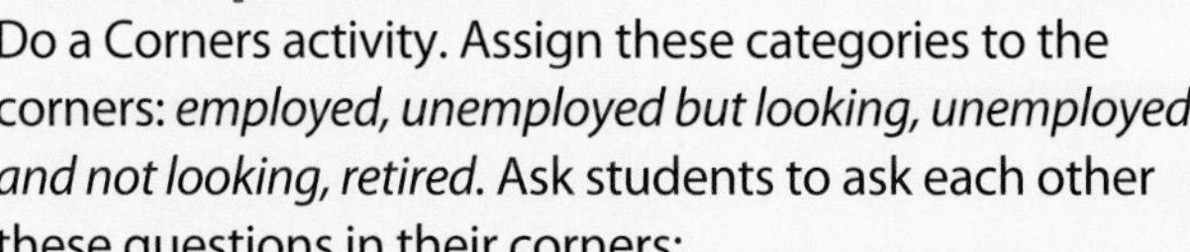

Do a Corners activity. Assign these categories to the corners: *employed, unemployed but looking, unemployed and not looking, retired.* Ask students to ask each other these questions in their corners:

Employed: *Where do you work? When do you start work?*
Unemployed: *What job do you want? Where do you want to work?*
Not employed, Retired: *What do you do? Where do you live?*

Introduction 3–5 mins. ■■■

Tell students that you teach. Also, tell them that you take roll and talk to students. Write these two duties on the board. Write *duties* above the phrases. State the goal: *Today, we will identify job duties.*

Presentation 1 12–15 mins. ■■■

Go over the pictures in Exercise A and help students with the vocabulary, especially verbs. Review the simple present. Point out that it is necessary in these sentences to use the final *s*.

A. Listen and write.

LISTENING SCRIPT

CD 2 TR 40

1. *Receptionists have many responsibilities. They schedule meetings and talk to customers. They also answer the phone.*
2. *Administrative assistants are very important. They do many things. One of the important things they do is send memos.*
3. *A salesperson is important. He or she talks to customers and answers their questions.*
4. *Custodians work in many different places. The custodian at the elementary school mops the floor, cleans the rooms, and changes the light bulbs.*

Practice 1 7–10 mins. ■■■

B. What do they do? Listen and write.

Have students cover Exercise A. Teach the expression *What do you do?* Explain that sometimes we answer with a job title and sometimes describe our duties. Play the recording for the example. Then, have students complete the chart as they listen.

LISTENING SCRIPT

CD 2 TR 41

1. *An administrative assistant has important responsibilities. He or she sends memos, for one thing.*
2. *Custodians work in many different places. The custodian at an elementary school mops floors.*
3. *Receptionists have many responsibilities. For example, a receptionist in an office answers phones.*
4. *A salesperson is important. He or she talks to customers and does many other things.*
5. *Cashiers are usually in the front of a store or business. A cashier in a supermarket makes change as well as many other things.*
6. *A manager is responsible for seeing that all goes well in a business. He or she supervises other employees.*
7. *A nurse in a hospital helps the doctors as much as possible.*

Evaluation 1 3–7 min s. ■■■

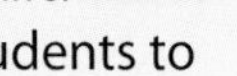

Re-create the chart on the board and ask students to complete it.

Presentation 2

15–20 mins.

C. Read.

Ask students to look at the pictures and read about what each person does. Ask them to think about what else each person does on their job.

Practice 2

10–15 mins.

D. APPLY Complete the chart.

Help students learn the new vocabulary. Show students how a receptionist can have more than one duty (schedule meetings and answer phones). Ask students what else a receptionist might do. Encourage students to look at the chart.

Go over the chart with students and make sure they understand how to read it. To make sure they understand, ask them comprehension questions such as: *What does an administrative assistant do?*

If you feel your students are ready, you might teach them how to use *and* as well as when to use commas. Write sentences on the board. Here are two example sentences: *A receptionist answers phones, talks to customers, and schedules meetings. A custodian mops and takes breaks.*

Now, ask *yes/no* questions. Remind students of the intonation. Go over the examples as a class.

E. Answer the questions. Check (✓) *Yes* or *No*. Practice with a partner.

Evaluation 2

3–5 mins.

Go over the answers as a class by having different students ask and answer the questions.

INSTRUCTOR'S NOTES

C. Read.

A receptionist schedules meetings.

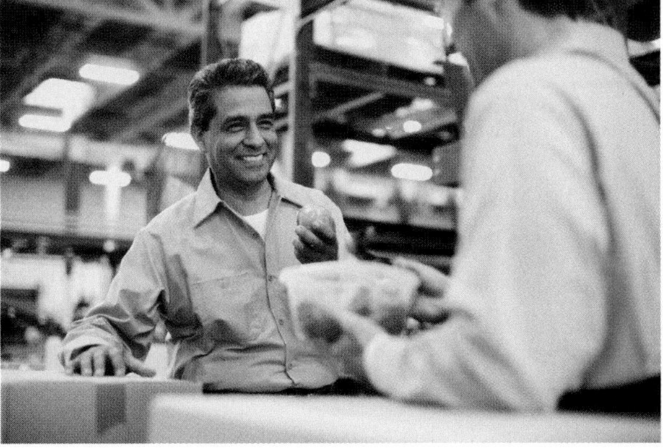

Sometimes, workers take breaks.

D. APPLY Complete the chart. Answers will vary.

	mops	answers phones	talks to customers	sends memos	takes breaks	schedules meetings
salesperson		x	x		x	
administrative assistant		x		x	x	x
receptionist		x	x		x	x
custodian	x				x	

YES/NO QUESTIONS

Does he clean?

Does she schedule meetings?

Does he talk to customers?

E. Answer the questions. Check (✓) *Yes* or *No*. Practice with a partner. Answers will vary.

	Yes	No
1. Does a salesperson supervise employees?		✓
2. Does an administrative assistant take breaks?	✓	
3. Does a custodian talk to customers?		✓
4. Does a receptionist talk to customers?	✓	
5. Does a salesperson mop the floors?		✓

F. Read.

Can			
Subject	***Can***	**Verb (base)**	**Example sentence**
I, You, He, She, It, We, They	can	send	I can send memos.
		change	He can change a light bulb.

Can't			
Subject	***Can't***	**Verb (base)**	**Example sentence**
I, You, He, She, It, We, They	can't	send	I can't send memos.
		change	He can't change a light bulb.

G. Complete the sentences with *can* + the verb.

1. He can file (file) papers.
2. They can send (send) memos.
3. I can mop (mop) the floor.
4. You can answer (answer) phones.

H. Complete the sentences with *can't* + the verb.

1. We can't take (take) breaks.
2. They can't type (type).
3. I can't talk (talk) to customers.
4. She can't file (file).

I. APPLY Write what you *can* and *can't* do. Use words from this lesson. Answers will vary.

1. I can ______.
2. ______.

1. I can't ______.
2. ______.

Presentation 3

7–10 mins.

F. Read.

Go over the charts with students. You may wish to introduce some grammar terminology at this point, such as *base form* and *negative*.

For shorter classes, ask students to do Exercises G and H for homework.

BEST PRACTICE

Reviewing grammar charts

Although charts provide valuable information, student often need to do more than reading and memorizing to have a better understanding of the grammar points they will cover in subsequent exercises.

In order to engage students in reviewing the charts, teachers can ask for volunteers to present the information to the class. They can also ask students to substitute the subjects and the verbs to create their own example sentences. These new examples can be shared with the class by having students write them on the board. Personalizing the grammar charts will help students better retain the information presented.

Practice 3

10–15 mins.

G. Complete the sentences with *can* + the verb.

H. Complete the sentences with *can't* + the verb.

Evaluation 3

5–7 mins.

Check the students' book work and go over the answers as a class.

Application

15–20 mins.

I. APPLY Write what you *can* and *can't* do. Use words from this lesson.

This activity is to help students evaluate what they might be able to do in a job setting. Encourage them to use vocabulary from this lesson.

Refer students to *Stand Out Basic Workbook, Unit 7, Lesson 3* for more practice with *can* and *can't*.

Go to the *Activity Bank* online for suggestions on promoting digital literacy and using the Internet to enhance this lesson.

MULTILEVEL WORKSHEETS

Lesson 3, Worksheet 1: Duties

Lesson 3, Worksheet 2: Using *can* and *can't*

INSTRUCTOR'S NOTES

AT-A-GLANCE **PREP**

Goal: Read evaluations
Grammar: Negative and affirmative with the verb *Be*
Academic Strategies: Focused listening
Vocabulary: *well, on time, signature, friendly, helpful, careful, cheerful*

Agenda

- Review things you can and can't do.
- Read evaluations.
- Learn new words on evaluations.
- Read about performances.
- Evaluate yourself.

Resources

Multilevel Worksheet: Lesson 4, Worksheet 1
Workbook: Unit 7, Lesson 4
Audio: CD 2, Track 42
Heinle Picture Dictionary: Working, pages 150–151

Pacing

- 1.5 hour classes
- 2.5 hour classes
- 3⁺ hour classes

STANDARDS CORRELATIONS

CCRS: RI1, RI7, SL1, SL2, L1, L2, RF3
CASAS: 4.4.4
SCANS: **Basic Skills** Reading, writing, listening, speaking
Information Acquire and evaluate information, organize and maintain information, interpret and communicate information
EFF: **Communication** Read with understanding, convey ideas in writing, speak so others can understand, listen actively, observe critically
Lifelong Learning Reflect and evaluate

Warm-up and Review

10–15 mins.

Review *can* and *can't*. Ask students to get in groups of four or five and report what they *can* do well and what they *can't* do well.

Ask students to identify what jobs they might be able to do. You may want to write other skills, not taught in the previous lesson, that students might be able to do on the board. For example, you might write: *cook, serve food, clean,* and *speak another language*. Write jobs that might be associated with these words.

Introduction

15–20 mins.

Ask students what they can do to be better students. Make a list on the board of their ideas. These ideas might include listening carefully and coming to class on time. State the goal: *Today, we will read employment evaluations.*

Presentation 1

15–20 mins.

A. Read.

Go over the evaluation with students. Make sure they understand all the new vocabulary. Ask them questions about Emilio. Talk about the word *well*. This lesson is about doing things well, but you might also want to introduce *not well* here. Ask students which one of the four areas they think is most important.

Ask students to get into groups and rank the four areas from most important to least important. Everyone in the group must agree. When students finish, take a class poll. There is no correct answer, so validate all student answers.

Practice 1

7–10 mins.

B. ANALYZE What does a good student do? Circle.

Ask students to do this in their groups as well and rank their answers like they did in Presentation 1.

C. COLLABORATE In groups, add more ideas.

Ask: *What does a good student do?* Tell them to look over their answers from Exercise B again Then, ask students to add more ideas.

Evaluation 1

10–12 mins.

Ask groups to report to the class. Write a sentence on the board to facilitate this: *We think* listens *is number one.*

LESSON 4 You're doing great!

WORKPLACE CONNECTION
Exercise C: Make decisions and solve problems

GOAL Read evaluations

A. Read.

Name: Emilio Sanchez		
Work Evaluation		
	Yes	**No**
1. Helps customers	✓	
2. Comes to work on time	✓	
3. Speaks English well	✓	
4. Follows directions well	✓	
Manager Signature: *Calvin Carter*		

B. ANALYZE What does a good student do? Circle.

sends memos	(does homework)	(practices English)
(listens)	talks to customers	(takes lunch breaks)
cleans the office	(comes to school on time)	(follows directions)
schedules meetings	(reads in class)	(writes in class)

C. COLLABORATE In groups, add more ideas. Answers will vary.

____

____

____

____

____

____

D. Read.

Simple Present: *Be*		
Subject	***Be***	**Example sentence**
I	am	I **am** friendly.
He, She, It	is	She **is** helpful.
We, You, They	are	They **are** careful.

Simple Present: *Be* (negative)		
Subject	***Be (Negative)***	**Example sentence**
I	am not	I **am not** cheerful.
He, She, It	is not	She **is not** helpful.
We, You, They	are not	They **are not** friendly.

E. Write the correct form of the verb *Be*.

1. Emilio ____is____ friendly with the customers.
2. Carolina ____is____ not cheerful.
3. We ____are____ helpful.
4. They ____are____ not careful.

F. Listen and check.

CD 2
TR 42

Name: Alice Eriksson		
Work Evaluation		
	Yes	**No**
1. Is careful		✓
2. Is friendly	✓	
3. Is helpful		✓
4. Is cheerful	✓	
Manager Signature: Jan Brown		

Presentation 2

15–20 mins.

Write *friendly* on the board. Ask students who they think is the friendliest student in the class. If they don't know the word, help them understand it. Have a class vote and make a class award for the person voted to be the friendliest.

D. Read.

Ask students to open their books. Go over the new vocabulary and how to use it in a sentence. Review the verb *Be* in both the affirmative and the negative.

Reinforce the example sentences by asking questions about who in the class is cheerful and who is helpful. Ask students what jobs would require a person to be careful. You might encourage them to go back in the unit to find examples of jobs. Add more jobs to their list like police officers, fire fighters, accountants, etc.

E. Write the correct form of the verb *Be*.

This is still presentation, so go over the activity as a class to make sure all students understand the basic structure.

Look at the Evaluation form for Exercise F. Ask students to evaluate themselves. They don't have to write or say anything, but some students may volunteer the information. Make sure they use *am*. Reinforce what they say with *we* when you share a characteristic with them.

Prepare students for practice by reviewing the principles of focused listening.

Practice 2

7–10 mins.

F. Listen and check.

Play the recording three times. Allow students to discuss answers between the times you play the recordings.

LISTENING SCRIPT

CD 2
TR 42

I evaluated Alice today. She is a very good worker and I think she is a good employee because, overall, her attitude is very good. She is always happy and cheerful. This is important because the customers see this and it helps them to feel good about our store. Alice is not always helpful, though, because she is new and doesn't know very much about the job. In time, she will get better. Alice and Jim are not careful enough. They were responsible for the lamp being broken in the lighting section. I have asked Alice to work on being more careful around the displays. Alice has a very good attitude. She talks to the customers and is very friendly. Overall, I am happy with Alice's work.

Evaluation 2

5–10 mins.

Go over the answers with students. You may need to play the recording again to confirm the answers. Ask students more about the listening excerpt to identify how much more they understand.

BEST PRACTICE

Evaluating student levels

There are times throughout instruction when you may choose to ask questions and find out if students can perform at a higher level. Some students may be learning at a faster rate than others and you may find it useful to identify them.

In focused listening activities, students are expected to identify key words. They are not expected to understand the entire passage. Nevertheless, some students may understand more than what is required.

Presentation 3

10–15 mins. ■■■

Ask students to close their books. Read the paragraph to them. By now students have probably learned *sometimes* and *always,* but make sure they understand what the two words mean. Write *Davit Deluse* on the board. Explain to them that this is a name.

Write the following words on the board: *works, helps, friendly,* and *careful.*

Read the paragraph out loud again. Ask students to raise their hands and put them down again immediately every time they hear one of the words.

BEST PRACTICE

Kinesthetic learners

Learners can be predominantly visual, auditory, tactile, global, or analytic. The *Stand Out* approach addresses each learning style and suggests a variety of teaching methods so students with different needs and learning styles can better benefit from instruction.

Kinesthetic learners learn better when they move around or manipulate things. They tend to remember more when they act something out. In the ESL classroom, kinesthetic learners learn better if they are asked to physically respond to questions or information. This can be as simple as following TPR commands or raising their hands or as complicated as acting out a play.

G. Read.

Go over the reading. If you have time, leave the information you have written on the board and give a quick dictation. While students are doing this activity, you might ask them to cover Exercise H so they don't do the practice activity before you ask them to.

For shorter classes, ask students to do Exercise H for homework.

Practice 3

7–10 mins. ■

H. EVALUATE Read about Davit again in Exercise G and complete the evaluation.

Ask students to check *Yes* or *No* based on the reading.

Evaluation 3

5–7 mins. ■

Check students' book work.

Application

20–30 mins. ■■■

I. APPLY Complete an evaluation for yourself at school.

In this activity, students write about themselves.

MULTILEVEL WORKSHEET

Lesson 4, Worksheet 1: Reading Evaluations

Refer students to *Stand Out Basic Workbook, Unit 7, Lesson 4* for more practice with the verb *Be* and characteristics.

Go to the *Activity Bank* online for suggestions on promoting digital literacy and using the Internet to enhance this lesson.

INSTRUCTOR'S NOTES

G. **Read.**

Davit Deluse is a salesperson. He works Monday through Friday. He always helps customers, and he is always friendly. Sometimes he is not careful with clothing, and sometimes he doesn't come to work on time.

H. **EVALUATE** **Read about Davit again in Exercise G and complete the evaluation.**

Name: Davit Deluse		
Work Evaluation		
	Yes	**No**
1. Helps customers	✓	
2. Comes to work on time		✓
3. Is friendly	✓	
4. Is careful		✓
Manager Signature: *Calvin Carter*		

I. **APPLY** **Complete an evaluation for yourself at school.** Answers will vary.

School Evaluation		
	Yes	**No**
1. I come to school on time.		
2. I follow directions.		
3. I do my homework.		
4. I am cheerful and friendly.		

LESSON 5 Please send the memo

GOAL ■ Follow directions

CD 2
TR 43

A. Listen and point.

1. Don't smoke.

2. Wash your hands.

3. Don't eat in the office.

Fred, please
answer the phones.

4. Fred, please answer the phones.

Fred, please
send the memos.

5. Fred, please send the memos.

Fred, please
schedule a meeting.

6. Fred, please schedule a meeting.

B. Read the signs and notes in Exercise A. Circle *Yes* or *No*.

1. Smoke.	Yes	**No**
2. Wash hands.	**Yes**	No
3. Eat.	Yes	**No**
4. Answer the phones.	**Yes**	No
5. Send the memos.	**Yes**	No
6. Schedule a meeting.	**Yes**	No

AT-A-GLANCE **PREP**

Goal: Follow directions
Grammar: Imperatives
Academic Strategy: Focused listening
Vocabulary: *don'ts, dos, answer, wash, send*

Agenda

- Make awards for cheerful and helpful students.
- Read signs.
- Practice following directions.
- Read a job description.
- Write classroom dos and don'ts.

Resources

Multilevel Worksheet: Lesson 5, Worksheet 1
Workbook: Unit 7, Lesson 5
Audio: CD 2, Track 43
Heinle Picture Dictionary: Factory, pages 156–157

Pacing

■ 1.5 hour classes ■ 2.5 hour classes
■ 3⁺ hour classes

STANDARDS CORRELATIONS

CCRS: RI1, RI7, SL1, SL2, L1, L2, RF3
CASAS: 4.4.4, 4.8.1, 4.8.3
***SCANS:* Basic Skills** Reading, writing, listening, speaking
Resources Allocate human resources
Information Acquire and evaluate information, organize and maintain information, interpret and communicate information
Interpersonal Participate as a member of a team
***EFF:* Communication** Read with understanding, convey ideas in writing, speak so others can understand, listen actively, observe critically
Decision Making Solve problems, make decisions, plan
Interpersonal Cooperate with others, advocate and influence, resolve conflict and negotiate, guide others

Warm-up and Review

10–15 mins.

As a class, prepare awards for the most cheerful and the most helpful students. Have an election and give out the awards.

Introduction

15–20 mins.

Pantomime the signs and messages on this page. Students should have their books closed. Write each direction on the board as students call it out. Then, ask a student to say each direction and react by pantomiming as if he/she is commanding you. State the goal: *Today, we will read signs and follow directions.*

Presentation 1

15–20 mins.

A. Listen and point.

Do this activity as a class. You may introduce the terms *negative* and *affirmative* to students if you think they will understand. Write the two word pairs *negative* and *no* and *affirmative* and *yes.*

LISTENING SCRIPT
The listening script matches the items in Exercise A.

Look around the room for any signs. Identify any other safety signs that may be on campus. Ask students what other messages a manager or supervisor might leave for employees.

Practice 1

10–15 mins. 

B. Read the signs and notes in Exercise A. Circle *Yes* or *No*.

Have students circle *yes* or *no* based on the signs and notes.

Ask students to pantomime to a group the different verbs and have them say the commands listed in Exercise B, either negative or affirmative. Ask students to form groups and play charades.

Evaluation 1

3–5 mins. 

Observe students as they play charades.

BEST PRACTICE

Whole-class charades

Any charade game can be expanded to a whole-class activity. This is a particularly attractive feature for teachers who want to do both group and whole-class work at the same time.

1. Divide students into groups.
2. Write clues on strips of paper and place them in an envelope.
3. Ask one group member at a time to come up to act out the clue on the strip for the class to guess. *(Group members guess the clue of their own teammate.)*
4. Allow groups to take turns guessing. Decide beforehand how many guesses groups are allowed.
5. Keep count. The group with the most correct guesses wins the game.

Presentation 2

20–30 mins.

C. Read.

Read the charts with students. Help them understand that we don't say the subject pronoun *you* with commands. Review words that are associated with the actions. For example, *wash* can be associated with *hands, the table, the car,* etc. Remind students that they learned this structure earlier in Unit 6 on page 140.

Review the other vocabulary words and associate them with actions.

D. Complete the sentences.

Do this activity together with students as reinforcement.

Prepare students for the practice by going over the two dialogs in Exercise E. Show students how they might substitute information.

BEST PRACTICE

Sentence completion exercises

A sentence completion exercise is like a fun puzzle. Students need to have a good idea of what the completed sentences will look like in order to complete the activity. Sentence completion is an effective way to test vocabulary, grammar, and syntax at the same time. It can be limited to just filling in the correct word or open-ended, which allows students to test their creativity while staying focused on the grammar points at hand. Exercises can also be very communicative both during and after completion. Students can work together in pairs or in small groups and later share their answers as a class.

Practice 2

7–10 mins.

E. Read and practice the conversations. Use the commands in Exercise C.

Evaluation 2

5–7 mins.

Ask volunteers to present the conversations for the class.

INSTRUCTOR'S NOTES

C. Read.

Affirmative Commands			
	Verb		**Example sentence**
~~You~~	wash	your hands	Wash your hands.
	answer	the phones	Answer the phones.
	send	the memos	Send the memos.

Negative Commands				
	Verb			**Example sentence**
~~You~~	don't	smoke		Don't smoke.
		eat		Don't eat.
		send	the memos	Don't send the memos.

D. Complete the sentences.

1. Wash *your hands*.
2. Send *the memos*.
3. Answer *the phones*.
4. Don't *eat in the office*.

E. Read and practice the conversations. Use the commands in Exercise C.

Manager: How are you, Isabel?
Isabel: I'm fine, thank you.
Manager: Please send the memos.
Isabel: Yes, of course.

Manager: How are you, Isabel?
Isabel: I'm fine, thank you.
Manager: Please don't eat in the office.
Isabel: No, of course not.

WORKPLACE CONNECTION
Exercises G and H: Collect and organize information
Exercise H: Make decisions and solve problems; Combine ideas and information

F. **INTERPRET** Read.

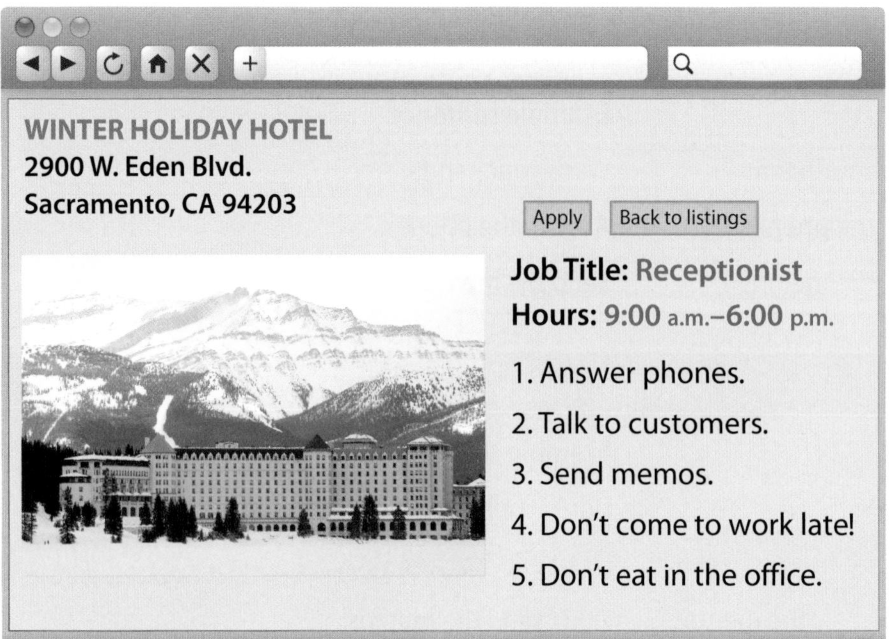

WINTER HOLIDAY HOTEL
2900 W. Eden Blvd.
Sacramento, CA 94203
Apply
Back to listings
Job Title: Receptionist
Hours: 9:00 a.m.–6:00 p.m.
1. Answer phones.
2. Talk to customers.
3. Send memos.
4. Don't come to work late!
5. Don't eat in the office.

G. **Look at the job description in Exercise F. Write the commands.**

Do's	Don'ts
Answer phones.	Don't come to work late.
Talk to customers.	Don't eat in the office.
Send memos.	

H. **CREATE** **In groups, write classroom *do's* and *don'ts*.** Answers will vary.

Classroom Do's	Classroom Don'ts
Listen.	

Presentation 3

7–10 mins.

F. INTERPRET Read.

Go over the job description with students. Ask them questions about it including the following: *What is the job title? When does the receptionist work? What are some of the duties?*

BEST PRACTICE

Working with realia

The picture in Exercise F is a type of realia *(the real object or a model of the real object)* used to build real-world knowledge. One of the purposes of using realia is to give students the opportunity to use more than one of their senses in learning: *see, touch, hear,* etc. Another purpose is to allow students to experience and learn vocabulary in context. Teachers can expound on Exercise F by asking students to find a real job ad in a newspaper or on the Internet to share with the class. Students can work in pairs, comparing information and making lists of the commands that appear in each. Using a real object will help students to connect with and better internalize the content.

Practice 3

10–15 mins.

G. Look at the job descriptions in Exercise F. Write the commands.

Ask students to write the information in the spaces provided. Then, in groups, ask students to determine what responsibilities are most important.

Evaluation 3

10 mins.

Check students' book work.

Application

10–15 mins.

H. CREATE In groups, write classroom *do's* and *don'ts*.

When they finish, ask groups to report to the class.

Refer students to *Stand Out Basic Workbook, Unit 7, Lesson 5* for more practice with the imperative.

Go to the *Activity Bank* online for suggestions on promoting digital literacy and using the Internet to enhance this lesson.

MULTILEVEL WORKSHEET

Lesson 5, Worksheet 1: Commands

INSTRUCTOR'S NOTES

Our son is going to get a job!

Before You Watch

- Ask students what you do when you want to find a job. Discuss as a class.

A. Look at the picture and answer the questions.

- Ask the questions and elicit answers.
- Ask students if they, or anyone they know, have a job similar to Hector's. Ask what their job duties are.

While You Watch

B. Watch the video and complete the dialog. Use the words in the box.

- Go over the vocabulary in the box, explaining the words students don't know.
- Ask students to watch the video and complete the conversation between Hector and Mr. and Mrs. Sanchez.
- Play the video once and ask students to watch and listen. Then, play the video again so that students can complete the exercise.

Check Your Understanding

C. Show the correct order of the events by writing a number next to each sentence.

- Ask students to put the events from the video in the correct order.
- Read the example and point out that this is the first event that takes place.
- Play the video. Then, play the video once more so that students can check their answers.

BEST PRACTICE

There are many ways to use video in the classroom. Students should rarely watch a video without some kind of task. You might introduce comprehension questions before they watch so they know what they are looking for. Below are a few techniques that you may try for variety beyond the comprehension checks and other ideas already presented in this lesson.

Freeze Frame: Pause the video during viewing and use it like a picture dictionary, identifying and expanding on the vocabulary.

Silent Viewing: Show the video in segments without sound so students can guess at the storyline. This helps them to understand that listening is more than just the words people say.

Prediction Techniques: Show portions of the video and ask students to predict what will come next.

Listening without Viewing: This helps students create their own image of what is happening. After a discussion, allow students to watch the video and the sound together.

Back-to-Back: In pairs, one student faces the video and the other faces away. Play the video without sound and ask the student viewing to report to the student who is facing away what is happening.

Summary Strips: Create strips of sentences that describe the events. Have students watch the video and then put the strips in the correct order, or ask students to predict the story line before watching and then check their answers. The Activity Bank has summary strips for each video in *Stand Out*.

LIFESKILLS

Our son is going to get a job!

Before You Watch

A. Look at the picture and answer the questions.

1. What job does Hector have? receptionist
2. What is he doing? answering the phone

While You Watch

B. Watch the video and complete the dialog. Use the words in the box.

cleans	custodian	mops	~~receptionist~~	takes

Hector: Why not? What does a (1) receptionist do?

Mrs. Sanchez: A receptionist answers phones and (2) takes messages.

Hector: Nah, I don't think so. What about a custodian? What does a (3) custodian do?

Mr. Sanchez: A custodian mops the floors and (4) cleans windows.

Hector: (5) Mops the floor?

Check Your Understanding

C. Show the correct order of the events by writing a number next to each sentence.

a. 2 Hector reads an ad for a custodian.
b. 4 Hector reads ads for sales clerks.
c. 1 Mrs. Sanchez tells Hector what a receptionist does.
d. 3 Mr. Sanchez says what a custodian does.
e. 5 Hector calls Mateo on his cell phone.

Review

Learner Log
I can identify occupations.
☐ Yes ☐ No ☐ Maybe

A. Write the name of the job.

1.
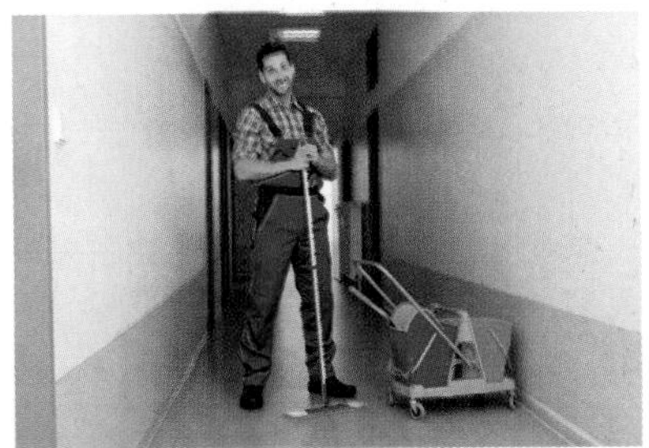
custodian

2.

teacher

3.

receptionist

4.

salesperson

5.

cashier

6.

bus driver

7.

doctor

8.

manager

B. Point to a picture in Exercise A. Ask a partner about the job.

Student A: What does he do?
Student B: He's a custodian.

AT-A-GLANCE **PREP**

Goal: All unit objectives
Grammar: All unit grammar
Academic Strategies: Focused listening, reviewing, evaluating, developing study skills
Vocabulary: All unit vocabulary

Agenda

- Discuss unit objectives.
- Complete the review.

Pacing

- 1.5 hour classes
- 2.5 hour classes
- 3+ hour classes

STANDARDS CORRELATIONS

CCRS: RI1, SL2, L1, L2, RF3

CASAS: 4.1.3, 4.1.8, 4.4.1, 4.8.1, 4.8.3, 7.4.1, 7.4.2, 7.4.3

SCANS: **Basic Skills** Reading, writing, listening, speaking

Information Acquire and evaluate information, organize and maintain information, interpret and communicate information

Thinking Skills See things in the mind's eye

EFF: **Communication** Speak so others can understand

Lifelong Learning Take responsibility for learning, reflect and evaluate

Warm-up and Review

7–10 mins.

With their books closed, ask students to help you make a list on the board of all the vocabulary they can come up with from the unit. Then, have a competition where students in groups find and write the page number for each item on the list. The first group to have the correct page number for each item wins.

Introduction

5 mins.

Write all the goals on the board from Unit 7. Show students the first page of every lesson so they understand that today will be review. Complete the agenda.

Note: Depending on the length of the term, you may decide to have students do Presentation and Practice for homework and then review student work as the warm-up for another class meeting.

Presentation

10–15 mins.

This presentation and practice will cover the first three pages of the review. Quickly go to the first page of each lesson. Discuss the goal of each. Ask simple questions to remind students what they have learned.

Practice

15–20 mins.

A. Write the name of the job. (Lesson 1)

B. Point to a picture in Exercise A. Ask a partner about the job. (Lesson 1)

BEST PRACTICE

Recycling/Review

The review process and the project that follows are part of the recycling/review process. Students at this level often need to be reintroduced to concepts to solidify what they have learned. Many concepts are learned and forgotten while learning other new concepts. This is because students learn, but are not necessarily ready to acquire language concepts.

Therefore, it becomes very important to review and to show students how to review on their own. It is also important to recycle the new concepts in different contexts.

Practice *(continued)*

C. **Match the job with the duty. Draw a line. (Lessons 1 and 3)**

D. **Write *when, where, what,* or *who*. Responses can be used more than once. (Lesson 2)**

INSTRUCTOR'S NOTES

Learner Log

I can give information about work. ▪ Yes ▪ No ▪ Maybe

I can identify job duties. ▪ Yes ▪ No ▪ Maybe

C. Match the job with the duty. Draw a line.

1.

2.

3.

4.

a. sends memos

b. makes change

c. changes light bulbs

d. talks to customers

D. Write *when, where, what,* or *who.* Responses can be used more than once.

1. ____When____ does the store open? The store opens at 10:00 a.m.
2. ____Where____ do you take a break? I take a break in the cafeteria.
3. ____Where____ do you work? I work in Sacramento.
4. ____Who____ is your manager? His name is Martin.
5. ____What____ does she do? She's a nurse.

Learner Log

I can read evaluations.
☐ Yes ☐ No ☐ Maybe

I can follow directions.
☐ Yes ☐ No ☐ Maybe

E. Identify the signs.

1. Don't smoke.

2. Don't eat.

3. Wash your hands.

F. COMPARE What can you do? What can your partner do? Complete the chart.

Answers will vary.

EXAMPLES: I can speak English well.
I can follow directions.
I can schedule meetings.

I can

We can

My partner can

Practice *(continued)*

E. Identify the signs. (Lesson 5)

F. COMPARE What can you do? What can your partner do? Complete the chart. (Lesson 3)

Evaluation

15 mins.

Go around the room and check on students' progress. Help individuals when needed. If you see consistent errors among several students, interrupt the class and give a mini lesson or review to help students feel comfortable with the concept.

Learner Log

Review the concepts of the Learner Log. Make sure students understand the concepts and how to do the log including the checkmarks.

BEST PRACTICE

Learner Logs

Learner Logs function to help students in many different ways.

1. They serve as part of the review process.
2. They help students to gain confidence and document what they have learned. In this way, students see that they are progressing and want to move forward in learning.
3. They provide students with a tool that they can use over and over to check and recheck their understanding. In this way, students become independent learners.

Application

Ask students to write down their favorite lesson or page in the unit.

Assessment

Use the Stand Out Assessment CD-ROM with ExamView© to create a post-test for Unit 7.

INSTRUCTOR'S NOTES

WORKPLACE CONNECTION

Combine ideas and information; Make decisions; Exercise leadership roles; Manage time; Complete tasks as assigned; Interact appropriately with team members; Collect and gather information; Interpret and communicate information; Apply technology

STANDARDS CORRELATIONS

CCRS: RI1, SL2, L1, L2, RF3

CASAS: 2.2.3, 4.8.1

***SCANS:* Basic Skills** Reading, writing, listening, speaking

Resources Allocate time, allocate money, allocate materials and facility resources, allocate human resources

Information Acquire and evaluate information, organize and maintain information, interpret and communicate information, use computers to process information

Interpersonal Participate as a member of a team, teach others, serve clients and customers, exercise leadership, negotiate to arrive at a decision, work with cultural diversity

Systems Understand systems, monitor and correct performance, improve and design systems

Thinking Skills Think creatively, make decisions, solve problems, see things in the mind's eye

Personal Qualities Responsibility, sociability, self-management

***EFF:* Communication** Read with understanding, convey ideas in writing, speak so others can understand, listen actively, observe critically

Decision Making Solve problems, make decisions, plan

Interpersonal Cooperate with others, advocate and influence, resolve conflict and negotiate, guide others

Lifelong Learning Take responsibility for learning, reflect and evaluate

Introduction

In this project, students will work in teams to create a company, incorporating the vocabulary they have learned from this unit.

Stage 1

15–20 mins.

COLLABORATE Form a team with four or five students.

Discuss the art on the student book page.

Help students to assign positions in their groups. On the spot, students will have to choose who will be the leader of their group. Review the responsibility of a leader and ask students to write the name of their leader in their books. Do the same with the remaining positions: artist, writer, and spokesperson.

Stage 2

3–5 mins.

What is the name of your company? What is your company logo? Make a cover page.

Help students as needed. Bring in some logos from companies in your community for students to look at.

Stage 3

40–50 mins.

What are the jobs in the company?

Make sure students distinguish between their roles on the team and their jobs in the company.

Stage 4

10–30 mins.

Write three job descriptions for jobs in your company.

You can use Multilevel Worksheets for this project.

Stage 5

10–30 mins.

Present your company to the class.

Ask teams to practice their presentations before they give them to the class. Videotaping the presentations can greatly enhance the learning experience.

BEST PRACTICE

Digital literacy

Projects are a perfect place to allow students opportunities to use other forms of presentations beyond pictures they create. Digital literacy is becoming more necessary as a life skill. Encourage students to create presentations using pictures from the Internet. They might also consider using other digital presentation tools.

TEAM PROJECT Start a company

1. **COLLABORATE** Form a team with four or five students. In your team, you need:

Position	Job description	Student name
Student 1: Team Leader	Check that everyone speaks English. Check that everyone participates.	
Student 2: Writer	Write job descriptions.	
Student 3: Artist	Make a cover page with the name of your company and a logo.	
Students 4/5: Spokespeople	Prepare a presentation.	

2. What is the name of your company?
   What is your company logo? Make a cover page.
3. What are the jobs in the company?
4. Write three job descriptions for jobs in your company.
5. Present your company to the class.

Offices for new companies sometimes look different from normal offices.

About the Explorer

Gabby Salazar is a conservation photographer from Greensboro, North Carolina. She has won numerous awards and accolades including a National Geographic Young Explorers Grant—a grant to cover the cost of fieldwork for young people with great ideas. Gabby has been fascinated by photography since a young age and has traveled all over the world to photograph nature. She is especially interested in rare and interesting plants and animals. Gabby is also interested in the conservation of the nature she photographs. As a public speaker, she educates people on how they can preserve the natural world.

About the Photo

This photo shows Gabby with a luna moth in Merrill Creek Resevoir, Washington, New Jersey. With a wingspan of over four and a half inches, the luna moth is one of the largest moths in North America. The moths fly only at night in the spring and early summer and are considered endangered. Gabby works as a motivational speaker for young people in different parts of the United States, and being able to share photos of endangered species allows her to raise awareness to issues people may not be aware of.

- Introduce the explorer. Tell students they are going to read about Gabby Salazar.

A. PREDICT Look at the picture and answer the questions.

- Ask students to look at the picture and answer the questions.

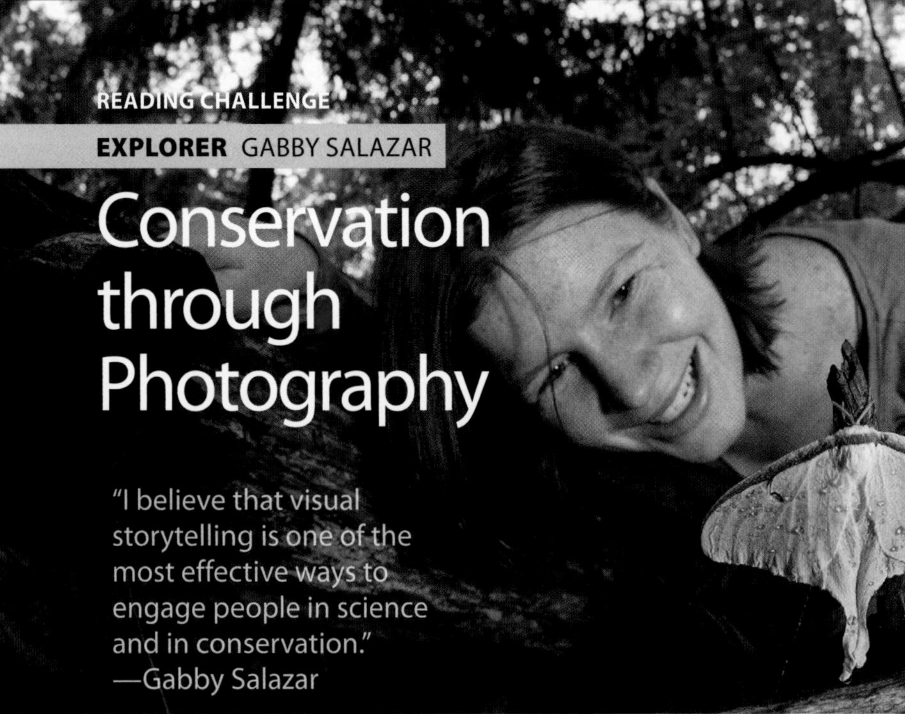

READING CHALLENGE
EXPLORER GABBY SALAZAR
Conservation through Photography
"I believe that visual storytelling is one of the most effective ways to engage people in science and in conservation."
—Gabby Salazar

A. PREDICT Look at the picture and answer the questions. *Answers will vary.*

1. Where is Gabby?
2. What do you think her job is?
3. What are her job duties?

B. SURVEY Ask three classmates what they do. Complete the sentences. *Answers will vary.*

1. ___Ana___ is a ___cook___. He/(She) ___makes food___
2. ______ is a ______. He/She ______
3. ______ is a ______. He/She ______
4. ______ is a ______. He/She ______

CCRS FOR READING

RI1, RI2, RI7, SL1, SL2, L5

WORKPLACE CONNECTION
Exercise E: Collect and organize information
Exercise F: Make decisions and solve problems

C. **Read about Gabby Salazar.**

Gabby Salazar is a nature photographer from North Carolina. She likes to take photos of rare and interesting plants, animals, and insects. She can take good photos, so good that she wins awards and her photos appear in magazines! Gabby can also speak well to people. With her photos, Gabby teaches people how to care for the natural world.

D. **What two things can Gabby do? Write one thing you can do.**

1. Gabby can *take good photos*.
2. Gabby can *speak well to people*.
3. I can *Answers will vary.*

E. BRAINSTORM **What can people take pictures of? Complete the chart.** *Answers will vary.*

People	Nature	Buildings	Events
children	plants	bridges	weddings

Photographs

F. APPLY **What do you take pictures of? Discuss in a group.** *Answers will vary.*

EXAMPLE: I take pictures of my children to show to my friends.

READING STRATEGIES

Active Reading

When students underline or circle key words and ideas in a reading passage, they are practicing active reading. Active reading keeps the information stronger in students' minds and makes it easier to recall later. It also keeps students focused on the material.

- Read the title and the quote. Then, ask students to check their answers to the questions. Ask if they want to change their predictions.
- Discuss students' predictions as a class.

B. SURVEY Ask three classmates what they do. Complete the sentences.

- Tell students they will make a survey.
- Explain that they will ask three students what type of jobs they have.
- Ask students to finish the sentences with truthful information about the three students they interviewed.

C. Read about Gabby Salazar.

- Ask students to read the passage about Gabby Salazar.
- Ask students to underline or circle the words they do not know. Then, explain the unfamiliar vocabulary.

D. What two things can Gabby do? Write one thing you can do.

E. BRAINSTORM What can people take pictures of? Complete the chart.

- Ask students what people usually take pictures of. Discuss as a class.
- Ask students to complete the table with their own answers.
- Have students share their answers with a partner.

F. APPLY What do you take pictures of? Discuss in a group.

UNIT 8

Lifelong Learning and Review

About the Photo

Paul Nicklen took this photo. He is a biologist and a photographer from Canada. The photo shows Alberto Nava and Susan Bird in an underwater cave examining the remains of "Naia." "Naia" was the name given to a teenage girl who died between 12,000 and 13,000 years ago. The divers believe that "Naia" lived in the cave below the Yucatán Peninsula in Mexico before it was flooded. This discovery was able to confirm the origin of Native Americans given their face shape. It is commonly held among geneticists that Native Americans were descendants of Siberians who migrated south.

- Introduce the unit. Ask students if they think that learning continues after finishing school or outside the classroom. Have students share their opinions.
- Ask students to look at the photo and answer the questions.

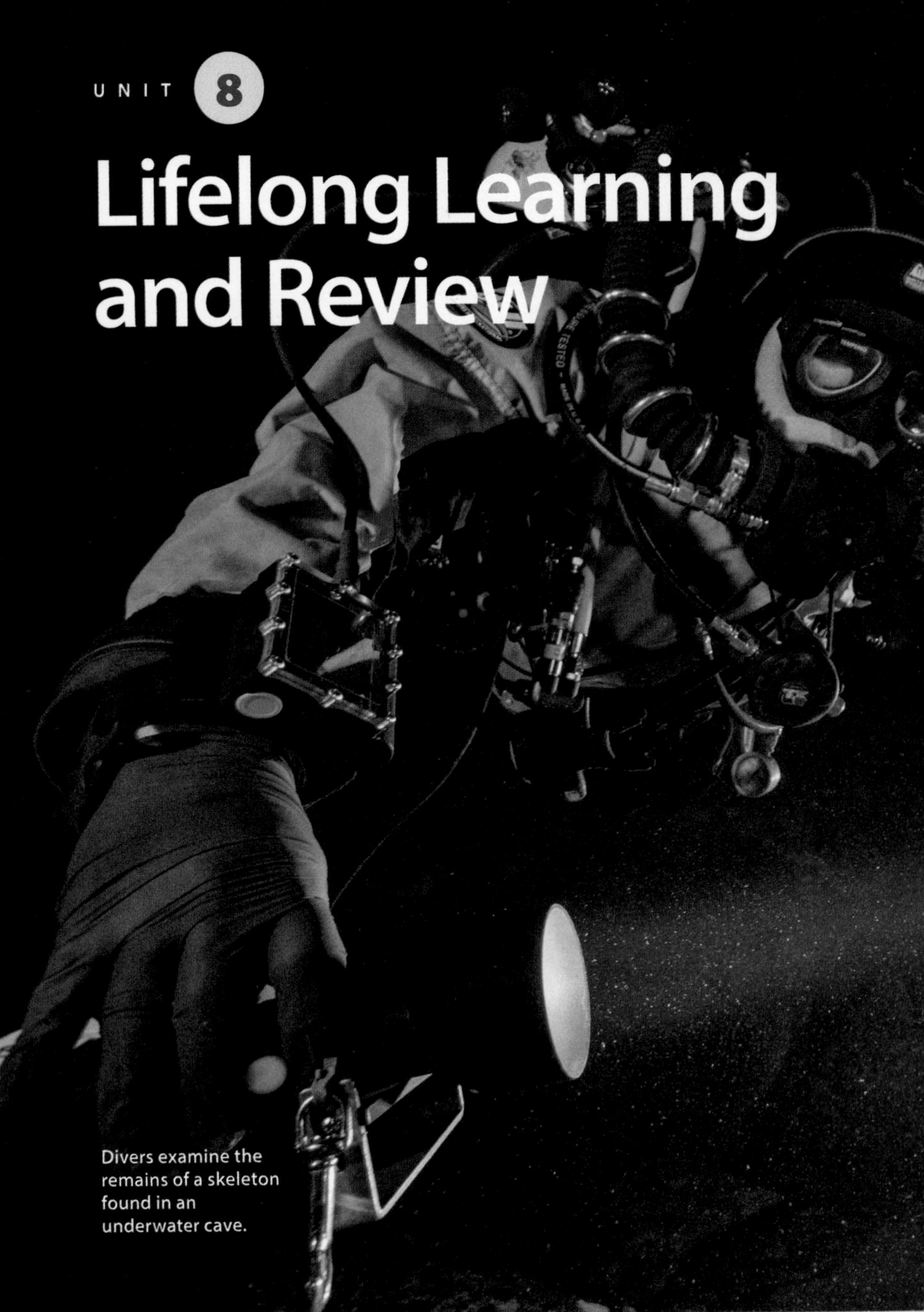

Divers examine the remains of a skeleton found in an underwater cave.

UNIT OUTCOMES	GRAMMAR	VOCABULARY	EL CIVICS
• Organize study materials • Make purchases • Give and follow directions • Make goals • Develop a study schedule	• The verb *Be* • Imperatives • Information questions: *where* • Prepositions of location • Simple present	• Study tools: *binders, dividers, notebook, pencils, pens, sheets of paper*	The skills students learn in this unit can be applied to the following EL Civics competency areas: • Educational systems • Community resources • Health and nutrition • Employment

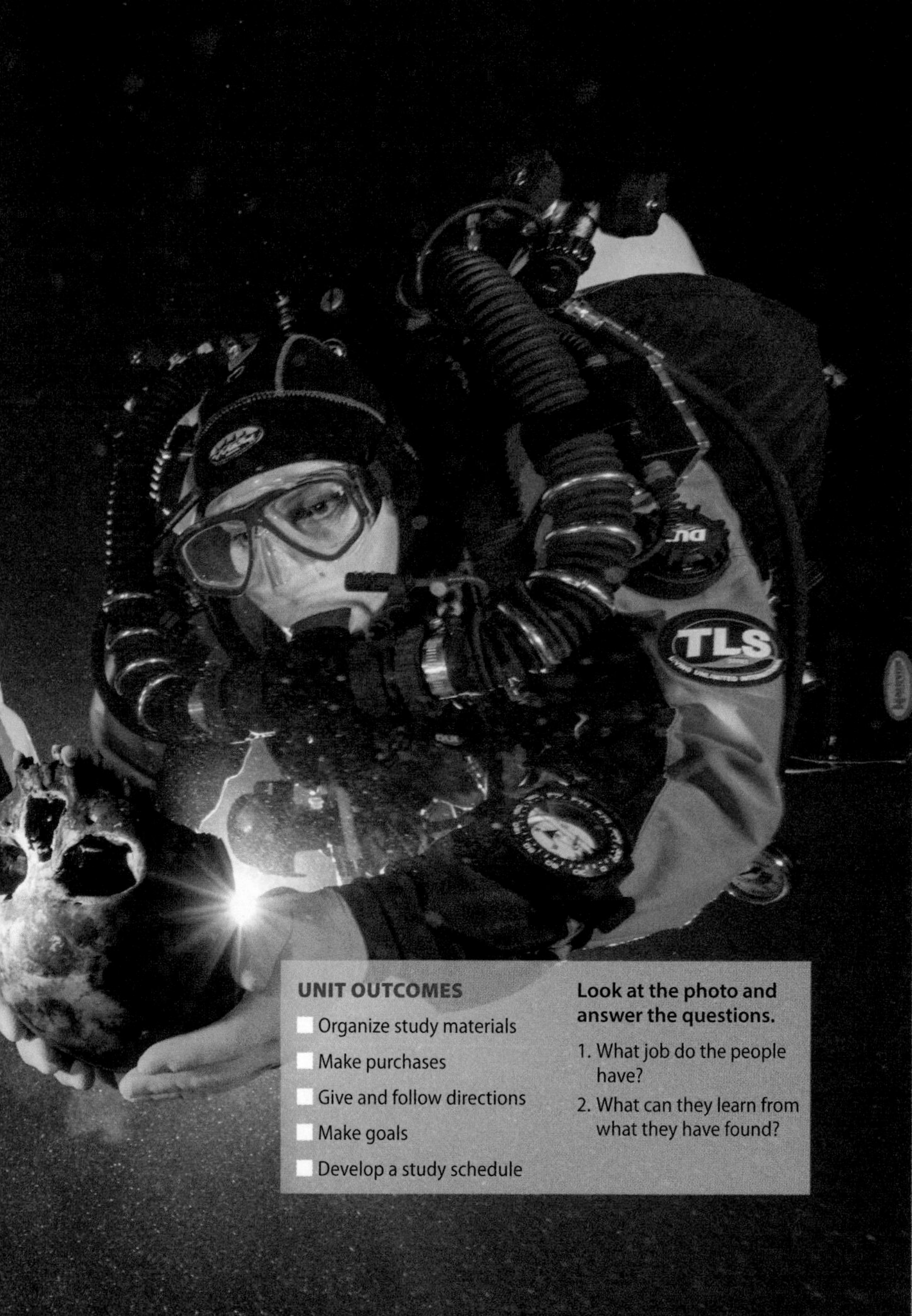

TLS
UNIT OUTCOMES
Organize study materials
Make purchases
Give and follow directions
Make goals
Develop a study schedule
Look at the photo and answer the questions.
1. What job do the people have?
2. What can they learn from what they have found?

- Read the caption. Ask students to brainstorm and think of other examples where people learn something.
- Go over the unit outcomes. Ask students what they are already familiar with. Discuss as a class.

Life Skills Link

In this unit, students will revisit what they have learned throughout the previous units and lay the groundwork for further study and language development.

Workplace Link

All lessons and units in *Stand Out* include basic communication skills and interpersonal skills important for the workplace. They are not individually identified. Other workplace skills are indicated. They include, collecting and organizing information, making decisions and solving problems, and combining ideas and information.

CASAS	SCANS	CCRS
Lesson 1: 0.2.1, 0.2.2, 7.1.4 Lesson 2: 1.1.6, 1.2.1, 1.3.1, 1.6.4, 7.1.4 Lesson 3: 2.1.1, 2.2.1, 7.1.4 Lesson 4: 0.2.1, 3.5.9, 6.7.2, 7.1.1, 7.1.2, 7.1.4 Lesson 5: 4.1.1, 4.4.4, 7.1.1, 7.1.4 Review: 7.4.2, 7.4.3 Team Project: 2.2.3, 4.8.1	Many SCANs skills are incorporated in the unit with an emphasis on: • Acquiring and evaluating information • Organizing and maintaining information • Interpreting and communicating information • Basic skills • Self-management	RI1, SL1, SL2, SL4, L1, L2, RF2, RF3

LESSON 1 Let's get organized!

GOAL Organize study materials

A. Listen and repeat.

CD 2
TR 44

binder

sticky notes

dividers

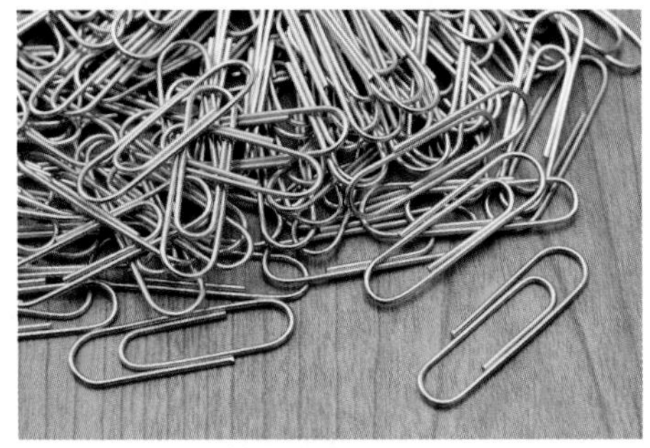
paper clips

sheets of lined paper

highlighter pen

B. COLLABORATE In a group, write more items you use to organize your study materials. Answers will vary.

______________________ ______________________

______________________ ______________________

______________________ ______________________

AT-A-GLANCE **PREP**

Goal: Organize study materials
Grammar: The verb *Be*
Academic Strategies: Focused listening, test-taking skills, organization skills
Vocabulary: *binder, inch, sheet, divider, lined paper, personal profile*

Agenda

- Discuss what makes a good student.
- Discuss organization materials.
- Organize a binder.
- Complete a personal profile.

Resources

Multilevel Worksheet: Lesson 1, Worksheet 1
Workbook: Unit 8, Lesson 1
Audio: CD 2, Tracks 44–45
Heinle Picture Dictionary: Classroom, pages 18–19
Stand Out Basic Assessment CD-ROM with ExamView®

Pacing

- 1.5 hour classes
- 2.5 hour classes
- 3+ hour classes

STANDARDS CORRELATIONS

CCRS: SL1, SL2, L1, L2, RF2, RF3
CASAS: 0.2.1, 0.2.2, 7.1.4
SCANS: **Basic Skills** Reading, writing, listening, speaking
Resources Allocate materials and facility resources, allocate human resources
Information Acquire and evaluate information, organize and maintain information, interpret and communicate information
Interpersonal Participate as a member of a team
Systems Understand systems
Thinking Skills Think creatively
Personal Qualities Responsibility, self-management
EFF: **Communication** Read with understanding, convey ideas in writing, speak so others can understand, listen actively, observe critically
Decision Making Solve problems and make decisions
Interpersonal Cooperate with others, guide others
Lifelong Learning Take responsibility for learning, reflect and evaluate

Preassessment *(optional)*

Use the Stand Out Basic Assessment CD-ROM with ExamView® to create a pretest for Unit 8.

Note: Unit 8 is composed of review lessons that also take students through the development of a study binder, which will help them review concepts in the book after the term is complete.

Warm-up and Review

15–20 mins.

Ask: *What makes a good student?* Make a list on the board of the students' answers. To get them started, you may wish to write some of your ideas on the board such as: *Come to school every day. Study at home.* Ask students to rank the ideas from the most important to the least important, first individually and then as a class.

Introduction

3–7 mins.

Tell students that to be a good student you should be organized. Help them understand the meaning of *organized* by writing the word on the board. To make it clearer, show them some examples of organization and disorganization, like a messily organized binder and a neat, orderly one with dividers. State the goal: *Today, we will identify ways to organize study materials.*

Presentation 1

20–30 mins.

A. Listen and repeat.

Ask students questions about the pictures such as: *What is this? Who has this? What's it for?*

LISTENING SCRIPT

CD 2 TR 44

The listening script matches the list of items in Exercise A.

B. COLLABORATE In a group, write more items you use to organize your study materials.

Help students think of things to write in this activity. Get them started by giving them some suggestions such as *file cabinet* and *pencils.*

Prepare students to do the listening activity by going over the pictures they see in the exercise items.

Practice 1

7–10 mins.

C. Listen and choose the correct answer.

Play the recording two times and allow students to discuss their answers between listenings.

LISTENING SCRIPT

CD 2 TR 45

1. **Liang:** *The teacher wants us to make special binders to study after school is finished.*
   Octavio: *Yes, I know. We have to go to the store and buy some things. I don't think it will be expensive.*
   Liang: *We need binders first.*
   Octavio: *What size do we need?*
   Liang: *I think we need 1 1/2 inch binders.*
   Octavio: *That sounds right. They shouldn't be too big.*
2. **Liang:** *We need dividers, too.*
   Octavio: *What are dividers?*
   Liang: *You know, the heavy paper to make sections in your binder.*
   Octavio: *Oh, yeah. How many do we need?*
   Liang: *We need a set of five dividers.*
3. **Octavio:** *What else do we need?*
   Liang: *We need paper for each section.*
   Octavio: *How many sheets do we need?*
   Liang: *Two hundred sheets, I think.*
   Octavio: *That sounds right.*

BEST PRACTICE

Listening for specific information

When listening for specific information in a recording, tell students that it is not important that they understand every word they hear. Rather, they should focus on listening carefully for the specific information they need to complete the exercise. Before playing the recording, read the directions and explain what students should listen for. Remind students to pay special attention if the recording contains numbers, measurements, or amounts.

Play the recording once to familiarize students. Then, play the recording again so students can focus on listening for specific details. If needed, play the recording multiple times.

If the recording is long or has several parts, stop between segments to give students time to work on their answers. Repeat each segment if needed.

Evaluation 1

3 mins.

Check students' book work.

Presentation 2

10–15 mins.

Ask students to refer to the table of contents in their books. Go over it with them. Show them where the page numbers are. Then, ask them to go to the appendix in the book and look at the vocabulary lists on pages 212–213. Ask them what two words are most important to them in the first two units. Refer them to Exercise D and ask them to write those two words in the space provided. Explain to students that each divider in the binder represents a different section in the book. Point out the tabs.

Practice 2

8–10 mins.

D. Look through Units 1–7. For your binder, write the page numbers and two words for each section.

Remind students to check the vocabulary list in the appendix.

Evaluation 2

3 mins.

Ask students to share their answers and display their dividers if possible.

INSTRUCTOR'S NOTES

C. Listen and choose the correct answer.

CD 2
TR 45

1. What size binder do they need?
   - ☐ 1 inch
   - ☑ 1 ½ inches
   - ☐ 3 inches
2. How many dividers do they need?
   - ☐ one divider
   - ☐ three dividers
   - ☑ five dividers
3. How many sheets of lined paper do they need?
   - ☐ 50 sheets
   - ☐ 100 sheets
   - ☑ 200 sheets

D. Look through Units 1–7. For your binder, write the page numbers and two words for each section.

Section	Reference pages	Example vocabulary
Basic Communication (Pre-Unit, Unit 1, and Unit 2)	2–59	
Consumer Economics (Unit 3 and Unit 4)	60–107	
Community Resources (Unit 5)	112–135	
Health (Unit 6)	136–159	
Occupational Knowledge (Unit 7)	160–183	

E. Interview and write about your partner. Report to a group. Answers will vary.

1. What's your name? ______
2. Where do you live? ______
3. What is your phone number? ______
4. What is your date of birth? ______
5. Are you married? ______
6. Where are you from? ______

F. CREATE Make a personal profile like the one below on a separate piece of paper. Use it as the first page of your binder.

PERSONAL PROFILE

School: ______

Teacher: ______

First Name: ______

Middle Name: ______

Last Name: ______

Address: ______

City: ______

State: ______

Zip: ______

Country: ______

Marital Status *(circle)*: **Single** **Married** **Divorced**

Presentation 3

10–15 mins.

Remind students of all the questions they learned in Units 1 and 2. Walk around the room and ask students questions as review.

Go over each question in Exercise E. Explain to students that this activity will prepare them to start their own binders.

Help students with pronunciation and question intonation. If students are ready, you might write key words on the board, have them close their books, and ask them for the questions based solely on the key words.

Review the verb *Be* in preparation for Practice 3.

Practice 3

10–15 mins.

E. Interview and write about your partner. Report to a group.

Ask students to report to their groups about their partners.

Evaluation 3

5–7 mins.

Ask volunteers to present their interviews in front of the class.

Application

15–20 mins.

F. CREATE Make a personal profile like the one below on a separate piece of paper. Use it as the first page of your binder.

Ask students to create their own personal profile like in the introductory page of a date planner using the sample provided, or ask them to complete the form provided in the Activity Bank.

Refer students to *Stand Out Basic Workbook, Unit 8, Lesson 1* for more practice with the verb *Be*.

Go to the *Activity Bank* online for suggestions on promoting digital literacy and using the Internet to enhance this lesson.

MULTILEVEL WORKSHEET

Lesson 1, Worksheet 1: Personal Profile

INSTRUCTOR'S NOTES

AT-A-GLANCE **PREP**

Goal: Make purchases
Grammar: *How much is, How much are*
Academic Strategy: Focused listening
Vocabulary: *package, set, dozen, ballpoint pen, colored, box*

Agenda

- Talk about places to shop.
- Read an ad.
- Complete a receipt.
- List food and clothing you buy.
- Make a section for Consumer Economics in your binder.

Resources

Multilevel Worksheet: Lesson 2, Worksheet 1
Workbook: Unit 8, Lesson 2
Audio: CD 2, Tracks 46–47
Heinle Picture Dictionary: Money and Shopping, pages 8–9; Food, pages 82–103; Clothing, pages 104–117

Pacing

■ 1.5 hour classes ■ 2.5 hour classes ■ 3⁺ hour classes

STANDARDS CORRELATIONS

CCRS: RI1, SL1, SL2, L1, L2, RF3
CASAS: 1.1.6, 1.2.1, 1.3.1, 1.6.4, 7.1.4
SCANS: **Basic Skills** Reading, writing, listening, speaking
Resources Allocate money
Information Acquire and evaluate information, organize and maintain information, interpret and communicate information
Interpersonal Participate as a member of a team, teach others
Thinking Skills Think creatively, make decisions
Personal Qualities Responsibility, sociability, self-management
EFF: **Communication** Read with understanding, convey ideas in writing, speak so others can understand, listen actively, observe critically
Decision Making Solve problems and make decisions, plan
Interpersonal Cooperate with others, guide others
Lifelong Learning Take responsibility for learning, reflect and evaluate

Warm-up and Review — 15–20 mins.

Ask students to work in groups and share the information they wrote on their personal profiles from the previous class.

Introduction — 5–7 mins.

Ask students where they buy food, clothing, and other items. Write the names of the stores on the board and take an informal poll to see what the most popular stores are. State the goal: *Today, we will review making purchases.* Help students understand what a *purchase* is. Use the word *buy* and give some examples.

Presentation 1 — 30–40 mins.

A. Read the advertisement.

Go over the ad with students. There is a lot of "extra" vocabulary that they may not need, but since they will be confronted by these words when they go off to make real purchases, help them discern what is important.

Review questions with *How much is* and *How much are.*

B. Listen to the conversation about the ad and practice the conversation.

Help students understand the basic format of the question and the words that may be unknown to them, such as *set.*

Ask students to look at the ad in Exercise A while you play the recording the first time. Then, play the recording once or twice more so students can practice the conversation.

LISTENING SCRIPT

CD 2 TR 46

The listening script matches the conversation in Exercise B.

LESSON 2 I need paper

WORKPLACE CONNECTION
Exercise B: Manage money

GOAL ■ Make purchases

A. Read the advertisement.

IS / ARE
How much **is** the paper?
How much **are** the notebooks?

B. Listen to the conversation about the ad and practice the conversation.

CD 2
TR 46

Customer: Excuse me, how much are the dividers?
Salesperson: They are $2.00 for a set of nine.
Customer: Thanks. I need one set, please.

WORKPLACE CONNECTION
Exercise D: Perform basic computations; Manage money
Exercise F: Apply technology to a task

C. Listen and repeat.

CD 2 TR 47

INCHES
a two-inch binder = a 2″ binder

I need …
a box of pencils.
a two-inch binder.
a set of five colored dividers.
a package of paper.
a box of ballpoint pens.
a notebook.

D. Look at the ad in Exercise A and write three more items you want. Write the total.

Answers will vary.

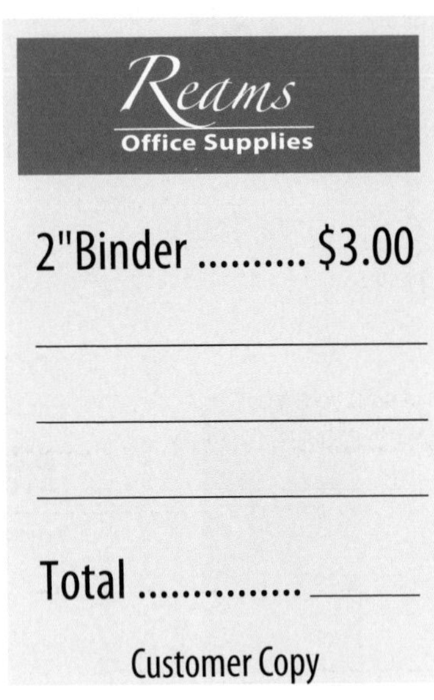

Reams
Office Supplies

2"Binder $3.00

____

____

____

Total .... ______

Customer Copy

E. Practice the conversation. Use the information in Exercise A to make new conversations.

Salesperson: What do you need?
Customer: I need a two-inch binder.
Salesperson: They are over here.
Customer: How much are they?
Salesperson: They are $3.00 each.

F. APPLY Visit an office supply store in person or online and check prices.

C. Listen and repeat.

Go over each sentence with students. Help them with new vocabulary.

LISTENING SCRIPT
CD 2 TR 47
The listening script matches the list of statements in Exercise C.

Practice 1

5–7 mins.

D. Look at the ad in Exercise A and write three more items you want. Write the total.

Ask students to complete the receipt by using the information in Exercise A.

Evaluation 1

15–20 mins.

Check students' book work.

Presentation 2

Practice the conversation in Exercise E with a volunteer. Make sure students understand how to substitute information from Exercises A and C.

Practice 2

10–15 mins.

E. Practice the conversation. Use the information in Exercise A to make new conversations.

Do the conversation with students one time so that they understand what to do before you ask them to work in pairs.

Evaluation 2

3–5 mins.

Ask volunteers to present their conversations in front of the class.

F. APPLY Visit an office supply store in person or online and check prices.

If possible, take the class on a field trip to a local office supply store.

BEST PRACTICE

Researching outside of class

Occasionally you may ask students to research some information outside of class. This is an excellent opportunity to build students' interest and motivation. It also encourages independent thinking and allows students time to evaluate their own comprehension of the lessons so far.

If an activity requires students to collect information outside of class, encourage students to note their findings in both traditional and nontraditional ways (if possible). Beyond writing information in their notebooks, students can be encouraged to take pictures, bring in realia, bookmark websites, etc. It is important to take advantage of the individual learning experience and turn it into a shared or a collective experience. This gives students needed feedback and also provides some degree of accountability.

INSTRUCTOR'S NOTES

Presentation 3

10–15 mins.

Again, ask students where they buy food and clothing. Make a list on the board of different places they go.

Practice 3

30–40 mins.

G. In a group, make a list of food you can buy in a supermarket.

Help as needed.

H. In a group, make a list of clothing you can buy in a clothing store.

Help as needed.

I. Look at Exercise E. Write and practice new conversations about your lists in Exercises G and H.

Help as needed.

Evaluation 3

3–5 mins.

Ask for volunteers to present their conversations in front of the class.

Application

10–15 mins.

J. CREATE Look back at Units 3 and 4. Prepare a section about *Consumer Economics* in your binder.

Ask students to create their own Consumer Economics summary page for their binder, using the sample provided, or ask them to complete the forms provided in the Activity Bank for this unit.

Refer students to *Stand Out Basic Workbook, Unit 8, Lesson 2* for more practice with *How much is* and *How much are*.

Go to the *Activity Bank* online for suggestions on promoting digital literacy and using the Internet to enhance this lesson.

MULTILEVEL WORKSHEET

Lesson 2, Worksheet 1: Consumer Economics

INSTRUCTOR'S NOTES

WORKPLACE CONNECTION
Exercises G and H: Collect and organize information
Exercise J: Combine ideas and information

G. **In a group, make a list of food you can buy in a supermarket.**

Answers will vary.

Food	Price

H. **In a group, make a list of clothing you can buy in a clothing store.**

Answers will vary.

Clothing	Price

I. **Look at Exercise E. Write and practice new conversations about your lists in Exercises G and H.**

J. **CREATE** **Look back at Units 3 and 4. Prepare a section about *Consumer Economics* in your binder.**

Clothing Vocabulary

______________________ ______________________

______________________ ______________________

______________________ ______________________

Food Vocabulary

______________________ ______________________

______________________ ______________________

______________________ ______________________

Questions and Sentences

____

____

____

____

____

LESSON 3 Where's the office supply store?

GOAL ■ Give and follow directions

A. PREDICT Look at the picture. What is happening?

B. Listen to the conversation. Write.

CD 2 TR 48

Woman: Excuse me, where is Reams Office Supplies?

Man: It's on First Street.

Woman: Where's First Street?

Man: Go straight on this street. Turn ____right____ on Main Street and ____left____ on First. It's ____next to____ the electronics store.

Woman: Thanks.

AT-A-GLANCE **PREP**

Goal: Give and follow directions
Grammar: Prepositions
Academic Strategy: Focused listening
Vocabulary: Office supplies

Agenda

- Make conversations about shopping.
- Practice giving directions.
- Read a phone directory.
- Draw a map.
- Make a section for Community in your binder.

Resources

Multilevel Worksheet: Lesson 3, Worksheet 1
Workbook: Unit 8, Lesson 3
Audio: CD 2, Track 48
Heinle Picture Dictionary: Community, pages 46–61

Pacing

- 1.5 hour classes
- 2.5 hour classes
- 3⁺ hour classes

STANDARDS CORRELATIONS

CCRS: RI1, RI7, SL2, L1, L2, RF3
CASAS: 2.1.1, 2.2.1, 7.1.4
SCANS: **Basic Skills** Reading, writing, listening
Information Acquire and evaluate information, organize and maintain information, interpret and communicate information
Interpersonal Participate as a member of a team, teach others
Personal Qualities Responsibility, sociability, self-management
EFF: **Communication** Read with understanding, convey ideas in writing, speak so others can understand, listen actively, observe critically
Lifelong Learning Take responsibility for learning, reflect and evaluate

Warm-up and Review
15–20 mins.

Ask students to share some of the conversations they completed in Exercise I on page 191.

Introduction
3–5 mins.

Ask students where an office supply store is near the school. Help them understand that an office supply store is a store where they can buy all the materials they need for their binders. State the goal: *Today, we will review how to give and follow directions.*

Presentation 1
40–50 mins.

A. PREDICT Look at the picture. What is happening?

Ask students to look at the picture and tell you what is happening in it. Have them guess what the woman is asking. It's fine if students look at the conversation in Exercise B at this stage.

Go over the conversation with students in Exercise B. Explain to them that they will be listening to the conversation and filling in the missing information.

Practice 1
5–10 mins.

B. Listen to the conversation. Write.

LISTENING SCRIPT

CD 2 TR 48

The listening script matches the conversation in Exercise B.

Evaluation 1
5–7 mins.

Check students' book work. Review *right, left,* and *straight*. Have two students perform the dialog with gestures in front of the class.

INSTRUCTOR'S NOTES

Presentation 2

20–30 mins.

C. INTERPRET Read.

Help students find the phone number and address for Reams Office Supplies. Ask other questions about other places in the directory.

D. Read the conversation.

Prepare students to do Exercise E.

Practice 2

10–15 mins.

E. Practice the conversation in Exercise D. Use the information in Exercise C to make new conversations.

Evaluation 2

7–10 mins.

Ask for volunteers to present their conversations in front of the class. There are many opportunities for students to perform unique conversations. Try to get all students in class to perform at least once.

BEST PRACTICE

Working with pictures

Teachers can have students do a lot with a picture. If time permits, add one or more of the following activities to a picture-based exercise:

* Ask students to create captions for the picture.
* Have students create thought bubbles predicting what each person is saying.
* Ask students to brainstorm vocabulary they know that might go with the picture, then have them categorize the words.
* Have students take turns describing the picture to partners.
* Ask students to re-create the picture and the dialog that goes with it.

INSTRUCTOR'S NOTES

C. INTERPRET **Read.**

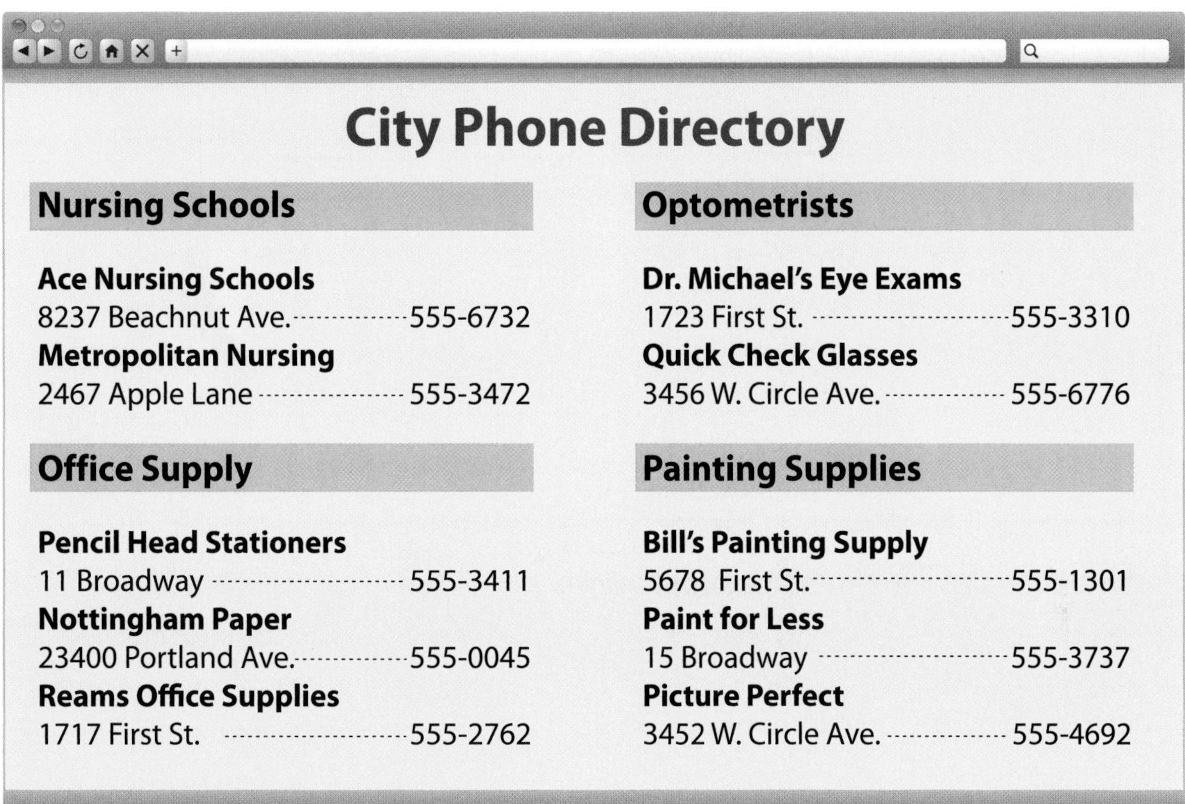

City Phone Directory

Nursing Schools

Ace Nursing Schools
8237 Beachnut Ave. 555-6732
Metropolitan Nursing
2467 Apple Lane 555-3472

Office Supply

Pencil Head Stationers
11 Broadway 555-3411
Nottingham Paper
23400 Portland Ave. 555-0045
Reams Office Supplies
1717 First St. 555-2762

Optometrists

Dr. Michael's Eye Exams
1723 First St. 555-3310
Quick Check Glasses
3456 W. Circle Ave. 555-6776

Painting Supplies

Bill's Painting Supply
5678 First St. 555-1301
Paint for Less
15 Broadway 555-3737
Picture Perfect
3452 W. Circle Ave. 555-4692

D. Read the conversation.

Man: Excuse me, where is Reams Office Supplies?
Woman: It's on First Street.
Man: What's the address?
Woman: It's 1717 First Street.
Man: Thanks.

E. Practice the conversation in Exercise D. Use the information in Exercise C to make new conversations.

F. CREATE Draw a map from your school to an office supply store in your community.

Answers will vary.

PREPOSITIONS

It's *next* to the bank.

It's *between* the bank and the store.

It's *on* the corner.

G. Write directions to the office supply store. Answers will vary.

____

____

____

____

H. Look back at Unit 5. Prepare a section about *Community* in your binder.

Important Vocabulary

______________________ ______________________

______________________ ______________________

______________________ ______________________

Questions and Sentences

____

____

____

____

____

Presentation 3

15–20 mins.

F. CREATE Draw a map from your school to an office supply store in your community.

Do this exercise with the class. Use the board to draw a map to a local office supply store or another store where students can buy the materials for their binders. Remind students of the prepositions they might use in Practice 3.

Practice 3

7–10 mins.

G. Write directions to the office supply store.

Help as needed.

Evaluation 3

5–7 mins.

Have students write their directions on the board.

Application

7-10 mins.

H. Look back at Unit 5. Prepare a section about *Community* in your binder.

Ask students to create their own Community Resource summary page for their binder, using the sample provided, or ask them to complete the forms provided in the Activity Bank for this unit.

Refer students to *Stand Out Basic Workbook, Unit 8, Lesson 3* for more practice with prepositions of location.

Go to the *Activity Bank* online for suggestions on promoting digital literacy and using the Internet to enhance this lesson.

MULTILEVEL WORKSHEET

Lesson 3, Worksheet 1: Community

BEST PRACTICE

Drawing maps

Not everyone is an artist. Some students feel uneasy about their drawing skills, so activities that require them should be approached with some degree of lightheartedness and flexibility.

Remind students that a map is not a painting and that a map can be very simple. Show them examples of maps that would be easy to draw.

Allow students to work in pairs to advance the activity. One student can draw and the other students can add and check specific details. Students tend to be more at ease when working on maps together. They also tend to pay more attention to specific information.

INSTRUCTOR'S NOTES

AT-A-GLANCE **PREP**

Goal: Make goals
Grammar: Simple present
Academic Strategies: Focused listening, study skills
Vocabulary: *goals, a day, a week, every, study, watch, poll*

Agenda

- Take a class poll about sleeping habits.
- Listen and read about goals.
- Read about a class poll.
- Take a class poll.
- Write goals.
- Make a section for Health in your binder.

Resources

Multilevel Worksheet: Lesson 4, Worksheet 1
Workbook: Unit 8, Lesson 4
Audio: CD 2, Track 49
Heinle Picture Dictionary: Health, pages 132–145

Pacing

■ 1.5 hour classes ■ 2.5 hour classes
■ 3^+ hour classes

STANDARDS CORRELATIONS

CCRS: RI1, RI2, RI7, W2, SL1, SL2, L1, L2, RF3
CASAS: 0.2.1, 3.5.9, 6.7.2, 7.1.1, 7.1.2, 7.1.4
SCANS: **Basic Skills** Reading, writing, listening, speaking
Resources Allocate time, allocate materials and facility resources, allocate human resources
Information Acquire and evaluate information, organize and maintain information, interpret and communicate information
Interpersonal Participate as a member of a team, teach others
Personal Qualities Responsibility, sociability, self-management
EFF: **Communication** Read with understanding, convey ideas in writing, speak so others can understand, listen actively, observe critically
Lifelong Learning Take responsibility for learning, reflect and evaluate

Warm-up and Review 15–20 mins.

Take a poll and determine how many hours students sleep a night. Make the results into a bar graph.

Introduction 5–7 mins.

Ask students how many hours of sleep is healthy and write their idea down as a goal. State the goal: *Today, we will make goals, including study goals.*

Presentation 1 15–20 mins.

A. Read Carina's goals.

Go over each goal with the class. Prepare students for focused listening. They will hear Liang talk about three goals. Students should put a check by the goals they hear.

Practice 1 10–15 mins.

B. Listen and check Liang's three goals.

Play the recording three times. Let students discuss answers. Ask groups to rank the goals.

LISTENING SCRIPT

CD 2 TR 49

I have many goals. There are a lot of things that I want to accomplish. Right now, I'm focusing on daily goals. First, I need to exercise every day. I want to get up early and exercise one hour a day. It's important to be physically fit. I suppose that it's important to be prepared for school every day, too, so I'm going to study a lot. I plan to study for one hour every day, even if I'm tired after work. I need to learn English and studying will help me do it faster. Somehow, I need to get plenty of sleep, too. Right now, I only sleep six hours a night, but my goal is to get eight hours of sleep. I hope I can do it. That's my goal. With all these goals, I will be healthy and have great success at school.

C. Talk about Carina's and Liang's goals.

Students are rarely asked to speak with minimal guidance at this level. Be sure to help students when needed and monitor their discussions.

Evaluation 1 3–5 mins.

Check students' answers. Ask the class to rank Liang's and Carina's goals.

LESSON 4 Sleep eight hours a night

GOAL Make goals

A. Read Carina's goals.

My Goals

- ☑ Sleep eight hours a night.
- ☐ Go to school every day.
- ☐ Exercise one hour a day.
- ☑ Eat three good meals a day.
- ☐ Study English at home one hour a day.
- ☑ Read an article in English online.
- ☐ Watch the news in English online.

B. Listen and check Liang's three goals.

CD 2 TR 49

- ☑ Sleep eight hours a night.
- ☐ Go to school every day.
- ☑ Exercise one hour a day.
- ☐ Eat three good meals a day.
- ☑ Study English at home one hour a day.
- ☐ Read an article in English online.
- ☐ Watch the news in English online.

C. Talk about Carina's and Liang's goals.

EXAMPLE: Liang's goal is to sleep eight hours a night.

Exercising one hour a day is a good health habit.

D. **INTERPRET** Study the two graphs about Liang's class.

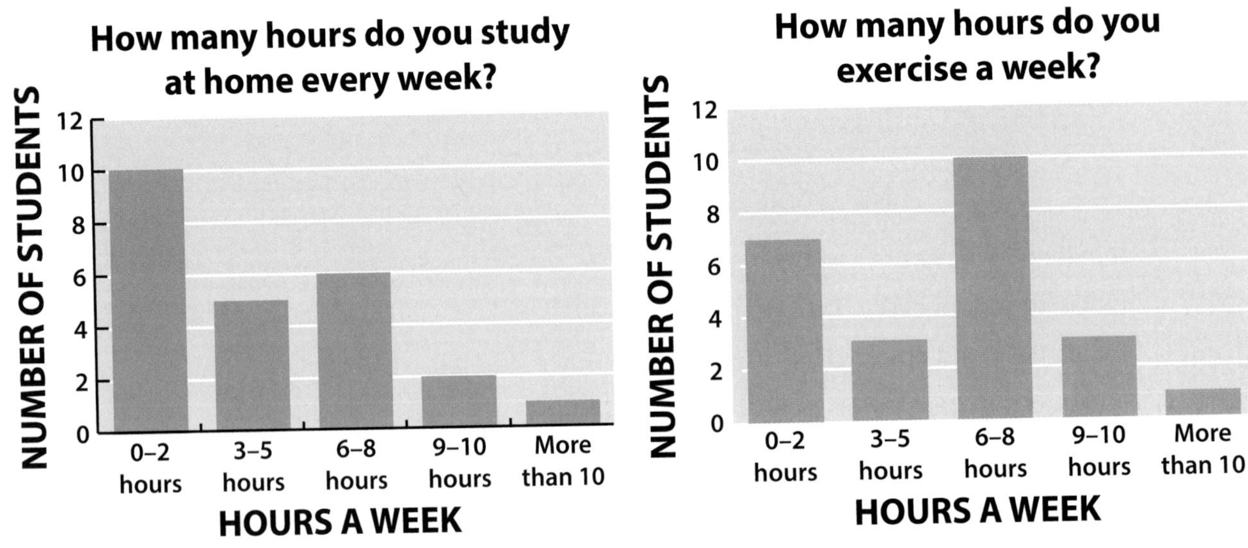

E. **SURVEY** Take a class poll. Ask, "How many hours do you study at home every week?" Create a bar graph with the information. Answers will vary.

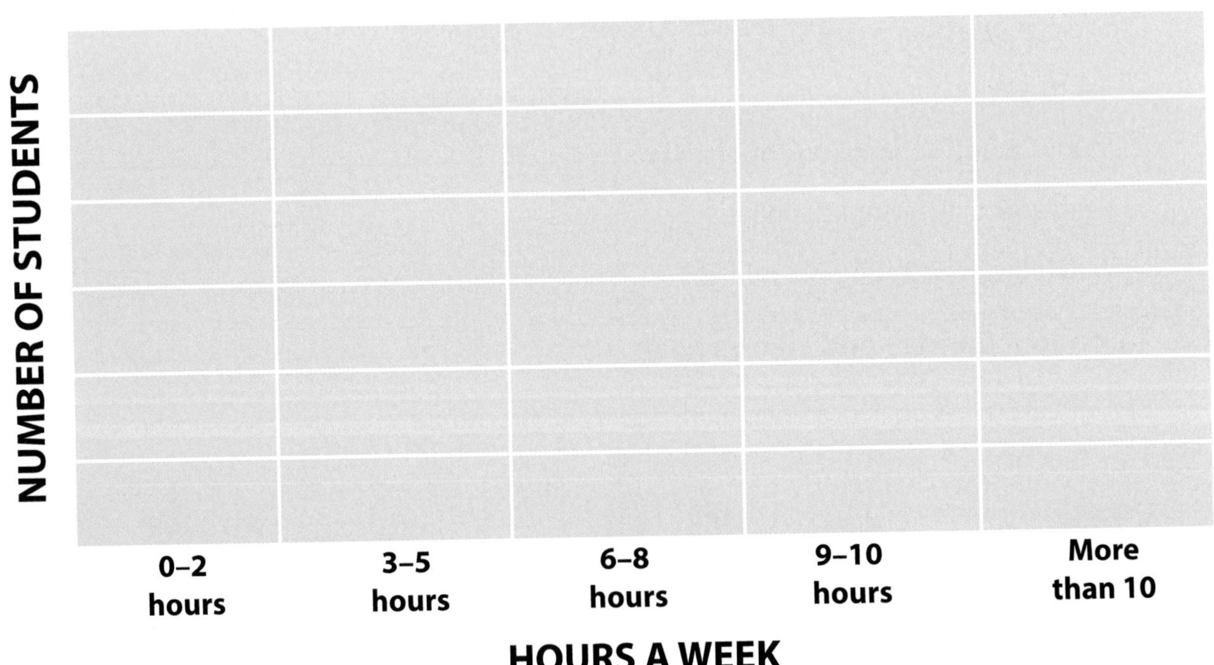

Presentation 2

15–20 mins.

D. INTERPRET Study the two graphs about Liang's class.

Go over the graphs with students and make sure they understand the information by asking them information questions.

BEST PRACTICE

Bar graphs

Students may initially judge bar graphs as being difficult to interpret. Assure them that bar graphs are some of the easiest ways to compare things between different groups or even to track changes over a period of time.

When teaching with bar graphs, always give students a sufficient amount of time to understand the information presented. Point out what is being compared or tracked in plenty examples until students see how simple bar graphs are.

1. First, explain to students that the title tells us what information we can find on the graph.
2. Then, tell students that there are two sides to the bar graph (a horizontal line and a vertical line). Ask them to look closely at what type of information is presented on each side.
3. Next, explain that the scale tells us how much or how many. Have them look at the numbers.
4. Then, point out that the height of the bar gives us the value of each item.

It is important that students feel confident with this visual method of presenting information before they start creating their own bar graphs. Help students by giving them a theme or a question to investigate. Suggest that students use an easy research method such as a survey. If students have been shown the different segments that make up a bar graph, they should be ready to share their collected information in this visual format.

Practice 2

15–20 mins.

E. SURVEY Take a class poll. Ask, "How many hours do you study at home a week?" Create a bar graph with the information.

Evaluation 2

5–7 mins.

Check students' book work.

INSTRUCTOR'S NOTES

Presentation 3

10–15 mins.

Ask students to close their books and discuss their personal goals. Ask them how many hours they sleep and how many hours they wish they could sleep. Help them to see that what they do and their goals can be the same or different. Ask the class as a whole each of the questions in Exercise F.

Ask students to open their books and go over each question with them. Review information-question intonation and the simple present.

Practice 3

15–20 mins.

F. Interview a partner. Write his or her answers.

Help as needed.

Evaluation 3

5–7 mins.

Ask volunteers to report their partners' answers to the class.

Application

15–20 mins.

G. APPLY Write your goals.

Help as needed.

H. CREATE Look back at Unit 6. Prepare a section about *Health* in your binder.

Ask students to create their own Health summary page for their binder, using the sample provided, or ask them to complete the form provided in the Activity Bank for this unit.

Refer students to *Stand Out Basic Workbook, Unit 8, Lesson 4* for more practice with the simple present.

Go to the *Activity Bank* online for suggestions on promoting digital literacy and using the Internet to enhance this lesson.

MULTILEVEL WORKSHEET

Lesson 4, Worksheet 1: Health

INSTRUCTOR'S NOTES

F. **Interview a partner. Write his or her answers.** Answers will vary.

1. How many hours do you exercise every week? ______
2. How many hours do you sleep every night? ______
3. How many hours do you study every day? ______
4. How many meals do you eat every day? ______
5. How many days do you go to school a week? ______

G. **APPLY** **Write your goals.** Answers will vary.

______
______
______
______
______
______

H. **CREATE** **Look back at Unit 6. Prepare a section about *Health* in your binder.**

Important Vocabulary

______ ______
______ ______
______ ______

Questions and Sentences

______
______
______
______
______

WORKPLACE CONNECTION
Exercise B: Collect and organize information

LESSON 5 When can I study?

GOAL ■ Develop a study schedule

A. Listen and point to the student and the teacher.

CD 2 TR 50

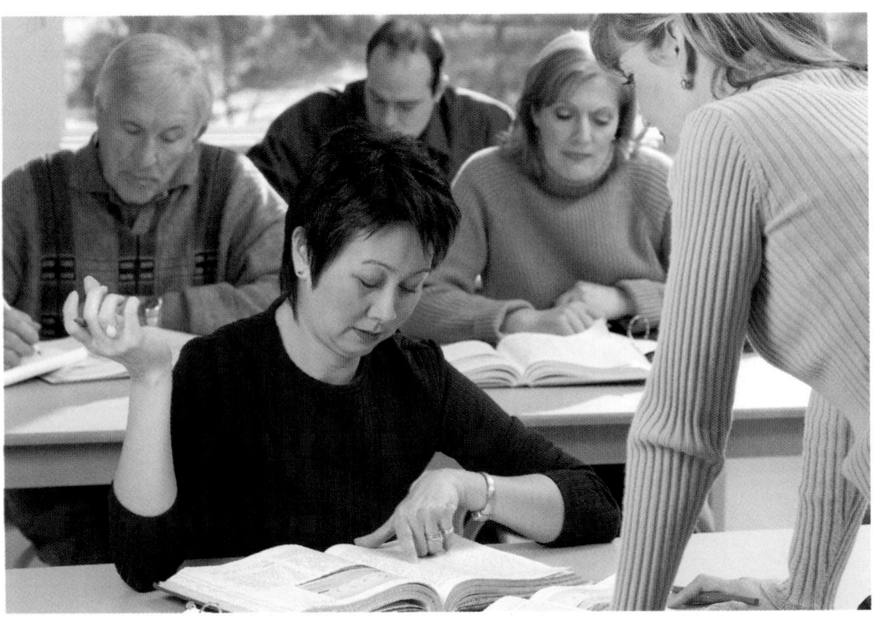

B. CLASSIFY Look at the teacher and student duties. Complete the table.

~~help students~~	study at home	come to class on time
study new words	prepare lessons	do homework

Student duties	Teacher duties
help students	help students
study at home	come to class on time
come to class on time	prepare lessons
study new words	
do homework	

C. Add more duties to the table in Exercise B.

AT-A-GLANCE **PREP**

Goal: Develop a study schedule
Grammar: Simple present
Academic Strategies: Focused listening, study skills
Vocabulary: *homework, prepare, evaluation, at home, schedule, organize*

Agenda

- Make a list of characteristics for good workers.
- Discuss what teachers and students do.
- Read a schedule.
- Complete a schedule.
- Read an evaluation.
- Complete an evaluation.
- Add a section for Occupational Knowledge in your binder.

Resources

Multilevel Worksheet: Lesson 5, Worksheet 1
Workbook: Unit 8, Lesson 5
Audio: CD 2, Track 50
Heinle Picture Dictionary: School, pages 22–23

Pacing

■ 1.5 hour classes ■ 2.5 hour classes ■ 3+ hour classes

STANDARDS CORRELATIONS

CCRS: RI1, SL1, SI2, L1, L2, L5
CASAS: 4.1.1, 4.4.4, 7.1.1, 7.1.4
SCANS: **Basic Skills** Reading, writing, listening
Resources Allocate human resources
Information Acquire and evaluate information, organize and maintain information, interpret and communicate information
Interpersonal Participate as a member of a team, teach others
Personal Qualities Responsibility, sociability, self-management
EFF: **Communication** Read with understanding, convey ideas in writing, speak so others can understand, listen actively, observe critically
Lifelong Learning Take responsibility for learning, reflect and evaluate

Warm-up and Review 10–15 mins.

Ask students what makes a good worker. Make a list of their ideas on the board.

Introduction 15–20 mins.

Ask students if they study at home. Explain that it is best to study at the same time every day. State the goal: *Today, we will develop a study schedule.*

Presentation 1 7–10 mins.

A. Listen and point to the student and the teacher.

Ask students to look at the picture. Ask: *Who are these people? Where are they? What are they doing?*

Ask students to listen to the recording and identify which duty is being spoken about. Play the recording at least two times. Then, go over the other duties mentioned in the recording and make sure students understand them.

LISTENING SCRIPT

CD 2
TR 50

Teachers and students share many duties, or responsibilities. Among them are several very important things. For example, teachers and students should come to class on time. Students don't like to come early and find that the teacher is late. The teacher should come with a prepared lesson every day. That's also very important. Students have more confidence in a teacher who is prepared. The teacher teaches the students, but students can also teach each other. Students should study at home. There is a lot that they can study. For example, they can study new words at home. Sometimes the teacher gives homework. Students who do their homework learn English faster.

Practice 1 10–15 mins.

B. CLASSIFY Look at the teacher and student duties. Complete the table.

Ask students to work in groups or pairs. Help them see that some duties fit in both categories.

C. Add more duties to the table in Exercise B.

Ask students in groups to add to the lists.

Evaluation 1 3–5 mins.

Discuss the lists with students.

Presentation 2

15–20 mins.

D. INTERPRET **Read and talk about the schedule. When does Liang work? When does Liang study?**

Read the chart with students. Help them to understand what a schedule is. Ask them questions about Liang's schedule. For example: *When does Liang eat lunch?* Help students see that Liang studies at the same time every day.

Review the simple present and show students the spelling for *studies.*

E. Answer the questions.

Go over the questions with students.

Practice 2

15–20 mins.

F. CREATE **Complete your schedule.**

Ask students to use Liang's schedule in Exercise D as a model.

Evaluation 2

10 mins.

Ask students questions about their schedules.

BEST PRACTICE

Schedules

The pedagogical value of working with schedules should not be underestimated. They are excellent tools for practicing and reviewing grammar and vocabulary. They are also useful for developing speaking, listening, reading, and writing skills.

For example, Exercise D gives students the opportunity to read and speak when they answer the questions. Students can work in pairs or groups to discuss what takes place in the schedule. Students also review important vocabulary for time formats, days of the week, meals, and daily duties such as work and study. In addition, students practice grammar tenses by describing events in the past, present, and future.

INSTRUCTOR'S NOTES

D. INTERPRET Read and talk about the schedule. When does Liang work? When does Liang study?

LIANG'S SCHEDULE

	Sunday	Monday	Tuesday	Wednesday	Thursday	Friday	Saturday
6:00 a.m.	Breakfast	Breakfast	Breakfast	Breakfast	Breakfast	Breakfast	Breakfast
9:00 a.m.		School	School	School	School	Study	Study
11:00 a.m.	Lunch	Lunch	Lunch	Lunch	Lunch	Lunch	Lunch
1:00 p.m.		Study	Study	Study	Study	Study	Study
3:00 p.m.							
5:00 p.m.		Work	Work	Work	Work	Work	
7:00 p.m.	Dinner	Dinner	Dinner	Dinner	Dinner	Dinner	Dinner
9:00 p.m.							

E. Answer the questions. Answers will vary.

1. When do you study at school? ______________________________
2. When do you study at home? ______________________________
3. When do you work? ______________________________
4. When do you eat breakfast, lunch, and dinner? __________, __________, __________

F. CREATE Complete your schedule. Answers will vary.

MY SCHEDULE

	Sunday	Monday	Tuesday	Wednesday	Thursday	Friday	Saturday

G. Read and talk about Liang's evaluation.

Name: Liang Ochoa

Studies at home	(Yes)	No
Comes to class on time	Yes	(No)
Speaks English in class	Yes	(No)
Is organized	(Yes)	No

Teacher's signature: Jennifer Douglas

H. Ask questions about Liang.

EXAMPLE: Does Liang study at home?

Answers will vary.

I. EVALUATE Complete an evaluation about yourself. Ask your teacher to sign it.

Name: ____________________

Studies at home	Yes	No
Comes to class on time	Yes	No
Speaks English in class	Yes	No
Is organized	Yes	No

Teacher's signature: ____________________

J. Look back at Unit 7. Prepare a section about *Occupational Knowledge* in your binder.

Important Vocabulary

____________________ ____________________

____________________ ____________________

____________________ ____________________

Questions and Sentences

____

____

____

Presentation 3

10–15 mins.

G. Read and talk about Liang's evaluation.

Go over Liang's evaluation with students. This evaluation is about whether Liang is a good student or not.

H. Ask questions about Liang.

Help as needed.

Practice 3

10–15 mins.

I. EVALUATE Complete an evaluation about yourself. Ask your teacher to sign it.

Evaluation 3

5–7 mins.

Ask students about their evaluations and observe their book work.

Application

20–30 mins.

J. Look back at Unit 7. Prepare a section about *Occupational Knowledge* in your binder.

Ask students to create their own Occupational Knowledge summary page for their binder, using the sample provided, or ask them to complete the form provided in the Activity Bank.

Refer students to *Stand Out Basic Workbook, Unit 8, Lesson 5* for more practice with the simple present.

Go to the *Activity Bank* online for suggestions on promoting digital literacy and using the Internet to enhance this lesson.

MULTILEVEL WORKSHEET

Lesson 5, Worksheet 1: Occupational Knowledge

INSTRUCTOR'S NOTES

It's easy to get organized

Before You Watch

- Ask students if they think they are organized. Ask: *Why or why not?* Then, ask: *What things do you use to help you get organized?* Discuss as a class.

A. Look at the picture and answer the questions.

- Ask the questions and elicit answers.
- Ask students how they organize their materials for class.

While You Watch

B. Watch the video and complete the dialog. Use the words in the box.

- Ask students to watch the video and complete the conversation between Hector and Mateo.
- Review the words in the box. Explain vocabulary that students do not understand.
- Play the video twice. Use the pause button when necessary.

Check Your Understanding

C. Show the correct order of the events by writing a number next to each sentence.

- Ask students to put the events from the video in order.
- Read the example and point out that this is the first event that takes place.
- Play the video again. Then, play the video once more so that students can check their answers.

BEST PRACTICE

There are many ways to use video in the classroom. Students should rarely watch a video without some kind of task. You might introduce comprehension questions before they watch so they know what they are looking for. Below are a few techniques that you may try for variety beyond the comprehension checks and other ideas already presented in this lesson.

Freeze Frame: Pause the video during viewing and use it like a picture dictionary, identifying and expanding on the vocabulary.

Silent Viewing: Show the video in segments without sound so students can guess at the storyline. This helps them to understand that listening is more than just the words people say.

Prediction Techniques: Show portions of the video and ask students to predict what will come next.

Listening without Viewing: This helps students create their own image of what is happening. After a discussion, allow students to watch the video and the sound together.

Back-to-Back: In pairs, one student faces the video and the other faces away. Play the video without sound and ask the student viewing to report to the student who is facing away what is happening.

Summary Strips: Create strips of sentences that describe the events. Have students watch the video and then put the strips in the correct order, or ask students to predict the story line before watching and then check their answers. The Activity Bank has summary strips for each video in *Stand Out*.

LIFESKILLS It's easy to get organized

Before You Watch

A. Look at the picture and answer the questions.

1. Where are Hector and Mateo?
   They are in class.
2. What's wrong with Mateo?
   He is disorganized.

While You Watch

B. Watch the video and complete the dialog. Use the words in the box.

dividers	have	need	notebook	~~organized~~	What

Hector: Look, Mateo. It's easy to get (1) ___organized___. You just put everything in a binder with dividers.

Mateo: How many (2) ___dividers___ do I need?

Hector: How many classes do you (3) ___have___?

Mateo: Five—I have five classes.

Hector: Then you (4) ___need___ five dividers, one for each class. Here, I'll give you some of my dividers.

Mateo: (5) ___What___ else do you think I need?

Hector: You need pencils, pens, a package of paper, and a (6) ___notebook___.

Check Your Understanding

C. Show the correct order of the events by writing a number next to each sentence.

a. ___3___ Mateo can't find his vocabulary list.

b. ___4___ Hector tells Mateo what he needs to get organized.

c. ___5___ Hector gives Mateo some dividers for his notebook.

d. ___1___ Mrs. Smith gives the class an extra reading.

e. ___2___ Mrs. Smith leaves the classroom.

Review

A. Match. Draw a line.

1. January, ________________, March	a. dairy
2. This person answers phones in an office.	b. address
3. It is at the end of your arm.	c. aspirin
4. your home	d. bank
5. milk, cheese, butter	e. bread
6. not sunny	f. dime
7. medicine for a headache	g. doctor
8. a place for money	h. February
9. food for a sandwich	i. hand
10. ten cents	j. June
11. This person can work in a hospital.	k. cloudy
12. May, ________________, July	l. receptionist
13. clothing for winter	m. ride
14. a place to buy food	n. shoes
15. You wear them on your feet.	o. supermarket
16. You ________________ a bicycle.	p. sweater

B. Write three words for each unit. *Answers will vary.*

Unit	Words	Unit	Words
Personal information	________ ________ ________	Our Community	________ ________ ________
Our Class	________ ________ ________	Healthy Living	________ ________ ________
Food	________ ________ ________	Work	________ ________ ________
Clothing	________ ________ ________	Lifelong Learning and Review	________ ________ ________

AT-A-GLANCE **PREP**

Goal: All unit objectives
Grammar: All unit grammar
Academic Strategies: Focused listening, reviewing, evaluating, developing study skills
Vocabulary: All unit vocabulary

Agenda

- Discuss unit objectives.
- Complete the review.

Pacing

- 1.5 hour classes
- 2.5 hour classes
- 3+ hour classes

STANDARDS CORRELATIONS

CCRS: L1, L2
CASAS: 7.4.2, 7.4.3
SCANS: **Basic Skills** Reading, writing, listening, speaking
Information Acquire and evaluate information, organize and maintain information, interpret and communicate information
Thinking Skills See things in the mind's eye
EFF: **Communication** Speak so others can understand
Lifelong Learning Take responsibility for learning, reflect and evaluate

Warm-up and Review

7–10 mins.

With their books closed, ask students to help you make a list on the board of all the vocabulary from the unit. Then, have a competition where students in groups find and write the page number for each item on the list. The first group to have the correct page number for each item wins. Explain that this review will also include going through the entire book for information.

Introduction

5 mins.

Write all the goals on the board from Unit 8. Show students the first page of every lesson so they understand that today will be review. Complete the agenda.

Note: Depending on the length of the term, you may decide to have students do Presentation and Practice for homework and then review as the warm-up for another class.

Presentation

10–15 mins.

This presentation and practice will cover the first three pages of the review. Quickly, go to the first page of each lesson. Discuss the objective of each. Ask simple questions to remind students what they have learned.

Practice

15–20 mins.

A. Match. Draw a line.

B. Write three words for each unit.

Ask students to complete the table finding the words in the units indicated.

BEST PRACTICE

Recycling/Review

The review and the project that follows are part of the recycling/review process. Students at this level often need to be reintroduced to concepts to solidify what they have learned. Many concepts are forgotten while learning other new concepts. This is because students are not necessarily ready to acquire language concepts.

Therefore, it is very important to review and to show students how to review on their own. It is also important to recycle new concepts in different contexts.

INSTRUCTOR'S NOTES

Practice *(continued)*

C. Find the page number from the Vocabulary List on pages 212 and 213 and write the sentence.

Additional Task: Choose a nearby market as a class. Create a map on the board to practice giving directions and map-reading skills.

D. Find two new words from the Vocabulary List on pages 212 and 213.

INSTRUCTOR'S NOTES

C. Find the page number from the Vocabulary List on pages 212 and 213 and write the sentence.

Phrase: marital status

Page number: 20

Sentence: He is single.

Phrase: extra large

Page number: 93

Sentence: Answers will vary.

Phrase: go straight

Page number: 127

Sentence: Answers will vary.

Word: checkup

Page number: 138

Sentence: Answers will vary.

D. Find two new words from the Vocabulary List on pages 212 and 213. Answers will vary.

Word: ____________________

Page number: ______

Sentence: ____

Word: ____________________

Page number: ______

Sentence: ____

E. Use the Grammar Reference on pages 214–216 and fill in the blanks.

1. a. I ______am______ married.
   b. We ______are______ students.
   c. You ______are______ hungry.
   d. They ______are______ thirsty.
   e. She ______is______ single.
2. a. I ____________ milk. Answers will vary.
   b. We ____________ a bowl of soup.
   c. You ____________ vegetables.
   d. They ____________ tacos.
   e. She ____________ a sandwich.
3. a. ______Wash______ your hands.
   b. ______Answer______ the phones.
   c. ______Schedule______ meetings.
4. a. I can ____________. Answers will vary.
   b. Aki and Adriano can ____________.
   c. We can't ____________.
   d. The teacher can't ____________.

F. Write the plural forms.

Singular	Plural
pear	pears
cookie	cookies
banana	bananas
egg	eggs
tomato	tomatoes

Practice *(continued)*

E. Use the Grammar Reference on pages 214–216 and fill in the blanks.

F. Write the plural forms.

You might want to extend the task by reviewing the singular and plural forms of articles of clothing or other foods studied.

Evaluation

15 mins.

Go around the room and check on students' progress. Help individuals when needed. If you see consistent errors among several students, interrupt the class and give a mini lesson or review to help students feel comfortable with the concept.

Learner Log

Review the concepts of the Learner Log. Make sure students understand the concepts and how to do the log including the check marks.

BEST PRACTICE

Learner Logs

Learner Logs function to help students in many different ways.

1. They serve as part of the review process.
2. They help students to gain confidence and document what they have learned. In this way, students see that they are progressing and want to move forward in learning.
3. They provide students with a tool that they can use over and over to check and recheck their understanding. In this way, students become independent learners.

Application

Ask students to write down their favorite lesson or page in the unit.

Assessment

Use the Stand Out Assessment CD-ROM with ExamView© to create a post-test for Unit 8.

INSTRUCTOR'S NOTES

WORKPLACE CONNECTION

Combine ideas and information; Make decisions; Exercise leadership roles; Manage time; Complete tasks as assigned; Interact appropriately with team members; Collect and gather information; Interpret and communicate information; Apply technology

STANDARDS CORRELATIONS

CCRS: SL1, SL2

CASAS: 2.2.3, 4.8.1

***SCANS:* Basic Skills** Reading, writing, listening, speaking

Resources Allocate time, allocate money, allocate materials and facility resources, allocate human resources

Information Acquire and evaluate information, organize and maintain information, interpret and communicate information, use computers to process information

Interpersonal Participate as a member of a team, teach others, serve clients and customers, exercise leadership, negotiate to arrive at a decision, work with cultural diversity

Systems Understand systems, monitor and correct performance, improve and design systems

Thinking Skills Think creatively, make decisions, solve problems, see things in the mind's eye

Personal Qualities Responsibility, sociability, self-management

***EFF:* Communication** Read with understanding, convey ideas in writing, speak so others can understand, listen actively, observe critically

Decision Making Solve problems and make decisions, plan

Interpersonal Cooperate with others, advocate and influence, resolve conflict and negotiate, guide others

Lifelong Learning Take responsibility for learning, reflect and evaluate

Introduction

In this project, students will work as a team to create a study guide for new students. They will present their binders to the class as a final class project.

Stage 1

15–20 mins.

COLLABORATE Form a team with four or five students.

Discuss the art on the student book page.

Help students to assign positions in their groups. On the spot, students will have to choose who will be the leader of their group. Review the responsibility of a leader and ask students to write the name of their leader in their books. Do the same with the remaining positions: artist, writer, and spokesperson.

Stage 2

20–30 mins.

Complete your binder from this unit. Share the information from your binder with your group.

Ask students individually to complete the sections of the binders they developed in this unit and to share what they have completed with the group.

Stage 3

40–50 mins.

Use your binders to make a team binder. This will be a study guide for new students.

Ask students in groups to design a sample binder for new students who might come into the class late in the term. It will be used as a study guide. They will use the worksheets in the Activity Bank for this unit.

Stage 4

10–30 mins.

Decorate the study guide.

Ask students to decorate the binder pages and add pages that the team thinks might be helpful.

Stage 5

10–30 mins.

Present your study guide to the class.

Ask teams to practice their presentation before they give it. Recording student presentations on video can greatly enhance the learning experience.

BEST PRACTICE

Digital literacy

Projects are a perfect place to allow students opportunities to use other forms of presentations beyond pictures they create. Digital literacy is becoming more necessary as a life skill. Encourage students to create presentations using pictures from the Internet. They might also consider using other digital presentation tools.

Create a study guide

1. **COLLABORATE** Form a team with four or five students. In your team, you need:

Position	Job description	Student name
Student 1: Team Leader	Check that everyone speaks English. Check that everyone participates.	
Student 2: Writer	Organize and add sections to the study guide.	
Student 3: Artist	Decorate the study guide.	
Students 4/5: Spokespeople	Prepare a presentation.	

2. Complete your binder from this unit. Share the information from your binder with your group.
3. Use your binders to make a team binder. This will be a study guide for new students.
4. Decorate the study guide.
5. Present your study guide to the class.

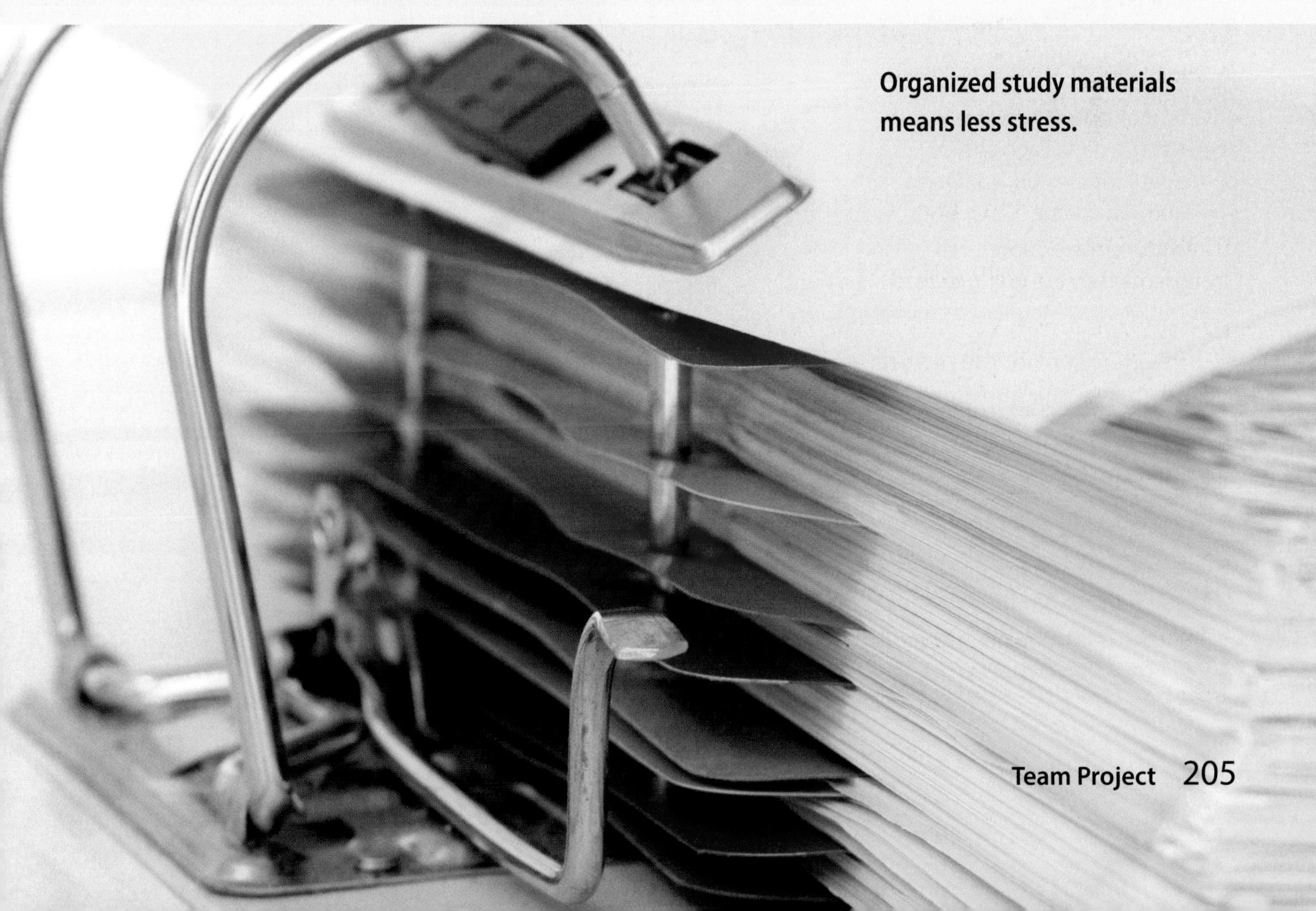

Organized study materials means less stress.

About the Explorer

Maritza Morales Casanova is an environmentalist from Mérida in Yucatán, Mexico. Her aim is to raise environmental awareness among children with the hope of shaping future leaders. Maritza has been trying to raise awareness from a very young age. When she was ten years old, she founded HUNAB (Humanity United to Nature in Harmony for Beauty, Welfare, and Goodness). Her project grew, and now at the Ceiba Pentandra Park, children learn how to care for the environment. Maritza believes in shaping the future leaders, and she empowers some of the children as teachers at the park.

About the Photo

This photo was taken at the Ceiba Pentandra Park. It shows Maritza and a group of children gathered around a pond. They are learning about how to care for the oceans and the organisms that live in them. Learning how to care for the oceans is just one environmental issue children learn about at the park. Each section of the park focuses on a different environmental issue.

- Introduce the explorer. Tell students they are going to read about Maritza Morales Casanova.

A. PREDICT Look at the picture and answer the questions.

- Ask students to look at the picture and answer the questions.
- Read the title and ask students what they think it means for the children in the photo.
- Read the quote and ask students what they think Maritza means.

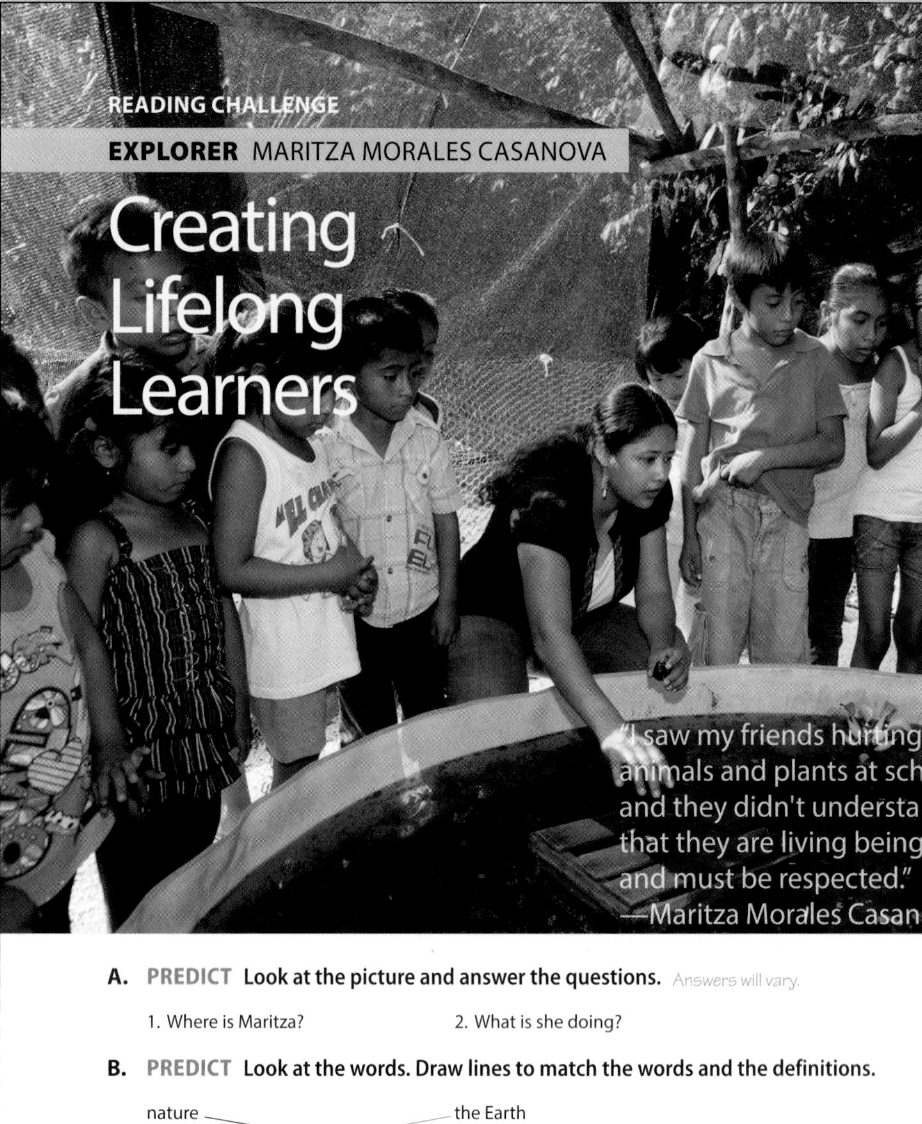

READING CHALLENGE
EXPLORER MARITZA MORALES CASANOVA
Creating Lifelong Learners
"I saw my friends hurting animals and plants at sch
and they didn't understa
that they are living being
and must be respected."
—Maritza Morales Casan

A. PREDICT Look at the picture and answer the questions. Answers will vary.

1. Where is Maritza?
2. What is she doing?

B. PREDICT Look at the words. Draw lines to match the words and the definitions.

nature	the Earth
the planet	living things like plants and animals
lifelong learning	help someone or something be safe
take care	don't stop learning

206 Unit 8

CCRS FOR READING

RI1, RI2, SL2

WORKPLACE CONNECTION
Exercise F: Collect and organize information

C. Read about Maritza Morales Casanova.

Maritza Morales Casanova is a teacher. She believes the nature around us is important. At the Ceiba Pentandra Park in Mexico, she and her fellow teachers show people how to take care of the planet. She wants everyone to learn and continue learning. She teaches her students to be lifelong learners. That's why most of the teachers at the park are children!

D. Answer the questions about the paragraph.

1. ***What does Maritza do?***
   She's a *teacher*.
2. ***What*** is the name of the park?
   Ceiba Pentandra is the name of the park.
3. ***Where*** is the park?
   The park is in Mexico.
4. ***Who*** are the teachers?
   Children are the teachers.

E. Practice asking and answering the questions in Exercise D.

F. SURVEY Ask five students about their favorite subjects. Complete the table. Write any new subjects in the spaces provided. *Answers will vary.*

A. What is your favorite subject?
B. My favorite subject is science.

Name	English	Math	Science	History	______	______
Maritza			✓			

B. PREDICT Look at the words. Draw lines to match the words and the definitions.

- Read the words. Then, ask students to match them with the correct definitions.
- Ask students to check their answers with a partner.
- Review answers and discuss as a class.

C. Read about Maritza Morales Casanova.

- Ask students to read the passage about Maritza Morales Casanova.
- Show students the location of Ceiba Pentandra Park or Yucatán, Mexico on a map if possible.

D. Answer the questions about the paragraph.

Ask students to answer the questions about the paragraph.

E. Practice asking and answering the questions in Exercise D.

Have students practice asking and answering the questions in Exercise D.

F. SURVEY Ask five students about their favorite subjects. Complete the table. Write any new subjects in the spaces provided.

- Tell students that they are going to make a survey.
- Have students ask five students about their favorite subjects using the conversation as a guide.
- Ask students to complete the table. Then, have them add any new subjects.

READING STRATEGIES

Questions

Questions about a reading can be very effective. They motivate students to read and draw their attention to what they will learn. Questions also help students check their comprehension and relate what they will learn to what they already know.

About the Photo

This photo shows a woman alongside a reindeer dressed in traditional Sami clothing. The Sami are indigenous people who inhabit the Arctic regions of Norway, Finland, Sweden, and some parts of Russia. This region is also known as Lapland. The Sami people have lived in these far northern regions for thousands of years and even though many live regular lives, there are still some who adhere to a traditional style of living. This includes herding reindeer for transport and food, living in tents, and wearing Gákti—traditional clothing worn during ceremonies and while working with reindeer.

VIDEO CHALLENGE

People of the Reindeer

A Sami woman with a reindeer

Over the last four units, you have learned about different types of housing and transportation. You have also learned about different types of jobs. Now you will meet the Sami people from the Arctic region of Finland. The Sami people have a special type of housing and a very different type of transportation.

208 People of the Reindeer

Before You Watch

A. Read the sentences. Match the word in bold to its meaning.

1. My **journey** was interesting because I visited many places in northern Europe.
2. We always sleep outside in a **tent** when we travel with our animals.
3. The **reindeer** usually eat the grass under the soft snow.
4. My people's **tradition** is to wear bright clothing with red and yellow colors.

a. things people do for a long time that never change ___tradition___
b. a large animal with antlers that lives in cold places ___reindeer___
c. a type of housing for outside used when you travel ___tent___
d. traveling from one place to another ___journey___

B. You are going to watch a video. Look at the pictures and read the captions. Match.

a. 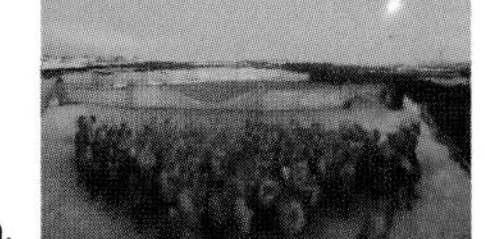
b. 
c. 

1. These Sami people have traditional clothing. ___c___
2. On a journey, the Sami people live in tents. ___b___
3. The Sami people work with their reindeer. ___a___

C. Look at the pictures and read the captions in Exercise B again. What do you think the video is going to be about? Circle your choice. Answers will vary.

a. The food the Sami people eat.
b. Winter snowstorms in northern Europe.
c. How the Sami people live and work.
d. The life of reindeer in the Arctic countries.

Before You Watch

- Read the title of the video, *People of the Reindeer*. Ask students to describe this animal. Then, ask students where they think this animal lives.

A. Read the sentences. Match the word in bold to its meaning.

- Ask students to read the sentences on their own, paying attention to the words in bold. Then, ask students to match the words to their correct meanings.
- Ask students to work with a partner and make new sentences with the words in bold.
- Have volunteers write their sentences on the board. Read and check for the correct meanings as a class.

B. You are going to watch a video. Look at the pictures and read the captions. Match.

- Ask students to look at the pictures and read the captions below. Then, ask students to match the correct caption with each picture. Check answers as a class.

C. Look at the pictures and read the captions in Exercise B again. What do you think the video is going to be about? Circle your choice.

- Tell students that they are going to watch a video called *People of the Reindeer*. Then, have them read the captions in Exercise B again. Ask: *What do you think the video is going to be about?* Have students circle their choice(s). Discuss as a class.

VIDEO CHALLENGE

While You Watch

A. Was your prediction correct? What is the video about? Complete the sentence in your own words.

Play the video and have students watch. Then, ask students if their prediction about the video in Exercise C on page 209 is correct. Ask students to write their prediction on the line. Have students share their answers with the class.

B. Watch the video again. Circle the word you hear in each statement.

- Tell students they will complete the sentences with the correct words they hear in the video. Ask students to read the sentences on their own.
- Play the video again and ask students to watch and listen while keeping the sentences in mind.
- Play the video once again to allow students to choose their answers. Then, have students check their answers with a partner.

C. Put the events in order. Write the correct number on the line.

Ask students to watch the video again to put the events in order. Ask students to read over the events before they watch. Have a volunteer read the events in the correct order. Play the video again to check the sequence of events if necessary.

While You Watch

A. Was your prediction correct? What is the video about? Complete the sentence in your own words.

The video is about how the Sami people live and work.

B. Watch the video again. Circle the word you hear in each statement.

1. The Sami people's reindeer move in (winter / spring).
2. The (farmers / children) travel with the reindeer, too.
3. This snow is hard. After (snowy / sunny) weather, it is soft.
4. (Soft / Hard) snow is good for the reindeer.
5. Well, that's all. It's time to (work / sleep).

C. Put the events in order. Write the correct number on the line.

1 a. The Sami people move the reindeer together.
4 b. A Sami man eats at the table in his home.
6 c. A Sami man sits on the snow with his dog.
5 d. A Sami baby in bright clothing plays outside.
3 e. A Sami woman works outside her house.
2 f. A Sami man sits next to a fire inside his tent.

After You Watch

A. Describe the video. Complete each sentence with the correct verb.

working	eating	burning	sitting	running

1. The Sami child is eating berries.
2. The reindeer are running in the snow.
3. The Sami woman is working in the yard.
4. The fire is burning inside the *goahti*.
5. The Sami man is sitting next to his dog.

210 People of the Reindeer

B. What did you learn about the Sami people? Classify the words and phrases in the table. Check the correct category.

	Type of housing	Daily duty	Food
make a fire		✓	
reindeer meat			✓
take care of children		✓	
goahti	✓		
berries			✓
move reindeer together		✓	
pack tents		✓	
flatbread			✓
watch the reindeer		✓	

C. Look at the picture. Who do you know that uses a tent? Does the person live in the tent all the time? What is the tent used for? Answers will vary.

EXAMPLE: We use a tent when we go camping and sleep in the woods. My family and I do not live in our tent. We live in a three-bedroom house. Answers will vary.

D. Work in small groups. Describe a long journey that you made. Where did you go or come from? Share with the class.

EXAMPLE: My family and I traveled from Florida to New York. We drove in our car for 19 hours.

STRATEGIES

Comprehension While Viewing

There are several strategies that teachers can use *while viewing* to help students better understand videos. These involve manipulation of the video to suit your needs:

1. **Stop or pause** the video while watching.
2. **Rewind the video** to clarify meaning and understanding.
3. **Watch the video** again with different objectives or purposes in mind.
4. **Adjust the viewing speed** (if possible) to focus on specific visuals.

After You Watch

- Ask students to describe the Sami *goahti*. Then, ask them if it is the same or different than the Mongolian *ger*.

A. Describe the video. Complete each sentence with the correct verb.

Ask students to describe the video by completing each sentence with the correct word. Ask students to share their answers with the class.

B. What did you learn about the Sami people? Classify the words and phrases in the table. Check the correct category.

Ask students what they learned about the Sami people from the video. Review the information in the table. Then, have them classify the words and phrases by checking the correct category. Ask students to share their answers in small groups.

C. Look at the picture. Who do you know that uses a tent? Does the person live in the tent all the time? What is the tent used for?

Ask students to look at the picture of the Sami *goahti*. Then, read the questions. Ask students to write their answer using the example as a guide. Have students share their answers with a partner.

D. Work in small groups. Describe a long journey that you made. Where did you go or come from? Share with the class.

Ask students to read the example and write their answer on the lines. Have students share their experiences with the class.

STAND OUT VOCABULARY LIST

PRE-UNIT
Greetings
bye 3
goodbye 3
hello 3
hi 3
Study verbs
check 11
circle 7
listen 9
point 6
read 9
repeat 10
write 10

UNIT 1
Calendar
date 27
month 26
year 26
Months
April 26
August 26
December 26
February 26
January 26
July 26
June 26
March 26
May 26
November 26
October 26
September 26
Marital status
divorced 20
married 20
single 20
Personal information
address 23
application 31
birthplace 18
city 23
date of birth 27
from 17
live 19
name 14
state 23
zip code 23

UNIT 2
phone number 38
schedule 47
time 48
Classroom words
book 41
board 41
bookcase 41
computer 41
desk 41
file cabinet 41
CD 45
notebook 45
pen 45
pencil 45
plant 41
sit 46
stand 46
trash can 41
Location
behind 42
between 42
in 42
in the front 42
next to 42
on 42
Weather
cloudy 50
cold 50
foggy 50
hot 50
rainy 50
snowy 50
sunny 50
windy 50

UNIT 3
Dinner 65
hungry 65
thirsty 66
Food
apple 63
banana 63
bread 63
broccoli 71
butter 63
cake 74
candy 74
carrot 67
cheese 63
chicken 63
chips 67
chocolate 74
cookie 67
egg 63
fries 65
fruit 70
ground beef 68
ham 62
hamburger 65
ice cream 74
lettuce 63
mayonnaise 63
milk 63
onion 68
orange 63
pear 69
pepper 69
pie 74
potato 63
rice 65
salt 68
sandwich 62
spaghetti 68
taco 65
tomato 63
tuna fish 62
turkey 63
vegetables 65
water 63
yogurt 74
Measurements and containers
bag 69
can 69
jar 68
package 68
pound 68
Supermarket
dairy 71
fish 71
meat 71

UNIT 4
Clothing
blouse 87
coat 87
dress 87
pants 86
shirt 86
shoes 86
shorts 87
socks 87
sweater 87
Colors
black 93
brown 93
blue 93
gray 93
green 93
orange 93
pink 93
purple 93
red 93
white 93
yellow 93
Money
dime 95
dollar 95
nickel 95
penny 95
quarter 95
Shopping
cash register 95
extra large 93
large 93
medium 93
receipt 97
sale 98
size 93
small 93

UNIT 5
Directions
go straight 127
stop 127
turn left 127
turn right 127
Housing
apartment 117
condominium 118
house 117
mobile home 117
Places in the community
bank 126
bookstore 126

STAND OUT GRAMMAR REFERENCE

Simple Present		
Subject	**Verb**	**Example sentence**
I, You, We, They	live take ride walk	I **live** in Mexico. You **take** the bus. We **ride** a bicycle. They **walk** to school.
He, She, It	lives takes rides walks	He **lives** in Irvine. He **takes** the bus. She **rides** a bicycle. She **walks** to work.

Simple Present		
Subject	**Verb**	**Example sentence**
I, You, We, They	eat	I **eat** three meals a day.
He, She, It	sleeps	She **sleeps** seven hours a night.

Negative Simple Present			
Subject	**Verb**		**Example sentence**
I, You, We, They	**don't**	eat	We **don't eat** three meals a day.
He, She, It	**doesn't**	sleep~~s~~	He **doesn't sleep** seven hours a night.

Simple Present: *Be*		
Subject	***Be***	**Example sentence**
I	am	I **am** friendly.
He, She, It	is	She **is** friendly.
We, You, They	are	They **are** friendly.

Simple Present: *Be* (negative)		
Subject	***Be (Negative)***	**Example sentence**
I	am not	I **am not** friendly.
He, She, It	is not	She **is not** friendly.
We, You, They	are not	They **are not** friendly.

Simple Present: *Have*		
Subject	***Have***	**Example sentence**
I, You, We, They	have	I **have** two shirts.
He, She	has	She **has** a dress.

Possessive Adjectives

Subject	Possessive adjective	Example sentence
I	My	**My** phone number is 555-3456.
You	Your	**Your** address is 2359 Maple Drive.
He	His	**His** name is Edgar.
She	Her	**Her** name is Julie.
We	Our	**Our** last name is Perez.
They	Their	**Their** teacher is Mr. Jackson.

Prepositions of Location

a. It's **in the front of** the store.

b. It's **in the corner of** the store.

c. It's **in the middle of** the store.

d. It's **in the back of** the store.

e. It's **on the left side of** the store.

f. It's **on the right side of** the store.

How much and *How many*

Question		Answer
How much	(money) is the sweater?	It is $33.00.
How many	coats do you want?	I want three coats.

Yes/No Questions

Question	Answer
Do you buy clothing at a department store?	Yes, I do. No, I don't.
Do you buy food at a supermarket?	
Do you buy shoes at a shoe store?	

Imperatives

	Subject	Verb
Please	~~you~~	read open let me (look) sit down stand up

Present Continuous (right now)			
Subject	***Be*** **verb**	**Base +** ***ing***	**Example sentence**
I	am	talking	I **am talking.**
He, She, It	is	sleeping	He **is sleeping.**
We, You, They	are	waiting	They **are waiting.**

Information Questions	
Question word	**Type of answer**
What	information (receptionist)
Where	a place (Johnson Company)
When	a time or day (9–6) (Monday–Friday)
Who	a person (Martin)

Can			
Subject	***Can***	**Verb (base)**	**Example sentence**
I, You, He, She, It, We, They	can	type	I can type.
		mop	He can mop floors.

Can't			
Subject	***Can't***	**Verb (base)**	**Example sentence**
I, You, He, She, It, We, They	can't	type	I can't type.
		mop	He can't mop floors.

Affirmative Commands			
	Verb		**Example sentence**
~~You~~	wash	your hands	Wash your hands.
	answer	the phones	Answer the phones.
	type	letters	Type the letters.

Negative Commands				
	Verb			**Example sentence**
~~You~~	don't	wash	your hands	Don't wash your hands.
		answer	the phones	Don't answer the phones.
		type	letters	Don't type the letters.

PHOTO CREDITS

01 (tl) Portra Images/Getty Images, **(tc)** Portra Images/Getty Images, **(tr)** Mark Edward Atkinson/ Tracey Lee/Getty Images, **(bl)** Hero Images/Getty Images, **(bc)** Jade/Getty Images, **(br)** Seth Joel/ Getty Images; **02 (b)** Erica Shires/Crave/Corbis; **06 (tl)** Andrey Orletsky/Shutterstock.com, **(tr)** Blvdone/Shutterstock.com; **07 (tl)** Photos.com, **(tc)** IndexOpen, **(tc)** Photos.com, **(tr)** Photos. com; **09 (bl)** arisara/Shutterstock.com, **(bc)** Africa Studio/Shutterstock.com, **(br)** Champion Studio/ Shutterstock.com; **10 (tc)** Champion Studio/ Shutterstock.com, **(tc)** OliverSved/Shutterstock.com, **(cl)** arisara/Shutterstock.com, **(c)** BeautyBlowFlow/ Shutterstock.com, **(cr)** Africa Studio/Shutterstock. com, **(br)** Champion Studio/Shutterstock.com; **12–13** YOAN VALAT/Corbis Wire/Corbis; **14** Inspiron.Dell. Vector/Shutterstock.com; **20 (tl)** Oliver Eltinger/ Fancy/Corbis, **(cr)** Fiona Conrad/Crave/Corbis, **(bl)** VStock/Alamy; **21 (cl)** Photos.com, **(c)** ImageSource/ SuperStock, **(cr)** BananaStock/Alamy; **23 (t)** Fotoluminate LLC/Shutterstock.com, **(b)** Vacclav/ Shutterstock.com; **24 (t)** Beboy/Shutterstock.com, **(c)** Mark Segal/Index Stock Imagery/Getty Images, **(b)** Bob Mahoney/The Image Works; **27** GORDON WILTSIE/National Geographic Creative; **28** artcphotos/ Shutterstock.com; **29** ©Cengage Learning; **30** A and N Photography/Shutterstock.com; **31 (bl)** VStock / Alamy, **(bc)** Fiona Conrad/Crave/Corbis, **(br)** Oliver Eltinger/Fancy/Corbis; **32 (tl)** michaeljung/ Shutterstock.com, **(tr)** Diego Cervo/Shutterstock. com, **(cl)** Dmitry Kalinovsky/Shutterstock.com, **(cr)** eurobanks/Shutterstock.com; **34 (tl)** MIKEY SCHAEFER/National Geographic Creative, **(tr)** Courtesy of Sarah Marquis, **(cl)** Rolando Pujol/EPA/ Newscom, **(cr)** Rolex Awards/François Schaer; **36–37** ED KASHI/National Geographic Creative; **45 (tl)** optimarc/Shutterstock.com, **(tc)** Vladislav Lyutov/ Shutterstock.com, **(tr)** Africa Studio/Shutterstock. com, **(cl)** naipung/Shutterstock.com, **(c)**

Early Spring/Shutterstock.com, **(cr)** Jason / Alamy, **(bl)** Wavebreakmedia/Shutterstock.com, **(bc)** Rangizzz/Shutterstock.com, **(br)** Christian Delbert/Shutterstock.com; **48** Jarrod Ligrani/ Shutterstock.com; **50 (tl)** Manamana/Shutterstock. com, **(tr)** Meunierd/Shutterstock.com, **(cr)** Nadezda Stoyanova/Shutterstock.com, **(bl)** john norman / Alamy, **(bc)** ivylingpy/Shutterstock. com, **(br)** Tupungato/Shutterstock.com; **52 (tl)** sirirak kaewgorn/Shutterstock.com, **(tc)** S_Photo/ Shutterstock.com, **(tc)** Peshkova/Shutterstock.com, **(tr)** fototi photography/Shutterstock.com;

53 ©Cengage Learning; **56 (tl)** Photos.com, **(cl)** Photos.com, **(cl)** Rido/Shutterstock.com, **(bl)** Photos.com; **57** Anibal Trejo/Shutterstock.com; **58** National Geographic Creative; **60-61** GERD LUDWIG/National Geographic Creative; **65 (bl)** J Shepherd/Ocean/Corbis, **(bc)** NatashaPhoto/ Shutterstock.com, **(bc)** Foodio/Shutterstock.com, **(br)** Ildi Papp/Shutterstock.com

67 (tl) Tei Sinthipsomboon/Shutterstock.com, **(tc)** Ozgur Coskun/Shutterstock.com, **(tc)** Kati Molin/Shutterstock.com, **(tr)** Christian Draghici/ Shutterstock.com, **(cl)** Ramon Antinolo/Shutterstock. com, **(c)** Valentyn Volkov/Shutterstock.com, **(cr)** science photo/Shutterstock.com

68 (tl) Nitr/Shutterstock.com; **69 (tl)** Guzel Studio/ Shutterstock.com, **(cl)** Guzel Studio/Shutterstock. com, **(c)** Guzel Studio/Shutterstock.com, **(tr)** Pack/ Shutterstock.com **(c)** Pack/Shutterstock.com, **(cr)** Pack/Shutterstock.com; **70 (tl)** Ramon Antinolo/ Shutterstock.com, **(tr)** Ramon Antinolo/Shutterstock. com, **(tl)** Kati Molin/Shutterstock.com **(tr)** Tei Sinthipsomboon/Shutterstock.com, **(cl)** Candus Camera/Shutterstock.com, **(cr)** Ozgur Coskun/ Shutterstock.com, **(cl)** K2 PhotoStudio/Shutterstock. com, **(cr)** Mmkarabella/Shutterstock.com, **(1)** Photos. com, **(2)** Photos.com, **(3)** Photos.com, **(4)** IndexOpen; **72 (tr)** Nick Rains/Terra/Corbis; **74 (tl)** Africa Studio/ Shutterstock.com, **(tc)** Brent Hofacker/Shutterstock. com, **(tc)** Dusan Zidar/Shutterstock.com, **(tr)** Amarita/Shutterstock.com, **(cl)** HandmadePictures/ Shutterstock.com, **(c)** Brent Hofacker/Shutterstock. com, **(cr)** Africa Studio/Shutterstock.com; **75 (bl)** Rhienna Cutler/Getty Images, **(bc)** Ronnie Kaufman/ Getty Images, **(br)** glyn/Shutterstock.com; **77** © Cengage Learning, **78 (tl)** Candus Camera/ Shutterstock.com, **(tc)** Brent Hofacker/Shutterstock. com, **(tr)** Amarita/Shutterstock.com

(cl) Christian Draghici/Shutterstock.com, **(c)** Brent Hofacker/Shutterstock.com, **(cr)** Mmkarabella/ Shutterstock.com; **81 (b)** kongsak sumano/ Shutterstock.com; **82 (t)** ©Catherine Jaffee/National Geographic Creative; **(br)** Shaiith/Shutterstock. com; **84–85** The Licensing Project/Offset; **87 (cl)** Photos.com, **(C)** Photos.com, **(cl)** IndexOpen, **(c)** Jack Hollingsworth/Blend Images/Getty Images, **(cr)** Thomas Northcut/Photodisc/Getty Images, **(bl)** D. Hurst/Alamy, **(bc)** Photos.com, **(br)** Clipart; **91** Fiphoto/Shutterstock.com; **93** Radius/Corbis; **95 (tl)** RTimages/Shutterstock.com, **(tc)** RTimages/ Shutterstock.com, **(tr)** RTimages/Shutterstock.com, **(cl)** United States Government/Public Domain, **(c)** United States Government/Public Domain, **(cr)** United States Government/Public Domain, **(c)** United States Government/Public Domain, **(cr)** United States Government/Public Domain, **(cr)** United States Government/Public Domain, **(cr)** United States Government/Public Domain, **(cr)** United States Government/Public Domain, **(c)** United States Government/Public Domain, **(bl)** United States Government/Public Domain, **(bc)** United States Government/Public Domain, **(bc)** United States Government/Public Domain, **(bc)** United States Government/Public Domain, **(bc)** United States Government/Public Domain, **(br)** United States Government/Public Domain; **96 (tr)** United States Government/Public Domain, **(tr)** United States Government/Public Domain, **(tr)** United States Government/Public Domain, **(tr)** United States Government/Public Domain, **(tr)** United States Government/Public Domain, **(tr)** United States Government/Public Domain, **(cr)** United States Government/Public Domain, **(cr)** United States Government/Public Domain, **(cr)** United States Government/Public Domain, **(cr)** United States Government/Public Domain, **(br)** United States Government/Public Domain, **(br)** United States Government/Public Domain; **97 (tl)** Photos.com, **(tr)** Photos.com, **(cl)** Photos.com, **(cr)** IndexOpen, **(bl)** Photos.com, **(br)** Jack Hollingsworth/Blend Images/ Getty Images; **98** Oscar Hernandez; **101** ©Cengage Learning; **102 (1)** Photos.com; **(2)** Photos.com, **(3)** Thomas Northcut/Photodisc/Getty Images, **(4)** Photos.com, **(5)** Photos.com, **(6)** IndexOpen, **(7)** Jack Hollingsworth/Blend Images/Getty Images, **(8)** D. Hurst/Alamy; **103 (b)** Jorge Salcedo/ Shutterstock.com; **105** Africa Studio/Shutterstock. com; **106** Courtesy of Sarah Marquis; **107** Chrupka/ Shutterstock.com; **108** Pedrosala/Shutterstock.com; **111** Mark Leong/Redux; **113–114** © Liesl Marelli;

114 (1) fiphoto/Shutterstock.com, **(2)** Niki Love/ Shutterstock.com, **(3)** fiphoto/Shutterstock.com, **(4)** Dotshock/Shutterstock.com, **(5)** Mangostock/ Shutterstock.com, **(6)** Panna Studio/Shutterstock.com; **118 (tl)** Rodenberg Photography/Shutterstock.com, **(tc)** Tim Collins/Shutterstock.com, **(tr)** Rudy Umans/ Shutterstock.com; **119 (tl)** Kevin Peterson/Photodisc/ Getty Images, **(tc)** Hemera Photodisc, **(tr)** Hemera Photodisc; **120 (tl)** zentilia/Shutterstock.com, **(tl)** Art Konovalov/Shutterstock.com, **(cl)** guroldinneden/ Shutterstock.com, **(tc)** luckyraccoon/Shutterstock.com

(c) after6pm/Shutterstock.com; **123 (tl)** kristian sekulic/Getty Images, **(tc)** Maridav/Shutterstock. com, **(tr)** lightpoet/Shutterstock.com; **129** ©Cengage Learning, **131 (tl)** lzf/Shutterstock.com, **(tr)** blvdone/ Shutterstock.com; **133** Radius Images/Alamy; **134** Mikey Schaefer/National Geographic Creative; **136–137** Corneliu Cazacu; **139** BROOKE WHATNALL/ National Geographic Creative; **141 (tl)** Gpointstudio/ Shutterstock.com, **(tc)** wavebreakmedia/Shutterstock. com, **(tr)** Maskot/Getty Images, **(cl)** Alexander Raths/ Shutterstock.com, **(c)** Stefano Cavoretto/Shutterstock. com, **(cr)** Photographee.eu/Shutterstock.com; **142 (b)** lofoto/Shutterstock.com; **149 (tl)** Mark Anderson/Rubberball/Alamy, **(tc)** Amy Eckert/ UpperCut Images/Getty Images, **(tr)** EDHAR/ Shutterstock.com; **153** © Cengage Learning; **154** ALEX TREADWAY/National Geographic Creative; **158** Ernesto Mastrascusa/EPA/Newscom; **160–161** Abner Kingman / Aurora Photos; **165 (tl)** Helen King/Comet/Corbis, **(cl)** Ian Lishman/Juice/Corbis, **(bl)** Oskari Porkka/Shutterstock.com; **167** auremar/ Shutterstock.com;

168 (1) Helen King/Comet/Corbis, **(2)** StockLite/ Shutterstock.com, **(3)** Hiya Images/Fancy/Corbis, **(4)**

Oskari Porkka/Shutterstock.com; **169 (tl)** Racorn/ Shutterstock.com, **(tr)** Tim Pannell/Crave/Corbis; **171** kzenon/iStock/Getty Images Plus/Getty Images; **172** Dmitry Kalinovsky/Shutterstock.com; **173** Eliza Snow/E+/Getty Images; **174 (tl)** Piyato/Shutterstock. com, **(tc)** Walther S/Shutterstock.com, **(tr)** Arcady/ Shutterstock.com; **176 (tl)** Elena Elisseeva/ Shutterstock.com; **177 (tr)** ©Cengage Learning

178 (1) Andrey_Popov/Shutterstock.com, **(2)** light poet/Shutterstock.com, **(3)** racorn/Shutterstock. com, **(4)** Karramba Production/Shutterstock. com, **(5)** Dmitry Kalinovsky/Shutterstock.com, **(6)** Cultura/Zero Creatives/Getty Images, **(7)** Pressmaster/Shutterstock.com, **(8)** wavebreakmedia/ Shutterstock.com; **179 (1)** Oskari Porkka/ Shutterstock.com, **(2)** StockLite/Shutterstock.com, **(3)** Hiya Images/Fancy/Corbis, **(4)** michaeljung/ Shutterstock.com; **180 (1)** Piyato/Shutterstock. com, **(2)** Arcady/Shutterstock.com, **(3)** Walther S/ Shutterstock.com; **181 (b)** Catherine Karnow/ Encyclopedia/Corbis; **182** Rick Stanley/National Geographic Creative; **184–185** PAUL NICKLEN/ National Geographic Creative; **186 (tl)** kyoshino/ Getty Images, **(cl)** Feng Yu/Shutterstock.com, **(bl)** Warwick Lister-Kaye/Getty Images, **(tr)** leungchopan/ Shutterstock.com, **(cr)** kai keisuke/Shutterstock. com, **(br)** robophobic/Shutterstock.com; **192** By Ian Miles-Flashpoint Pictures/Alamy; **195** hiroshitoyoda/ Shutterstock.com; **198** AbleStock/Index Stock Imagery/Photolibrary; **201** ©Cengage Learning; **205** rtbilder/Shutterstock.com; **206** Rolex Awards/ François Schaer; **208** PhotoDisc/Getty Images; **209 (cl)** ©Cengage Learning **(c)** ©Cengage Learning, **(cr)** ©Cengage Learning; **211** ©Cengage Learning;

STAND OUT SKILLS INDEX

STAND OUT VIDEO SCRIPTS

UNIT 1: Lifeskills Video: Nice to meet you

Hector: Mateo! It's about time.
Mateo: Well excuse me for being late, Mr. Sanchez.
Hector: Please, call me Hector.
Mateo: Of course, Mr. Hector.
Hector: Whatever. Just chill.
Mateo: Where is everybody?
Hector: I think the teacher is coming. She's a little late.
Mateo: What is her name?
Hector: Mrs. Smith, I think.
Mateo: *Mrs.* or *Ms.?*
Hector: Mrs. She's married to Mr. Smith, the math instructor. Shh! Here she comes.
Mrs. Smith: Good morning. Are you here for Business 101?
Hector: We sure are. Are you the instructor?
Mrs. Smith: Yes, I am. My name is Mrs. Smith. What's your name?
Hector: My name is Hector Sanchez.
Mrs. Smith: And what about you? What's your name?
Mateo: Mateo Trujillo, at your service.
Naomi: And my name's Naomi Takayama.
Mrs. Smith: Hello, Naomi. It's nice to meet you. Please come in and take a seat. These are your classmates. This is Hector, and this is Mateo.
Naomi: Hi! Nice to meet you.
Hector: Nice to meet you.
Mateo: Nice to meet you too.
Mrs. Smith: Before we start, I'd like to tell you a little bit about myself.
My family is from Ireland. I was born in Boston, Massachusetts, and I moved to California ten years ago. I'm married and I live in Glendale. What about you, Naomi? Where are you from?
Naomi: I'm from Pasadena. My mom's from LA, but my dad's from Japan. He's an engineer. Let's see . . . What else can I tell you . . .
Mrs. Smith: Do you work?
Naomi: Oh, yes. I work at a diner, the "Blue Wave." I'm a waitress. I love my job.
Mrs. Smith: Hector?
Hector: Me? I don't have a job, not yet. But I have parents. My dad's from Mexico and my mom's from Turkey. I've lived in Glendale my whole life. Mateo's my best friend.
Mateo: That's right. Hector's like my brother—my *little* brother.
Mrs. Smith: Are you from Glendale, too?
Mateo: No, I'm from Puerto Rico, but I moved here when I was a little kid.
Mrs. Smith: Well, it's nice to meet you all. Welcome to class. I look forward to being your instructor this semester.

UNIT 2: Lifeskills Video: It's raining hard

Hector: It's ten after three. Where is everybody? Three o'clock class canceled because of bad weather. Oh, no. What do I do now?
Mateo: Whew! It's raining hard outside.
Hector: I know. It's cold and wet and rainy.
Mateo: Am I late?
Hector: No, we're the only ones here.
Mateo: Where's the instructor?
Hector: She's not here. The class is canceled because of bad weather.
Mateo: Shoot! What will we do now?
Hector: I'm not sure. Naomi! Are you OK?
Naomi: Oh, my gosh! It is so windy outside. The wind is blowing hard. It blew my umbrella inside out. Where is everybody?
Mateo: The class is canceled because of the storm. The instructor didn't come to class. Nobody came to class—except us.
Naomi: Oh. So, now what?
Hector: We wait?
Naomi: For how long?
Hector: I guess we have to wait until the rain stops.
Mateo: Shh! Did you hear that?
Naomi: Thunder! The storm is getting stronger. Let's leave now, you guys.
Hector: Are you sure? It's raining and the wind is blowing. Let's wait a little while longer.
Mateo: I agree with Naomi. Let's leave now before the storm gets worse.
Hector: OK, if you think so. Just let me put on my rain poncho.
Naomi: My umbrella is wrecked.
Hector: Here. Use my umbrella.
Naomi: Are you sure?
Hector: Don't worry. It's fine.
Naomi: What are you going to use?
Hector: I have a poncho. I'll be fine.
Mateo: I've got my umbrella. Are you guys ready?
Naomi: I think so.
Hector: Ready, set, let's go!

UNIT 3: Lifeskills Video: What's for lunch?

Hector: I am really hungry.
Mateo: Me too. The menu looks good. What should we have?
Hector: French fries . . . onion rings . . . hamburgers . . . cheeseburgers . . . tacos . . . chips . . . They all look so good.
Mateo: French fries, onion rings, and a hamburger? Are you sure?
Hector: Sure, why not?
Mateo: Well, it's not very good for you. I'm going to have the salad. You need to eat fresh vegetables every day, you know? Hello?
Hector: I'm really thirsty, too. I think I'll have a soda.
Mateo: Go ahead, knock yourself out.
Naomi: Hey, you guys! How are you?
Hector: I'm really hungry.
Naomi: Well, you've come to the right place.
Hector: What's for lunch?
Naomi: Our special today is chicken and rice. The pasta with tomato sauce is really good, too. Do you need some time to think about it?

Hector: Nah, I've already decided. I'll have a cheeseburger, French fries, onion rings, and a glass of soda.
Naomi: Wow, you really are hungry.
How about you Mateo? What would you like?
Mateo: What's in the chicken salad?
Naomi: The chicken salad has carrots and mushrooms.
Mateo: That sounds good. Can I have some tomatoes with it too?
Naomi: Sure. What would you like to drink?
Mateo: I'll have iced tea—with no sugar.
Naomi: Let's see . . . cheeseburger, French fries, onion rings, chicken salad with tomatoes, a glass of soda, and an iced tea, no sugar. I'll be right back.
Naomi: Here's your salad and iced tea.
Mateo: Yum! It looks delicious.
Naomi: And here's your cheeseburger, French fries, and onion rings, and your soda. Are you sure you can eat all that?
Hector: No problem.
Naomi: Alright, then. Enjoy your meal.
Naomi: How was it?
Mateo: Great. The chicken salad was delicious.
Naomi: Oh, good. I'm glad you liked it. How about you, Hector?
Hector: Yeah, it was good. Too good. What's for dessert?
Naomi: We have vanilla ice cream, chocolate cake, and apple pie. What would you like?
Mateo: I'll have a slice of chocolate cake.
Naomi: The cake is good. I think you'll like it. How about you, Hector?
Hector: I'll have . . . nothing. I want dessert, but I'm just too full.
Naomi: I'm not surprised. You ate a big lunch. I'll be right back with your dessert, Mateo.

UNIT 4: Lifeskills Video: That's a good deal
Mateo: Can I help you?
Hector: Mateo! So this is where you work. Are you a sales clerk?
Mateo: We like to call ourselves "sales technicians" And pretty soon I'll be promoted to manager.
Mr. Sanchez: Hector's still looking for a job. As a matter of fact, that's why we're here. He needs a new suit.
Hector: Yeah, something nice but not too formal.
Mateo: Well, you're looking in the right place. And you're in luck, because all these clothes are 30% off.
Hector: Wow! So how much is this jacket, with the discount?
Mateo: Well let's see . . . The price tag says $160. Thirty percent is $48. So that means the coat is only $112.
Mr. Sanchez: That's a pretty good deal.
Hector: My dad's paying for it, so the cheaper the better.
Mateo: Well this coat is even cheaper. It's only $150.
Mr. Sanchez: With the discount, that's $105.
Mateo: Exactly.
Hector: I like it, I think. Yes, I definitely like it. Now I need some pants, and a tie.
Mateo: Here's a nice pair of pants. The normal price is $40, but today they're on sale. They're only $25. And here's a blue tie. Blue is a good color to wear to an interview.
Hector: Ten dollars. I've never bought a tie before. Is that the usual price?
Mateo: Well, the normal price is $18. You save $8 per tie.
Hector: In that case, I'll get two. A blue one and a red one. Now all I need is a shirt.
Mateo: What size do you wear?
Hector: I usually wear medium. But sometimes I wear a large. It all depends on the shirt.
Mateo: Here's a white dress shirt. It's large. But I think this is the right size for you. And it goes with your suit.
Hector: How much is it?
Mateo: It's $22.50. The normal price is $27.50. You save $5.00. All together you're saving $86.
Hector: I'm sure my dad's happy to hear that . . . Dad?
Mr. Sanchez: What do you think of this? It's only $20.
Hector: A yellow polo shirt? To go with my suit?
Mr. Sanchez: I wasn't talking about you. I meant for me.

Video Challenge 1: A Mongolian Family
Narrator: This is Ochkhuu's home. It's a ger in Ulaanbaatar. Ochkhuu's daughter, Anuka, is six years old. Ochkhuu's wife's name is Norvoo. Norvoo's family isn't from the city. These are her parents. Their ger is in the country.
This is Jaya, Norvoo's father. He's a farmer.
Jaya and his wife, Chantsal, are 65 years old. They are happy in the country.
Jaya's life and Ochkhuu's life are very different.
Ochkhuu is a taxi driver now.

UNIT 5: Lifeskills Video: Do you live around here?
Naomi: Hector, hi!
Hector: Naomi, hey! How are you?
Naomi: Good, thanks. What a surprise to see you here. Do you live around here?
Hector: Yes, I do. I live on Oak Street. What about you? Where do you live?
Naomi: I live on Maple Street.
Hector: Maple Street. That's near Chestnut Street, isn't it?
Naomi: I think so. I'm still learning the names of all the streets. I just moved here.
Hector: Glendale's a small town. You'll get used to it pretty soon.
Naomi: I hope so. Where are you going?
Hector: I'm taking the bus to school.
Naomi: Oh, so am I.
Hector: Good, we can take the bus together.
Naomi: Which bus do we take?
Hector: Here, let me show you. We're here, see?
Naomi: By the hospital?
Hector: Right. First we take the Number 11, get off at the Galleria Mall, and then we take the Number 3 to Glendale Community College. It's that easy.
Naomi: We take the Number 11 to the mall, then we take the Number 3 to campus . . . So, what time does the Number 11 come?
Hector: The next one is 11:50. It should be here any minute. I think I see it coming.

Naomi: Here it is. So, did you do the homework last night . . .
Naomi: Hi, Hector! What a coincidence! Taking the bus to school?
Hector: Yes, I am taking the Number 11.
Naomi: Wait, don't tell me. First we take the Number 11 to the mall. Then we take the Number 3 to campus.
Hector: Ah, so you're an expert now!
Naomi: I'm still learning the schedule, though. How often does the Number 3 leave the mall?
Hector: It leaves every 20 minutes. There's one at 12: 15.
Naomi: Well, it's 20 past 12 now. I think we missed that one. Oh, well. The next one will be here at 12:35.
Hector: See what I said? You are becoming an expert now.
Passerby: Excuse me, do you know how I get to the Galleria Mall?
Naomi: Yes, take the Number 11 bus.
Passerby: When does it get here?
Naomi: It comes every 20 minutes, and the next one should be at 1:15.
Passerby: Thank you.
Naomi: You're welcome.

UNIT 6: Lifeskills Video: I've got lots of stress
Dr. Badaoui: Good morning, Victor. How are you?
Mr. Sanchez: Well, Dr. Badaoui, I'm not sure. That's why I'm here.
Dr. Badaoui: I'm sure everything will be fine. Let's start by checking your vital signs.
Mr. Sanchez: OK.
Dr. Badaoui: Your heart rate is normal. Can you open your mouth and go "ahh"?
Mr. Sanchez: Ahhh.
Dr. Badaoui: Good . . . Now let me look inside your ear.
Mr. Sanchez: What do you see?
Dr. Badaoui: Everything looks fine. All your vital signs are normal. Tell me, what brings you in today?
Mr. Sanchez: Well, I'm very tired all the time. I don't have any energy.
Dr. Badaoui: Do you get enough sleep?
Mr. Sanchez: I get about 5 hours of sleep every night.
Dr. Badaoui: Five hours? That's not very much.
Mr. Sanchez: I know, I know.
Dr. Badaoui: What time do you go to bed?
Mr. Sanchez: I usually go to bed about 11 o'clock. But I can't sleep because I think too much.
Dr. Badaoui: What kinds of things do you think about?
Mr. Sanchez: Oh, my job, problems at work, money, bills. I just think and think about everything. So then I get up and watch TV.
Dr. Badaoui: I see. Do you have any other symptoms?
Mr. Sanchez: Sometimes I have headaches in the middle of the day.
Dr. Badaoui: Do you take anything for these headaches?
Mr. Sanchez: Yes, I take aspirin.
Dr. Badaoui: How many aspirin do you take a day?
Mr. Sanchez: I take about 3 aspirin a day, sometimes 5 or 6.
Dr. Badaoui: You can take ibuprofen for your headaches too.
Mr. Sanchez: Ibuprofen?
Dr. Badaoui: Yes, it's a pain reliever. You can buy ibuprofen at the drug store. Just make sure you take it as prescribed.
Mr. Sanchez: OK . . . So what do you think, doctor? Why do I have all these symptoms?
Dr. Badaoui: Inability to sleep . . . headaches . . . these are symptoms of stress.
Mr. Sanchez: Stress! You can say that again. I've got lots of stress in my life. So what am I supposed to do about it?
Dr. Badaoui: Having good, healthy habits can really help a lot.
Mr. Sanchez: For example?
Dr. Badaoui: Getting enough sleep is important. You should have at least 7 hours of sleep every night. Try going to bed a little earlier. Exercise can help you sleep, too.
Mr. Sanchez: I haven't exercised in years.
Dr. Badaoui: To start, try walking. Walking is an excellent form of exercise.
Mr. Sanchez: I suppose I could do that. Why not?
Dr. Badaoui: Try drinking more water, too. You should drink at least six glasses of water every day. Drinking more water may help with your headaches.
Mr. Sanchez: I'll try doing that. Thank you, Dr. Badaoui. I appreciate your help.
Dr. Badaoui: Anytime, Victor. And please, call me if you still have any symptoms.

UNIT 7: Lifeskills Video: Our son is going to get a job!
Hector: Hey, Ma, what does a receptionist do?
Mrs. Sanchez: That's an odd question. Why do you want to know?
Hector: I'm looking at job ads.
Mrs. Sanchez: Job ads? Are you really thinking about getting a job?
Hector: Yep, it's about time. I need some money of my own.
Mrs. Sanchez: I think that's a wonderful idea. But I'm not sure you'd like the job of a receptionist.
Hector: Why not? What does a receptionist do?
Mrs. Sanchez: A receptionist answers phones and takes messages.
Hector: Hello? OK, three o'clock, alright. Um, oh, hold on one second actually. . . Hello. Yes. Um-hmm. Can you, ok . . . Hello? Alright, OK . . . Hold on just a second if you would here, while I staple this . . . OK, thank you . . . alright. So, um-uh. I don't think so. What about a custodian? What does a custodian do?
Mr. Sanchez: A custodian mops the floor and cleans windows.
Hector: Mops the floor . . .
Mr. Sanchez: I have an idea.
Hector: What's that?
Mr. Sanchez: What about being a salesperson?
Hector: I never really thought about it.

Mr. Sanchez: Well, you should think about it. It's a good place to start. That was my first job.
Let's ask your father what he thinks. Did you hear the news?
Mr. Sanchez: What news?
Mrs. Sanchez: Our son is going to get a job!
Mr. Sanchez: That's old news. Hector told me about that a long time ago. I helped him buy some clothes for his interview. Didn't he tell you?
Mrs. Sanchez: I'm always the last person to know! Well, anyway, he's looking at the classified ads. He wants to be a salesclerk. Isn't that a great idea?
Mr. Sanchez: It depends.
Hector: Depends on what?
Mr. Sanchez: Well, sales clerks work long hours. Can you stand on your feet for a long time?
Hector: Sure, why not?
Mrs. Sanchez: You have to be good with customers, too.
Hector: Oh, that's easy. I know how to talk to people.
Mrs. Sanchez: Take a look and see what you find.
Hector: A couple of stores right here in Glendale are looking for sales clerks.
Mr. Sanchez: You should compare the salaries and benefits.
Hector: Here's one. It pays $10.50 an hour. But it doesn't say anything about benefits.
Mrs. Sanchez: You know what that means.
Mr. Sanchez: It doesn't have any benefits. What about the next one?
Hector: Patel's Clothing Store. That sounds familiar.
Mrs. Sanchez: Oh yes, it's at the mall.
Hector: Oh, yeah. That's where Mateo works. Let's see how much money he makes! Only ten dollars an hour . . . Poor Mateo.
Mr. Sanchez: Yes, but look at the benefits. It says you get 1 week of paid vacation.
Mrs. Sanchez: What about health insurance?
Mr. Sanchez: It doesn't say. You should probably ask Mateo . . . Hector?
Hector: Hello? Mateo.

UNIT 8: Lifeskills Video: It's easy to get organized
Teacher: OK, class. Here is your assignment for next time. Please read pages 45 to 62 in your textbook. Then, write a summary of the chapter and bring the summary to class. And here is some extra reading for you, also. It's an article I found on the Internet. I thought you might like it.
Mateo: Do we have to read this?
Teacher: No, you don't have to read it. But it might be a good idea. Who knows? You just might learn something important.
Naomi: She means it might be on the test.
Teacher: Maybe it will and maybe it won't. Oh, and one more thing. Here is a list of terms you should know. You need to know all these words for the test.
Hector: When is the test, by the way?
Teacher: On Wednesday the 29th. Are there any more questions? OK, then. See you next time.
Naomi: Did you hear that? We have to read pages 45 to 62 in our book.
Hector: And write a summary.
Naomi: And memorize all the vocabulary terms.
Mateo: What vocabulary?
Naomi: The list that Mrs. Smith gave us.
Mateo: You mean this one?
Naomi: No, that's from last week. Don't you have the list she gave us today?
Mateo: I know I have it somewhere. I just can't find it right now.
Hector: Look, Mateo. It's easy to get organized. You just put everything in a binder with dividers.
Mateo: How many dividers do I need?
Hector: How many classes do you have?
Mateo: Five—I have five classes.
Hector: Then you need five dividers, one for each class. Here, I'll give you some of my dividers.
Mateo: What else do you think I need?
Naomi: You need pencils, pens, a package of paper, and a notebook.
Mateo: Pencils, pens, a package of paper, a notebook.

Video Challenge 2: People of the Reindeer
Narrator: The Sami people's reindeer move in spring. The Sami people go with them. These are Nils Peder Gaup's reindeer.
On the journey, the people live in tents.
These Sami people have traditional lives.
The children travel with the reindeer too.
Sami man: This snow is hard. After snowy weather, it is soft. Soft snow is good for the reindeer.
Well, that's all. It's time to sleep.

WORKBOOK ANSWER KEY

PRE-UNIT: WELCOME
Lesson 1: Say hello!
B.1. Hi! 2. Welcome to our class. 3. Hello! 4. How are you? 5. Fine! How are you?
D. Answers will vary. Sample answer:
Safa: Hello, I am Safa.
Hans: Hi, I am Hans.
Safa: Nice to meet to meet you, Hans.
Hans: Nice to meet you, too.
F. 1. I'm Silvia. 2. I'm Oscar. 3. I'm Ruby. 4. I'm Orlando. 5. I'm Taylor. 6. I'm Satsuki.
G. Answers will vary. Sample answer:
Duong: Hello.
Eva: Hi, I'm Eva.
Duong: Nice to meet you. I'm Duong.
Eva: Nice to meet you, too.
H. I'm a student.

Lesson 2: Phone numbers
B. 1. one 2. two 3. three 4. four 5. five 6. six 7. seven 8. eight 9. nine 10. ten
D. 1. Satsuki: (310) 555-1225 2. Ms. Adams: (619) 555-7843 3. Elsa: (714) 555-9856 4. Mirna: (562) 555-3534 5. Maria: (617) 555-7798 6. Orlando: (508) 555-4375
F. 1. It's 893-7234. 2. It's 777-3245. 3. It's 555-2235. 4. It's 327-8564. 5. It's 981-4392. 6. It's 972-2224. 7. It's 283-9764. 8. It's 765-2876.
G. 1. Satsuki: (310) 555-1225 2. Ms. Adams: (619) 555-7843 3. Elsa: (714) 555-9856 4. Mirna: (562) 555-3534 5. Maria: (617) 555-7798 6. Orlando: (508) 555-4375
H. Answers will vary.

Lesson 3: Class work
B. a book, paper, a name, a word, the teacher, the answer
C. 1. True 2. False 3. False 4. True
E. 1. Read 2. Write 3. Listen 4. Point 5. Repeat 6. Circle 7. Check
F. read: a book, a word; write: a word, your name; listen to: a radio, the teacher; check: the answer
G. 1. a book 2. a word 3. a radio 4. the teacher 5. a word 6. your name 7. the answer
H. 1. 5 2. Answers will vary. 3. pencil, pencil, pencil

UNIT 1: PERSONAL INFORMATION
Lesson 1: What's your name?
B. Man: Matias, Binh; Woman: Irma, Christine; Student: Matias, Irma, Christine, Binh
C. 1. teacher 2. student 3. students 4. friends 5. teacher 6. friends 7. teacher 8. friends/students
D. 1. Henry 2. Ana 3. Joseph 4. Marie 5. John 6. Albert 7. Nika
E. Answers will vary
G. 1. He 2. She 3. They 4. I 5. We 6. It
H. 1. He 2. She 3. We 4. He 5. They
I. Answers will vary.

Lesson 2: Where are you from?
B. 1. USA 2. Tunisia 3. China 4. Vietnam 5. Brazil 6. Mexico
C. 1. the United States, teacher 2. student, Japan 3. students, Colombia
E. 1. Long Beach 2. Torrance 3. Long Beach 4. San Pedro 5. San Pedro 6. Torrance
G. 1. lives 2. lives 3. live 4. live 5. lives 6. live 7. live 8. live 9. live 10. lives
H. 1. lives 2. lives 3. live 4. live
F. Answers will vary.

Lesson 3: Are you married?
B. 1. b 2. a 3. c
C. 1. single 2. divorced 3. married
E. Martha: married; Martin: single; Alex and Marie: married; Maria: divorced
G. 1. is 2. are 3. is 4. is 5. are 6. are 7. is 8. are 9. is 10. are 11. are 12. is 13. is 14. am 15. is 16. are
H. 1. is married, is from China 2. is single, is from Saudi Arabia 3. is divorced, is from Guatemala 4. is single, is from France
I. Answers will vary.

Lesson 4: What's your address
A. Name: Amal Jahshan; Address: 8237 Augustin Street; City: Irvine; State: CA; Zip code: 92602
B. Name: Amal Jahshan; Address: 8237 Augustin Street; City: Irvine; State: CA; Zip code: 92602
D. Return Address: Saul Andrade; 2239 Benton Way; Boston, MA; 02111 Mailing Address: Ava Tanaka; 44 Pio Pico Ave.; Dallas, TX; 75204
F. 1. It's 2. It's 3. He's 4. I'm 5. It's 6. She's 7. It's 8. I'm 9. I'm 10. She's
G. The name is Ava Tanaka. The address is 44 Pio Pico Ave. The city is Dallas. The state is TX.
The zip code is 75204.
H. Answers will vary.

Lesson 5: What's your date of birth?
A. Answers will vary
B. January 25th 1-25-YYYY 1/25/YYYY
February 6th 2-6-YYYY 2/6/YYYY
March 19th 3-19-YYYY 3/19/YYYY
April 17th 4-17-YYYY 4/17/YYYY
May 26th 5-26-YYYY 5/26/YYYY
June 24th 6-24-YYYY 6/24/YYYY
July 21st 7-21-YYYY 7/21/YYYY
August 16th 8-16-YYYY 8/16/YYYY
September 24th 9-24-YYYY 9/24/YYYY
October 30th 10-30-YYYY 10/30/YYYY
November 19th 11-19-YYYY 11/19/YYYY
December 4th 12-4-YYYY 12/4/YYYY
D. Address: 2346 Wilbur Place, Seattle, Washington, 98103; Birthplace: Osaka, Japan; Date of Birth: January 17, 1962
F. 1. c 2. a 3. b 4. e 5. f 6. d
G. What's your address? What's your name? What's your date of birth? What's your phone number?
H. Answers will vary.

Practice Test
A. 1. a 2. d
B. 1. c 2. b

UNIT 2: OUR CLASS

Lesson 1: Introduce yourself and others

B.

Felipe: This is Gabriela. She is the teacher.
Duong: Nice to meet you, Gabriela. I'm Duong.
Gabriela: Nice to meet you, too.

Gabriela: I want to introduce Duong. He is a student.
Felipe: Nice to meet you, Duong. I'm Felipe.
Duong: Nice to meet you, too.

Felipe: Meet Eva. She is a student.
Gabriela: Nice to meet you, Eva. I'm Gabriela.
Eva: Nice to meet you, too.

Duong: This is Eva and I am Duong. We are students.
Felipe: Nice to meet you, Duong and Eva. I am Felipe.
Duong: Nice to meet you.
Eva: Yes, nice to meet you, too.

E. 1. 23567 West Ave. 2. Nakamura 3. Russia 4. 92714
G. 1. Her 2. His 3. Their 4. My 5. Her 6. Their 7. His 8. Our
H. 1. Her address is 23567 West Ave. 2. His phone number is 555-8934. 3. Their native country is Vietnam. 4. Our teacher is Mrs. Jones. 5. My teacher is Mrs. Jones 6. My last name is Nakamura. 7. Our phone number is 555-6734. 8. Our native countries are Japan and Vietnam. 9. My last name is Calvin. 10. Her date of birth is 09-13-1975.
I. Answers will vary.

Lesson 2: Where's the pencil sharpener?

A. book; magazine; bookcase; plant; board; door; desk; file cabinets; trash can
B. 1. board 2. book 3. bookcase 4. desk 5. door 6. file cabinets 7. magazine 8. plant 9. trash can
C. Answers will vary.
E. 1. the plant 2. the pencil 3. the clock 4. the clock
F. 1. in front of 2. in 3. in back of 4. on
G. Answers will vary.

Lesson 3: What are you doing?

A. Listen to: the teacher, a CD, music; Talk to: the teacher, a friend; Read: a book, a note, a magazine; Write: on a sheet of paper, a note, in a notebook
B. Answers will vary.
C. 1. is writing 2. is reading 3. is sitting 4. is talking 5. is listening 6. is standing 7. is writing 8. is reading
E. 1. Mario is reading a book. 2. Eva is sitting in a chair. 3. Kenji is writing on a sheet of paper. 4. John is listening to a digital music player. .
F. 1. is listening 2. is talking 3. is standing 4. is writing 5. is sitting 6. is reading 7. is writing 8. is talking 9. is listening 10. is talking
G. Answers will vary.

Lesson 4: When is English class?

A. English Class: 8:30 a.m.; Lunch: 1:00 p.m.; Pronunciation Class: 3:00 p.m.; Work: 5:30 p.m.
B. 1. It's at 8:30 a.m. 2. It's at 1:00 p.m. 3. It's at 3:00 p.m. 4. It's at 5:30 p.m.
C. It's six thirty; It's five o'clock; It's two thirty; It's nine o'clock; It's four o'clock; It's seven thirty
D. Answers will vary.
F. 1. When's work? It's at 7:00 a.m. 2. When's dinner? It's at 6:00 p.m. 3. When's school? It's at 8:00 p.m. 4. When's breakfast? It's at 6:30 a.m. 5. When's lunch? It's at 12:30 p.m. 6. When's bedtime? It's at 10:30 p.m.
G. 1. It's at 8:30 a.m. 2. It's at 1:00 p.m. 3. It's at 3:00 p.m. 4. It's at 5:30 p.m.
H. Answers will vary.

Lesson 5: It's cold today

A. 1. rain coat 2. scarf 3. flip flops 4. t-shirt
B. Answers will vary.
C. Hot: sandals, t-shirt; Sunny: sandals, t-shirts; Cold: coat, scarf, sweater; Rainy: raincoat, umbrella
E. 1. need 2. need 3. need 4. needs 5. needs 6. needs 7. need 8. needs
F. 1. needs 2. needs 3. need 4. need 5. need 6. need 7. needs 8. need
G. needs; needs; need

Practice Test

A. 1. a 2. b
B. 1. c 2. b

UNIT 3: FOOD

Lesson 1: Let's eat!

B. 1. tomato 2. banana 3. eggs 4. sandwich 5. apple
C. Meat/Fish: tuna, turkey, chicken; Fruits/Vegetables: apples, potatoes, bananas, oranges, tomatoes; Drinks: milk,water
F. 1. tomato sauce 2. tomato sauce 3. green beans,peas 4. pears 5. corn 6. pears, tuna
G. 1.next to the corn 2. next to tomato sauce, under the green beans 3. between the green beans and the peas 4. next to the tomato sauce, under the peas 5. between the pears and the tuna 6. over the pears, next to the corn

Lesson 2: I'm hungry

B. Answers will vary.
C. Answers will vary.
D. Answers will vary.
F. 1. are 2. am 3. are 4. are 5. is 6. are 7. are 8. are 9. is 10. is 11. is 12. is
G. 1. are not 2. am not 3. are not 4. are not 5. is not 6. are not 7.are not 8. are not 9. is not 10. is not 11. is not 12. is not

Lesson 3: Let's have spaghetti

B. bag, can, jar, package, pound
C. cans, bags, jar
D. beans; bags of potato chips; peanut butter
F. 1. apples 2. sandwiches 3. tomatoes 4. jars 5. bags 6. onions 7. eggs 8. bottles 9. boxes 10. packages 11. radishes 12. potatoes
G. 1. eggs, onion 2. carrots, tomato 3. banana, apple 4. potato, carrots
H. 2 cans of tomato sauce; 1 package of spaghetti; 5 pounds of ground beef; 3 eggs; 4 potatoes; 6 bananas
I. cans; package; pounds; eggs; potatoes; bananas

Lesson 4: Simple Present: What's for dinner?
B. Lien: chicken, green beans, eggs, chocolate cake, rice, soup, lettuce; Molly: fish, broccoli, onions, cheese, rice, soup, lettuce
D. Meat/Fish: turkey, chicken, fish; Vegetables: lettuce, broccoli, carrots, green beans; Fruit: bananas, pears, oranges; Dairy: milk, yogurt
F. 1. want 2. want 3. wants 4. want 5. want 6. wants 7. wants 8. want 9. want 10. wants
G. 1. wants 2. wants 3. want 4. want 5. wants 6. want
H. Answers will vary.

Lesson 5: What do you like?
B. Answers will vary.
C. Answers will vary.
D. 1. Saul likes chocolate cake. 2. Amadeo eats pie. 3 Yoshi eats yogurt. 4. Chen likes fruit. 5. Rhonda likes cookies. 6. Sue eats ice cream.
F. 1. like 2. eat 3. need 4. likes 5. need 6. eats 7. want 8. likes 9. need
G. 1. needs 2. wants 3. like 4. eat 5. want 6. like 7. eats 8. need
H. Answers will vary.

Practice Test
A. 1. b 2. c
B. 1. b 2. c

UNIT 4: CLOTHING
Lesson 1: What's on sale?
A. 1. next to $19: sweater 2. next to $150: coat 3. next to $47: boots 4. next to $9: scarf 5. next to $22: gloves 6. next to $12: baseball cap 7. next to $10: t-shirt 8. next to $18: shorts 9. next to $8: sunglasses 10. next to $28: sandals
B. Winter clothing: sweater, coat, boots, scarf, gloves; Summer clothing: baseball cap, t-shirt, shorts, sunglasses, sandals
C. 1. scarf 2. coat 3. gloves 4. sweater 5. boots 6. baseball cap 7. t-shirt 8. shorts 9. sandals 10. sunglasses
E. 1. has 2. have 3. has 4. have 5. have 6. have 7. have 8. have
G. 1. need 2. want 3. have 4. has 5. need 6. has 7. have 8. have

Lesson 2: Where's the fitting room?
A. Answers will vary.
B. 1. women's 2. men's 3. women's 4. children's 5. teen boys' 6. teen girls'
C. 1. in the women's section 2. in the men's section 3. in the women's section 4. in the children's section 5. in the teen boys' section 6. in the teen girls' section
E. 1. a 2. b 3. b 4. c
F. Answers will vary.

Lesson 3: What colors do you like?
B. 1. ten 2. red and blue 3. fifteen 4. black 5. seven 6. eight 7. green, red, and black 8. white and yellow 9. four 10. blue and green
D. Leti: dress, 8, yellow; Gaspar: shirt, medium, green; Pedro: sweater, small, blue
F. 1. There are 2. There are 3. There is 4. There are 5. There is 6. There are
G. 1. There are three small shirts. 2. There are two medium shirts. 3. There is one large shirt.
H. Answers will vary.

Lesson 4: That's $5.00
A. 1. $28.25 2. $59.50 3. $62.50 4. $87.75 5. $33.50 6. $41.50
B. 1. one $20 bill, one $5 bill, three $1 bills, one quarter 2. two $20 bills, one $10 bill, one $5 bill, four $1 bills, two quarters 3. three $20 bills, two $1 bills, two quarters 4. four $20 bills, one $5 bill, two $1 bills, three quarters 5. one $20 bill, one $10 bill, three $1 bills, two quarters 6. two $20 bills, one $1 bill, two quarters
D. 1. $28.00 2. $22.50 3. $33.00
F. 1. are, are 2. is, is 3. are, are 4. is, is 5. is, is 6. are, are
G. How much is...the shirt / the blouse / the dress / the sweater? How much are...the shoes / the shorts / the sweaters / the shirts?
H. Answers will vary.

Lesson 5: How much are the shoes?
B. 1. $33 2. $12 3. $285 4. $84 5. $12 6. $17 7. $12 8. $17 9. $36 10. $24
C. 1. Marcus needs four shirts. 2. He needs one pair of boots. 3. He needs two pairs of blue jeans. 4. He needs two pairs of socks.
E. 1. How much 2. How much 3. How many 4. How much 5. How many 6. How many
F. 1. b 2. a 3. c 4. a 5. a 6. c

Practice Test
A. 1. a 2. c
B. 1 b 2. c

UNIT 5: OUR COMMUNITY
Lesson 1: Where we live
A. 1. c 2. d 3. b 4. a
B. 1. bank 2. bookstore 3. clothing store 4. convenience store 5. department store 6. electronics store 7. fast-food 8. hotel 9. pharmacy 10. restaurant 11. shoe store 12. supermarket
C. 1. b 2. c 3. c 4. c 5. b
D. Answers will vary.
F. 1. No, I don't. 2. No, I don't. 3. Yes, I do. 4. No, I don't. 5. Yes, I do. 6. No, I don't.
G. 1. Do you 2. Do you 3. Do you 4. Do you 5. Do you 6. Do you
H. Answers will vary.
I. Answers will vary.

Lesson 2: Where do you live?
B. 1. Pat, house, $1,450 2. Pedro, apartment, $800 3. no contact, condo, $950 4. Jackie, mobile home, $650 5. no contact, apartment, $600 6. Eva, house, $1,500
C. 1. lives in a house. 2. lives in a mobile home. 3. lives in an apartment.
E. In: California, Los Angeles, mobile home, house; On: Birch Street, Walker Drive, West Palm St., Second Street
F. 1. in 2. in 3. on 4. on 5. in 6. in
G. I live <u>in</u> a house. I live <u>on</u> Market St. <u>in</u> San Francisco.
H. Answers will vary.

Lesson 3: *Come, Go*
A. 1. car – drive 2. train – take 3. bus – take 4. bicycle – ride
B. Answers will vary.
C. Saud: takes the bus, pharmacy; Margaret: takes the train, school; Nina: drives a car, doctor
E. 1. comes 2. goes 3. goes
F. 1. comes 2. goes 3. go 4. come 5. come 6. go 7. go 8. comes
G. Answers will vary.

Lesson 4: She takes the train
A. Answers will vary.
B. 1. is 2. is 3. are 4. are 5. are 6. am
E. 1. drives 2. takes 3. takes
F. 1. lives, takes 2. live, take 3. live in 4. rides, bicycle 5. Carina lives 6. drive to school
G. 1. rides 2. ride 3. drives 4. walk 5. take 6. lives 7. walk 8. live

Lesson 5: Where's the store?
A. 1. Big's Foods 2. St. John's Pharmacy 3. Second Street 4. Perry Avenue
B. 1. b 2. a 3. b
C. (a) The school is on Hampton Street next to Food Mart. (b) The hospital is on First Street next to the pharmacy. (c) Her apartment is next to the train tracks.
E. 1. b 2. d 3. a 4. c
F. 1. Go straight. Turn right on Second Street. Turn left on First Street. Stop. 2. Turn around. Go straight. Turn left. Turn right on Birch Avenue. Stop. It's next to the market.
G. Answers will vary.

Practice Test
1. d 2. b 3. a 4. c

UNIT 6: HEALTHY LIVING
Lesson 1: I need a checkup
A. 1. eyes 2. head 3. arm 4. foot 5. mouth 6. nose 7. hand 8. leg
C. 1. c 2. a 3. d 4. b
F. 1. b 2. e 3. a 4. c 5. d
G. Answers will vary.

Lesson 2: I'm sick!
A. 1. China 2. He has a headache, a fever, and a sore throat. 3. He speaks only a little English.
B. 1. Headache 2. Fever 3. Sore throat
C. Answers will vary.
D. 1. Humberto 2. Humberto; Chen 3. Omar 4. Chen
F. 1. is 2. has 3. has 4. are 5. is 6. is 7. have 8. has 9. have 10. are
H. 1. sees; once a year 2. have; once a year 3. visit; two times a year 4. visits; once a year 5. go; once a year 6. goes; three times a year 7. has; two times a year 8. sees; three times a year

Lesson 3: You need aspirin
A. 1. Hang Tran 2. Cold 3. 3:00 pm 4. 555-3765 5. backache 6. Elsa 7. 555-5842 8. 2:15 pm
B. headache, aspirin; cold, cold medicine; stomachache, antacid
C. 1. aspirin 2. aspirin 3. cough syrup 4. cough drop
E. 1. last photo 2. first photo 3. middle photo
F. 1. aspirin 2. antacid 3. cough syrup
G. 1. has, needs 2. has, needs 3. have, need cough drops 4. have, need antacid 5. have, need aspirin 6. have, need cold medicine 7. have, need aspirin 8. has, needs aspirin 9. have, need aspirin 10. has, needs cold medicine

Lesson 4: Exercise every day!
B. Julia: sleeps 8 hours a night, gets a checkup once a year, is in good health; Both: exercises, eats breakfast, lunch, and dinner; Delmar: smokes, sleeps five hours a night, is unhealthy
C. 1. eight 2. 30 3. three 4. two times a year
E. 1. don't 2. doesn't 3. don't 4. doesn't 5. don't 6. don't 7. doesn't 8. doesn't
F. 1. doesn't eat 2. don't have 3. don't sleep 4. doesn't exercise
G. 1. exercises 2. doesn't see 3. sleep 4. don't 5. eat

Lesson 5: I have an appointment
A. Mark: talking to each other; Hector: talking to each other; John: talking to each other; Brian: talking on the phone; Nancy: reading a magazine; Fran: reading a magazine; Receptionist: writing information
B. 1. Ben 2. Doreen, Rosa 3. Antonio 4. receptionist
D. 1. is 2. is 3. are 4. are 5. am 6. is 7. are 8. are 9. is 10. are
E. 1. is writing 2. are reading 3. are talking 4. is talking 5. is waiting 6. are waiting 7. is sitting

Practice Test
A. 1. b 2. b
B. 1. a 2. d

UNIT 7: WORK
Lesson 1: Do you work?
A. 1. is a cashier, in a supermarket 2. is a teacher, in a school 3. is a receptionist, in an office 4. is a salesperson, in a clothing store 5. is a custodian, in an office building 6. is a nurse, in a hospital
B. Supermarket: cashier, manager; Office: secretary, receptionist, manager, salesperson; Hospital: nurse, doctor; Restaurant: server, cashier, manager; School: student, teacher, custodian, principal
E. 1. works 2. work 3. work 4. work 5. work 6. works 7. work 8. works
F. 1. B: He works for Fast-Xpress Delivery. 2. B: She works at Freemont School. 3. B: Ivan works at Freemont School. 4. B: They work at Freemont School.

Lesson 2: When do you go to work?
A. 1. a 2. a 3. b 4. c
B. Ben: nurse, works Monday-Thursday, helps the doctor; Both: work in a hospital, work 7 a.m.-7 p.m., helps patients; Hue: doctor, works Friday-Sunday, supervises
D. 1. Roxy's Department Store 2. at 6:30 P.M. 3. She's a nurse. 4. Mr. Peabody 5. at 3:30 P.M. 6. Lien
E. 1. g 2. d 3. a 4. b 5. h 6. c 7. e 8. f

Lesson 3: What do you do?
A. 1. b. 2. e. 3. a. 4. c. 5. d. 6. f.
B. 1. A salesperson talks to customers. 2. A student studies in school. 3. A teacher works in a school. 4. A cashier

works in a supermarket. 5. A nurse works in a hospital. 6. A manager works in an office.

C. doctor: takes care of patients; nurse: takes care of patients, helps the doctor; receptionist: sends memos, schedules meetings; custodian: cleans

D. 1. A doctor takes care of patients. 2. A nurse takes care of patients and helps the doctor. 3. A receptionist sends memos and schedules meetings. 4. A custodian cleans.

E. gardener: works outside; delivery person: delivers packages, talks to people; receptionist: answers phones, talks to people; cashier: counts money, talks to people

F. 1. A gardener works outside. 2. A delivery person delivers packages and talks to people. 3. A receptionist answers phones and talks to people. 4. A cashier counts money and talks to people.

I. 1. can 2. can 3. can 4. can't 5. can 6. can 7. can 8. can't

J. 1. can't come 2. can speak 3. can drive 4. can help 5. can schedule

K. Answers will vary.

Lesson 4: You're doing great!

B. 1. Kenny Gomez 2. yes 3. June 27th 4. yes 5. National Sales Corporation 6. yes

D. 1. Peter Langdon 2. Calvin Carter 3. yes 4. no

F. 1. is 2. is 3. am 4. are 5. are 6. are

G. 1. is not 2. are not 3. is 4. are 5. is not 6. is not

H. Answers will vary.

Lesson 5: Please send the memo

A. Do's: ask for help, speak only English, do homework, practice every day, help others; Don'ts: leave early, eat in the classroom, speak in your language, come late to class

B. speak, do, come to class, not to leave, do not eat

D. Do's: come to work on time, help customers, speak English; Don'ts: eat in the store, leave early, smoke in the store

F. 1. d, l 2. a, c, j 3. b, f, h 4. c, k 5. f, l 6. b, e, g, h

G. Receptionist: 1. Don't 2. Answer 3. Talk 4. Don't come 5. Don't take; Student: 1. Don't come 2. Do 3. Speak 4. Don't forget 5. Ask

Practice Test

A. 1. c 2. b

B. 1. a 2. d

UNIT 8: LIFELONG LEARNING AND REVIEW

Lesson 1: Let's get organized

A. Julia: single, Mexico; Hasna: married, Saudi Arabia; Dalmar: single, Haiti; Eva: divorced, Croatia; Gabriela: single, Colombia Felipe: married, Mexico

B. Answers will vary.

D. 1. am 2. is 3. are 4. are 5. is 6. is 7. are 8. is 9. am 10. are

E. Answers will vary.

F. Answers will vary.

Lesson 2: I need paper

A. 540, a dozen, pencils, $1.00; 201, a dozen, pens, $2.00; 75, 10 pack, 9-tab dividers, $12.00; 33, each, binders, $2.00; 310, package, paper, $2.00; 140, each, notebooks, $3.00

B. 1. $1.00 a dozen 2. $2.00 a dozen 3. $12.00 for a 10 pack 4. $2.00 each 5. $2.00 per package 6. $3.00 each

C. 1. how many 2. a description 3. the price for one

E. 1. c 2. j 3. a 4. e 5. h 6. g 7. i 8. b 9. d 10. f

F. 1. are 2. are 3. is 4. is 5. are 6. is 7. are 8. are

G. Answers will vary.

Lesson 3: Where's the office supply store

A. 1. 555-3472 2. 555-3224 3. Library (Public) 4. 122 Jefferson St. 5. 151 E. Broadway 6. Police Department

B. 1. First Street 2. Main Street 3. Grand Street

D. El Marco Restaurant: next to Elegant Clothing, on the corner of Main Street and First Street; St. John's Pharmacy: next to St. John's Hospital, between St. John's Hospital and Save-a-lot Foods; Pete's Burgers: next to American Café, on the corner of First Street and Grand Street; American Café: next to Pete's Burgers, on the corner of Grand Street and Second Street; St. John's Hospital: next to St. John's Pharmacy, between El Marco Restaurant and St. John's Pharmacy, on the corner of First Street and Main Street

E. 1. on 2. on the corner 3. next to 4. next to 5. on 6. on the corner of 7. St. John's Pharmacy 8. El Marco Restaurant

F. Answers will vary.

Lesson 4: Sleep eight hours a night

A. Frank: sleep, eight hours, exercise two hours a day, read an English newspaper every day; Both: go to school every day, watch TV in English; Cathy: sleep seven hours, exercise one hour a day, read the Internet in English every day

B. 1. two 2. five 3. Answers will vary.

D. 1. exercises 2. sleep 3. studies 4. study 5. works 6. walk

E. 1. exercises 2. study 3. sleep 4. eats 5. studies 6. eats

F. Answers will vary.

Lesson 5: When can I study?

A. 1. Ali studies at school on Monday, Wednesday, and Friday. 2. Ali works Monday through Friday. 3. Ali studies at home Sunday through Friday. 4. Ali has dinner at 5:00PM all week. 5. Ali does not go to school on Saturday.

B. 2 times a week: walk; 3 times a week: exercise; 4 times a week: school; 5 times a week: lunch, study

D. 1. eats 2. exercises 3. work 4. study 5. have 6. exercise

E. eats, goes, eats, studies

F. Answers will vary.

Practice Test

A. 1. a 2. b

B. 1. b 2. c

LESSON PLANNER METHODOLOGY

The *Stand Out* Lesson Planner methodology ensures success!

Stand Out ensures student success through good lesson planning and instruction. Each of the five Lessons in every Unit has a lesson plan. Unlike most textbooks, the Lesson Planner was written before the student book materials. A lot of learning occurs with the student books closed so by writing the lesson plans first, we could ensure that each objective was clearly achieved. Each lesson plan follows a systematic and proven format:

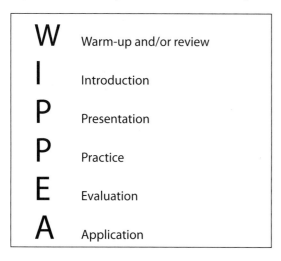

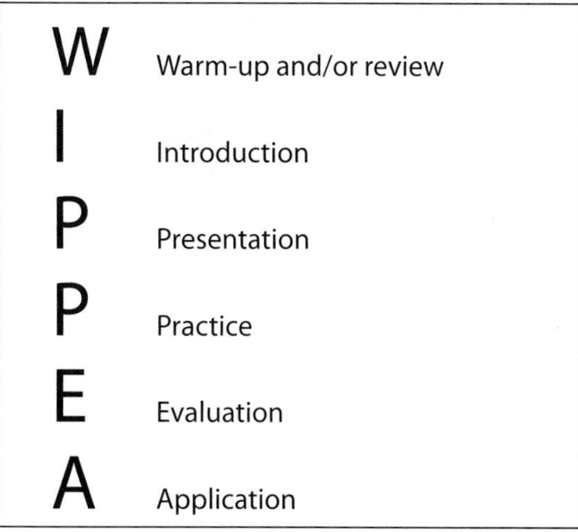

Warm-up and/or review
The warm-up activities establish a context and purpose to the lesson. Exercises use previously learned content and materials that are familiar to students from previous lessons.

Introduction
In the introduction step, exercises focus the students' attention on the goals of the lesson by asking questions, showing visuals, telling a story, etc. Instructors should state the objective of the lesson and tell students what they will be doing. The objective should address what students are expected to be able to do by the end of the lesson.

Presentation
The presentation activities provide students with the building blocks and skills they need to achieve the objectives set in the introduction. The exercises introduce new information to the students through visuals, realia, description, listenings, explanation, or written text. This is the time to check students' comprehension.

Practice
Practice activities provide meaningful tasks for students to practice what they have just learned through different activities. These activities can be done as a class, in small groups, pairs, or individually. All of these activities are student centered and involve cooperative learning. Instructors should model each activity, monitor progress, and provide feedback.

Evaluation
Evaluation ensures that students are successful. Instructors should evaluate students on attainment of the objective set at the start of the lesson. This can be done by oral, written, or demonstrated performance. At this point, if students need more practice, instructors can go back and do additional practice activities before moving onto the application.

Application
Application activities help students apply new knowledge to their own lives or new situations. This is one of the most important steps of the lesson plan. If students can accomplish the application task, it will build their confidence to be able to sue what they've learned out in the community. The Team Projects are an application of unit objectives that involves task-based activities with a product.

In addition to each lesson plan following the WIPPEA model, each Unit in *Stand Out* follows this same approach. The first lesson is always in Introduction to the Unit, introducing new vocabulary and the basic concepts that will be expanded upon in the unit. The following four lessons are the Presentations and Practices for the unit topic. Following the five lessons is a Review lesson, which allows students to do more practice with everything they already learned. The final lesson is an Application for everything they learned in the unit, a team project.

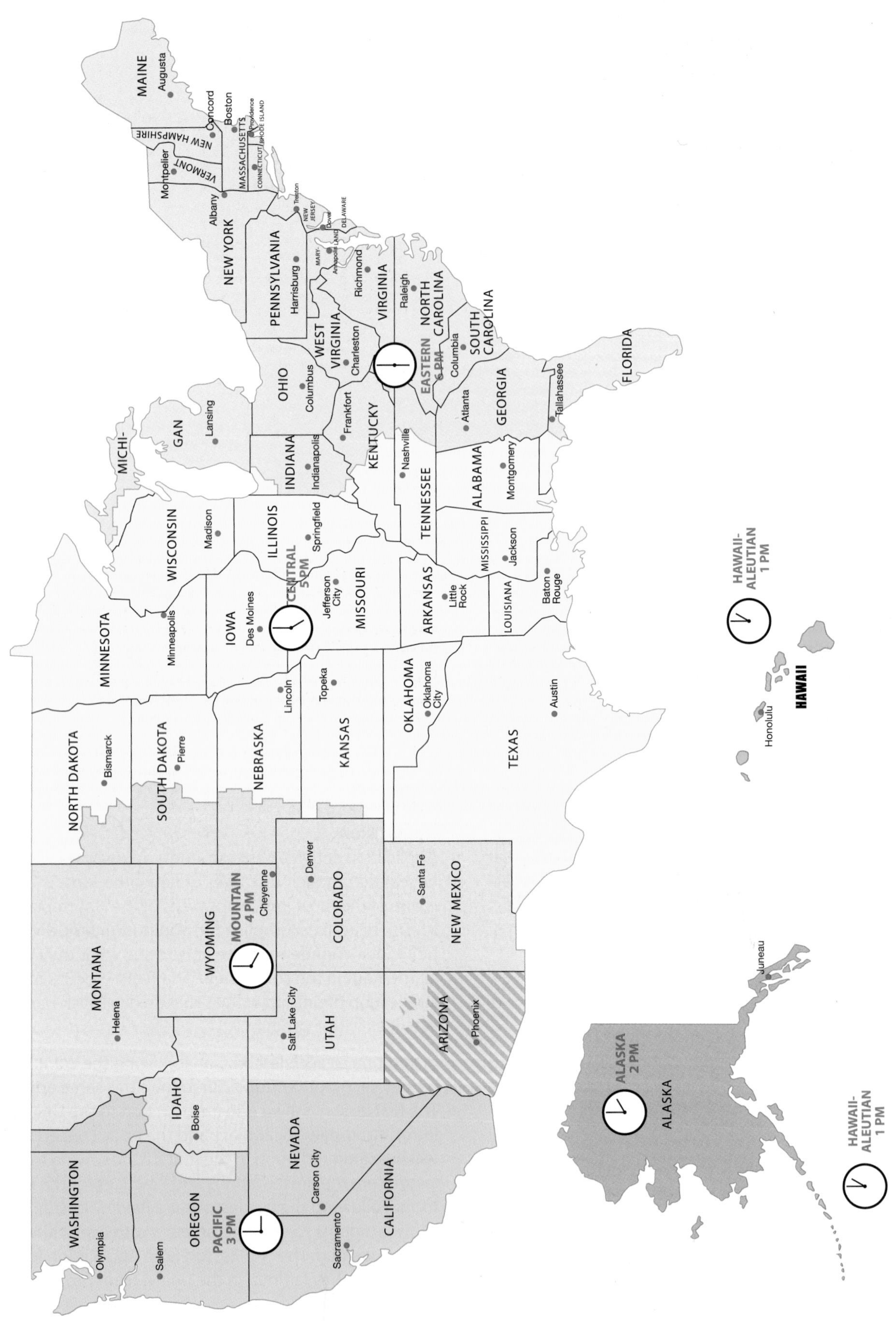

MAINE
Augusta
NEW HAMPSHIRE
Concord
VERMONT
Montpelier
MASSACHUSETTS
Boston
CONNECTICUT
RHODE ISLAND
Providence
NEW YORK
Albany
PENNSYLVANIA
Harrisburg
NEW JERSEY
Trenton
DELAWARE
Dover
MARYLAND
Annapolis
VIRGINIA
Richmond
WEST VIRGINIA
Charleston
NORTH CAROLINA
Raleigh
SOUTH CAROLINA
Columbia
EASTERN
6 PM
GEORGIA
Atlanta
FLORIDA
Tallahassee
OHIO
Columbus
MICHIGAN
Lansing
INDIANA
Indianapolis
KENTUCKY
Frankfort
TENNESSEE
Nashville
ALABAMA
Montgomery
MISSISSIPPI
Jackson
WISCONSIN
Madison
ILLINOIS
Springfield
CENTRAL
5 PM
MINNESOTA
Minneapolis
IOWA
Des Moines
MISSOURI
Jefferson City
ARKANSAS
Little Rock
LOUISIANA
Baton Rouge
NORTH DAKOTA
Bismarck
SOUTH DAKOTA
Pierre
NEBRASKA
Lincoln
KANSAS
Topeka
OKLAHOMA
Oklahoma City
TEXAS
Austin
MONTANA
Helena
WYOMING
Cheyenne
MOUNTAIN
4 PM
COLORADO
Denver
NEW MEXICO
Santa Fe
IDAHO
Boise
UTAH
Salt Lake City
ARIZONA
Phoenix
WASHINGTON
Olympia
OREGON
Salem
PACIFIC
3 PM
NEVADA
Carson City
CALIFORNIA
Sacramento
ALASKA
2 PM
ALASKA
Juneau
HAWAII-
ALEUTIAN
1 PM
HAWAII
Honolulu
HAWAII-
ALEUTIAN
1 PM